THINKING WITH THE CHURCH

Thinking with the Church

ESSAYS IN HISTORICAL THEOLOGY

B. A. Gerrish

WILLIAM B. EERDMANS PUBLISHING COMPANY
GRAND RAPIDS, MICHIGAN / CAMBRIDGE, U.K.

Published 2010 by

Wm. B. Eerdmans Publishing Co.

2140 Oak Industrial Drive N.E., Grand Rapids, Michigan 49505 /

P.O. Box 163, Cambridge CB3 9PU U.K.

Printed in the United States of America

15 14 13 12 11 10   7 6 5 4 3 2 1

Library of Congress Cataloging-in-Publication Data

Gerrish, B. A. (Brian Albert), 1931-

Thinking with the church: essays in historical theology / B.A. Gerrish.

p.   cm.

Includes index.

ISBN 978-0-8028-6452-9 (cloth: alk. paper)

1. Theology — History.   I. Title.

BR118.G45   2010

230.09 — dc22

2009043727

www.eerdmans.com

To DD

for the first twenty years

Contents

CONTENTS

Preface

Three of the essays in this collection (Chaps. 3, 9, and 10) have not previously been published. Chapters 9 and 10 were written as the first two of my Schaff Lectures on the idea of atonement, delivered at Pittsburgh Theological Seminary in 1998. The initial version of Chapter 3, on the Atheism Controversy, was written a very long time ago: in 1981 it was presented as part of my second Tate-Willson Lecture at Southern Methodist University. At that time, I had planned to develop the Tate-Willson Lectures into a book, but over the years other projects moved to the top of my agenda. Much of the lecture material did appear piece by piece in various published essays, including, from the second lecture, a critical appraisal of the allegedly fictionalist opinions of Forberg, whose article provoked the Atheism Controversy. The obvious omission from these published fragments was Fichte — all the more culpable because the Germans commonly refer to the Atheism Controversy precisely as *Fichte's* Atheism Controversy. Chapter 3 belatedly attempts to atone for this omission.

All the other chapters were first published in a variety of places — journals, symposia, and an encyclopedia. The present book brings these scattered publications together. They touch on several major themes in Christian theology. The themes in Parts I-II, though the treatment of them is largely historical, belong to philosophical theology, and in a systematic or dogmatic work they would most likely be brought under questions of "prolegomena": What is religion? What is revelation? No one who knows me will be surprised that John Calvin is, in a measure, my lodestar for navigating through these preliminary questions —

though perhaps not always in ways he would approve. Part III turns directly to historical interpretation of the Calvinist (or "Reformed") tradition, viewed in the very diverse work of three of its foremost representatives: Calvin himself, Friedrich Schleiermacher, and Charles Hodge. Finally, Parts IV-V then deal with particular Christian doctrines on which the diversity of the Calvinist tradition is apparent: atonement, the Eucharist, and grace, starting once again with historical interpretation but not excluding the critical engagement that, in my view, belongs to the task of historical theology.

I can well imagine that not every reader will begin with chapter 1; some will want to turn first to later chapters, as their historical or theological interest moves them. I need not object. Naturally, I would like the book to be taken as a whole, and I believe that it really is a coherent whole — and not only by reason of the ubiquity of John Calvin and the way I understand historical theology as critical conversation with the church. Still, the individual parts, precisely because of their particular origins, are sufficiently self-contained to be read individually or in more than one sequence.

I should note that throughout the book I have availed myself of standard English translations of sources in Latin, French, and German, where available, but have regularly checked them against the originals. Where no reference is made to an existing English version, the translation is mine.

My thanks are due for permission to reprint essays that originally appeared in other publications. Acknowledgments to the copyright holders are provided in the Introduction. Except as noted, biblical quotations follow the New Revised Standard Version.

Abbreviations

AA   Immanuel Kant, *Kants gesammelte Schriften*
         (Akademieausgabe). Berlin: Königlich Preussische (later
         Deutsche) Akademie der Wissenschaften, 1900-.

BC   *The Book of Concord: The Confessions of the Evangelical Lu-
         theran Church.* Trans. and ed. Theodore G. Tappert. Phila-
         delphia: Muhlenberg, 1959.

BELK   *Die Bekenntnisschriften der evangelisch-lutherischen Kirche.*
         4th ed. Göttingen: Vandenhoeck & Ruprecht, 1959.

BS   Philip Schaff, *Bibliotheca Symbolica Ecclesiae Universalis:
         The Creeds of Christendom, with a History and Critical
         Notes.* 6th ed., ed. David S. Schaff. 3 vols. New York:
         Harper, 1931.

CC   Calvin's Commentaries. Trans. Calvin Translation Society
         (Edinburgh, 1844-56). Reprinted in 22 vols. Grand Rapids:
         Baker, 1981.

CG   Friedrich Daniel Ernst Schleiermacher, *Der christliche
         Glaube, nach den Grundsätzen der evangelischen Kirche im
         Zusammenhange dargestellt.* 2nd ed., 1830-31. KGA I, 13/1-2.
         Cited by section (§) and (where needed) subsection, fol-
         lowed in parentheses by the corresponding pages in the
         English translation. *The Christian Faith.* Trans. H. R.
         Mackintosh, J. S. Stewart, et al. Edinburgh: T&T Clark,
         1928; reprinted 1999.

CO   *Ioannis Calvini opera quae supersunt omnia.* Ed. Wilhelm

xi

Baum, Eduard Cunitz, and Eduard Reuss. 59 vols. *Corpus Reformatorum,* vols. 29-87. Brunswick: C. A. Schwetschke & Son (M. Bruhn), 1863-1900.

FSW   *Ludwig Feuerbachs sämmtliche Werke.* Ed. Wilhelm Bolin and Friedrich Jodl. 13 vols. in twelve. Stuttgart: Frommann, 1959-64. A facsimile reprint of the original ten-volume edition (1903-1911) with two additional volumes, one a double vol., edited by Hans-Martin Sass.

GD   Karl Barth, *The Göttingen Dogmatics.* See *UCR.*

ICR   John Calvin, *Institutio Christianae religionis.* Cited in the definitive 1559 edition by book, chapter, and (where needed) section, followed in parentheses by the corresponding pages in the standard English translation. *Institutes of the Christian Religion.* Ed. John T. McNeill, trans. Ford Lewis Battles. 2 vols. LCC 20-21. Philadelphia: Westminster, 1960.

KD   Friedrich Schleiermacher, *Kurze Darstellung des theologischen Studiums zum Behuf einleitender Vorlesungen.* 2nd ed. Berlin, 1830. KGA I, 6:317-446. Eng. trans., *Brief Outline on the Study of Theology.* Trans., with introductions and notes, by Terrence N. Tice. Richmond: John Knox, 1966.

KGA   Friedrich Schleiermacher. *Kritische Gesamtausgabe.* Vols. 1-. Berlin: Walter de Gruyter, 1980-. Cited by division, volume, and page.

KS   Friedrich Schleiermacher, *Kleine Schriften und Predigten.* Ed. Hayo Gerdes and Emanuel Hirsch. 3 vols. Berlin: Walter de Gruyter, 1969-70.

LCC   The Library of Christian Classics. Ed. John Baillie, John T. McNeill, and Henry P. Van Dusen. 26 vols. Philadelphia: Westminster, 1953-66.

LW   Luther's Works (American Edition). Ed. Jaroslav Pelikan and Helmut T. Lehmann. 55 vols. St. Louis: Concordia and Philadelphia: Fortress, 1955-86.

LWZ   Latin Works of Huldreich Zwingli. Ed. Samuel Macauley Jackson et al. 3 vols. Vol. 1, *The Latin Works and the Corre-*

	spondence of Huldreich Zwingli, New York: G. P. Putnam's Sons, 1912. Vols. 2-3, Philadelphia: Heidelberg, 1922-29. Vols. 2 and 3 reprinted, *On Providence and Other Essays* and *Commentary on True and False Religion.* Durham, NC: Labyrinth, 1983, 1981.
MPL	J.-P. Migne, *Patrologiae cursus completus, Series Latina.* 221 vols. Paris, 1844-1900.
NPNF	A Select Library of the Nicene and Post-Nicene Fathers of the Christian Church. Ed. Philip Schaff. 14 vols. New York, 1886-90. Reprinted, Grand Rapids: Eerdmans, 1969-75.
OS	*Joannis Calvini opera selecta.* Ed. Peter Barth, Wilhelm Niesel, and Doris Scheuner. 5 vols. Munich: Chr. Kaiser, 1926-52.
SG	Thomas Aquinas, *Summa contra Gentiles* (or *contra Gentes*). Cited by book, chapter, and section.
ST	Thomas Aquinas, *Summa theologiae* (or *Summa theologica*). Cited by part, question, article, and (where needed) objection (obj.) or reply (ad), followed in parentheses by volume and page numbers in the English translation. *Summa Theologica* (First Complete American Edition). 3 vols. Trans. Fathers of the English Dominican Province. New York: Benziger Brothers, 1947. In Chaps. 7-9, where there is no possibility of confusion with Thomas's *Summa,* the abbreviation *ST* is used for Charles Hodge, *Systematic Theology.* 3 vols. 1871-72. Reprinted, Grand Rapids: Eerdmans, 1981.
SW	*Friedrich Schleiermachers sämmtliche Werke.* 31 vols. Berlin: Georg Reimer, 1834-64. Cited by division, volume, and page.
TT	Calvin's Tracts and Treatises. Trans. Henry Beveridge. 3 vols. Edinburgh, 1844-51. Reprinted, Grand Rapids: Eerdmans, 1958. Also included as vols. 1-3 in Selected Works of John Calvin: Tracts and Letters. 7 vols. Grand Rapids: Baker, 1983.
UCR	Karl Barth, *Unterricht in der christlichen Religion.* Lectures

at Göttingen University, 1924-25. 3 vols. Ed. Hannelotte Reiffen (vol. 1) and Hinrich Stoevesandt (vols. 2-3). *Karl Barth Gesamtausgabe,* vols. 17, 20, 38. Zurich: Theologischer Verlag, 1985, 1990, 2003. Sections §§1-18 trans. Geoffrey Bromiley as *The Göttingen Dogmatics: Instruction in the Christian Religion,* vol. 1. Grand Rapids: Eerdmans, 1991. Cited as *GD.*

WA   *D. Martin Luthers Werke: Kritische Gesamtausgabe* (Weimarer Ausgabe). Weimar, 1883-.

WADB   Ibid. *Deutsche Bibel.*

ZW   *Huldreich Zwinglis sämtliche Werke.* Ed. Emil Egli and Georg Finsler. 14 vols. *Corpus Reformatorum,* vols. 88-101. Berlin: C. A. Schwetschke & Son, 1905-63.

Introduction

To define the task of historical theology, we could hardly do better than borrow an expression from the *Spiritual Exercises* of Ignatius Loyola: historical theology is "thinking with the church" *(sentire cum ecclesia)*. But we need not take it in quite his sense. For Ignatius, thinking with the church meant thinking what the church thinks even, if need be, against our own insight. One of the permanent gains of the Enlightenment, by contrast, is the principle that each of us, according to our limited abilities, must do our own thinking, not delegating the responsibility to another. But there has to be something to think about, and others to think with. The Christian tradition offers a wealth of answers to perennial human questioning: the task of historical theology is not only to give an account of them, but also, as far as possible, to engage them critically. In this sense it is "*thinking* with the church."

Historical theologians go about their task assuming, not the authority of what the church says, but the likelihood that it is worth thinking about; and their "church" will be made up, at least in principle, of all those leading thinkers to whom we owe the proven classics of the Christian tradition. Their critics, too, will not be excluded from the conversation. The only exclusions will be imposed by the undoubted limits of our lesser minds; and the inclination we all have to devote our best energies to one part of the tradition rather than another, though it has its temptations, may in practice lend depth to the conversation. So understood, the historical theologian's thinking with the church provides a bridge from historical inquiry to the constructive work of the systematic theologian.

I

In the Western world, the eighteenth century was the watershed between medieval and modern thought about *revelation*. "Revelation and the Religion of Reason" (Chap. 1) reviews some of the most important options for religious thought in the so-called Age of Reason. The Deist Controversy in England led to a reversal of the old belief that the weakness or perversity of human reason required revelation to supplement and correct it: the Deists countered that every claim to possess a revelation is subject to rational scrutiny. Fundamental to their approach was the view that naive privileging of Christian discourse, resting as it did on the assumed possession of an unparalleled revelation, had to yield to a pluralist interpretation of Christianity as one religion among others.

There were, of course, eminent churchmen — Samuel Clarke (1675-1729), George Berkeley (1685-1753), Joseph Butler (1692-1752), and others — who met the Deists on their own ground; and there were others who were content with a bare fideism that rejected the subordination of faith to reason. But among the critics some thought that religion, whether natural or supposedly revealed, was a superseded stage in human development. The skepticism of David Hume (1711-1776) and the dogmatic atheism of Baron d'Holbach (1723-1789) are sometimes taken for the dead end of religious thought. In actual fact, the closing years of the eighteenth century witnessed the first beginnings of one of the most creative and constructive periods in the history of Christian theology. New directions were opened up. Immanuel Kant (1724-1804) located the proper ground of religion in morality, not in metaphysics and cosmology, where the old proofs for the existence of God had looked for it. Friedrich Schleiermacher (1768-1834) sought to interpret Christian faith as a distinctive modification of a feeling or intuition that is common to every religion — indeed, to every human self-consciousness. And he acknowledged the persuasion of the Deists that religious pluralism belongs to the proper starting point for a reconstruction of Christian theology. How successful he may have been in dealing with pluralism, is hotly debated. But the unprecedented encounter of Christians with "other religions" in the twentieth and twenty-first centuries has made pluralism in religion one of the most urgent issues for present-day theology.[1]

---

1. "Natural and Revealed Religion," in *The Cambridge History of Eighteenth-Century*

Introduction

The thrust and parry of arguments about revelation in the Age of Reason cannot be reduced to a single formula, but it becomes clear that without a concept of revelation the enterprise of Christian theology hardly seems possible. Obviously, if one is to move beyond historical description and interpretation, the first task will be to define more carefully the concept of revelation that seems to be in trouble; then, if *some* concept of revelation remains indispensable to the theological enterprise, to ask how we might go about rethinking the old one.

The classical view of revelation, found (with variations) in Thomas Aquinas (ca. 1225-1274) and Martin Luther (1483-1546), took it to mean information supernaturally imparted. Although the old belief about revelation was certainly represented by one strand in John Calvin (1509-1564), a fresh concept might be developed out of his comparison of God's Word to the provision of spectacles for the elderly or visually impaired: revelation is divinely improved vision, not the supernatural communication of truths about God that are inaccessible to reason. In Calvin's own use of the simile, the spectacles were the Scriptures of the Old and New Testaments, and the prescription was only for a privileged few, the elect — those whom God "pleased to gather more closely and intimately to himself." Schleiermacher, I think, was right to include in the introduction to his dogmatics a *generic* concept of revelation: that is, a formal concept applicable to Christianity and other religions as well, nothing being initially presupposed about material resemblances or differences. Hence (in Chap. 2) I adapt Calvin's simile to a broader frame of reference, and I develop a revised concept of revelation in dialogue with good friends and colleagues, each of whom honored me with an address on the occasion of my retirement: Van Harvey, who spoke for Ludwig Feuerbach (1804-1872); Bruce McCormack, for Karl Barth (1886-1968); and Walter Wyman, for Schleiermacher (with reservations). Despite the difficulties posed for Christian theology by allowing that revelation occurs in every religion, I end with a defense of *special* revelation.[2]

Philosophy, ed. Knud Haakonssen, 2 vols. (Cambridge: Cambridge University Press, 2006), 2:641-65. © Cambridge University Press 2006. Reprinted with permission. My chapter was intended to provide a general introduction to the third section of this composite volume: "Philosophy and Theology."

2. "Errors and Insights in the Understanding of Revelation: A Provisional Response," *Journal of Religion* 78 (1998): 64-88. © 1998 by The University of Chicago. Re-

II

In eighteenth-century Germany, the pervasive influence of Kant's moral interpretation of religion gave rise to debate about *faith and morals* in the Atheism Controversy (1798-99), precipitated by an anonymous father's admonition to his student son that if, with the atheist, you take away belief in God, moral chaos will result. There is an extensive and growing German literature on the controversy. But it has not (to the best of my knowledge) attracted much attention in English — not even for the light it sheds on the development of Fichte's philosophy of transcendental idealism (Chap. 3).

J. G. Fichte (1762-1814) held that the proper starting point for all our knowledge is not, as commonly supposed, perception of the world of sense but analysis of human selfhood (the "absolute ego"), and that this analysis establishes the fundamentally moral character of our existence. The real atheism, so he argues, is the idolatrous belief in God as a separate being, invoked to support moral order. By "God" we should rather mean the moral order itself, which cannot be denied and in which each of us has to find a place. For all the obvious differences between them, the Atheism Controversy and the earlier Pantheism Controversy (begun in 1785) shared a marked shift away from a dualistic to a monistic understanding of God and the world. With Fichte, as with Johann Gottfried von Herder (1744-1803), the task of a philosophical theology becomes explicitly revisionist: it is not solely a matter of either criticizing or defending an inherited idea of God, but rather of rethinking it in the light of the nisus to monism that characterized some of the profoundest thought of the day. And with the changing idea of deity went a changed understanding of the fundamental problem of religion: no longer "How can I get a gracious God?" but "Where do I fit in the grand scheme of things?"[3]

Fichte's colleague Friedrich Karl Forberg (1770-1848) developed the Kantian philosophy in a very different direction, and perhaps he was more faithful to Kant's intentions. He argued that religious belief, rightly interpreted, is strictly practical: it is not the factual assertion that God or

---

printed with permission. The presentations delivered by Harvey, McCormack, and Wyman are printed in the same number of the journal.

3. "Idolatrous Faith: Fichte's Atheism Controversy." Tate-Willson Lecture II, 1981; previously unpublished.

a moral world order (a "kingdom of God") actually exists but rather, as purely practical, only binds us to act *as if* there were a God or a moral order. Religion is moral commitment in the guise of metaphysical assertions. Nevertheless, Forberg granted that while morality does not need metaphysics to ground it, reflection on the autonomous moral imperative leads inescapably to a theistic worldview — to a God who is the principle of moral order. Invoking God to guarantee virtue gets things exactly the wrong way around: the movement of thought is from morality to metaphysics, not from a theistic metaphysics to a well-founded morality. For himself Forberg, unlike Fichte, had no real interest in working out a worldview on the foundation of morality, but he left the door open for just such a "moral theology." And in response to Forberg's argument, I suggest (in Chap. 4) that a better meaning of "practical belief" would be, not a belief that says nothing at all about the way the world goes, but factual belief that *arises out of* moral experience.[4]

It is precisely the moral strand in religious belief that shows the inadequacy of the attempt made by Ludwig Feuerbach (1804-1872) to understand religion as the product of an obsessive desire for happiness. Van Harvey's recent study argues that Feuerbach's theory of religion in *The Essence of Religion* (1848), is more persuasive than the earlier — and better known — projection theory in *The Essence of Christianity* (1841). ("Projection" was George Eliot's translation of the German *Vergegenständlichung,* "objectification," the psychological mechanism by which purely human ideals are objectified in an imaginary divinity.) The later theory sought to understand religion as reaction to the encounter with nature. It was certainly a merit of Feuerbach's explanation that he recognized the inadequacy of the old view of religion as grounded solely in *fear* of natural phenomena: account must also be taken of other emotions stirred by nature — the feeling of release from fear and anxiety, the feeling of delight, joy, love, and gratitude. Missing, however, in Feuerbach's interpretation of religion was due attention to confrontation with a moral imperative. Once again, Calvin is enlisted (in Chap. 5) — this time for his firm emphasis on moral demand, or faith as obedi-

4. "Toward a Moral Theology: Forberg on Practical Belief," *Criterion* 29 (1990): 10-13. © 1990 by The University of Chicago (The Divinity School). Reprinted with permission. A shortened version of an informal address on work in progress, given on 9 February 1989 in the Divinity School of the University of Chicago.

ence. Although he could describe human nature as a veritable factory of idols, he understood true religion as conforming to an order that is given, not manufactured, and he understood this order as mediating the demand of a divine will. This is not to assume, without argument, that Calvin was right about religion, but simply to point to a major — perhaps fatal — deficiency in the later theory of Feuerbach.[5]

III

Calvin has already made his appearance in Parts I and II. Part III turns directly to *the Calvinist tradition* and (in Chap. 6) offers some very brief remarks on Calvin's relation to Augustine, Bernard, Luther, Schleiermacher, and Barth, especially on grace and election. Calvin's debts to his predecessors Augustine (354-430) and Bernard (1090-1153) are generally acknowledged and have been examined in depth in a number of recent studies. His affection for these two "fathers" of the church led him to claim them for the evangelical side in the conflict with Rome, and he insisted that his apparent differences from them on "free will" and "merit" were merely semantic: their use of the terms could be improved, but they really meant what he, too, believed about the bondage of the will and the gratuitous favor of God.

Textbook judgments on Calvin's relation to his contemporary Martin Luther, on the other hand, are still distorted, in some respects, by the legacy of denominational controversies between the Lutherans and the Reformed and the failure to distinguish clearly enough between Calvin and Ulrich Zwingli (1484-1531). There was unquestionably a difference of accent when Luther and Calvin spoke of the role of law in the Christian life, but on the sacrament of the Lord's Supper Calvin stood close to Luther, and even closer to Augustine; he judged Zwingli's opinion to be simply "profane."

Chapter 6 concludes with observations on Calvin's heritage in the theologies of Schleiermacher and Barth. (I return to Schleiermacher

5. "Feuerbach's Religious Illusion," *Christian Century* 114 (1997): 362-67; a review article on Van A. Harvey, *Feuerbach and the Interpretation of Religion,* Cambridge Studies in Religion and Critical Thought, vol. 1 (Cambridge: Cambridge University Press, 1995). Copyright © 1997 by the *Christian Century.* Reprinted by permission from the April 9, 1997, issue of the *Christian Century.*

and the legacy of Calvin in Chapter 8.) Particularly interesting is the way these heirs of Calvin dealt with the doctrine of election. They were agreed on the fundamental importance of the doctrine: Schleiermacher undertook to defend it in a remarkable essay, and Barth identified it as nothing less than the sum of the gospel. But neither of them could approve of Calvin's double predestination of some to eternal life and others to eternal death: they were of one mind in affirming that it is *humanity* that is elect in Jesus Christ. If this seems like quite a liberty to take with the Calvinist heritage, they could have appealed to Calvin's own principle that we must form in the manner we think best whatever is handed on by us. His descendants are faithful to his memory when they take the Calvinist tradition to be progressive.[6]

But what *is* Calvinism? Charles Hodge (1797-1878) is usually taken as the foremost nineteenth-century spokesman of Calvinism in America. He set the pattern among American evangelicals of excluding Schleiermacher from the Reformed family (or even from the Christian family!), whereas in Germany Alexander Schweizer (1808-1888) praised Schleiermacher as the actual renewer of Reformed theology after its decline during the eighteenth century. Hodge appeared on the theological scene (Chap. 7) at a time of bitter controversy over the new German theology and biblical scholarship. His comments, mostly negative, on German theology in general and Schleiermacher in particular are fascinating — sometimes amusing, whenever he has recourse to ethnological comparisons of the German and the Anglo-American "minds." Despite some ungrudging praise for Schleiermacher's piety and personality, he could see nothing in his thought but a pantheistic threat to sound, biblical theology. Whether Hodge understood Schleiermacher, or even read him with care, is open to doubt. But his stature and influence have lent his name to a strong anti-Schleiermacherian stream in American theology.[7]

Schleiermacher and Hodge both paid their respects to Calvin. A

6. "The Place of Calvin in Christian Theology," in *The Cambridge Companion to John Calvin,* ed. Donald K. McKim (Cambridge: Cambridge University Press, 2004), pp. 289-304. © Cambridge University Press, 2004. Reprinted with permission.

7. "Charles Hodge and the Europeans," in *Charles Hodge Revisited: A Critical Appraisal of His Life and Work,* ed. John W. Stewart and James H. Moorhead (Grand Rapids: Eerdmans, 2002), pp. 129-58. © 2002 Wm. B. Eerdmans Publishing Co. Papers from a symposium held on the campuses of Princeton University and Princeton Theological Seminary, 22-24 October 1997.

comparison of their actual references to Calvin (in Chap. 8) suggests that "the Calvinist tradition" is in part a construct, capable of development in more than one direction. When Schleiermacher spoke of the development of doctrine, he was not making a historical observation that Christian doctrine has in fact developed, but defining the task of the theologian, which is precisely the further development of received doctrine, not mindless transmission of it. Development, for him, was not a problem but a duty. Hodge, by contrast, thought of tradition in static terms, and he could only say yes (usually) or no (occasionally) to the legacy of Calvin: he did not take it up as something worth developing. For this reason, it is pertinent to note that Calvin himself, at any rate in his attitude toward Luther, claimed the right to affirm a developing, not a static, tradition. He thought of himself not as bound to Luther's every word, but as traveling along the path that Luther had opened up.[8]

IV

The final two parts of the present volume move closer to the heart of Christian belief and show how two particular Christian doctrines — atonement and the Eucharist — exemplify divergent Calvinist traditions. "Theories of *atonement*" may sound like an archaic theme, but the question it seeks to answer concerns the central Christian conviction, on which everything else turns, that "in Christ God was reconciling the world to himself" (2 Cor. 5:19). It is hard to imagine that there might be any argument about that, though there are certainly other ways of saying it. And if that is so, then the central question for Christian theology can only be: What does it mean to confess with the apostle Paul that an activity of God occurred in Jesus Christ that brought about a new relationship between God and an estranged, or even hostile, world?

It is probably the idea of vicarious satisfaction or penal substitution that still dominates official Protestant teaching on atonement, and those who reject it, or have silent reservations about it, are often at a loss to

---

8. "Constructing Tradition: Schleiermacher, Hodge, and the Theological Legacy of Calvin," in *The Legacy of John Calvin: Papers Presented at the 12th Colloquium of the Calvin Studies Society, April 22-24 1999,* ed. David Foxgrover (Grand Rapids: CRC Product Services, 2000), pp. 158-75. © Calvin Studies Society, 2000. Reprinted with permission.

say what they could commend in its place. By "vicarious satisfaction" is meant the theory that the death of Christ satisfied the penalty imposed on sinful humanity by a just God. Hodge's *Systematic Theology* contains one of the most detailed apologies for the theory of vicarious satisfaction (or one version of it) in the English language (Chap. 9). He did not want to say, with Calvin, that the Son of God actually experienced the torments of a condemned man: his suffering was rather a "just equivalent" to the penalties due to condemned sinners. This was perhaps a significant departure from Calvin, though Hodge did not expressly say so. But, be that as it may, Hodge's thoughts on atonement were centered entirely on the *death* of Christ, understood as executing a transaction between God the Father and God the Son that gave the divine love room to operate without compromising the divine justice.[9]

By contrast, John Williamson Nevin (1803-1886), Hodge's one-time pupil and theological adversary, saw reconciliation brought about by the incarnation, through which the divine *life* of Christ flowed into humanity and, in the life of the church, still does (Chap. 10). It is not by a transaction between the first and second persons of the Trinity ("outside us"), but rather by participation in the quickening power of Christ's person ("in us") that humanity is saved. Whereas Hodge's legal metaphors moved within the orbit of the Latin theological tradition, Nevin's exuberant organic or biological metaphors brought him close to the old Greek fathers with their notion of deification — and close to none other than John Calvin, whose teaching on the Lord's Supper affirmed that Christ "transfuses into us the life-giving vigor of his flesh." The meaning of Christ's death, in Nevin's view, can be understood only in its connection with the incarnation: it is then rightly seen as, with the resurrection, the final victory of life over sin and hell.

Hodge and Nevin agreed that their quarrel had its roots in the differences between Zwingli and Calvin, the original creators of the Reformed tradition (or "traditions," plural). Calvin himself drew attention to two ways in which "the life-giving flesh" of Christ (John 6:51-58) was being interpreted by the Reformers. In the one view (Zwingli's), the flesh of Christ was life-giving only in the sense that it was crucified for our salvation; in the other view (Calvin's), Christ's flesh gives life to believers be-

---

9. "Charles Hodge on the Death of Christ." Schaff Lecture I, 1998; previously unpublished.

cause they are joined with him in a sacred union that the sacrament of the Lord's Supper nurtures and increases. As the contrast reappears in Hodge and Nevin, it must be admitted that neither view is above criticism, but Nevin's — which shows a clear affinity with the "participatory" strand in Calvin's understanding of the work of Christ — deserves more recognition than it has received. Is it capable of development as a possible alternative to the dominant doctrine of penal substitution? And Nevin makes the important suggestion that the way the sacrament of the Lord's Supper is understood will govern one's understanding of other theological themes, including the work of Christ.[10] It is to the Eucharist, then, and the grace it confers that we turn, finally, in Part V.

V

The meaning of *the Eucharist* was one of the most hotly debated issues of the sixteenth century. By 1520 Luther had decided that the Roman Catholic Mass was a fearful perversion of the Lord's institution at the Last Supper. Christ did not institute a sacrifice but a testament, by which he promised forgiveness of sins to his disciples, and he added a sign as confirmation of the promise: the presence of his body and blood under the elements of bread and wine. Vehement though his denunciation of the Roman Mass certainly was, Luther's anger was fiercer still when he learned that Ulrich Zwingli rejected the real presence and the very notion of a means of grace. Zwingli agreed that the Lord's Supper is not a sacrifice: it is *remembrance* of a sacrifice. The body and blood of Christ are not, therefore, in the elements: to eat and drink the body and blood is to look back to the cross and *believe,* with gratitude, that Christ died for our sins. Receiving the elements cannot save us, or else, in Zwingli's view, we would have to surrender the fundamental Reformation principle that we are saved by faith alone *(sola fide)*.

Calvin found Zwingli's explanation of the Eucharist no less wrongheaded than Luther did. The Johannine language of eating the flesh of the Son of Man meant something quite different to him; and it is crucial to recognize that what was at stake for him was not simply the mode of

---

10. "John Williamson Nevin on the Life of Christ." Schaff Lecture II, 1998; previously unpublished.

Christ's presence when the Sacrament is celebrated, but the manner in which the Christian is related to Christ all the time. Zwingli was of course right to insist that eating the flesh of the Son of Man is figurative, but in Calvin's view he was wrong about the meaning of the figure. For Calvin, it meant that the believer is related to Christ not merely by believing, but by an intimate union that draws life from him; and he held that the sacramental signs are not merely reminders of past grace, but means by which the living Christ offers himself anew to his people as the food of their souls.

Calvin's eucharistic theology aligned him closely with Martin Bucer (1491-1551) and Peter Martyr Vermigli (1500-1562), and their lead was followed — if hesitantly — by the English reformer Thomas Cranmer (1489-1556). Chapter 11 was originally designed as a comprehensive review of the various ways in which the Eucharist was understood in the time of the Reformation, laying out the options even-handedly. It takes account not only of the Lutherans, the Zwinglians, and the Calvinists, but also of Tridentine Catholicism and the so-called Left Wing of the Reformation (Anabaptists, Spiritualists, and Rationalists). For the purpose of the present volume, it serves to set Calvin's contribution in its sixteenth-century context, drawing the lines that show where he faced his adversaries and where he found his friends.[11]

Implicit in the eucharistic controversies were divergent understandings of *the grace of Christ* (Chap. 12). Many historians and ecumenical theologians these days, both Roman Catholic and Protestant, commend Luther as champion of the Catholic witness to the absolute priority of grace against a semi-Pelagian deviation from it in late medieval scholasticism. But the suspicion lingers that, by their heavy emphasis on grace alone *(sola gratia),* the Protestants neglected the Christian's sanctification and obligation to do good works. In actual fact, Luther taught that in addition to the wholly unmerited *grace* that justifies the sinner God grants the *gift* of healing from the sickness of sin; and Calvin spoke expressly of a "*double* grace" received by participation in Christ — reconciliation and renewal. This is not to say that no differences on the grace of Christ distinguish Protestants from Roman Catholics. Precisely be-

---

11. "Eucharist," in *The Oxford Encyclopedia of the Reformation,* ed. Hans J. Hillerbrand, 4 vols. (New York: Oxford University Press, 1996), 2:71-81. Reprinted by permission of Oxford University Press, Inc.

cause Luther made the *Word* of God — the gospel — the paramount means of grace, whereas in the medieval tradition grace was mediated by the sacraments, disagreements were bound to arise, whether or not ecumenical theology can now overcome them.

There remains for both communions, Roman Catholic and Protestant alike, the problem of divine grace and human responsibility, inherited from Augustine. The Pauline questions, "What do you have that you did not receive? And if you received it, why do you boast as if it were not a gift?" (I Cor. 4:7) were the foundation of Augustine's piety of thankfulness. But relentless logic led him to conclude that even the choice by which one person receives grace, while another doesn't, must be wholly the gift of God, grounded solely in predestination. And where does that leave human freedom? Luther's adoption of the aphorism of John Wycliffe (ca. 1325-1384) condemned by the Council of Constance (1414-1418), "Everything happens by absolute necessity," only underscores the problem. The question for our "thinking with the church" is whether post-Reformation Protestantism, in surrendering predestination, has preserved the confession of God's sovereign grace.[12]

---

12. "Sovereign Grace: Is Reformed Theology Obsolete?" *Interpretation* 57 (2003): 45-57. © 2003 by Union Theological Seminary and Presbyterian School of Christian Education. Reprinted with permission.

PART ONE

Revelation

CHAPTER I

Revelation and the Religion of Reason

So-called natural religion is usually so refined and has such philosophical and moral manners that it allows little of the unique
character of religion to shine through.

Friedrich Schleiermacher, *On Religion*

The importance of the eighteenth-century Age of Reason for interpreting religion is commonly recognized; but how its importance is perceived depends on where one sees its outcome. It was a time of intense
disagreement about the nature and worth of religion. A student at Cambridge in the early years of the following century — say, around 1810 —
would have been confident that the redoubtable Archdeacon Paley had
finally vindicated religion, both natural and revealed, against a hundred
years of criticisms. The doors of the church and the academy were still
open for business as usual. Today's admirer of the Enlightenment is
more likely to find the representative figure in the skeptical David Hume
or the acid Voltaire, their exposure of frail arguments and pious absurdi-
ties being taken as the final antidote to conventional religion. Yet others
may think that at the end of the eighteenth century the meager religious
insights of the Enlightenment, such as they were, were taken up into the
grander visions of Herder, Goethe, Schleiermacher, and Hegel. Still,
there would be general agreement that the eighteenth century raised
good questions about religion, whoever is held to have come up with the
best answers.

Old theological controversies endured; frequently, they became entangled in domestic politics. But the main interest of the period for religious thought arises out of questions brought to the forum of public debate by the Deists. The participants in the debate, including both the defenders and the critics of religion, held overconfident opinions that time would prove to be much more parochial than they imagined. On all sides, limited perceptions of the essence, benefits, and defects of religion were naively universalized, and obstinate stereotypes of a complex and elusive mode of human behavior were bequeathed to future generations. But, for all that, the contestants opened up *approaches* to religion that were characteristically modern. One part of their legacy was what we would call today a "non-theological" approach, and another was the transformation of theology itself.

An enormous body of literature was generated by the eighteenth-century debates on religion. A few attempts have been made to put together anthologies of representative selections.[1] But much of the literature is accessible today only in research libraries; little more than a small fragment exists in modern reprints or critical editions. The field of eighteenth-century religious studies is currently receiving unprecedented scholarly attention, partly from scholars in search of the roots of the philosophy of religion and the science (or history) of religion as distinctively modern disciplines. (The theologians are usually more interested in the nineteenth century, especially the first three decades, a time when Christian theology enjoyed in Germany one of the most creative periods of its entire history.) It is hardly possible to present a comprehensive survey of the field here. All that is attempted is to place together in context the more important issues and thinkers. From the theological point of view (as from others), the century is open-ended both at its beginning and at its close. However, one might roughly identify a period that runs from John Locke's *The Reasonableness of Christianity* (1695) to Friedrich Schleiermacher's *On Religion: Speeches to its Cultured*

---

1. John Martin Creed and John Sandwith Boys Smith, *Religious Thought in the Eighteenth Century, Illustrated from Writers of the Period* (Cambridge: Cambridge University Press, 1934); E. Graham Waring, *Deism and Natural Religion: A Source Book* (New York: Frederick Ungar, 1967); Peter Gay, *Deism: An Anthology* (Princeton: D. Van Nostrand, 1968). For the secondary literature, see the extensive bibliographies in the volume from which the present chapter is taken: Knud Haakonssen, ed., *The Cambridge History of Eighteenth-Century Philosophy*, 2 vols. (Cambridge: Cambridge University Press, 2006), 2:1141-1341.

Despisers (German 1799), which clearly marks the transition from the old Christian apologetics to the new. Interest falls naturally on two main themes: the Deist Controversy in England and new theological beginnings in Germany. But first, it will be as well to sketch the intellectual environment in which Deism was born: it was a time of religious turmoil and of the emergence of liberal and radical theological traditions.

I. The Theological Situation

The sixteenth-century struggle for reform of the Western church ended in the creation of new churches. After years of appalling armed conflict, the existence of separate churches or "confessions" could only be an acknowledged fact. In Germany, where the Protestant Reformation had begun, the refinement and defense of confessional traditions engaged much of the theologians' energies throughout the seventeenth century. But by the eighteenth century theological disagreement ceased to shape the international situation, and the churches largely assumed the role of supports for the political establishments of their respective lands. The very plurality of churches and the existence of dissenting minorities within them encouraged the spirit of toleration that revulsion against dogmatism and religious wars had provoked. A liberal religious tradition emerged. It held the promise of fresh theological directions, transcending the old party lines, even if it sometimes sank into a dry formalism, against which more passionate varieties of religiousness protested. And the extraordinary expansion of knowledge about the human species, other lands, and the wider cosmos further encouraged the openness of the liberal spirit. There was no warfare of science and religion, but there was a crisis of authority in both religion and science.

1. The "Men of Moderation"

Toleration of dissenting minorities did not come easily or quickly. By the Edict of Nantes (1598), Henry IV ended the French wars of religion and granted the Huguenots the right to free exercise of the Reformed or Calvinist religion in designated locations. But Bourbon hostility to the Huguenots led to further armed conflict, and in 1685 the edict was re-

5

voked by Louis XIV, in whose reign the Huguenot exodus from France began. In the German Empire, the pattern of accommodation between the churches was foreshadowed by the Peace of Augsburg (1555), which affirmed the right of every Lutheran or Roman Catholic ruler to determine the religion of his own domain. The Calvinists were not included in the settlement, and dissenters were confronted with a harsh choice: either to conform or to sell everything and migrate. Only in the imperial free cities could Lutherans and Roman Catholics expect to live together. But "territorialism," rather than strict toleration, was still the solution that brought the Thirty Years' War to an end (Peace of Westphalia, 1648). This time the rights of the Calvinists were recognized, but the Anabaptists had no acknowledged homeland.

In the English-speaking world, toleration came sooner in two of the American colonies than in the motherland. Founded by Lord Baltimore as a refuge for English Catholics (1634), Maryland extended its welcome to Protestants as well; and Rhode Island's history began when Puritan separatist Roger Williams bought land from the Indians at "Providence" (1636) and pledged religious freedom to "those distressed for cause of conscience." In England itself, Oliver Cromwell's dream of an inclusive church settlement, which would have given equal recognition to a variety of religious viewpoints and have left the rest alone, did not survive him. With the restoration of the monarchy (1660) came the return of the episcopal establishment, and the Act of Uniformity (1662) deprived an estimated 1,800 Puritan clergy of their pastoral charges. The accession of William and Mary and the Toleration Act (1689) removed some of the more severe penalties of the law from most nonconformists, but not from Roman Catholics or Unitarians.

The antithesis of "establishment" and "nonconformity" was never overcome, but the course of theological reflection in the Anglican church did reinforce the legal requirement of toleration. During the fearful religious conflicts of seventeenth-century England, a third stream of religious thought can be identified, self-consciously disowning the dogmatism of the high churchmen and the dogmatism of their Puritan adversaries. The "men of moderation," also called in derision "Latitudinarians," were minimalists in their creed and urged modesty and open-mindedness in the pursuit of uncertain questions. Immensely important though they were for the course of religious thought in the eighteenth century, it is arguable that they won the cause of moderation only at a price: religion came to be widely understood as a private matter for the individual conscience, faith as free assent to a minimum of morally useful beliefs, and churches as voluntary associations for the propagation of beliefs and the promotion of virtue.

This, indeed, was the position John Locke (1632-1704) spoke for in *A Letter concerning Toleration,* published in the same year as the Toleration Act. Religion, he held, is an inward persuasion of the mind. No one can be coerced into accepting a particular religion, since the nature of the understanding is such that "it cannot be compell'd to the belief of any thing by outward force." A church is a voluntary society, which a man is as free to leave as he was to enter, according to the way he judges its doctrine and worship.[2] For Locke, it was plainly doctrine that came first — religious beliefs to which free intellectual assent could be given. And there were not very many of them. In *The Reasonableness of Christianity* he assures us that the only faith and repentance God requires of us are belief that Jesus is the Messiah ("the one great Point") and a "sincere Endeavour after Righteousness, in obeying his Law." It is true that other great doctrines are "dropt here and there" in the New Testament epistles, but they are not fundamental articles of faith and must not be thought necessary to salvation. Locke's religion was for plain, laboring men — suited to vulgar capacities and unencumbered with the niceties of the schools.[3]

While it simplified religion, perhaps too drastically, the liberal or latitudinarian mentality cultivated the spirit of free inquiry. The thesis that Puritan ideals gave a strong impetus to the scientific revolution continues to be widely debated, for and against, but some historians of science argue that Latitudinarian attitudes must have been much more propitious to the scientific enterprise. In Restoration Cambridge, after the publication of Isaac Newton's *Principia mathematica* (1687), a "holy alliance" between moderate churchmanship and Newtonian natural philosophy fostered a buoyant rational theology, and Newton's eminent disciple Samuel Clarke was firmly persuaded that the new science left the atheists with no place to hide.

2. John Locke, *Epistola de tolerantia,* published anonymously in Latin (Gouda, 1689) and translated into English by William Popple: see John Locke, *A Letter concerning Toleration* (1689), ed. James H. Tully (Indianapolis: Hackett, 1983), pp. 27-28.

3. John Locke, *The Reasonableness of Christianity as Delivered in the Scriptures* (anon., London, 1695); ed. John C. Higgins-Biddle in the Clarendon Edition of the Works of John Locke (Oxford: Clarendon, 1999), pp. 104, 119, 132, 166, 169.

2. Radical Religious Thought

In at least one respect, however, theological discourse in the Age of Reason was to take a turn that the seventeenth-century Latitudinarians did not anticipate. Whereas they wanted to calm theological rancor by reducing the number of essential Christian beliefs, others, more radical than they, decided that the entire inner-Christian quarrel was hopelessly parochial, the real problem being how to relate Christianity itself and all other religions to a presumed universal essence of religion. Whether God prefers the church to be presbyterian or episcopal faded into triviality beside the question whether he has chosen to reveal himself only to contentious Christians. This is the question already raised in the seventeenth century by Lord Herbert of Cherbury (1583-1648), sometimes called "the father of Deism."

In the enlarged edition of his epistemological study on truth (1645), Herbert inserted a discussion of religion and revelation in which he argued that the only doctrines known to be true are those that command universal assent: "common notions" that God has given in all times and places to all people. Every religion has some portion of the truth, but corrupted by error, so that we have to separate the truth by applying Herbert's method: we discover the common notions by surveying all the religions of the world comparatively, or, more expeditiously, by examining the contents of our own minds. Herbert's five religious notions are: that there is a Supreme Deity; that this Sovereign Deity ought to be worshiped; that the best part of divine worship is virtue conjoined with piety; that all vices and crimes should be expiated by repentance; and that there are rewards and punishments after this life. The true catholic church, outside of which there is indeed no salvation, is constituted by these common notions, and it embraces people of all times and places. Every particular church's truth depends on how far it is separated from this one.[4] A similar belief in a normative, universally accessible essence of religion was defended later by Matthew Tindal in the Deist Controversy.

A second variety of radical religious thought also led beyond the

---

4. Lord Herbert of Cherbury (Baron Edward Herbert), *De veritate,* enlarged ed. (London, 1645); ed. with an English translation by Meyrick H. Carré, University of Bristol Studies, no. 6 (Bristol: J. W. Arrowsmith, 1937; reprinted London: Routledge/Thoemmes, 1992), chaps. 9-10. The first edition was published in Paris in 1624.

Latitudinarians by inquiring into the psychology, rather than the episte-mology, of religious belief. An interest in the emotional sources of belief had been sparked by the way Thomas Hobbes (1588-1679) treated the subject in his *Leviathan* (1651). Hobbes endorsed the opinion of the Ro-man poet Statius (though not by name) that fear first made the gods — "in the ignorance of causes," Hobbes adds. But he acknowledged that monotheism, at least, had a rational impulse behind it: precisely the de-sire to know the causes of things.[5] The coincidence of religious fanati-cism and early studies of physiology in the seventeenth century, such as Robert Burton's pioneering work on melancholy, invited a further pos-sibility: that religion, or at least "enthusiasm," is a sickness. In *The Natu-ral History of Superstition* (1709) by John Trenchard (1662-1723) we find a clinical scrutiny of "enthusiasm" as an emotional disorder with a phys-iological base. One suspects that, despite the cautious title of his work, Trenchard would be willing to include the orthodox zealots in his diag-nosis along with the enthusiasts: the cause of their unyielding temper, too, is perhaps an intoxication with "Vapours ascending from the lower Regions of [the] Body."[6] Hume, at any rate, who thought such a matter worthy of a philosopher's attention, titled his own venture into the field, quite simply, *The Natural History of Religion* (1757). But is it really a mat-ter for philosophy — or theology — at all?

3. Theology, Natural and Revealed

In our day, theology, the philosophy of religion, the history of religions, and the scientific study of religion have become separate disciplines. Sometimes they are perceived as mutually antagonistic. It would be an anachronism to read these terminological distinctions back into the eighteenth century, even though it was then that the material differ-ences began to emerge. A hint of the need for new nomenclature can be discerned in the Deists' revival of a very ancient Stoic distinction, which they attributed to Varro, between three kinds of theology: mythical, nat-

5. Thomas Hobbes, *Leviathan* (London, 1651), I, xii; ed. Richard Tuck (Cambridge: Cambridge University Press, 1996), pp. 76-77.
6. John Trenchard, *The Natural History of Superstition* (London, 1709), p. 50. Trenchard nevertheless believed that a rational religion, which improves the faculties, is entirely possible (p. 16).

ural or rational, and civil or political. It might also strike us as conceptually tidier to distinguish theology from religion, and science from philosophy. But that, too, would be to impose more order on the sources than they display. Francis Bacon, it is true, began the drive to detach the natural sciences from sacred theology; but he called science "natural philosophy," as did Newton still, a century later. And if we consult Dr. Johnson's *Dictionary,* we find theology itself was assumed to be a science. He equates "theology" with "divinity" and illustrates his meaning from Richard Hooker: "Theology, what is it but the science of things divine?"[7] Properly speaking, it may be, "religion" denotes a mode of human behavior, "theology" one of the intellectual disciplines (sciences) that concern themselves with religion. But no such clarification was current in the eighteenth century.

In the seventeenth-century schools of divinity, the word "theology" was sometimes applied (as *theologia archetypa*) to God's knowledge of himself. But as human knowledge of God *(theologia ectypa),* theology was "discourse about God and divine things" — a definition warranted, according to the Lutheran Johann Andreas Quenstedt (1617-1688), by the etymology of the word. The general field of theological study was broken down into several subdisciplines: Johann Friedrich Koenig (1619-1664), for example, another Lutheran divine, distinguished exegetical, didactic (systematic), polemical, homiletic, casuistic, and ecclesiastical theology. Such divisions persist throughout the eighteenth century. But they barely hint at the new distinctions that were to emerge; rather, they betray the clerical connection of theological study, and it must be remembered that the universities, including Oxford and Cambridge, were still seminaries of the established churches.

Much more important philosophically was the contrast commonly drawn between natural and revealed theology, or natural and revealed religion. Against the Socinian view that the soul is a tabula rasa at birth, the orthodox divines of the seventeenth century affirmed the existence of an innate notion of God, closely connected with the voice of conscience. They further held that the innate notion of God assumed deter-

---

7. The quotation is from Richard Hooker (1586-1647), *Of the Laws of Ecclesiastical Polity,* 8 bks. (London, 1593-1662), III, viii [11]; reprint of bks. I-V, with an intro. by Christopher Morris, 2 vols., Everyman's Library, pp. 201-2 (London: J. M. Dent & Sons, 1954), 1:319.

minate characteristics through observation of nature, understood as
general revelation, and in particular through meditation on human nature (the microcosm, or world in miniature). But they deemed all knowledge of God derived from nature insufficient for salvation, because the
good pleasure of God cannot be firmly grasped apart from God's self-
communication in Scripture, which is *special revelation.* Reason untouched by grace is not a neutral instrument of inquiry: it is biased and
blinded by the vested interests of the sinful will and must not be regarded as the criterion of what is true in religion. The truths of revelation cannot be conceived by reason. But reason, when enlightened by
grace and revelation, has the ability to apprehend these truths and the
duty to defend them by proving that revelation has in fact occurred.

There is room in this scheme for rational explication of both natural
and revealed religion, and there are a few mixed articles that are accessible in part to philosophy as well as to theology. In practice, however, the
distinction between natural and revealed theology required only a perfunctory treatment of the former in a prolegomenon to theology
proper. Moreover, theology was taken to be, like medicine, preeminently a practical discipline. Just as the goal of medicine is not knowledge of the body but health, so theology is directed to the worship of
God and human blessedness. Indeed, as Quenstedt pointed out, theology is a *discipline* only in a secondary sense: in its primary sense it is a
disposition (a "habit") of the mind.[8] It is easy to see why the orthodox divines could use the words "theology" and "religion" interchangeably:
theology was not disinterested academic inquiry but belonged to the
practice of piety. It is also easy to understand that the critics of divinity
wondered if it was not, after all, the "enlightened" reason of the divines
that was at the disposal of self-interest — the self-interest of piety.

Purists may insist that "natural theology" and "natural religion" are
not synonymous terms. The idea of a natural theology goes back to
Plato's attempt to show that certain truths about God can be strictly
demonstrated; and it plays, of course, a significant role in medieval
scholasticism, notably in the "five ways" by which Thomas Aquinas
sought to prove the existence of God. Natural religion, by contrast, is

8. Johann Andreas Quenstedt, cited in Heinrich Schmid, *The Doctrinal Theology of
the Evangelical Lutheran Church,* trans. Charles A. Hay and Henry E. Jacobs (1875; reprinted, Minneapolis: Augsburg, 1961), p. 19.

rooted in Stoic thought. Here the claim is that buried under the various doctrines and practices of the rival religions are a few beliefs held in common by all, and that these alone are the essentials of religion, all else being accidental accretions. It is the Stoic concept, taken up by Lord Herbert of Cherbury, that becomes primary in the Deist Controversy, but it was not sharply differentiated from the Platonic concept. The organ by which natural religion comes into existence was held to be reason, and it was an understandable step to add that reason, as ratiocination, could prove at least some of the propositions of natural religion. In practice, the terms were used indifferently. The title of Hume's celebrated work is *Dialogues concerning Natural Religion* (1779). But the dialogues themselves belong largely to the argumentative genre of the theistic proofs, and they do in fact speak expressly of "natural and revealed *theology*" as well as "natural *religion*," the terms not being clearly distinguished. Hume's other investigation, into the origin of religion in human nature (the *Natural History of Religion*), certainly owes a great deal to eighteenth-century preoccupation with nature and natural explanations, but it is an enterprise that would in due course be transferred from natural theology to the social sciences.

The eighteenth century did not invent the contrast between natural and revealed theology, but in the course of the Deist Controversy the inherited priority was reversed. The insufficiency of the light of nature had formerly been the basis of the Protestant appeal to Scripture: reason was unambiguously subordinated to revelation, and the mainline theologians did not expect to discover beyond Christianity anything but superstition and idolatry. Indeed, that is what the Puritans found in Roman Catholicism and even, in smaller measure, in Anglicanism. They agreed with Calvin's verdict that human nature is a "perpetual factory of idols," and that only Scripture can clarify "the otherwise confused knowledge of God in our minds." Perhaps the weak link in the argument was the enlistment of reason to prove that revelation had indeed occurred, despite the caution with which Calvin had tried to make the case.[9] The Deists, at any rate, wanted to give reason this task — without caution — and more.

Durable questions of revealed theology continued to occupy church divines in the eighteenth century. They debated ecclesiastical authority,

9. John Calvin, *ICR* I, xi.8 (1:108); vi.1 (1:70); viii.1-2 (1:81-83).

the doctrines of the Trinity and the person of Christ, original sin, election and free will, efficacious grace, the Eucharist, and so on. The Jansenist controversy in France, originally about the Augustinian doctrine of grace, became endlessly entangled in the party politics of church and state, not least because the Jansenists took up the ancient demand of Gallicanism for limitation of papal sovereignty over the French church. In England, the incursions of anti-Trinitarianism stirred up continual debates about the deity of Christ. Even establishment theologians such as Samuel Clarke were suspected of Arianism, as, more forgivably, was Sir Isaac Newton. Presbyterians became unitarian by droves, and they found an able leader in the chemist-theologian Joseph Priestly. In Reformed Geneva, Voltaire discovered that all the leading ministers were Socinian.

The Trinitarian debate was plainly connected with the simplification of religion that the age demanded. Some ecclesiastical controversies were by no means cut off from the main trends of secular thought. Hobbesians and Calvinists, for example, invoked similar psychological arguments to refute "free will" (as commonly understood). Jonathan Edwards (1703-1758), possibly the greatest Reformed theologian of the eighteenth century, certainly the greatest in the English-speaking world, was equally at home in Christian doctrine and philosophical argument. He had been "entertained and delighted" with Locke's *Essay concerning Human Understanding* (1690) at the age of fourteen, and he undertook his great treatise on free will not only as a refutation of the insidious peril of Arminianism, but also as a philosophical study of moral agency. The liveliness of the debates about the Trinity, free will, and other perennial issues in Christian theology did not diminish. But Deism forced other, newer questions on the attention of the theologians, and they were much more radical questions, raising doubts about the truth of Christianity.

II. The Deist Controversy

Deism was an international phenomenon: the list of representative names includes, among others, John Toland and Matthew Tindal in England, Voltaire in France, Hermann Samuel Reimarus in Germany, and Thomas Paine in America. Unfortunately, however, the description "Deist," like so many others in the history of ideas, turns out to be elusive. In present-day usage a "deist" is someone who believes in an absentee deity: that is, in a God who fashioned the intricate machinery of the universe, then left it to run by its own immanent laws. It is far from clear that all the Deists were deists in this sense, although the mechanistic world-picture of Newtonian science unquestionably pushed theistic thinking in that direction. At any rate, the term "deists," as used by philosophers of religion today, does not give the defining characteristic of the historical group as a whole. Better, perhaps, is the description often associated with it: "freethinkers," those who refused to submit their thoughts — even on religion — to ecclesiastical authorities. It is then convenient to use the expression "Deist Controversy" simply to refer to two constantly recurring *quaestiones disputatae* that moved to the forefront of theological reflection in England during the first half of the eighteenth century. Both questions had to do with the claims of Christian revelation: the first was whether any such revelation was needed; the second, whether, as a matter of fact, a revelation had occurred.

The twofold problem of revelation lay already, just beneath the surface, in the work of John Locke, who in this respect was a transitional figure between orthodoxy and Deism. The chapter on "enthusiasm" that he added to the fourth edition of *An Essay concerning Human Understanding* (1700) does not depart radically from the orthodox divines, but it underscores the duties of reason just enough to be the harbinger of something new. The mark of a sincere lover of truth is "not entertaining any Proposition with greater assurance than the Proofs it is built upon will warrant." This, to be sure, means that "*Reason* must be our last Judge and Guide in every Thing." But Locke implies no opposition between reason and revelation. Reason is natural revelation; "*Revelation* is natural *Reason* enlarged by a new set of Discoveries communicated by GOD immediately...." Reason may not reject a supposedly revealed proposition simply on the grounds that its truth would never be "made out by natural Principles." Its task, rather, is to determine whether in truth the proposition comes from God. And how does reason do that? By noting the miraculous signs that attest a genuine revelation. Even where these are presently lacking, we still have the revelation of Scripture, which has already been attested, and the common dictates of right reason to guide us.[10]

10. John Locke, *An Essay concerning Human Understanding,* 4th ed. (London, 1700), IV, xix, §§1, 4, 14-16; ed. Peter H. Nidditch in the Clarendon Edition of the Works of John

It is precisely the assumptions of this confident argument against enthusiasm (that is, against the vain assurance of immediate, unauthenticated revelation) that the Deist Controversy opened to objection. If reason is able to judge revelation, are there really any new discoveries that revelation can bring to us? And is it in fact the case that the Christian Scriptures have been sufficiently attested as divine revelation? The two objections, obviously, belong together. But we may say that the first was acutely raised by Toland and Tindal; the second, by Anthony Collins, Thomas Woolston, Conyers Middleton, and others. The often caustic, always subversive arguments of the Deists provoked an astonishing quantity of orthodox replies. (There were around one hundred and fifty refutations of Tindal alone.) But in retrospect one is bound to view the entire controversy as a mere pause on the way from orthodox Christian faith to thoroughgoing skepticism. Correspondingly, the defense moves from detailed counterargument to a weary — or indignant — fideism.

1. The Critique of Revelation

John Toland's *Christianity not Mysterious* (1696), published anonymously, is commonly identified as the spark that fired the Deist Controversy, albeit Toland denied he was a Deist. (He preferred to represent himself as simply a good Anglican.) Revelation, he argued, is not mysterious; on the contrary, reason is given us as the instrument for comprehending it. When the New Testament speaks of "mysteries," it means things that were mysterious before they were revealed, but are not mysterious anymore. Reason is the candle, the guide, the judge that God has lodged within every man who comes into the world. With its aid even the vulgar can understand the gospel of Christ; what they cannot understand is the willful mystification of the gospel by clergymen, who want to keep them in subjection. "The uncorrupted Doctrines of *Christianity* are not above their Reach or Comprehension, but the Gibberish of your *Divinity Schools* they understand not."[11]

Locke (Oxford: Clarendon, 1975; pb. ed., with changes in the editorial material only, 1979), pp. 697-98, 704-6.

11. John Toland (1670-1722), *Christianity not Mysterious: Or, a Treatise Shewing, That there is nothing in the Gospel Contrary to Reason, Nor Above it, And that no Christian Doc-*

It is easy to surmise what the next step in the controversy is likely to be, but Toland shows himself reluctant to take it. "Others will say," he writes, "that this Notion of *Faith* makes *Revelation* useless. But, pray, how so? for the Question is not, whether we could discover all the Objects of our *Faith* by Ratiocination. . . . But I assert, that what is once reveal'd we must as well understand as any other Matter in the World."[12] The step from which Toland held back was firmly taken in Matthew Tindal's *Christianity as Old as the Creation* (1730), often referred to as "the Deists' Bible." For Tindal, the question was exactly what Toland said it wasn't: whether we could discover the objects of our faith without a revelation. To be sure, Tindal proceeded cautiously. He styled himself a "Christian Deist" and placed on the back of his title page a quotation from an esteemed churchman, Thomas Sherlock, then Bishop of Bangor: "The Religion of the Gospel, is the true original Religion of Reason and Nature. — And its Precepts declarative of that original Religion, which was as old as the Creation." Tindal's book, written in the form of a dialogue, is an extended commentary on this assertion in fourteen chapters, the last of which is a response to Samuel Clarke. The core of the argument is already evident in Tindal's subtitle: the gospel is simply a republication of natural religion.[13]

Whether or not an orthodox construction could be placed on the bishop's words, Tindal's argument is plainly designed to make one wonder whether the alleged republication of natural religion was necessary, or even a good idea. He takes his departure from the complaint of the clergy that the people have become cool to the speculative points of Christianity and are being misled by the low-church advocates of natural religion into magnifying mere sincerity, which places all religions on the same level. Tindal's response is that natural religion and revealed are actually the same in content, but the "Ecclesiasticks" have made revelation into an instrument of control and a cause of dissension. Rightly understood, everyone is perfectly capable of knowing the law of reason, or the religion of nature. The difficulty is that throughout Christian history the leaders of the church have done more to obscure natural reli-

trine can be properly call'd a Mystery (anon., London, 1696); facsimile reprint, ed. Günter Gawlick (Stuttgart-Bad Cannstatt: Friedrich Frommann, 1964), III, 4, §67.

12. Toland, *Christianity not Mysterious*, §66.

13. Matthew Tindal (1655-1733), *Christianity as Old as the Creation: or, The Gospel, a Republication of the Religion of Nature* (London, 1730); facsimile reprint, ed. Günter Gawlick (Stuttgart-Bad Cannstatt: Frommann-Holzboog, 1967).

gion than to promote it. The Scriptures themselves are partly to blame, because they confuse us with their obscurity; indeed, if taken literally, they mislead us with an imperfect morality, and virtue, after all, is what true religion is about. They even record mistakes; and if the apostles were wrong about Christ's speedy return, how can we be sure they were not wrong about other matters, too?

Tindal ends his book with an interesting threefold distinction that points toward Kant's *Religion within the Boundaries of Mere Reason* (German 1793). First, there are "Things, which, by their internal Excellency, shew themselves to be the Will of an infinitely wise, and good God." Second, there are "Things, which have no Worth in themselves; yet because those that have, can't many Times be perform'd without them, these are to be consider'd as Means to an End." Finally, there are things that are neither means nor ends, but mere superstitions. The second class of things is, of course, the most intriguing. While Tindal thought a great deal of organized religion was designed only to impose on a credulous laity, he was willing to concede an instrumental value to at least some outward forms of ecclesiastical piety. The important thing is not to forget what they are for: to promote the inward religion of the things in the first class. It is then possible to treat them as useful but mutable — to be varied according to human discretion. "He that carries these Distinctions in his Mind, will have a truer Notion of Religion, than if he had read all the *Schoolmen, Fathers,* and *Councils.*"

By the time we reach Tindal, the appeal to reason has taken a radical turn. No longer the organ for understanding revelation, reason is the actual source of whatever religious truth we have, and therefore the critical instrument by which we determine just how much truth any "instituted religion" may fairly claim for itself. The Christian Deist confesses that Christianity contains the true religion of reason, but he must admit that the Scriptures sometimes get in the way of the very religion they are supposed to "republish." The reversal of the old dogmatic superordination of Scripture to reason is complete, and it invites a thoroughgoing critical reappraisal of the Bible.

Reappraisal took the form, at least in part, of a direct assault on what had been the two main weapons in the Christian apologetic arsenal ever since the apostolic preaching recorded in the Acts of the Apostles: the fulfilment of prophecy and the performance of miracles. (See, for example, Peter's sermon on the Day of Pentecost in Acts 2:14-36.)

But it is not possible here to follow the case of Anthony Collins against the literal fulfilment of Old Testament prophecies in Jesus, or the case of Thomas Woolston against a literal interpretation of Jesus' miracles and resurrection from death. The importance of their subversive labors lies generally in their attempt to specify the fundamental principles of historical understanding. (The same holds for Conyers Middleton's work on post-canonical miracle stories.) The single most fundamental principle of all had been laid down already by John Toland: that there is no different rule to be followed in the interpretation of Scripture than is common to all other books.

2. The Defense of Revelation

There was no shortage of replies to the scandalous Deist literature. Apologists rose up by dozens — partly, it is said, because publication held out the hope of ecclesiastical advancement. Only a fraction of the counter-treatises is read anymore. But much of it was widely acclaimed in its own time, and some, at least, has the marks of enduring wisdom. The apologists adopted many different strategies. Even before the century began, *Charles Leslie* brought out *A short and easie Method with the Deists* (1698), which disposed of the troublemakers with four rules as to the truth of matters of fact done before our time. A matter attested must have been (1) sensible and (2) public, and (3) must have resulted in monuments and observances that (4) go back to the time when it was done. *Thomas Sherlock* won renown for works defending the fulfillment of prophecy and the historicity of Jesus' resurrection. But *Soame Jenyns,* later in the century, wisely conceded that miracles could no longer bear the weight Christian apologists had formerly placed on them. The marvels recorded in the New Testament must have been convincing proofs to those who witnessed them, but today they will be most credible to someone who is convinced already of the religion they were at first intended to support. Hence we should begin by showing the internal marks of divinity stamped on the Christian religion and, in particular, the personal character of its Author.[14]

14. See the selections from Leslie, Sherlock, and Jenyns in Creed and Boys Smith, *Religious Thought,* pp. 51-55, 61-64, 67-75, 82-86.

Some of the brightest luminaries of the English church were drawn into the fray, including Samuel Clarke, George Berkeley, and Joseph Butler. Clarke despised the Deists as closet atheists, who, under the pretense of Deism, ridiculed all that was truly excellent even in natural religion. In the introduction to his second series of Boyle Lectures, *The Unchangeable Obligations of Natural Religion* (1706), he insisted that an honest Deist would be well disposed to receive revelation when offered. But the "loose, vain, and frothy Discourses" of the pretended Deists, and above all their "vitious and immoral Lives," proved them to be mere atheists, incapable of judging the truth of Christianity. Nevertheless, Clarke did stoop to answer Charles Blount's argument against revelation, wherein "all the Deniers of Revelation agree with him": that what is not equally made known to *all* cannot be needful for *any*. Clarke's undaunted answer is that all, as a matter of fact, are not equal. Even the truths of natural religion, though discoverable by reason, are not accessible to those whose reasoning ability is deficient; and though reason inclines us to expect a revelation, God is not obliged to give it to everyone, or even to give it at all.[15]

A sprightly reply to the "freethinkers" was Bishop Berkeley's *Alciphron* (1732), written in Newport, Rhode Island, as he awaited news of his projected interracial college in Bermuda. The longest of his writings, it has been undeservedly neglected. In seven dialogues, Berkeley pays back the freethinkers in kind — with as much mischievous wit and acute argument as they had mustered against the establishment. He teases them as "minute philosophers" (an expression borrowed from Cicero) because they "diminish all the most valuable things, the thoughts, views, and hopes of men."[16] But he deals seriously with their arguments. Bernard Mandeville's cynical libertarianism and the Earl of Shaftesbury's notion of moral sense are fairly stated (in the persons of Lysicles and Alciphron) in entire dialogues they receive to themselves

15. Samuel Clarke, *A Discourse concerning the Unchangeable Obligations of Natural Religion, and the Truth and Certainty of the Christian Revelation*, Boyle Lectures 1705 (London, 1706); facsimile reprint (Stuttgart-Bad Cannstatt: Friedrich Frommann, 1964), intro. and prop. vii, §4.

16. George Berkeley, *Alciphron: Or, The Minute Phlosopher. In Seven Dialogues. Containing An Apology for the Christian Religion, against those who are called Free-Thinkers*, 2 vols. (London, 1732[1]); 3rd ed. (1752), dial. I, §10; *The Works of George Berkeley, Bishop of Cloyne*, ed. T. E. Jessop, vol. 3, ed. A. A. Luce and T. E. Jessop (London: Nelson, 1950), p. 46.

(dials. I, III). The fourth dialogue introduces the "divine visual language" proof of God's existence, already stated in Berkeley's *Principles of Human Knowledge* (1710): the totality of our experience consists in nothing but signs by which the Author of Nature speaks to us. And "this Visual Language proves, not a Creator merely [the Deist view], but a provident Governor, actually and intimately present. . . ."[17] The last three dialogues defend the utility and truth of Christianity against a wide range of current objections, including objections to the claim that the Scriptures are a divine revelation (dial. VI).

Berkeley's *Alciphron* anticipates the two main points in the apologetic work that came to eclipse it. He ("Crito") remarks that "probable arguments are a sufficient ground of faith" and goes on to say: "And it will be sufficient if such analogy appears between the dispensations of grace and nature as may make it probable (although much should be unaccountable in both) to suppose them derived from the same Author, and the workmanship of one and the same Hand."[18] This is exactly the line Samuel Butler takes in his *Analogy of Religion* (1736), by far the most famous book to come out of the Deist Controversy. Taking his cue from a remark by Origen of Alexandria, Butler argues that if Scripture comes from the Author of Nature, we can expect to find difficulties in revelation similar to those observed in the constitution and course of nature. Indeed, what we now know about nature yields instructive analogies to religion both natural and revealed. Biological transformations, such as the change of worms into flies, convince us that the future state affirmed by natural religion is entirely in accord with the analogy of nature. Similarly, the objection to revelation — that it is not given to all — ignores the plain evidence of nature that God does not in fact bestow the same favors on everyone. If we find problematic the idea of a special revelation disseminated but slowly over an infinite number of ages, at least it is in harmony with what we observe in the operations of nature.[19]

Butler's tentative tone and grave style are in striking contrast to the optimistic flow of Samuel Clarke's discourse. "To us," Butler's famous

17. Berkeley, *Alciphron*, IV, §14; *Works*, 3:160.

18. Berkeley, *Alciphron*, VI, §31; *Works*, 3:280-81.

19. Joseph Butler, *The Analogy of Religion, Natural and Revealed, to the Constitution and Course of Nature. To Which are added two brief dissertations* (London, 1736), intro., I.i, II.vi, and conclusion; reprinted as *The Analogy of Religion* (without the dissertations), intro. by Ernest C. Mossner (New York: Frederick Ungar, 1961), pp. 4, 11, 189-90, 256.

aphorism affirms, "probability is the very guide of life."[20] That is to say: probability, which is all we can hope for, is also as much as we need to get on with the business of living. Similarly, Berkeley had asked the rhetorical question: "Who ever supposed that scientifical proofs are necessary to make a Christian?"[21] Well, Samuel Clarke supposed they were at least possible: his method of arguing, he claimed, was "as near to Mathematical as the Nature of such a Discourse would allow." He was confident that the new science was wholly on God's side. Fresh discoveries in anatomy, physiology, and astronomy had left atheism "utterly ashamed to show its Head."[22] The shift from Clarke to Butler, from "mathematical" to "probable" arguments, is significant. Indeed, Butler's case is avowedly ad hominem. He does not try to show what the Deists (publicly, at least) did not deny, that there is an Author of Nature. Many of his contemporaries could greet his book as the final blow to Deism's reluctance to move beyond the truths of natural theology. But, on another reading of the situation, we might judge that the Deist Controversy ended when it was superseded by a more radical skepticism — and by the obverse of skepticism, which is fideism.

3. Skepticism and Fideism

The Deist Controversy was about revelation, the contestants on both sides "taking for proved, that there is an intelligent Author of Nature, and *natural* Governor of the world."[23] The question was whether or not the Author of Nature had favored some with a special revelation. Butler invoked his principle of analogy, not to prove that revelation had occurred, but to deflate objections to it. He recognized, however, that his method of reasoning invited a more negative conclusion: Anyone who,

20. Butler, *Analogy,* introduction; Mossner, p. 2.

21. Berkeley, *Alciphron,* VI, §31; *Works,* 3:280.

22. Samuel Clarke, *A Demonstration of the Being and Attributes of God: More Particularly in Answer to Mr. Hobbs, Spinoza, and their Followers,* Boyle Lectures 1704 (London, 1705), pref. and prop. xi; facsimile reprint (Stuttgart-Bad Cannstatt: Friedrich Frommann, 1964). The 1738 edition is reproduced in Clarke, *A Demonstration of the Being and Attributes of God and Other Writings,* ed. Ezio Vailati (Cambridge: Cambridge University Press, 1998).

23. Butler, *Analogy,* intro.; Mossner, p. 5.

considering the difficulties in Scripture, denies that it comes from God might, on similar grounds, deny that the world was formed by God. This was the road taken by a few in the second half of the century, notably Baron d'Holbach. But atheism in the strict sense — denial of the existence of a god or gods — was not characteristic of the time. Many more, unpersuaded by the endless marshaling of arguments, chose the path either to skepticism or to fideism. What they had in common was that they took more seriously than Butler himself his remark that probable evidence is "relative only to beings of limited capacities."[24] The question was about the limits of reason.

Best known and most read of the eighteenth-century philosophers in Britain is today, of course, David Hume. His contributions to religious thought are misrepresented when he is read out of context, but preferential treatment of him is fully justified: taken together, his writings on religion make up a comprehensive philosophy of religion.[25] This is not the place to enter into the many lively debates on his individual contributions, but precisely to see him, more broadly, in historical context. On the surface, at least, his *Natural History of Religion* seems to place him with those (such as Hobbes and Trenchard) who made a distinction between genuine or pure theism and the crude religion of the uninstructed masses. The springs of the one are reflective; and of the other, emotional. "The whole frame of nature bespeaks an intelligent author; and no rational enquirer can, after serious reflection, suspend his belief a moment with regard to the primary principles of genuine Theism and Religion."[26] But there are hints here and there that this testimony should be taken with a grain of salt, and in the *Dialogues concerning Natural Religion* Hume submits the foundation of theism in reason to a thorough critique, foreshadowed in the *Enquiry*.[27]

24. Butler, *Analogy;* Mossner, p. 2.

25. See David Hume, *Writings on Religion,* ed. Anthony Flew (LaSalle: Open Court, 1992); cf. Hume, *Principal Writings on Religion,* ed. J. C. A. Gaskin (New York: Oxford University Press, 1993). My references to Hume on religion cite the pages in Flew's (slightly modernized) texts.

26. David Hume, *Natural History of Religion* (first published in *Four Dissertations,* London, 1757), intro.; Flew, p. 107.

27. David Hume, *An Enquiry concerning Human Understanding* (first published as *Philosophical Essays concerning Human Understanding,* London, 1748); ed. T. L. Beauchamp in the Clarendon Edition of the Works of David Hume (Oxford: Clarendon, 2000), sec. XI.

The skeptical Philo in the *Dialogues* is not insensitive to the power of the cosmic image suggested by Newtonian science: the world as one great machine. The image invites the inference that the cause of order in the universe must be analogous to a human intelligence. But the analogy is very imperfect, and observation actually discloses "an infinite number of springs and principles" in nature. "What peculiar privilege has this little agitation of the brain which we call *thought,* that we must thus make it the model of the whole universe?" Such force as the evidence of rational order retains after these reflections does not permit us to think of nature's ulti-mate cause as either transcendent or benevolent. Nature may itself be "the necessarily-existent Being," and her purpose seems to extend no further than the preservation and propagation of species. She is blind, "pouring forth from her lap, without discernment or parental care, her maimed and abortive children." Hence, to worship this Nature-God is wholly inappro-priate, or rather: "*To know God,* says Seneca, *is to worship him.* All other worship is indeed absurd, superstitious, and even impious."[28]

Natural theology, as Hume saw it, is an attempt to carry our thoughts beyond the capacities of human understanding.[29] But he knew that the failure of argument to provide a satisfactory answer to ultimate questions would give rise to "Contempt of human Reason" and a long-ing for revelation — in short, to seeking all that religion requires in "Faith alone." Philo's parting word is this: "To be a philosophical Scep-tic is, in a man of Letters, the first and most essential Step towards being a sound, believing Christian."[30] No doubt we must allow for some irony, as in the famous conclusion to Hume's essay on miracles: that the Chris-tian religion can be believed only by the miracle of faith, mere reason be-ing "insufficient to convince us of its veracity."[31] Sometimes it is diffi-cult to judge whether or not a contemporary of Hume's, when appealing to faith against reason, is being ironical. Henry Dodwell's anonymous treatise *Christianity not Founded on Argument* (1741) is a masterpiece of ambiguity, and how his readers took it tells as much about them as about the author. However, there were those who affirmed the insufficiency of reason and the need for faith without irony or embarrassment.

28. David Hume, *Dialogues concerning Natural Religion* (published posthumously: London, 1779), parts II and IX-XII; Flew, pp. 208, 252, 261, 274, 290.
29. Hume, *Enquiry,* VII, i.
30. Hume, *Dialogues,* X, p. 265; XII, pp. 291-92.
31. Hume, "Of Miracles," *Enquiry,* X, ii; Flew, p. 88.

In the eyes of many, the eighteenth century was afflicted by a surfeit of reason. It was not merely that the never-ending clash of argument and counterargument became tedious; it tended, besides, to give a false impression of what religion is all about. The disagreement between the Deists and the orthodox was trivial compared to their common assumption that religion is a matter of truths to be demonstrated, partly by showing that they are socially beneficial — making better Englishmen. William Law's response to Tindal was to put reason on trial, and his verdict was in effect a return to the old orthodox view that autonomous reason is incompetent to pass judgment on "the fitness and reasonableness of God's proceedings with mankind."[32] Law exercised a strong influence on John Wesley, who found the chief evidence of Christianity's truth in the experience of "those who were blind, but now see . . . who were miserable, but now are happy."[33] In Wesley's sermons we hear, not about the probability or improbability of the "religious hypothesis" (as Cleanthes calls it in Hume's *Dialogues*), but rather about God's free grace, the new birth, and a faith that is not the cool assent of the head so much as the resting of the heart on Christ for salvation.[34]

And yet, neither Hume nor Wesley spoke the last word. The classic English works of Christian apologetics were written after Hume's classic refutations of the entire enterprise. Undismayed by "Mr. Hume's" objections, William Paley energetically defended miracles. The argument that no testimony for a miraculous happening can ever be believed against our common experience begs the question, Paley thinks, since a miracle is by definition an exception to common experience. The sole pertinent question is the reliability of the witnesses. And is it likely that anyone would suffer martyrdom for a fabricated story?[35] The defense of miracles was followed by Paley's venture into natural theology. The re-

32. William Law (1686-1761), *The Case of Reason, or Natural Religion, Fairly and Fully Stated: In Answer to a Book, entitul'd, Christianity as old as the Creation* (London, 1731); Waring, *Deism and Natural Religion*, p. 185.

33. John Wesley (1703-1791), "A Letter to the Reverend Dr. Conyers Middleton, Occasioned by His Late 'Free Enquiry' (4-24 January 1748-49); *The Works of John Wesley,* 14 vols. (1872; reprinted Grand Rapids: Zondervan, 1958), 10:1-79; quotation on p. 78.

34. Wesley, sermon 1: "Salvation by Faith" (1738); *Works,* 5:7-16.

35. William Paley (1743-1805), *A View of the Evidences of Christianity, in Three Parts,* 3 vols. (London, 1794), "preparatory considerations"; *The Works of William Paley, D.D., Archdeacon of Carlisle* (Philadelphia, 1857), pp. 271-73.

markable adaptation of parts to ends in nature bespeaks an intelligent contriver, as a watch requires a watchmaker. Even if the watch sometimes goes wrong, and even if we cannot see how every part conduces to the general effect, that does not invalidate our persuasion that a watch is a contrivance with a purpose.[36] But Paley did not have the last word either. Charles Darwin read him at Cambridge with deep respect, but later wrote: "The old argument of design in nature, as given by Paley, which formerly seemed to me so conclusive, fails, now that the law of natural selection has been discovered."[37]

III. New Beginnings in Theology

On the continent of Europe, religious thought in the eighteenth century partly mirrors the English controversies, partly moves beyond them. Initially, both France and Germany were debtors to England for the new questions about religion. But Paris became the capital of the Enlightenment, and the great *Encyclopédie* (1751-80) launched by Denis Diderot was in some ways its most characteristic product. Voltaire, more than anyone else, became the spokesman of the Age of Reason. But before the century was out, the first stirring of new beginnings in theology made their appearance in Germany, and the way was opened for the flowering of Christian thought in the nineteenth century.

1. Voltaire and Rousseau

Though he styled himself a "theist," Voltaire (1694-1778) did not believe that the Creator troubles himself with human affairs, or that the meaning of human existence turns around the expectation of an afterlife. Whereas Paley thought the main point of revelation was to furnish "authorised assurances" of a life to come,[38] Voltaire's outlook was con-

---

36. William Paley, *Natural Theology: Or, Evidences of the Existence and Attributes of the Deity, Collected from the Appearances of Nature* (London, 1802), "State of the Argument," chaps. i-ii; *Works*, pp. 387-90.

37. *The Autobiography of Charles Darwin 1809-1882*, ed. Nora Barlow (New York: W. W. Norton, 1969), p. 87; cf. p. 59.

38. Paley, *Evidences*, II, ii; *Works*, p. 330.

cisely stated in the closing words of *Candide* (1759): the tiresome explanations of Dr. Pangloss about the way everything is ordered for the best
are all very well, but we have to tend our garden. Immensely influential
though he was, Voltaire was not a greatly original thinker. Indeed, he
tried to pass off the anonymous first edition of his *Dictionnaire
philosophique* (1764) as largely a compilation of sentiments from English authors. Neither did his writings spark an open exchange of arguments like the Deist Controversy in England, partly because the leaders
of the French church preferred repression to argument.

In the "Profession of Faith of a Priest of Savoy" in *Émile* (1762),
Rousseau portrayed the conflict between Deistic sympathies and the
teaching of the Roman Catholic Church as an inward struggle of conscience.[39] A justly celebrated manifesto, it also documents Rousseau's
growing apprehension of a critique of religion more radical than his
own — the critique that carried Diderot from Deism to materialism.
The priest of Savoy trusts his heart more than the arguments of the philosophers, and in this respect Rousseau hints at the coming revolt
against Enlightenment rationalism. But it is the standard natural religion of the Deists — the religion of reason — that provides the content
of the priest's confession. Though he conforms outwardly to the church
and scrupulously performs the duties assigned to him, the only truths
he acknowledges are the moral truths of which his conscience tells him;
and they provide the measure by which he determines what is essential
in Christianity, or in any other religion. He simply does not trouble himself with dogmas that are without benefit to morality. At the same time,
like Voltaire, Rousseau's priest is appalled by the new materialist or nat-
uralist understanding of humanity (la Mettrie, Helvétius, d' Holbach),
which means total rejection of his own deistic faith along with the ecclesiastical faith he himself subjects to criticism.

2. Enlightenment Theology in Germany

Many have seen in the dogmatic atheism of d'Holbach's *System of Nature* (French 1770), which passes beyond the skepticism of Pierre Bayle

---

39. Jean-Jacques Rousseau (1712-1778), *Émile, ou De l'éducation* (Paris, 1762); trans.
and ed. Allan Bloom as *Émile, or On Education* (New York: Basic Books, 1979), pp. 266-313.

or even David Hume, the final outcome of the French enlightenment, perhaps of the Enlightenment in general. In Germany it was different. There the scattering of English ideas generated something new and positive in the understanding of religion. For one thing, the religious climate was more benign. The protest of Pietism against the dry intellectualism of orthodoxy had created a religious environment that nurtured a surprisingly large number of Germany's leading thinkers. Most of them saw themselves also as heirs of Martin Luther: his name was reverently invoked to underwrite a variety of mutually exclusive causes — including orthodoxy, the Pietism that rebelled against its formalism, and the rationalism that was critical of them both. Further, the course of the Enlightenment in Germany was decisively shaped by the teleological system of Gottfried Wilhelm Leibniz (1646-1716), whose watchword that we live in "the best of all possible worlds" was mercilessly ridiculed in Voltaire's *Candide*. The characteristic products of "enlightened" religious thought in Germany were not anticlericalism and skepticism, although undercurrents of both were certainly present. More representative in the earlier phase were further ventures in natural theology, or rational theism, notably the attempt of Christian Wolff, Leibniz's most distinguished follower, to reconcile mechanism and teleology, making room for God in his grand system of "rational philosophy."[40]

In the later phase of Enlightenment theology in Germany, from around the mid-century, the questions of natural theology and natural religion yielded first place to a church reform program that came to be called "Neology" ("new doctrine"). For their part, the followers of Wolff, whether or not they engaged directly in the explication of church doctrines, were convinced that he had shown the way to harmonize reason and revelation as mutually supplemental sources of theological information. They had no thought of revising orthodoxy. For the Neologists by contrast (A. F. W. Sack, J. F. W. Jerusalem, J. J. Spalding, and others), a revision of dogma was among the most urgent tasks of the day. They did not reject the concept of revelation but asked how far the official dogmas of the church succeeded in conveying the truths of revelation. Intricate doctrines such as the Trinity, which posed no great intellectual difficulties for the Wolffians, were now judged morally bar-

---

40. Christian Wolff (1679-1754), *Theologia naturalis methodo scientifica pertractata*, 2 vols. (Frankfurt, 1736-37).

ren, if not logically incoherent; others, such as original sin, were admitted to be an actual hindrance to spiritual improvement, as unbelievers had already noticed. The Neologists were eminently practical men, many of them active churchmen rather than academic theologians. They called for drastic simplification of ecclesiastical dogma in the interests of actual Christian experience. But some of them, notably Johann Salomo Semler (1725-1791: usually classed with the Neologists) undertook the critique of dogma partly in recognition of the historical limitations of all concrete expressions of religion in thought and language: neither dogma nor the Bible itself can be exempted from the relativity of time and place. Hence a free, "scientific" inquiry into the Christian tradition is entirely legitimate as well as needful to piety. It is here, rather than in the defense of a natural religion, that Neology owed its principal debt to the English Deists.

Besides the Neologists, others such as G. E. Lessing and H. S. Reimarus took up the Deist enterprise of a "free investigation" of the Scriptures. For Christian theologians, the historical-critical approach to the Bible was to prove more important, in the long run, than rational theism, which is naturally more intriguing to philosophers. True, one early impulse to critical study of Scripture had come from a philosopher, Benedict Spinoza (1632-1677), whose purpose in his *Tractatus Theologico-Politicus* (anon., 1670) was to distinguish a philosophical from a theological doctrine of God. But the new historical studies made a division within theology itself, programmatically formulated in J. P. Gabler's academic address (1787) on the proper distinction between biblical and dogmatic theology.[41] The ideal, at least, had come to be a descriptive study of biblical ideas that would be free from external presuppositions, philosophical as well as ecclesiastical. How well the ideal was realized may be open to doubt; Gabler himself *presupposed* that linguistic, literary, and historical examination of the individual books of the Bible would uncover a uniform, timeless biblical truth. But precisely because pure description of historical data was the goal, the emergence of a historical-critical theology is of less philosophical interest than the fate of natural theology and natural religion at the hands of Immanuel

---

41. Johann Philipp Gabler (1753-1826), "De iusto discrimine theologiae biblicae et dogmaticae," in *Johann Philipp Gabler's kleinere theologische Schriften,* edited by his sons, T. A. and J. G. Gabler, 2 parts (Ulm, 1831), II, pp. 179-98.

Kant and Friedrich Schleiermacher. For Kant, the only possible theology of reason was moral theology; and for Schleiermacher even Christian theology had to begin with analysis of human consciousness.

3. Kant's Moral Theology

Kant's strictures on rational theology in the transcendental dialectic of the *Critique of Pure Reason* arise from the application of his theory of knowledge to the idea of God.[42] The Kantian categories are strictly categories of *thought,* by which the mind organizes sense experience. But there is a persistent tendency of the mind to assume that its structure must be the structure of *being:* it projects the categories onto things-in-themselves. The logic of the mind is then transformed into a metaphysic of reality, and this is illusion. The same holds good for the ideas by which the mind seeks to unify the experience ordered by the categories, including the idea (or ideal) of God as the ultimate unifying ground of everything there is. After dismantling the proofs by which theists have tried to establish the existence of God, Kant concludes that for theoretical reason the concept of God is a "mere idea," justified not by its supposed reference to an actual object but by its usefulness in driving the quest for a single system of empirical knowledge.[43] However, he drops a hint that there is more to be said: "Consequently, if one did not ground [theology] on moral laws or use them as guides, there could be no theology of reason at all."[44]

What this means becomes clearer in several of Kant's later writings. We may point, by way of example, to his *Lectures on the Philosophical*

---

42. Immanuel Kant, *Kritik der reinen Vernunft,* cited by the two editions: A (1781), B (1787). Others of Kant's writings will be cited in the Akademieausgabe (AA). I have conformed the wording of my quotations to the English versions in the Cambridge Edition of the Works of Immanuel Kant, which is keyed to AA. The volume *Religion and Rationality* in the Cambridge Edition, trans. and ed. Allen W. Wood and George di Giovanni (Cambridge: Cambridge University Press, 1996), includes *Religion within the Boundaries of Mere Reason, The Conflict of the Faculties,* and *Lectures on the Philosophical Doctrine of Religion.*

43. Kant, *Kritik der reinen Vernunft,* A 670-71, B 698-99. Cf. the expression *focus imaginarius* in A 644, B 672.

44. Kant, *Kritik der reinen Vernunft,* A 636, B 664.

Doctrine of Religion, probably delivered in the winter semester 1783-84 and published posthumously. The lectures show Kant's familiarity with Hume's *Dialogues,* but his constant conversation partner is the Wolffian philosopher A. G. Baumgarten (1714-1762), whose natural theology (part three of his *Metaphysica,* 1739) Kant adopted as his main textbook. Defining theology broadly as "the system of our cognition of the highest being," he confines his attention to rational theology (the "theology of reason"), which sets out to see how far reason can get in attaining cognition of God without any help from revelation. Rational theology, so understood, falls into two parts. *Speculative theology* (part one) is organized according to the three traditional proofs of God's existence into onto-, cosmo-, and physicotheology. In adding *moral theology* (part two), Kant believed he was coining a new name for a field that had not previously been correctly distinguished. To be sure, the content of his moral theology was not without antecedents: Butler's writings, for instance, contain at least a suggestion of a natural theology grounded in moral experience. But Kant's claim to originality was largely justified.[45]

Speculative theology is not only parsimonious in what it can permit us to say about God, seeing that talk of God is of no use in explaining natural phenomena. It also tends to mislead us into forgetting that the question of God is a practical one, which has to do, above all, with the strength of our moral dispositions. Our morality, not our cosmology, needs the idea of God. In this way, Kant makes theology a theory of religion rather than a branch of metaphysics. Indeed, he can say forthrightly: "Religion is nothing but the application of theology to morality."[46] Our experience of nature ("natural theology" in Kant's narrow sense) does not produce the God that religion requires; it can only stir up fear of a very powerful being. But by way of moral experience reason furnishes the concept of God as the holy, just, and benevolent ruler of the world. "God," in short, is a *moral* concept, and *practically* necessary.[47]

---

45. Immanuel Kant, *Vorlesungen über die philosophische Religionslehre,* ed. Karl Heinrich Ludwig Pölitz (1817[1]), 2nd ed. (Leipzig, 1830; reprinted Darmstadt: Wissenschaftliche Buchgesellschaft, 1982), AA 28:993-1126; see p. 995. The heading to part one is "Transcendental Theology," but in his introduction Kant divides speculative theology into transcendental *and* natural theology: ontotheology is transcendental, cosmo- and physicotheology are natural (see esp. p. 1003).

46. Kant, *Philosophische Religionslehre,* p. 997.

47. Kant, *Philosophische Religionslehre,* p. 1071.

Just how and why morality needs the idea of God is spelled out in the doctrine of the three postulates of practical reason — freedom, immortality, and the existence of God — in the *Critique of Practical Reason* (German 1788). The argument is a delicate one, since it must not be taken to imply that morality *rests on* belief in God or the prospect of rewards in an afterlife. Moral obligation depends on nothing outside itself. But precisely because we ought to promote the highest good in the world, we necessarily presuppose its possibility, and we can only conceive of this possibility if we assume the existence of a supreme cause whose causality is appropriate to the nature of the moral life: which must mean, a highest intelligence. Kant concludes that by this route our cognition (*Erkenntnis,* not our theoretical knowledge) really is extended. But we must not claim to know the nature of the Supreme Being, whom we cannot experience as we experience objects in space and time. Theoretical reason can only *assume* that the concept of God has an object, or a possible object, even if the first *Critique* has shown that the traditional proofs failed to *demonstrate* it.[48]

Kant returns to his "moral proof" in his third critique, the *Critique of the Power of Judgment* (German 1790), part two: "Critique of Teleological Judgment." Man's moral nature, which raises him above the rest of nature as its ultimate goal *(Endzweck),* requires us to represent the supreme cause as moral, and this alone can give us a teleological principle — a final intention *(Endabsicht)* — adequate to ground a theology.[49] The consequent definition of religion as "the recognition of our duties as divine commands"[50] is taken up again in *Religion within the Boundaries of Mere Reason* (German 1793),[51] which earned Kant a royal rebuke from Frederick William II. There Kant indulges in some standard Enlightenment anti-clericalism. But he argues that the radical evil in humanity requires a collective remedy, and he grants that a church may be the vehicle of the ethical commonwealth at which the pure religion of reason aims. Reason, however, must submit every ecclesiastical belief and prac-

48. Kant, *Kritik der praktischen Vernunft* (Riga, 1788), AA 5:1-163; see pp. 125-26, 133-36.

49. Kant, *Kritik der Urtheilskraft* (Berlin and Libau, 1790[1]), 2nd ed. (1793), AA 5:165-485; see the appendix (§§79-91), pp. 416-85.

50. Kant, *Kritik der Urtheilskraft,* p. 481.

51. Kant, *Die Religion innerhalb der Grenzen der bloßen Vernunft* (Königsberg, 1793[1]), 2nd ed. (1794), AA 6:1-202; see pp. 153-54.

tice to critical scrutiny, if their moral core is not to be lost in idle super-stition.[52] Hence Kant not only transformed natural theology into moral theology: he also, in effect, implemented Tindal's program for making natural religion, or the religion of reason, a critical standard for judging the instrumental worth of so-called revealed religion. In short, he was able to view revealed religion as a "*wider* sphere of faith that includes the other, a *narrower* one [the pure religion of reason] within itself (not as two circles external to one another but as concentric circles)."[53]

4. Schleiermacher's Theology of Consciousness

Kant's *Religion within Boundaries* already moves beyond "enlightened" thinking in some respects (notably, in his emphasis on radical evil). Much further removed from the Enlightenment than Kant was Friedrich Schleiermacher, whose *On Religion: Speeches to Its Cultured Despisers* appeared anonymously at the close of the century. He wrote this, his first book, in the shadow of the Atheism Controversy, in which the Kantian critical philosophy provided the initial terms of debate. But he himself stood in the stream of ideas that flowed out of the earlier Pantheism (or Spinozist) Controversy, started by the quarrel between F. H. Jacobi and Moses Mendelssohn over the religious opinions of Lessing, who had died in 1781. Renewed interest in Spinoza led many to abandon the image of God as a mind outside a machine and to reconceive of deity as the ultimate animating force of nature. Goethe wrote to Jacobi (June 9, 1785): "[Spinoza] does not prove the existence of God; existence is God."[54] And Herder equated God, the primal force, with the luminous rational order discovered in nature by scientific enquiry: the divine activity is not arbitrary but necessary, identical with the law-governed

---

52. Kant, *Die Religion*, pp. 94-96, 109-12, 115-23, 167-69. A rational (i.e., strictly moral) interpretation of Scripture thus differs from the task of the biblical scholar, or biblical theologian, who is bound to busy himself with the statutory obligations and purported facts of a historical faith; and it does not ask what the author meant, but what reason can derive from the text for the benefit of morality (pp. 111-12). Cf. Kant, *Der Streit der Fakultäten* (1798), AA 7:5-94; see esp. pp. 36-37, 67.

53. Kant, *Die Religion*, pref. to 2nd ed., AA 6:12.

54. Johann Wolfgang von Goethe (1749-1832), *Briefwechsel zwischen Goethe und F. H. Jacobi*, ed. M. Jacobi (Leipzig, 1846), p. 85.

course of nature.[55] The world of this "neo-Spinozism" was the young Schleiermacher's world. He also shared with Herder the conviction that religion is not correct belief, nor correct behavior either, but the poetic expression of lively feeling.

Schleiermacher's *On Religion* could hardly have been written in an earlier century.[56] His question in the first two speeches is not about the soundest variety of Christian doctrine, but about the nature of religion. Not until the fifth and last speech does he try to show how religion, generically understood, is suitably manifested in Christianity. The defense of Christian faith is launched, not by arguing at the outset for a special revelation, but by insisting that religion in general is rooted in human nature, which is diminished when religion is despised or neglected.[57] But the religion Schleiermacher finds in humanity is not the *prisca theologia* ("original theology") of which some of the Deists spoke — the cluster of minimal beliefs that all thinking men have held since the beginning of history. With most of his friends, he shared Rousseau's and Hamann's protest against the abstract intellectualism of the Enlightenment: the whole person is more than thinking, understanding, and arguing. Religion renounces any claim to whatever belongs to the domain of science and metaphysics, and it cannot be reduced to morality or praxis either: it is an "indispensable third" alongside thinking and acting. What is it, then? Religion, or "piety," is the sense of the Infinite that surrounds and pervades us: the Infinite, not as the endless sum of finite things, but as the underlying unity that conditions the whole of which we are part. "Thus to accept everything individual as a part of the whole and everything limited as a

---

55. Johann Gottfried von Herder, *Gott: Einige Gespräche* (Gotha, 1787), in *Herders sämmtliche Werke,* ed. Bernhard Suphan, vol. 16 (Berlin: Weidmann, 1887); Eng. trans., *God, Some Conversations,* trans. and ed. Frederick H. Burkhardt, with cross-references to the pagination in Suphan's German edition (Indianapolis: Bobbs-Merrill, 1940), pp. 128-30, 133-34.

56. Friedrich Schleiermacher, *Über die Religion: Reden an die Gebildeten unter ihren Verächtern* (Berlin, 1799), KGA I,2:185-326; trans. and ed. Richard Crouter, Texts in German Philosophy (Cambridge: Cambridge University Press, 1988). The older English version by Oman was made from the third German edition (1821): Friedrich Schleiermacher, *On Religion: Speeches to Its Cultured Despisers,* trans. John Oman (1893; reprinted, without Oman's introduction, Louisville: Westminster/John Knox, 1994). The critical text in KGA I, 12:1-321 reproduces the fourth German edition (1831) but notes the minor differences from the third.

57. Schleiermacher, *Über die Religion,* speech I, KGA I, 2:197-98; Crouter, pp. 87-89.

representation of the infinite is religion." It matters little how the imagination moves us to conceptualize this "intuition and feeling" in an idea of God — or even if it leaves us with no idea of God at all.[58]

Schleiermacher thought that the enterprise of rational or natural *theology* was of no help to anyone who wanted to understand religion. The essence of religion is an elemental "feeling" *(Gefühl)* or "intuition" *(Anschauung)*, and our access to it is by observing the structure of consciousness — in the final analysis, our own consciousness.[59] Do we then have, by result, the natural *religion* that the Deists sought in all the "positive" religions? Schleiermacher's answer in the fifth speech is a firm no. To understand religion in its actual manifestations, we must abandon the vain wish for a single religion. Precisely because the essence of religion is not a quantity of common beliefs that can be extracted from the positive religions, everything particular being disdained as superfluous, Schleiermacher had no sympathy with the concept of natural religion or the use to which it had been put. It is an armchair construct: there is little of real religion in it, and it cannot exist on its own. Only in the positive religions is a genuine individual cultivation of the religious capacity possible.[60] With this conclusion, Schleiermacher helped to shape the agenda for a future philosophy of religions (plural) and a Christian theology that would accept religious pluralism as part of the legacy of the eighteenth century.

58. Schleiermacher, *Über die Religion,* speech II, KGA I, 2:207-16 (quotation on p. 214), 244-46; Crouter, pp. 97-107 (quotation on p. 105), 137-38. In his later dogmatic work, *Der christliche Glaube,* Schleiermacher shifted to the "feeling of absolute dependence" as the essence of religion (*CG,* §4 [p. 12]), but the continuity with the first edition is plain in this "explanation" in the third edition of *Über die Religion:* "We do not feel ourselves dependent on the Whole in so far as it is an aggregate of mutually conditioned parts of which we ourselves are one, but only in so far as underneath this coherence there is a unity conditioning all things and conditioning our relations to the other parts of the Whole" (trans. Oman, p. 106; German in KGA I, 12:134).

59. Schleiermacher, *Über die Religion,* speech I, KGA I, 2:201-2; Crouter, p. 92. This is not the place to enter into the debate about Schleiermacher's terms *Gefühl* and *Anschauung.* The advantage of the second term is that it points more clearly to an *object* of religious experience. But Schleiermacher retreated from it in the second edition of *Über die Religion,* partly because it could appear to make the essence of religion a kind of cognition.

60. Schleiermacher, *Über die Religion,* speech V, KGA I, 2:296-97, 308-12; Crouter, pp. 192-94, 204-8. My epigraph to the present chapter is taken from Crouter, p. 193 (German in KGA I, 2:296).

CHAPTER 2

Errors and Insights
in the Understanding of Revelation

You can hold before the elderly or blear-eyed, or any whose vision is clouded, even the most beautiful volume, and though they recognize it as something written, they will hardly be able to put two words together. But with the help of a pair of spectacles they will begin to read clearly. In the same way, Scripture focuses the otherwise confused knowledge of God in our minds, dispels the mist, and clearly shows us the true God.

John Calvin, *Institutes*

Why Great Spirit no send book to Injin, too?

James Fenimore Cooper ("Hist"), *The Deerslayer*

Conscience! Conscience! Divine instinct, immortal and celestial voice, certain guide of a being that is ignorant and limited but intelligent and free.

Jean-Jacques Rousseau, *Émile*

In our day, the confidence of the Enlightenment in a universal human rationality — everywhere and at all times the same — has been widely rejected. But the forceful criticisms made in the Age of Reason against Christian belief in a special revelation have not disappeared. The question remains whether the replies of the church's apologists have retained their persuasiveness, whether a better defense is possible, or whether a fresh start in our understanding of revelation is called for. The previous chapter sought to line up impartially the positions of the critics and the apologists in the Deist Controversy. I must now venture to offer a more critical appraisal of the many-sided debate, and to compare my own conclusions with the opinions of colleagues who speak for Feuerbach, Barth, and Schleiermacher. In proposing an alternative to the prevailing concept of revelation during the Deist Controversy, I shall be taking up a suggestion from Calvin, though I think it stands in need of modification.

I. The Classical Concept of Revelation

What we may call (for lack of a better term) the "classical" concept of revelation is bound up with the notion of a twofold knowledge of God. That there are two sources of religious knowledge, not just one, has been virtually the consensus of Christian theologians throughout the history of the church, but there has been less agreement on what the two sources are and how they are related to each other. Paul's argument in Romans 1–2 has commonly been the scriptural foundation of the discussion, or at least its point of departure. It may suffice for now, however, to start from the well-known formula of a twofold knowledge that divides the *Summa contra Gentiles* of Thomas Aquinas into two parts (books 1-3 and book 4, respectively). According to Thomas, some knowledge of divine things (e.g., that God exists) can be acquired by natural reason, which *ascends* to them through perception of lower, created things. Other knowledge pertinent to humanity's highest good (e.g., that God is triune) exceeds the capacity of the intellect; but the divine truth in such matters *descends* in the mode of revelation, yielding the knowledge of faith. Revelation, then, is the supernatural communication of truths inaccessible to natural cognition, and its subjective correlate is the faith or belief that assents to it.[1]

Somewhat different is Martin Luther's twofold knowledge of God,

---

1. Thomas Aquinas, *SG* I, iii.2, ix.1; IV, i.4-5, 9-11. In the fourth book Thomas actually writes of a *threefold* knowledge of things divine, adding to the other two the knowledge reserved for the eschatological vision (IV, i.5-6, 8).

general and special. Whereas the Thomistic version of a rational knowledge of divine things traces its lineage back to the natural *theology* of Plato and Aristotle, Luther's notion of a general knowledge of God has affinities rather with the Stoic tradition of natural *religion,* on which the apostle Paul seems to have drawn in Romans 1–2. Thomas's rational route to a limited knowledge of God is open only to a few: even the things demonstrable by reason must be taken on faith by those of us (the vast majority) who lack the talent, time, or energy for rational inquiry.[2] Luther's general knowledge, by contrast, is the possession of all. And it is Luther's version of the twofold knowledge of God that is formalized in seventeenth-century Protestant scholasticism as the contrast between general revelation and special revelation: the distinction is not drawn, as in Thomas, between a natural knowledge and a revealed knowledge, but between two kinds of revelation. There is an innate notion of God that assumes definite characteristics by observation of God's self-disclosure in the created order, including human nature. But it is insufficient for salvation because the good pleasure of God cannot be grasped apart from God's communication in Scripture, which provides Luther with the *proper* knowledge of God.[3] On either view, however, the Thomistic or the Lutheran, we may say that *"revelation" (or "special revelation") is the supernatural communication of truths about God that would otherwise remain hidden, and "faith" is assent to them* (though, of course, that may not be all that is meant by faith).

This remained the dominant understanding of faith and revelation throughout the seventeenth and eighteenth centuries, and it probably

---

2. Thomas, *SG* I, iv.2. Cf. Thomas, *ST* I, q. 1, art. 1 (1:1).

3. Martin Luther, *In epistolam S. Pauli ad Galatas Commentarius* (1535), WA 40/1:607; trans. as *Lectures on Galatians 1535,* LW 26:399. In later Protestant theology the terms vary: sometimes the contrast is between natural and supernatural revelation, sometimes between general and special revelation, and sometimes there seems to be a hesitation to call "revelation" what is given naturally and to all. With special and supernatural revelation David Hollaz (1648-1713), for instance, contrasts the general revelation or natural *manifestation* by which God makes himself known both through the innate light of nature and through effects conspicuous in the kingdom of nature. See Heinrich Schmid, *The Doctrinal Theology of the Evangelical Lutheran Church,* trans. Charles A. Hay and Henry E. Jacobs (1875; reprinted Minneapolis: Augsburg, 1961), p. 26. For a similar Calvinist statement, see the opening chapter of the Westminster Confession (1647), in which the *manifestation* of God by "the light of nature and the works of creation and providence" is contrasted with God's *revelation* of himself.

still is the dominant understanding today. There were of course variations, as we have seen (in Chapter 1) — besides the obvious difference
that some argued for, others against, revelation and faith in the classical
sense. *Herbert's* view hardly seemed to require revelation at all; in fact,
however, he did not exclude it but insisted that it had to be either universal or private, not the imposition of one contentious group on all humanity. He tells us in his autobiography how he himself prayed for a sign
when trying to decide whether or not to print his book on truth. His
prayer was rewarded with "a loud yet gentle noise" from heaven, which
he gratefully took to mean that he should publish. That, presumably,
was a notable example of private revelation. But private revelation is
close to the "enthusiasm" that *Trenchard* exposed as a sickness.
Trenchard notes that the enthusiast, feeling a storm of devotion coming
upon him, supposes himself graced with a supernatural revelation. His
inflexible temper and refusal to hear any criticism of his opinions could
be due, in actual fact, to an excess of black bile ("melancholy") in his system. Another variation was *Tindal's* opinion that the gospel is simply a
republication of the true, original religion of reason and nature. Obviously, this excludes revelation in the classical sense — something essential added to what we know of God by the light of nature. Similarly
Kant, though he often adopts the prevailing usage that claims "revelation" as the foundation of the church's faith, holds that anything in ecclesiastical faith that goes beyond the purely moral religion of reason is,
in itself, merely historical and unessential, even if it may serve as the
temporary vehicle of the religion of reason.

Some of the variations are only terminological; others are more
substantial. In any case, the common presupposition in them all is that
revelation is, or is supposed to be, additional information about God or
divine matters, available to human understanding only by a supernatural intervention. We may take from John Locke explicit definitions of
revelation and faith that clearly echo the classical concepts. *Revelation,*
he says, is natural reason "enlarged by a new set of Discoveries communicated by GOD immediately."[4] And *faith* is "the Assent to any Proposi-

---

4. John Locke, *An Essay concerning Human Understanding,* 4th ed. (London, 1700),
IV, xix, §4; ed. Peter H. Nidditch in the Clarendon Edition of the Works of John Locke
(Oxford: Clarendon, 1975; pb. ed., with changes in the editorial matter only, 1979),
p. 698.

tion, not . . . made out by the Deductions of Reason; but upon the Credit of the Proposer, as coming from GOD, in some extraordinary way of Communication."[5] The Deists and their adversaries alike presupposed that this is the meaning of revelation, and of faith or belief in it; the disagreement was over the question whether the claim to possess a revelation, so defined, was credible.

It is not difficult to see why the church's claim to have been favored with revelation ran into serious trouble in the Age of Reason. The problem was one side of the struggle against ecclesiastical authority, and the coincidence of three developments gave the struggle the precise form that it took: revulsion against all the bitter and often bloody conflicts within Christendom, increasing knowledge of a sophisticated religious world beyond Christendom, and a new understanding of the natural causes of events once supposed to be brought about by divine or demonic intervention. The very *concept* of revelation came under fire, and the beginnings of a historical approach to Scripture heightened the conflict by submitting the *credentials* of the Christian revelation to relentless criticism. For even if the idea of revelation — as the supernatural disclosure of truths about God to a privileged segment of humanity — could be made credible in principle, it still had to be asked whether a revelation had in fact occurred in Christianity (or in any other religion). And the orthodox Christian argument from miracles and the fulfilment of prophecy merely added a further pair of dubious concepts.

To view Christianity from the perspective of the English Deists is to see it as one religion among others, and that means reading the Bible with the same critical eye that we bring to our reading of any other book, sacred or secular. There can be no reason to grant privileged status to Christian claims or Christian literature, even though we may have a special interest in them simply because they are part of *our* history. On the contrary, the task will be to bring any religious claims whatever under the scrutiny of generally accepted standards of inquiry. And this, as no one has seen more clearly than Ernst Troeltsch, is to remove Christianity entirely from the domain of the "supernatural" (as usually understood).[6] The temptation is always present, of course, to move from antisupernaturalism (rejection of the belief that God sometimes interrupts

---

5. Locke, *Essay,* xviii, §2; Nidditch, p. 689.
6. On Troeltsch, see Secs. V-VI below.

the natural course of events) to naturalistic reductionism (the belief that there is no objective reality to which talk about God refers). But a realistic account of religious experience is not necessarily excluded: faith may be examined as, at least hypothetically, a response to a distinctive order of reality. What is excluded in principle is any untested assumption at the outset that Christianity is distinguished from all other religions as the sole recipient of an authoritative revelation, miraculously communicated, or as the object of a miraculous divine activity that is unparalleled in any other religious history.[7]

II. An Alternative Proposal

If a fresh beginning is required in our thoughts on revelation, what help can possibly be expected from Calvin, who came before the seventeenth- and eighteenth-century debate? The answer is that one strand in his understanding of revelation was free from the assumption shared by the protagonists on both sides, Deists and orthodox alike, that by "revelation" is meant the giving of information to be accepted by intellectual assent or belief. The content of special revelation, taken in that sense, is formally analogous to what is presumed to be given by general revelation — the religion of reason or of nature. Eighteenth-century theologians and their Deist opponents typically thought of natural religion as a *prisca theologia,* an original or primitive "theology," reducible to a short list of propositions. Special revelation was supposed to extend the list. It was also the shared assumption of both parties that to defend either the shorter or the longer list was to show the social utility of the beliefs proposed: that is, their effectiveness in making solid citizens.

It is not difficult to find statements in Calvin that share the understanding of revelation as informative. The Scriptures, he believed, communicate facts or truths we could not possibly have known without revelation, even if Adam had never fallen: for example, that the work of creation took six days. Here, plainly, revelation is information not otherwise available, imparted in a supernatural manner — in the example

---

7. It may not be superfluous to add that the point is purely methodological: it does not imply endorsement of any particular seventeenth- or eighteenth-century interpretation either of Christianity or of religion in general.

given, by God's speaking to Moses, who wrote it down. But Calvin could also say that the Scriptures are like a pair of spectacles by which we are enabled to view the world with a clearer vision, to see things as Adam must have seen them before disobedience clouded his eyesight. From this perspective, revelation is not supernaturally conveyed information but divinely improved vision.[8]

It is true that what Calvin had in mind when he used the simile of the spectacles was the knowledge of God *the Creator:* the Scriptures are like corrective lenses insofar as they enable us to perceive the true God in nature. I am not pretending to offer a comprehensive account of his doctrine of the Word of God, merely suggesting that the simile gives us an important clue to the way in which we might try to rethink the old idea of revelation. It is worth noting, however, that when he comes to the knowledge of God *the Redeemer,* Calvin defines faith — the correlate of revelation — as "recognition," not as assent or belief. What faith recognizes in the course of events is a fatherlike goodwill or, more simply, the "face" of God.[9] The recognition happens initially to an individual in the setting of the communion of saints — in the proclamation and hearing of the "promise," the special form of revelation in which Calvin was most interested. But the faith born of the Word or promise subsequently shapes the way the believer perceives and lives her entire life: it is not so much an act of assent (in the brain) as an abiding disposition (of the heart), living obediently as an adopted child of God.[10] We are surely justified in concluding that it was preeminently the gospel story (the *historia evangelica,* as he called it) that functioned for Calvin as a lens, enabling him to make out the paternal image in a narrative of obedience, suffering, and death, and to transfer this disclosure to the whole of Christian existence.

---

8. John Calvin, *ICR* I, vi.1 (the first epigraph to this Chapter; trans. mine). See also *ICR* I, xiv.1-2 (1:159-62), where the simile of the spectacles is repeated. Notice that the "volume" in Calvin's simile is the book of nature; it is not Scripture, which provides, rather, the corrective lenses for reading it.

9. Calvin, *ICR* III, ii.2, 14, 16, 28 (1:553, 560, 562, 573-74).

10. Calvin, *ICR* III, ii.8 (1:551-53); ii.29 (1:575-76). When Calvin remarks that assent itself rests on a devout disposition, he comes close to Thomas's understanding of faith as a *habitus* that produces acts of assent; but for Thomas this is because faith is formed by love, a notion that Calvin rejects (and possibly misunderstands). See B. A. Gerrish, *Saving and Secular Faith: An Invitation to Systematic Theology* (Minneapolis: Fortress, 1999), pp. 5-8.

If, then, Calvin's simile of the spectacles invites a revised definition of revelation as the counterpart of the old one, it will go something like this: *By "revelation" is meant a moment of disclosure that focuses our perception of our world and of ourselves, and "faith" is the enduring insight that corresponds to this disclosure.* There is no need to qualify this moment as "supernatural," and the proper response to it, we might say, is not "I believe it" but "Oh, I see!" That some such rethinking of the concepts of revelation and faith is sound will have to be made secure by experience: that is, by noting what seems actually to happen when someone goes to church, hears a sermon, and finds her way of seeing the world and living in the world decisively shaped by the disclosure and insight given in the Word. It will also need to be established that revelation in the revised sense is free from the objections that made the old concept unworkable. And a moment's reflection will show that revelation understood as an occasion of disclosure and insight does not occur only in church on Sunday morning and is not mediated solely by Scripture or preaching, or even by words. The concept may be taken as broad and generic, not designed to set the Christian proclamation apart. We must certainly be willing to ask, Why, then, *this* revelation rather than another? And how do we know that our supposed insight is not an illusion? But the *concept* of revelation, as revised with Calvin's help, is not as such greatly problematic, or at least not problematic in the same way as the old one. And that is all I am concerned to maintain for the present.[11]

Calvin himself was not interested in developing a general concept of revelation, but only in describing how the Scriptures function in the

---

11. I have discussed the concept of faith further in the study mentioned in the preceding footnote. I should say that, in addition to the clue I take from Calvin's simile of the spectacles, I was persuaded (during my student days) when I first became acquainted with John Oman's view of religious cognition as a mode of interpretation — a view developed in John Hick's *Faith and Knowledge: A Modern Introduction to the Problem of Religious Knowledge* (Ithaca: Cornell University Press, 1957). I was also captivated by the perceptive account of disclosure situations in Ian T. Ramsey, *Religious Language: An Empirical Placing of Theological Phrases* (London: SCM, 1957). Many years later, I read H. Richard Niebuhr's *The Meaning of Revelation* (1941; reprinted, New York: Macmillan, 1960), where I was delighted to find revelation in our history defined as "that special occasion which provides us with an image by means of which all the occasions of personal and common life become intelligible" (p. 80). See also the use of Wittgenstein's analysis of *seeing as* in John Hick, "Seeing-as and Religious Experience" (1983), reprinted in Terence Penelhum, ed., *Faith* (New York: Macmillan, 1989), pp. 183-92.

Christian knowledge of God as Creator and Redeemer. My remarks have already pressed beyond Calvin's horizon, and it is here that we have something to learn from Schleiermacher's pioneering attempt to develop a Christian theology in the context of religious pluralism. I must indicate next where I think Schleiermacher furthers the discussion — and where I think he invites dissent. It was his merit not to introduce the category of revelation simply in order to remove Christianity at the outset from the company of other religions. In *The Christian Faith* he speaks, like the orthodox Protestant divines, of a general divine manifestation in human nature and the order of creation. But, unlike them, he introduces special revelation as a generic concept that denotes the originating moment in every historical religion, Christianity included. Working with the old contrast between general and special revelation, he sets it in the new context of religious pluralism and historical understanding.[12] (Whether he *keeps* it there is the question to which I shall have to return.) To this extent, I think Schleiermacher's discussion marks a necessary advance over what must strike us, with the wisdom of hindsight, as the parochialism of Calvin. Moreover, Schleiermacher rightly sees no need to characterize the occurrence of the originating moment as strictly (or "absolutely") supernatural.[13]

It will be obvious, however, that in defining the faith that corresponds to revelation as "discernment," "recognition," or "insight," I am working with *cognitive* categories such as Schleiermacher wanted to avoid in specifying the content both of *general* revelation, given in the "feeling" of absolute dependence, and of *special* (historical) revelation, given not simply in doctrines but in the total impression of a founding personality.[14] And I must also demur when he excludes *moral* categories

12. "Accordingly we might say that the idea of revelation signifies the *originality* of the fact which lies at the foundation of a religious community" (*CG*, §10, postscript [p. 50]).

13. "The appearance of the Redeemer in history is, as divine revelation, neither an absolutely *(schlechthin)* supernatural nor an absolutely *(schlechthin)* supra-rational thing" (*CG*, §13 [p. 62]). It is "supernatural" in the qualified sense that a new beginning in history "can never be explained by the condition of the circle in which it appears and operates; for if it could, it would not be a starting-point" (§13.1 [p. 63]).

14. Schleiermacher, *CG*, §13.1 (p. 63). I do not need to pursue the point further, but it is surely evident that cognitive terms will be needed to describe the *reception* of the "original fact" *(die ursprüngliche Tatsache)*, as Schleiermacher understands it: that is, the impression the founder makes on the circle of his followers. It is also significant that in the

as well from "original revelation," as he calls it. The exclusion seems all the more remarkable when he tells us later — much later! — that conscience, too, is an original revelation of God.[15] In my own dogmatic efforts, I have sought to keep the idea of general revelation closer to the moral understanding of it in the older dogmatic tradition, including Calvin.[16] To put it in my own terms: Discernment situations that are properly termed "general revelation" stir our awareness of living in an ordered world, which, at least in our small corner, is a *moral* order that confronts us as a task or demand.[17] I have argued that this awareness, which I call "elemental faith" and take to be the counterpart of an elemental concept of God, is secure insofar as *order* is the presupposition of all scientific inquiry and *moral* order is presupposed in all our everyday discourse about right and wrong. While the spectacles of special revelation — for Christians, the *historia evangelica* — may be said to focus this dual awareness, the awareness given in general revelation is self-evidently the condition for the possibility of the special revelation that brings it to a focus.

From these remarks about the shortcomings of the classical idea of revelation and a possible way of revising it, the main lines of my re-

---

first edition of *Über die Religion,* as has often been noted, Schleiermacher characterizes the essence of religion (i.e., general revelation) as feeling and *Anschauung* (see p. 34 above). The German word is inescapably cognitive (the dictionaries give as one English equivalent "way of looking at or seeing"); but this is one reason why Schleiermacher shied away from it in subsequent editions.

15. Perhaps misleadingly, Schleiermacher actually describes as *ursprüngliche Offenbarung* (1) the universally human revelation given in the structure of consciousness, (2) the general revelation in nature or the world, (3) the revelation in conscience, and (4) the particular historical revelation in Jesus of Nazareth. See, respectively, *CG,* §4.4 (p. 17); §10, postscript (p. 51); §83.1 (p. 342); §103.2 (pp. 443, 445). See also Schleiermacher, *Über die Glaubenslehre: Zwei Sendschreiben an Lücke* (1829), KGA I/10:374-76; trans. James Duke and Francis Fiorenza as *On the Glaubenslehre: Two Letters to Dr. Lücke,* American Academy of Religion Texts and Translations Series, no. 3 (Chico: Scholars, 1981), pp. 78-79. "Original" may not have quite the same meaning in all four contexts, but perhaps a shared meaning is: not accidental but grounded in the divinely ordained way things are. Cf. the remarks on "original perfection" in *CG,* §57.1 (p. 234).

16. See esp. John Calvin, Comm. John 1:5; CO 47:6.

17. See my *Saving and Secular Faith,* chap. 3. I find Ramsey's way of describing the empirical anchorage of religious language especially apt: "'Conscience' (for Butler), the 'Moral Law' (for Kant) and 'Duty' (for Ross) are close logical kinsmen to the theologian's 'God,' and give good approximations to its logical placing" (*Religious Language,* p. 31).

sponse to Van Harvey and Bruce McCormack can readily be anticipated. For if I cannot see *Deus dixit* as the distinguishing characteristic
of the Christian witness (Karl Barth), I am not persuaded that all talk of
revelation is illusion (Ludwig Feuerbach). My response to Walter
Wyman is bound to be more complicated precisely because we are very
nearly agreed, but not quite.[18]

III. Feuerbach and Revelation as Illusion

No one in our day has probed more relentlessly than Van Harvey the
nagging questions that cluster around the theme of faith and history.
His book *The Historian and the Believer* (first published in 1966) has
been hailed with good reason as a twentieth-century theological classic.
In the introduction to the new edition, he still asserts that biblical criticism, especially research into the historical Jesus, is a skeleton in the
closet of Christian theology and adds: "The history of theology since
the middle of the nineteenth century may be seen as a series of unsuc-
cessful salvage operations mounted to deal with this problem."[19] Much
of the mid-nineteenth-century furor over faith and history was of
course precipitated by D. F. Strauss (1808-1874). In his more recent
work, however, Harvey has moved on, so to say, to another left-wing Hegelian: from Strauss to Feuerbach.[20] Strictly speaking, the focus shifts
from revelation and history to revelation and naturalistic reductionism.
But it was the purpose of our conference on "Revelation and History" to
explore the history of the idea of revelation as well as the conceptual
problems of revelation and historical thinking. Perhaps remembering
that I was once considered a Luther scholar, Harvey made his contribu-

18. Van A. Harvey, "Feuerbach on Luther's Doctrine of Revelation: An Essay in
Honor of Brian Gerrish," *Journal of Religion* 78 (1998): 3-17; Bruce L. McCormack, "Rev-
elation and History in Transfoundationalist Perspective: Karl Barth's Theological Episte-
mology in Conversation with a Schleiermacherian Tradition," pp. 18-37; Walter E.
Wyman, Jr., "Revelation and the Doctrine of Faith: Historical Revelation within the
Limits of Historical Consciousness," pp. 38-63.

19. Van A. Harvey, *The Historian and the Believer: The Morality of Historical Knowledge and Christian Belief,* with a new introduction by the author (Urbana and Chicago:
University of Illinois Press, 1996), p. ix.

20. Van A. Harvey, *Feuerbach and the Interpretation of Religion,* Cambridge Studies
in Religion and Critical Thought, vol. 1 (Cambridge: Cambridge University Press, 1995).

tion to our theme by looking into Feuerbach's ostensibly historical claim that Martin Luther's doctrine of revelation was wholly on his side.

If Harvey is correct, Feuerbach's appeal to Luther was something more than window dressing. In any case, in 1844 Feuerbach was developing a new interpretation of religion. The central theme of *The Essence of Christianity* (German 1841) had been "projection": the mechanism by which the characteristics of the human species are objectified in the idea of God. Soon after writing the book that made him famous, Feuerbach became more preoccupied with the inner drive that turns a person to belief in God. There was a double shift, we might say: from the human species to the individual, and from a psychological mechanism to the motivation for it. *The Essence of Faith according to Luther* (German 1844) falls into the transitional stage of Feuerbach's thinking, between *The Essence of Christianity* and his *Lectures on the Essence of Religion* (German 1848), the time when he was exploring the evidence that religion is powered by what Harvey sums up as "the felicity principle": that is, "the assumption . . . that the principal aim of religion is to secure the welfare or felicity of humanity in general and the self in particular."[21] Feuerbach discovered, or at least tried to show, that this is exactly the meaning of Luther's doctrine of revelation. For the revelation of God is the incarnation, which, together with the resurrection, is the perceptible proof that God is God "for us" or "for me" *(pro nobis, pro me)* and takes away the limits by which nature obstructs our blessedness, including the ultimate limit: death.[22] Harvey comments: "[I]n the Luther book, *Sinnlichkeit* [perceptibility] is the basis for the Christian certainty that the divine is truly beneficent. . . ."[23] Thus the essence of faith according

---

21. I take the definition of the felicity principle from Harvey's Feuerbach book (p. 69). Cf. Harvey, "Feuerbach on Luther's Doctrine," pp. 11-12.

22. Feuerbach didn't think Protestantism was very good at achieving victory over the ultimate limit. On Luther's own testimony, evangelical sermons actually increased the fear of death, changing an acute evil, Feuerbach comments, into a chronic one. See Feuerbach, "Comments upon Some Remarkable Statements by Luther," in Ludwig Feuerbach, *The Essence of Faith according to Luther* (hereafter *Luther*), trans. Melvin Cherno (New York: Harper & Row, 1967), p. 127. For the German see FSW 7:311-75. Harvey provides references to the new critical edition, Feuerbach's *Gesammelte Werke*, ed. Werner Schuffenhauer (Berlin: Akademie, 1981ff.), which will eventually supersede FSW for scholarly work on Feuerbach.

23. Harvey, "Feuerbach on Luther's Doctrine," p. 13 (reading "beneficent" for "beneficient").

to Luther was in effect the desire for blessedness, or the love of each individual for him- or herself.

Most of us, I suspect, shudder when we read the coup de grâce: the quotation in which Luther expressly points out that concern for others is a small thing in comparison with our own salvation.[24] We are reminded of the Calvinist (well, Puritan!) counterpart: Max Weber's citation of the place in John Bunyan's *Pilgrim's Progress* (part 1, 1678) where Christian stuffs his fingers in his ears, so as not to hear the entreaty of his wife and children, and runs off toward the celestial city crying, "Life! Life! Eternal Life."[25] Feuerbach's argument in *The Essence of Faith according to Luther* is not that Luther's mentality was peculiarly his own, but that it exemplified with uncommon clarity Christian faith in general. "Luther was the first to let out the secret of Christian faith."[26] Indeed, he gave away the secret of religion.

Was Feuerbach right about Luther? And was he right about religion? Obviously, I cannot venture more than a comment or two on each question.[27] The Luther book is hardly to be judged as an academic contribution to the history of theology, and it is perhaps beside the point to rummage for counter-citations in "the great Pandora's box" of the Weimar Edition, as Karl Barth called it,[28] to prove that Feuerbach's case was tendentious. Still, something needs to be said for the sake of our conversation on revelation and history. Actually, Feuerbach's thoughts on the role of *Sinnlichkeit* in Luther's theology (the Luther scholars might prefer to say *Leiblichkeit*) were by no means wrong-headed; they would be confirmed by a closer look at Luther's faith in the sacrament of Christ's body and blood. But Feuerbach's interpretation of the Lutheran *pro me* needs correction.

Three qualifications are called for. First, while the *pro me* may sometimes have nurtured an egocentric piety by which self-love is extended rather than cured, its original function was to assure the individual that she was not excluded from God's love for the world. First-

---

24. Feuerbach, *Luther,* p. 101.

25. Max Weber, *The Protestant Ethic and the Spirit of Capitalism* (German 1904-5), trans. Talcott Parsons (New York: Scribner's, 1958), p. 107.

26. Feuerbach, *Luther,* p. 50.

27. See further Chap. 5 below.

28. Karl Barth, "Nachwort," in Heinz Bolli, ed., *Schleiermacher-Auswahl, mit einem Nachwort von Karl Barth* (Munich and Hamburg: Siebenstern, 1968), p. 302.

person pronouns are commonplace in evangelical hymn books, but Luther understood well that, in his day, many with troubled consciences found it hard to use the first person at all — hard to be persuaded that God's love includes *me*.[29] Second, the *pro me* did not prevent him from identifying self-love as the essence not of faith but of sin,[30] and he could warn his pastoral charges that God receives his glory only when I put his kingdom first, not desiring it for the sake of my own blessedness but nonetheless finding my blessedness in commitment to his kingdom.[31] Third, it was precisely the thought that "God takes care of me" that, in Luther's view, freed the Christian for her neighbor. Feuerbach does not fairly represent the sequence: first faith, then love. It doesn't mean that I am more important than my neighbor; it means that eternal blessedness is both more important than earthly happiness and, in addition, the actual spring of loving action in the temporal domain, because I am available to others only when I am no longer consumed with anxiety about myself or my standing before God.[32] In short, what Luther heard in the Word of God — God's revelation — was a good deal more than can be subsumed under the felicity principle.

Feuerbach's reading of Luther went with the new theory of religion that was to be presented in the *Lectures on the Essence of Religion*. There he asserts more explicitly that the felicity principle (as Harvey calls it) is the fertile soil of wishful thinking in religion.[33] That God exists for me means that God does not *really* exist: I am just imagining and inventing the God I wish for. My imagination, driven by the desire for blessed-

---

29. See, e.g., Martin Luther, *Der Prophet Jona ausgelegt* (1526), WA 19:206. The question is not, as Feuerbach supposes (*Luther,* p. 64), whether God is *really* good, but whether God's goodness is *for me.*

30. Most notably in his *Vorlesung über den Römerbrief* (Latin 1515-16), to which Feuerbach would not have had access. See Chap. 12, n. 29, below.

31. Martin Luther, *Eine kurze und gute Auslegung des Vaterunsers vor sich und hinter sich* (1519), WA 6:21-22.

32. For this fundamental Lutheran insight, one need look no further than Luther's tract *De libertate Christiana* (1520): see WA 7:64-66; LW 31:364-68. Feuerbach doesn't quite get the point when he concedes that I must care for myself before I can care for others (*Luther,* p. 102). But that is close! And he also recognizes that, in Luther's scheme, I wish blessedness for others as well as myself (p. 115).

33. Hints of this reduction of faith to illusion will be found already in Feuerbach's Luther book (*Luther,* pp. 76, 79n., 95, 102-4, 112). "God is a blank tablet on which there is nothing written but what you yourself have written" (p. 107).

ness, helps me come to terms with the mysterious powers of nature by personalizing them, making them able to hear and to meet my needs. Harvey thinks this offers a more convincing critique of religion than the earlier projection theory. But the limitations of the critique are surely evident: it works better with some kinds of religious experience than with others. Feuerbach's thinking was shaped more than he realized by the religion closest to home.

A strong aversion to Protestant pietism made its appearance already in Feuerbach's early work, *Thoughts on Death and Immortality* (German 1830). Pietism, he believed, makes each person in her individuality the center of her own attention. He read Luther one-sidedly because he ransacked the Reformer's writings, especially his sermons and postils, only for more evidence of Protestant egocentrism — at its source. But it was a further mistake if he supposed that this gave him a theory of *religion.* There are religions that do not reassure us that everything is as we wish it to be, but admonish us to adjust ourselves to the way things inevitably are; and the function of religion has sometimes been to counter the individual's desires, wishes, and self-seeking with a moral demand that can hardly be construed as a product of *physical* nature. It is the sense of a *moral* order that leads the religious consciousness to represent the subject of revelation (the Revealer) as a commanding will. As he tells us himself, Harvey learned of such a "profound faith" from his Calvinist father.[34] But I do not see how his Feuerbach could incorporate it into his theory of religion.

IV. Karl Barth and Revelation as *Deus Dixit*

On the whole, nineteenth-century theologians seem to have worried less about Feuerbach than about Strauss. That may well be the right choice. But it may also betray more than a little theological myopia. The most influential Protestant theologian at the end of the century, Albrecht Ritschl, proposed a theory of religion that would have delighted Feuerbach: "In every religion what is sought, with the help of the superhuman spiritual power reverenced by man, is a solution of the contradiction in which man finds himself, as both a part of the world of na-

---

34. Harvey, *The Historian and the Believer,* p. xiv.

ture and a spiritual personality claiming to dominate nature."[35] It was to Luther's idea of the "kingship" of believers that Ritschl appealed in support of this theory.[36] And for his well-known doctrine of religious value-judgments, according to which "we know the nature of God and Christ only in their worth for us," he appealed to Luther's explanation of the First Commandment in his *Large Catechism* (German 1529), which Feuerbach also liked.[37] In one of his rare references to Feuerbach, Ritschl thought it enough to dismiss him with the remark that Christian faith cannot possibly be egoistic because it is connected with moral duty in the kingdom of God. But if that is a move in the right direction, Ritschl runs back into Feuerbach's open arms when he adds that moral conduct is not disinterested: "The vital point is that one realises as one's own interest the interest of others to whom the service is rendered."[38]

We owe it to Karl Barth more than anyone else that in the middle third of the twentieth century revelation was reaffirmed as the Word of God to which our thinking and living must be conformed. This is not to imply that no one else in the first third of the century protested against theologies that measure doctrines by their efficiency in satisfying the needs of the day. But the champions of an objective revelation were prone to compromise their case by identifying revelation with an infallible book, and the weight of historical-critical study of the Bible increasingly went against them. Protestant seminarians of my generation dis-

---

35. Albrecht Ritschl (1822-1889), *The Christian Doctrine of Justification and Reconciliation: The Positive Development of the Doctrine,* trans. H. R. Mackintosh and A. B. Macaulay from the 3rd German ed. (1900; reprinted, Clifton, N.J.: Reference Book Publishers, 1966), p. 199.

36. But Ritschl regrets that Luther's notion of "positive world-dominating freedom" in *De libertate Christiana* was wholly overshadowed in his later writings by the "negative sense of freedom from the law and from sin" (*Justification and Reconciliation,* p. 181).

37. Ritschl, *Justification and Reconciliation,* pp. 211-12; cf. Feuerbach, *Luther,* p. 51.

38. Ritschl, *Justification and Reconciliation,* p. 206. Fiorenza, however, notes approvingly that Ritschl, in his reply to Feuerbach, insisted on the social nature of religion. In Fiorenza's summing up: "[A]ny scientific observation of religion should necessarily take as its starting-point not the religion of an individual, but the religion of the community." Francis Schüssler Fiorenza, "The Responses of Barth and Ritschl to Feuerbach," *Sciences religieuses/Studies in Religion* 7,2 (1978): 149-66; see p. 156. As Fiorenza points out (p. 156 n. 25), Karl Marx saw the weakness of Feuerbach's treatment of religion at exactly this point.

covered in Karl Barth and Emil Brunner a view of Scripture as fallible human witness to the Word of God in Jesus Christ, and it seemed all the more persuasive to us because it was represented as the *real* understanding of Scripture (appearances sometimes to the contrary!) in the Protestant Reformers, especially Luther. *Deus dixit* and *Paulus dixit,* we learned, are not quite the same.

I think it is fair to say that we read Barth and Brunner — especially Brunner — in those days as mediating theologians in the Reformed (Calvinist) tradition. But we also learned that the place of Schleiermacher in the tradition was more than dubious. As the strident criticisms of Schleiermacher increased, so did my regard for him. Hence I welcome Bruce McCormack's groundbreaking work on Barth, which not only calls for conversation between the Barthians and the Schleiermacherians but also sees the respective heroes of each party standing in a mediating tradition, Reformed or not. This, of course, does not mean glossing over the break with "liberalism" that McCormack documents in his formidable study of Barth's theological progress.[39] But, as his contribution to our conference made clear, he is convinced that even after the break Barth was dealing with nineteenth-century problems and, up to a point, drawing on nineteenth-century solutions. In particular, Barth, like Schleiermacher before him, tried to formulate a doctrine of revelation that did not question Kant's limitation of theoretical knowing to what is "intuitable": that is, perceptible under the forms of intuition (space and time). His theology was in this respect, as in others, not so much neo-orthodox as modern: a theology of mediation and correlation.

However much I welcome McCormack's placement of Barth in the history of modern theology, I have some misgiving about what he sees as Barth's contribution to our theme. Nothing is to be gained by laboring the point McCormack freely admits: that Kant would not be impressed by the argument that God makes Godself intuitable in the incarnation without surrendering the unintuitability proper to God, since God's *hidden* presence in the life of Jesus can be recognized only as the Holy Spirit gives us eyes to see.[40] But one may well question the wisdom

39. Bruce L. McCormack, *Karl Barth's Critically Realistic Dialectical Theology: Its Genesis and Development, 1909-1936* (Oxford: Clarendon, 1995), the first of two volumes planned, clearly provides a benchmark for any further discussions of Barth's early career.

40. I take the formulation Barth gives in his Göttingen dogmatics: Karl Barth, *GD*

of solving an eighteenth-century problem by repeating sixteenth- and seventeenth-century formulas that had come under sharp attack in Kant's day. Schleiermacher, by contrast, conceded the Neologists' criticisms of the inherited christological dogmas and tried to *rethink* what it might mean to confess that God was in Christ without the scholastic abstractions, which, he believed, lost contact with the language of faith.[41] (It is no accident that the "Reformed version of an anhypostatic-enhypostatic Christology"[42] never found its way into the Reformed confessions of faith!) "Correlation" requires something more than the juxtaposition of the old and the new, neither one undergoing change. I was struck by some of the "if-then" sentences in McCormack's presentation. They may suffice to show the coherence of what is being said. But can they reassure the reader that she is confronted with something more than an astute dialectical exercise?

The Barthian riposte, no doubt, is that in Christian dogmatics the *fact* of revelation precedes any inquiry into its possibility. The *Deus dixit* is given, and so is the identity of God's life with the life of Jesus, which is the form of revelation. To ask *how* it is possible is not to ask *whether* it is possible or to reconsider our axiomatic starting point in God's becoming human: that would be to forsake the discipline of church dogmatics. For my part, I have no doubt that a lot of good theology is done from this

---

1:331-35. Cf. McCormack, "Revelation and History," pp. 27-32. By his affirmation that God in Christ fully entered the world of intuitability, Barth advanced beyond the contention of his second *Römerbrief* (1922) that God's revelation was the resurrection understood as an event without extension. See Barth, *The Epistle to the Romans,* trans. from the 6th ed. by Edwin C. Hoskins (London: Oxford University Press, 1933), pp. 29-31.

41. Schleiermacher desired christological formulas that "shall approximate to what can be presented to Christian congregations in religious teaching" (*CF,* §96.3 [p. 397]). One reason why McCormack does not speak of Schleiermacher's christology is that he compares Schleiermacher on the independence of *general* revelation with Barth on the independence of *special* revelation. As for McCormack's observations on Kant, it goes without saying that a great deal more could be said about Kant's thoughts on God, Christ, and religion. He will surely agree that we are not yet done with Kant when we say that he "reduced God to a regulative idea wholly lacking in content" (McCormack, "Revelation and History," p. 21). See my remarks on Kant's moral theology in Chapter 1, pp. 29-32 above.

42. McCormack, "Revelation and History," pp. 27-28. See further McCormack, *For Us and Our Salvation: Incarnation and Atonement in the Reformed Tradition,* Studies in Reformed Theology and History, vol. 1, no. 2 (Princeton: Princeton Theological Seminary, 1993), pp. 11-13.

standpoint, and I continue to learn from the greatest Reformed theologian of the last century. But what the seventeenth- and eighteenth-century critics of orthodoxy were saying, it seems to me, is that only our provincialism has prevented us from facing a *larger fact:* that there are, as Ernst Troeltsch put it, several nodal points in the history of humanity's encounter with transcendence, not one absolute center.[43] Once Christian theologians fully acknowledge *this* fact, it is bound to make a difference to the way they go about their business, not least to the way in which they think of revelation. We still need a (posthumous) debate between Barth and Troeltsch. On that I agree entirely with McCormack,[44] and it brings me to the last part of my response.

V. Schleiermacher on General and Special Revelation

I have left until last some rather more detailed comments on Walter Wyman's presentation. He sees the problem of revelation and history much as I see it, and he adds a hint at the direction he thinks we ought to take in our attempt to solve it. Like me, he is irresistibly drawn to Friedrich Schleiermacher and Ernst Troeltsch and the manner in which they framed our question.[45] It is not surprising that, after a telling epigraph from Schleiermacher and an astute posing of the apparent polar opposition between Wolfhart Pannenberg and Gordon Kaufman, Wyman launches into an exposition and critique of Scheiermacher's and Troeltsch's thoughts on revelation. Roughly speaking, he prefers Schleiermacher on general revelation, Troeltsch on historical revelation, and judges Schleiermacher's contribution more secure than Troeltsch's. With respect to Christian belief in a special revelation in Jesus Christ, he

43. Ernst Troeltsch (1865-1923), *Die Bedeutung der Geschichtlichkeit Jesu für den Glauben* (Tübingen: J. C. B. Mohr [Paul Siebeck], 1911), pp. 15, 22.

44. We cannot start the debate here, but I may at least say that I don't think Troeltsch's principle of correlation is a mere dogma (see McCormack, "Revelation and History," p. 36 n. 43). True, it is not exhaustively *testable* by historical method, but Troeltsch's point is that it is *presupposed* by historical method in the sense that it is implicit in the way modern historians actually do their work.

45. For the way in which Schleiermacher and Troeltsch recast the task of theology, one could hardly do better than turn to Wyman's book *The Concept of Glaubenslehre: Ernst Troeltsch and the Theological Heritage of Schleiermacher,* AAR Academy Series, no. 44 (Chico: Scholars, 1983).

ends on a largely negative note: not even Troeltsch, he thinks, succeeded in saving it. It is with his critique of Schleiermacher and Troeltsch, then, that I wish to conclude my response. I hesitate to follow Wyman in his apparent reduction of special to general revelation,[46] even though my thoughts and his reflect much the same conceptual framework.

Wyman is sympathetic, as am I, to Schleiermacher's understanding of *universal revelation* in the second of the speeches *On Religion,* which he cites in the first edition.[47] I think he is right in his verdict that Troeltsch, who internalized general revelation as the actual inward connection of the divine and human spirits, failed to improve on Schleiermacher's notion of the self-revelation of the Universe in every outward event.[48] Religion, Schleiermacher tells us, is grasping everything individual as part of the Whole, and any fresh, original intuition of the Whole is properly termed a "revelation" inasmuch as it is the work of the unceasing activity of the Universe on us. But the way in which one expresses the revelation, or conceptualizes its source as "God," depends on the individual imagination.[49] Wyman likes this line of thought, which leads later, in Schleiermacher's *The Christian Faith,* to the identification of the feeling of absolute dependence as an original revelation of God. He finds it attractive because it allows for variety in the forms of religious experience, even though the action of the Universe that evokes them is uniform. On the other hand, he doesn't endorse Schleiermacher's notion of a *historical revelation* in Jesus Christ, foreshadowed in the fifth speech and developed in the introduction to *The Christian Faith,* because it appears to violate the selfsame principle of cosmic uni-

46. Wyman's position is reminiscent of Matthew Tindal's estimate of Christianity as a "republication" of the religion of nature (see Chap. 1 above, pp. 16-17). But his acknowledged debt is to Schubert Ogden's notion of "re-presentation." I should note that in my response to Wyman I depart from his use of the qualifier "original." As I have indicated (n. 15 above), Schleiermacher himself doesn't confine the term "original revelation" to revelation in human consciousness or in nature. Hence I have reverted to the old antithesis of "general" and "special" revelation, and I use "universal" to refer more specifically to the general revelation in *nature* (the universe) and "historical" to refer to special revelation in *history.*

47. See Chap. 1 n. 56, above.

48. Wyman, "Revelation and the Doctrine of Faith," pp. 55-56. Wyman's objection is that Troeltsch's location of general revelation "in the intertwining of the divine and human in the depths of the human spirit" presupposes without argument a "metaphysics of spirit."

49. See Chap. 1, pp. 33-34, above.

formity. It is, in a word, a relic of discredited supernaturalism, which attributes two kinds of activity to God: one identical in scope with the orderly progress of the world, the other disrupting it. On historical revelation, then, Wyman prefers Troeltsch to Schleiermacher.[50]

By way of rejoinder to this criticism, more could surely be said in Schleiermacher's defense — whether or not the more is sufficient to make his understanding of God's revelation in Jesus a viable option. We need to distinguish his formal description of this (as of all other) revelation from the content he assigns to it. For one might wish to rule out the appearance of a perfect God-consciousness in Jesus (the essential content of the Christian revelation, according to Schleiermacher)[51] as irreconcilable with historical thinking, and yet still argue that the founding event of Christianity was a distinctive revelation of God in Jesus of Nazareth. In itself, the idea of an original fact that lies at the foundation of a religious community is presumably unexceptionable. Even Troeltsch's principles of criticism, analogy, and correlation did not prevent him from acknowledging genuine novelty in the historical process. The difficulty, however, is that Schleiermacher seems to undermine his own generic concept of revelation by refusing to leave Jesus as revealer in the same class as Moses and Mohammed. For him, the supernatural appearance of the Redeemer expressly annuls the principle of analogy.[52]

Schleiermacher would reply, I think: But so does the creation of the world, which, in the eternal purpose of God, includes the sending of the Redeemer. What is supernatural about the appearance of the Redeemer is that it results, not from an unparalleled divine intervention in the flow of history, but from God's one eternal decree. The decree to send Christ forth is one with the decree to create the human race. The supernatural

---

50. Troeltsch's critique of supernaturalism as a violation of the historical principles of criticism, analogy, and correlation is presented in his essay "Über historische und dogmatische Methode in der Theologie" (1900): Troeltsch, *Gesammelte Schriften,* 4 vols. (1921-25; reprinted Darmstadt: Wissenschaftliche Buchgesellschaft, 1980), 2:729-53; Eng. trans. in Ernst Troeltsch, *Religion in History,* trans. James Luther Adams and Walter F. Bense, Fortress Texts in Modern Theology (Minneapolis: Fortress, 1991), pp. 11-32.

51. "[T]he divine revelation through Him, however it is conceived, is always conceived as identical with his whole being *(Existenz)*" (*CG,* §14, postscript [p. 75]); "the God-consciousness in Him was absolutely clear and determined each moment, to the exclusion of all else" (§96.3 [p. 397]).

52. Schleiermacher, *CG,* §11.4 (p. 58).

in Christ is therefore not referred to a temporal act of God: it belongs rather to the timeless divine causality, in which creation and redemption coincide. The incarnation is the reason why everything in nature is as it is. If, then, creation may be said to be supernatural, or without analogy, so must the appearance of the Redeemer, which is the completion of the creation of humanity and holds the meaning of creation in itself.[53] Hence Schleiermacher can say, in impeccably orthodox language: "[I]n truth He [Christ] alone mediates . . . all revelation of God through the world. . . ."[54]

Still, though I think more needs to be said about Schleiermacher's "supernaturalism," I don't disagree with Wyman's preference for Troeltsch on historical revelation. I concede that Schleiermacher's identification of Christian revelation with the historical appearance of a perfect God-consciousness cannot stand up to the criticisms of historically minded theologians such as F. C. Baur, Strauss, and Troeltsch. I even concede, a bit more reluctantly, that Schleiermacher's account of what is supernatural about the appearance of the Redeemer, though ingenious and still worthy of consideration, is likely to strike the historically minded as an irrelevant dogmatic ploy — not as a secure line of defense. But I am unwilling to infer that a generic concept of historical revelation, as revised by Troeltsch, is unworkable, and in general this is Wyman's inclination, too — with the qualification I must move on to shortly. Schleiermacher defeats his own concept of historical revelation by removing Christ from the class of historical personalities. Troeltsch retrieves it by assuming that the revelation through Jesus is *formally* analogous to the revelations granted to Moses and Mohammed, whatever differences there undoubtedly are in the *content* of the messages they communicate.[55] Hence, Wyman decides, Troeltsch's understanding of revelation is not, like Schleiermacher's, vulnerable to historical science.

53. Schleiermacher, *CG*, §109.3 (p. 501); §164.2 (p. 724).

54. Schleiermacher, *CG*, §94.2 (p. 388).

55. It should be emphasized that for Schleiermacher historical revelation, wherever it occurs, is not initially in the form of "doctrine": the *ursprüngliche Tatsache* that establishes a religious communion is always the appearance of the founding personality, "a thinking being who works upon us directly as a distinctive existence by means of his total impression on us" (*CG*, §10, postscript [p. 50]). The respective revelations of Judaism, Christianity, and Islam are analogous in this respect. But the analogy breaks down at the point where Jesus is taken out of the company of Moses and Mohammed as the unique embodiment of the perfect God-consciousness.

Nevertheless, in his conclusion Wyman leaves us with a trouble-some question that jeopardizes the independent viability of any claim to a special, historical revelation and threatens to collapse it into the idea of general revelation. The question has to do with the notion of imaginative invention: not *whether,* but *how much* the imagination contributes to the interpretation of religious experience. Wyman has no wish to deny categorically that imaginative constructs can have an objective refer-ence, as Schleiermacher and Troeltsch both believed. Here I certainly agree. If the operation of imaginative invention were non-referential or wholly non-cognitive, then the constructs would have the status of pure *fictions,* generated wholly within the religious subject, and the idea of revelation would simply be out of place. No object would be revealed: subjective creations would be projected into thin air. The only objectiv-ity one might wish to claim for them would not lie in some transcendent divine reality, but in the existence of a historical tradition of imaginative construction in a particular religious community; the fictions would be communal or collective fictions. If, however, one takes the constructs to be *perspectives* ("perspectives on reality" is one of Wyman's expres-sions), there is no logical reason to exclude the concept of revelation. It is, of course, always possible that the object disclosed is falsely identi-fied by the religious consciousness, as the later Feuerbach argued. But this is not the path that Wyman wants to take.

VI. In Defense of Special Revelation

The issue for Wyman, if I understand him correctly, is not whether the work of the religious imagination can plausibly be taken as a response to the disclosure of ultimate reality. It is whether we can assign any more definite content to what is supposedly revealed in history than Schleier-macher assigns to *general* revelation — which is not much. Wyman re-marks on the epistemological modesty of Schleiermacher's theory of revelation in the first edition of *On Religion,* and he cites Van Harvey's comment that the key term *Anschauung* is compatible with agnosticism about the nature of what is intuited. And the question is: How can we move on from there to Troeltsch's claim that the ongoing career of Christian faith is a fresh, historical revelation and not (as I take Wyman to be asking) simply a developing interpretative perspective on the little that is given in general revelation? Wyman's answer is, We can't. Why not? Of course, any revelation claim whatever is open to questions about its supposedly transcendent source. The main difficulty Wyman perceives, however, is that a divine disclosure in history appears to presuppose a special divine act, besides the ordinary course of divinely sustained events, and Schleiermacher has taught us that there are *no* special acts of God. There is only the timeless, spaceless divine activity, which sustains the whole course of nature, and of which we are aware in our intuition of the Whole or in our feeling of absolute dependence.

If this line of reasoning is sound, then Troeltsch's view of *historical* revelation may have the merit of not imperiling the principle of analogy, but it is less secure than Schleiermacher's conception of *general* revelation, which at least has the advantage of being firmly grounded in an analysis of the structure of human existence and does not postulate any divine activity apart from the regular movement of the Whole. In the end, Schleiermacher's case for general revelation scores highest of all the options because it has two merits: it is not on collision course with historical thinking, and, more positively, it has a "fair chance" of proving credible when tested by philosophical argument. In sum: Wyman's adroit argument has first let Troeltsch undermine Schleiermacher's concept of historical revelation, then let Schleiermacher, in turn, drastically trim Troeltsch's modification of the same concept. Indeed, it becomes doubtful whether the expression "historical *revelation*" has a proper use at all. Maybe theology had better learn to do without it. All that is left is general revelation — and a human imagination busily generating beliefs and symbols out of the stuff of history while the mysterious deity has nothing more to say.

For now, I can contribute only two brief comments on this turn in the conversation. They have to do with the two theological criteria Wyman borrows from Schubert Ogden: appropriateness to the normative Christian witness and credibility according to universal conditions of truth. First, while I agree that the notion of particular acts of God in history is improperly anthropomorphic,[56] we must look more closely at

---

56. See Schleiermacher's succinct proposition on creation: *CG,* §41. An "act of God" has been the subject of extensive theological debate. See, e.g., the contributions in Owen C. Thomas, ed., *God's Activity in the World: The Contemporary Problem,* AAR Studies in Religion, no. 31 (Chico: Scholars, 1983).

the assumption that special revelation presupposes special divine acts and therefore fails the test of credibility. It depends on what "special" is taken to mean.[57] Recall Wyman's interpretation of Schleiermacher's thoughts on revelation in the speeches *On Religion*. Is it strictly true that the action of the universe on us is "uniform"? Even if we grant that nature's ceaseless activity reflects the uniform application of so-called laws, the products of the activity are diverse and so, accordingly, are their effects on ourselves. When these products become the occasions of revelation, they are by no means taken as equally significant. Some of them are "special," but not in the sense that nature works harder at them, or that by them the ordinary processes of nature are supplemented or suspended. Rather, they have special importance in forming our perception of the kind of universe we live in — and hence of its ultimate cause, ground, or first principle.

The analogy commonly invoked here proposes that we should not think of God's activity as resembling the interaction between one self and another, but as more like the relationship between a single self and its own psychic or bodily activities. Still anthropomorphic, no doubt! But more properly so, insofar as the comparison avoids misrepresenting God's activity as akin to the discrete actions of a finite agent in space and time. Christian theologians will presumably wish to insist that God is the enduring ground of all temporal events, including the acts of free agents. The analogy enables them, however, to make good sense of the concept of special or historical revelation. For although everything I do is my activity, it is obvious some of the things I do are better indications than others of my essential and characteristic self, and in this sense may be said to be, or to become, "special revelations" of who I am. I would be unwilling to surrender the credibility of a special, historical revelation of God before the possibility of rethinking the concept along these lines had been given (to borrow one of Wyman's expressions) a "fair chance."

Schleiermacher, it is true, though he proposes the analogy,[58] seems

---

57. Clearly, the problem is not unrelated to the problem of Schleiermacher's describing the appearance of the Redeemer as, in a sense, supernatural. Both problems are set by the admission that the divine activity cannot be construed as intervention in the regular course of events. The difference, however, is that now the question is not about one wholly non-analogous event (Schleiermacher), but about several special events that are admitted to be analogous to one another (Troeltsch).

58. Schleiermacher, *CG*, §52.2 (p. 206).

to jeopardize it by his insistence that while the divine causality is coextensive with natural causality *(dem Umfange nach ihr gleichgesetzt)*, it is nonetheless, as timeless and spaceless, a causality of a quite different kind.[59] Do we then have to say of God's activity, if not of nature's, that it is "uniform"? H. R. Mackintosh complained that "the causality of God is presented [by Schleiermacher] as operating in the world as an infinite, uniform and quite undeviating pressure, like that of a hydraulic apparatus, with its allotted equal weight on each square inch."[60] How could the diverse products of nature tell us anything special about a divine causality so conceived? How, indeed, could such an absolute causality operate on the world at all? The process theologians will assure us that there are better metaphysical foundations on which to rest the self-body analogy, and the "fair chance" I am asking for will need to take into account the neoclassical alternative, with which Wyman has strong sympathies. For now, I wish only to point out that if the analogy holds good, special revelation is not inconsistent with the view that God's activity *(Tätigkeit)* grounds every historical event and cannot properly be construed as a particular act *(Tat)*, or sequence of acts, *within* history. To this extent, special revelation is not excluded by the criterion of credibility.

My second comment has to do with Wyman's other theological criterion: appropriateness to the normative Christian witness. His proposal is that we think of creation as the "original revelation" of God, and that we need not attribute anything more to supposed historical revelations than imaginative interpretation of it. He then suggests that to take creation itself as the original revelation meets the criterion of appropriateness because "Christian faith is, among other things, also faith in

---

59. Schleiermacher, *CG*, §51 (p. 200).

60. Hugh Ross Mackintosh, *Types of Modern Theology: Schleiermacher to Barth* (London: Nisbet, 1937), p. 82. Schleiermacher's sharp differentiation of divine from natural causality did not inhibit his derivation of divine attributes from experience, though it qualified their status. They denote something particular or special not in God but in the way the feeling of absolute dependence is to be connected with God (*CG*, §50). As such, they are modes of the divine *causality* (§82, postscript [p. 341]). And yet they certainly assert something true about God, and one of them, love, is to be taken as the equivalent of God's being or nature (§167.1 [p. 730]). Schleiermacher's notion of the absolute divine causality, whether or not it should, did not in fact prevent him from thinking of individual divine attributes without divine intervention.

creation."[61] But the suggestion sounds a little disingenuous if the other things are in effect reduced to this one thing. Naturally, the move that I see beginning, at least, in Calvin demands a rethinking of the classical way of relating natural and revealed knowledge of God. If revelation is the self-communication of God received in the confidence and obedience of faith, then it cannot be quantified in the old manner, as though the revelation in Scripture were simply more information added to information already imparted. The God encountered in the biblical witness to Jesus Christ is the God revealed in the created order. Nevertheless, Calvin's distinction between "the knowledge of God the Creator" and "the knowledge of God the Redeemer in Christ" remains fundamental to Christian theology, even if it is neither a distinction between two gods nor a matter of an increasing quantity of information about the one true God.

Let me then turn to John Calvin once more. He is surely correct when he asserts: "[I]t is one thing to feel *(sentire)* that God as our Maker supports us by his power, governs us by his providence, nourishes us by his goodness, and attends us with all sorts of blessings — and another thing to embrace the grace of reconciliation offered to us in Christ."[62] For Calvin, the dividing line that made the knowledge of God twofold was the disobedience of Adam and Eve at the beginning of history. We don't need to follow him in the doctrine of a historical fall. The essential point is that, in everyman's and every woman's experience, revelation is given under the conditions of estrangement, God-forgetfulness, doubt, ennui, moral insensitivity, guilt, despair — all that is covered by the old-fashioned rubric "sin." Whether or not the context of estrangement and reconciliation requires us to think in terms of some added content to what is given in the general revelation of God will no doubt depend in part on our understanding of the redemption accomplished by Jesus of Nazareth, and I cannot enter adequately into that question here.[63] I am

61. Wyman, "Revelation and the Doctrine of Faith," p. 60.

62. Calvin, *ICR* I, ii.1 (1:40).

63. The ways of getting at the "more," if any, of Christian revelation are very diverse. For Calvin, redemption is restoration to prelapsarian piety, but with the significant difference that the goodness of God is now disclosed as the grace of forgiveness. For Schleiermacher, it is only in our experience of Christ that we know the *love* of God and perceive the world as a theater of redemption. For Rudolf Bultmann, while there is a "more" of the gospel, it does not lie in the *content* of revelation but rather in its *occurrence*

simply concerned to insist that the heart of the Christian theological enterprise is the theme of revelation and faith under the conditions that threaten faith and the conditions of its renewal. Not that Wyman intends to disregard these conditions; he would certainly agree that an adequate application of the test of appropriateness to the Christian witness would require us to keep them at the center.[64] And the security of our concept of revelation cannot be established without giving due weight to *both* criteria: appropriateness as well as credibility. But I suspect that, in practice, the quest for security tends to push us toward the epistemological problem of credibility, exposing us to Albrecht Ritschl's famous remark about theologians who remain standing in the court of the Gentiles.[65]

---

for me. And so we might go on. In my dogmatics lectures, I tried to allow for the "more" by speaking of "the distinctively Christian way of believing, in which elemental faith is confirmed, *specified,* and represented as filial trust in God 'the Father of Jesus Christ.'" Every attempt to identify the "more" of Christian revelation reflects a particular understanding of redemption. My own case turns around the conviction that the heart of Christ's saving work is precisely the gift of faith. But I would not say that Christian or saving faith is *only* "reassurance of primal or secular faith," nothing more (see Wyman, "Revelation and the Doctrine of Faith," n. 91).

64. Indeed, my comments on "appropriateness" were formulated in response to an earlier version of Wyman's paper. I welcome the explicit attention he gives to this criterion in the last two paragraphs of the published version; although he was not able to carry the discussion further in his paper, he does indicate the direction in which the conversation must go.

65. Quoted in Otto Ritschl, *Albrecht Ritschls Leben,* 2 vols. (Freiburg i.B. and Leipzig: J. C. B. Mohr, 1892-96), 2:106.

PART TWO

Faith and Morals

CHAPTER 3

Idolatrous Faith:
Fichte's Atheism Controversy

Real atheism . . . consists in this: that a man . . . is unwilling to obey the voice of his conscience until he thinks he foresees a good result.

The idea of God as a separate entity is impossible and contradictory.

J. G. Fichte, "On the Foundation of Our
Belief in a Divine Government of the World"

Late in the year 1798, copies of a printed pamphlet began to appear in Saxony titled *A Father's Letter to His Student Son concerning the Atheism of Fichte and Forberg*. Neither author nor publisher was named on the title page. The letter ended with the words "Your devoted father," followed by the initial G. Just who Father G was is not known. He must have believed devoutly in his mission since it is reported that the pamphlet could be obtained free of charge, presumably at the author's own expense. At the University of Jena, Fichte suspected one of his colleagues, Gruner, a medical man who had taken a strong dislike to him. Others suggested J. P. Gabler, a highly regarded theologian in Altdorf. But Gabler's vehement disavowal was all the more convincing because he wrote contemptuously of the pamphlet, judging it a vain attempt to refute a subtle and original thinker with commonplace, popular philosophy.

The true authorship of the pamphlet matters less than its contents. Under a motto taken from Romans 1:22, "Claiming to be wise, they became fools," the anxious father, whoever he was, wrote to warn his son of two articles that had just appeared in a philosophical journal: if widely disseminated, he said, the articles would have disastrous consequences for religion and morality alike. By publishing his warning, the father did more than anyone else to bring about the possibility he feared: he placed squarely before the public eye a discussion that might otherwise have lain unobtrusively buried in the pages of an academic journal. He, as much as the authors of the two articles, launched the Atheism Controversy. The argument of the father's letter (sec. I) and the course of the controversy he aroused (sec. II) are good indicators of the conventional world of religious thought in which Fichte proposed an unconventional concept of God (sec. III).[1]

I. The Father's Letter

In form, the pamphlet is a critical commentary on some key passages in the two offending articles, together with recommendations for more profitable reading.[2] The four recommended titles make a revealing selection. Apart from a satirical book on Fichte, titled *Life and Opinions of Sempronius Gundibert, a German Philosopher,* they are all standard works by theologians of the "enlightened" variety: the Neologists

1. There are two older collections of sources from the Atheism Controversy: Fritz Medicus, ed., *Johann Gottlieb Fichte: Die philosophischen Schriften zum Atheismusstreit, mit Forbergs Aufsatze 'Entwickelung des Begriffs der Religion'* (Leipzig: Felix Meiner, 1910), and, more inclusive, Hans Lindau, ed., *Die Schriften zu J. G. Fichte's Atheismus-Streit,* Bibliothek der Philosophen, vol. 4 (Munich: Georg Müller, 1912). More recent is a very comprehensive collection: Werner Röhr, ed., *Appellation an das Publikum: Dokumente zum Atheismusstreit um Fichte, Forberg, Niethammer — Jena, 1798/99* (Leipzig: Philipp Reclam, 1987), which I cite simply as "Röhr." For the course of the controversy, besides the editorial accounts in these three collections, I have relied on Fritz Medicus, *Fichtes Leben* (1914[1]), 2nd ed. (Leipzig: Felix Meiner, 1922), pp. 111-44, and Fritz Mauthner, *Der Atheismus und seine Geschichte im Abendlande,* 4 vols. (Stuttgart and Berlin: Deutsche Verlags-Anstalt, 1920-23), 4:23-72. One of the few accounts of Fichte's life and work known to me in English is Robert Adamson, *Fichte* (1903; reprinted, Freeport: Books for Libraries, 1969). Additions to the secondary literature in German since the present chapter was first written include Folkart Wittekind, *Religiosität als Bewußtseinsform: Fichtes Religionsphilosophie 1795-1800,* Beiträge zur evangelischen Theologie, vol. 114 (Gütersloh: Chr. Kaiser/Gütersloher Verlagshaus, 1993).

2. *Schreiben eines Vaters an seinen studierenden Sohn über den Fichtischen und Forbergischen Atheismus* (1798); Röhr, pp. 42-63.

Spalding and Jerusalem and the anonymous "fragmentist" Reimarus. The father's spiritual kinship is further established by a concluding rhetorical flourish about the enlightenment of his son's understanding and the ennoblement of his heart, to which ends the obscure and senseless sophistries of Kant and Fichte have nothing to contribute. Gloating over recent signs of disarray in the Kantian ranks, he confides to his son: "I must confess to you in all honesty, from the very first I predicted that the Critical Philosophy [i.e., Kant!] would not last long." And in his final sentence he ventures another prophecy: that the majority will in the end return to the land of sound reason and human understanding, and things will then be better.

With the wisdom of hindsight, we may find these predictions so wide of the mark that we wonder if the letter was a hoax. But all they really prove is that the father was no simple pietist, as one might suppose from others of his remarks, but rather a champion of the waning rationalism of the German Enlightenment. What he detected in the essays of Forberg and Fichte was age-old skepticism dressed up in a new jargon, and in his opinion the "enlightened" theologians already had the remedy. He was appalled to learn that atheism was being taught, in a Christian school and a Christian university, to future leaders of state and church. Not, he said, that he feared for his own son, whose intelligence he trusted enough to let him read and judge for himself. But some of his son's fellow-students would be more susceptible, because students often admire most what they can't understand and whatever sounds new.

"Atheism" means here, as it did in the famous trial of Socrates, not believing in the official religion or theology of the day. And by "God" the concerned father understood — analogically, as he expressly conceded — a highest being, distinct from the world, whose works are the purposive activity of omnipotence. If, then, theoretical atheism is defined as not believing in the god or gods of the prevailing religion, the father was entirely right: the two articles, as he pointed out, contained express denials of God as ordinarily understood, and they were therefore atheistic — even though one of them, at least, did proclaim a deity of sorts. But what of the disastrous consequences the two essays would supposedly have for morals?

The anxious father maintains the conventional belief, reinforced by the eighteenth century's theology of reason, that there is an inevitable link between religion and morality, and he appears more interested in the advantages of religious belief than in its grounds. To preach atheism, he thinks, is to rob immature youths of the principal support of virtue: which is, belief in God, immortality, and retribution to come. A man whose desires are drowning the voice of moral sense will welcome the word that there is no divine judge and no afterlife; if he has nothing either to fear or to hope for, he will be content with only the reputation of virtue. It is indeed already dubious morality to impart openly atheistic principles to future teachers in the church and the schools, who will then be required to teach — dishonestly, according to the principles they have learned — that there is a God.

But the father's main argument is this: to make young people dubious of belief in God is tantamount to sowing the seeds of immorality. Hence the importance he assigns to religion in the sense of a lively belief in God's moral governance of the world. In his support he can even point to the founder of the Critical Philosophy: despite his insistence on the self-sufficiency of morality, Kant held that the actual evil in human nature makes us receptive to a higher assistance, which is provided by religion. As a venture in religious politics, the pamphlet was a resounding success; the author had a broad consensus of popular piety and moral philosophy on his side.

II. The Atheism Controversy

Johann Gottlieb Fichte (1762-1814), to give him his full name, was a young, thirty-six-year-old professor of philosophy at the University of Jena. He had begun his career obscurely as a private tutor, but he leaped to fame when his first book, *Attempt at a Critique of All Revelation,* was published at Königsberg (German 1792). Apparently by accident, his name was omitted from the title page: the book was attributed to Kant, his philosophical model, and taken for a fourth critique. Kant himself, to whom Fichte had sent the manuscript with the inscription "To the philosopher," promptly disclosed the real author and gave him high commendation. A happier accident would be hard to imagine; Fichte's philosophical reputation was made in a day, and the call to a philosophy chair at Jena came soon afterward.

Fichte was no stranger to public controversy even before the scandal of his allegedly atheistic essay. He had also earned an ambiguous reputation as a radical in his politics, and the first book had been followed by two anonymous pamphlets defending freedom of thought and the principles of the French Revolution. Not long after his arrival in Jena (1794), he managed to give offense all around — to colleagues, clergy, and students alike. His philosophical views alienated some of his colleagues, and he shocked the Lutheran clergy by arranging a course of public lectures at 10 o'clock on Sunday mornings, when all good Germans should be in church. It was rumored that, like the revolutionaries in France, he proposed to replace the worship of God with a new cult of Reason. Neither the Weimar authorities nor the university senate could be persuaded to censure him, but it was deemed advisable to reschedule the lectures for 3 p.m. An energetic lecturer, Fichte attracted a growing number of enthusiastic students. But among the students, too, he made bitter enemies by advocating abolition of the fraternities. On New Year's Eve 1794, a student mob went on a rampage, smashing the windows of Fichte's house and shouting obscenities. Believing his life to be in danger, he fled with his wife to a temporary home outside the town, no doubt confirmed in his low opinion of the fraternities. Fichte seemed irresistibly destined for controversy of one kind or another.

As it happened, however, the Atheism Controversy was not precipitated by Fichte himself, but by his young friend and one-time colleague Friedrich Karl Forberg (1770-1848). Formerly a junior member of the Jena philosophy department, Forberg had accepted an appointment as assistant superintendent of a high school in nearby Saalfeld (1797). From there he sent Fichte an article titled "Development of the Concept of Religion," hoping it might be found worthy of publication in the philosophical journal of which Fichte was coeditor with Friedrich Immanuel Niethammer.[3] Parts of the essay, as Forberg later admitted, were written out of youthful devilry. But his central argument was serious enough: By making religion strictly a matter of *practical* belief, he wanted to show its independence of *theoretical* belief — independence, that is, of the truth or falsity of assertions about God and God's kingdom. Religion, as practical belief, is moral commitment in the guise of factual claims that are totally irrelevant to it — and highly dubious. It is

---

3. "Entwickelung des Begriffs der Religion," *Philosophisches Journal einer Gesellschaft teutscher Gelehrter* 8 (1798): 21-46; Röhr, pp. 23-38. Cited hereafter by the pagination in Röhr.

not a duty to *believe that* a moral world government exists, but only to *act as if* such an order existed.

Forberg imagined that this understanding of religion placed him on common Kantian ground with Fichte. But Fichte had grave reservations about the essay and first urged the author not to publish it. When pressed, he offered to publish it with his own annotations — a curious editorial service he had already performed for an earlier article by Forberg. But Forberg balked again. In the end, Fichte accepted the essay. But, convinced that he himself occupied a loftier philosophical plane than his young friend, he furnished an editorial companion piece, "On the Foundation of Our Belief in a Divine Government of the World," which sought to reaffirm, after a fashion, the cognitive claims of religious language.[4] And he placed his own essay first, presumably to spare gullible readers the pain of being led astray — however briefly — by Forberg.

The rest of the story is soon told. The government of Electoral Saxony responded to a complaint from the Dresden church consistory with a rescript (19 November 1798) instructing the universities of Leipzig and Wittenberg to confiscate the offending issue of the journal. Elector Frederick Augustus III urged neighboring states to take similar steps, and he informed Duke Charles Augustus of Saxe-Weimar-Eisenach that students from Electoral Saxony would be forbidden to attend the University of Jena unless appropriate measures were taken against the authors and editors of the two articles. Charles Augustus then instructed the university senate to initiate an inquiry.

Fichte made the outcome all but inevitable by two bluff, uncourtly publications in his defense. He asserted that any penalties imposed on him or Forberg would violate their academic freedom; and that because they had been accused publicly, they should be publicly judged. Hearing a rumor that the Weimar authorities were preparing to oblige him with an official directive, he added imprudence to imprudence by warning privy councilor Voigt in a letter that he would resign rather than submit to censure; others, he said, were resolved to leave the university with him, and there was talk about regrouping in a new institute. Deeply shocked, Goethe wrote in retrospect some months later that he would

---

4. "Über den Grund unsers Glaubens an eine göttliche Weltregierung," *Philosophisches Journal* 8 (1798): 1-20; Röhr, pp. 11-22.

have voted against his own son if he had permitted himself such language against a government (Goethe to J. G. Schlosser, 30 August 1799).

Not that the Weimar government showed any eagerness to discipline Fichte. It was the letter to Voigt that seemed to demand something more than a *pro forma* rebuke, although it was actually an item of personal correspondence. The rescript that finally disposed of the affair (29 March 1799) acknowledged that philosophical speculation could not be the object of a judicial verdict, and it merely authorized the university senate to reprimand the editors of the journal for lack of discretion. Only in a postscript was Fichte's offer of resignation noted and accepted. A petition from his loyal students, couched in more humble language than he himself could manage, pleaded with Duke Charles Augustus not to let them be deprived of their chief reason for being at Jena; after all, a public commitment had in effect been made to them in the university's lecture list. But the duke considered the matter closed and didn't wish to be further troubled with it. A second petition, which sought to have Fichte recalled after his dismissal, likewise fell on deaf ears. His career at Jena was finished — something Goethe, at least, was able to view with equanimity, because he had already decided that the future of Jena philosophy lay with Schelling. He is said to have remarked laconically: "If one star sets, the other rises."[5]

J. C. W. Augusti, the Kantian philosopher who was appointed Fichte's successor, contributed to the Atheism Controversy a satire titled *The Angel Gabriel and Johann Gottlieb Fichte*. In it the supposed writings of an uncomprehending Fichte are actually dictated to him by the angel. Once Fichte has earned the crown of martyrdom, the angel departs from him: which is to say that nothing more is to be expected of the disgraced philosopher. In retrospect, we know the angel was wrong. Fichte moved on to a new, more congenial home in Prussian Berlin, where he lived productively — with only a brief interruption occasioned by the war with Napoleon — for the rest of his days. From 1810 he enjoyed a second, albeit short, academic career at Frederick William III's new university. The king was one of the few personages who remained unruffled by the controversy. He had declined to join other German states in taking action against Forberg and Fichte. He did not anticipate any harmful consequences from their errors, he explained, since faith in

---

5. Medicus, *Schriften zum Atheismusstreit,* pp. xxii-xxiii.

God is made secure by God himself, and he did not wish a public prohibition to draw attention to a journal that was virtually unknown and unobtainable in his domains. Even when Fichte wanted to take up residence in Berlin, the king was unconcerned and remarked: "If it is true that he is engaged in hostilities with the dear God, the dear God may settle it with him: it's no concern of mine."[6]

Forberg, too, enjoyed a second career of sorts, but not as a philosopher of religion. He never retracted the views expressed in his 1798 article and defended in his *Apology*.[7] In 1821 he wrote: "In no circumstances of my life have I been in need of faith, and I intend to persevere in my unbelief to the end, which for me is a total end."[8] He moved on to other occupations and other interests. He is remembered, if not for his philosophical writings, at least for his illustrated and annotated collection of erotic texts, culled from classical literature when he became superintendent of the court library of Duke Ernest I of Saxe-Coburg-Saalfeld. "These trifles," he explains, "engaged our attention first as a mere pastime. We were led to them accidentally, as we roamed from subject to subject, for Philosophy, the garden we had hoped to set up our tent in for life, lies desolate."[9]

III. Fichte on Faith in Divine Governance

In the opening paragraphs of his article,[10] Fichte welcomed Forberg's contribution, though a little condescendingly. The essay of this "excel-

---

6. Lindau, *Atheismus-Streit*, p. xiii.

7. *Friedrich Carl Forbergs der Philosophie Doctors und des Lyceums zu Saalfeld Rectors Apologie seines angeblichen Atheismus* (Gotha, 1799); Röhr, pp. 272-358. Cited hereafter by the pagination in Röhr. An historical account of Forberg and an analysis of his argument in the article and the defense will be found in my essay "Practical Belief: Friedrich Karl Forberg (1770-1848) and the Fictionalist View of Religious Language" (1989), reprinted in *Continuing the Reformation,* chap. 6. See also Chap. 4 below.

8. German quoted from a letter of Forberg to H. E. G. Paulus by Mauthner, *Atheismus,* 4:62.

9. I quote from the preface as translated in Fred. Chas. Forberg, *Manual of Classical Erotology (De figuris Veneris),* Latin text and Eng. trans. by Julian Smithson (1884[1]; facsimile ed., 2 vols. in 1, New York: Grove, 1966), p. 5.

10. My parenthetic references to Fichte's "Über den Grund unsers Glaubens an eine göttliche Weltregierung" follow the pagination in Röhr.

lent philosophical author," he wrote, had given him an occasion to lay before a wider philosophical public, at least in outline, his own thoughts on the same theme, which till then he had presented only in his lectures. His task was made easier because much in Forberg's essay agreed with his own position. But he also found himself challenged to speak his mind because in other respects the essay did not so much contradict his position as fail to reach its level. This is the first and last mention of "the excellent philosophical author" (he is not mentioned by name). It becomes plain enough where Fichte is disagreeing with him. A common starting point in the philosophy of Kant is unmistakable, and yet the respective approaches of Fichte and Forberg are so strikingly different that they can only be described as antithetical. Perhaps Forberg did not see it that way: already in the previous year he had written that he agreed with Fichte's *Wissenschaftslehre* ("science of knowledge") provided he might understand "the absolute ego" as nothing more than a systematic fiction.[11] For Fichte, that would have been no small adjustment.

Fichte thought of his editorial companion piece as a corrective to Forberg's agnosticism — a correction made possible by a more constructive development of the Critical Philosophy. Curiously, it was Fichte's contribution that in some quarters aroused the greater public animosity; he was perceived as offering a negative answer to the question Forberg (ostensibly, at least) had left open, whether there is a God.

11. Quoted from the *Philosophisches Journal* (1797) by Medicus, *Schriften zum Atheismusstreit*, p. v. Hans Vaihinger (1852-1933) discovered in Forberg a sound interpreter of Kant's use of the *as if* formula and a forerunner of his own fictionalism. Hans Vaihinger, *Die Philosophie des Als Ob: System der theoretischen, praktsichen und religiösen Fiktionen der Menschheit auf Grund eines idealistischen Positivismus, mit einem Anhang über Kant und Nietzsche* (1911[1]), 9th and 10th eds. (Leipzig: Felix Meiner, 1927), pp. 736, 752 n. 2. The English translation by C[harles] K. Ogden, published in the International Library of Psychology, Philosophy, and Scientific Method with an autobiographical preface by Vaihinger (1924[1], 1935[2]), was made — with a number of omissions — from the 6th German ed. My references are to the ninth/tenth edition of the German. Ogden devoted another volume in the International Library of Psychology, Philosophy, and Scientific Method to Jeremy Bentham (1748-1832), a more important forerunner of fictionalism than Forberg but not well known to Vaihinger until shortly before his death. C. K. Ogden, *Bentham's Theory of Fictions* (1932[1]; 2d ed., London: Routledge & Kegan Paul, 1951). An interesting volume, written after Vaihinger, seeks to relate the theory of fictions to the genre of literary fiction: [John] Frank Kermode, *The Sense of an Ending: Studies in the Theory of Fiction* (New York: Oxford University Press, 1967); see pp. 39-41 on Vaihinger.

He was understandably indignant to find that the charges against him displayed, as he protested, not the slightest notion of what his system was all about. But since his conclusions were even stranger than Kant's, the critics were perhaps not entirely to be blamed.

The transcendental viewpoint of the of the *Wissenschaftslehre* had undergone its initial formulation in Fichte's early years at Jena, and in his reply to Forberg he brought the distinctive approach of transcendental idealism to bear on the problem his young friend had posed: What are the foundations of our belief in a divine world government? His answer was derived from the axiom that the ultimately real is not the world of things but the absolute ego *(das absolute Ich),* which cannot be perceived or even thought. Properly speaking, it cannot be grasped in consciousness at all; for consciousness is the *finite* self, the correlate of the not-self, which in turn exists as phenomenon only for consciousness. The absolute ego is antecedent to the objectified consciousness and its world. Hence the final reality can only be felt — or believed.

What has confounded previous discussion of his theme, according to Fichte, is the view that belief in God must be implanted in humanity by philosophical arguments. But where, in that case, do the philosophers get what they try to give us by their proofs? And how can they expect to find access in us without presupposing in us something analogous to their own belief? Philosophy cannot produce facts; it can only elucidate them. The belief in a moral world government cannot be established by proving it to the unbeliever; but the believer's conviction can be shown to be reasonable by deriving it from the necessary functions of common human reason. (Fichte is thinking of Kant's *practical* reason, which is immediately conscious of the moral law.) There can be no question of making up with hope what the proofs lack in persuasiveness. For the belief in a moral world government is not a hypothesis one decides to accept or not, as one sees fit; if grounded in reason, it is simply necessary (pp. 11-12).

The contrast with Forberg's approach, though not explicitly stated, is clear. Belief in a moral world government has, for Fichte, a quite different logical status. The necessity for it does not lie in a supposed logical inference from the existence and character of the world of sense; if one starts from the world of sense, treating *it* as absolute, there is no need to go beyond it to the hypothesis of an intelligent Maker, which is incoherent anyway. But from the transcendental viewpoint, there *is* no self-existent world: in everything, all we see is the re-flection of our own mental activity. We have to begin immediately with the *supersensible* world: which means, to find the ground of belief entirely in the workings of the ego — not just my ego or your ego, but the "absolute ego" of humanity. Fichte knows, of course, that this is by no means to devise a novel proof that works better than the old ones. The starting point of the *Wissenschaftslehre* can neither be proved nor conceptualized: it can only be immediately intuited *(läßt sich . . . nur unmittelbar anschauen),* because it is the axiom that all proof must fi-nally presuppose. If anyone lacks this intuition *(Anschauung),* Fichte can get nowhere with him (pp. 13-14).

The course of the argument, then, is to proceed from human ratio-nality, the activity of the absolute ego, to the assertion that this is the way things are[12] — unless we are willing to contradict our own nature and cast ourselves into intellectual chaos. For no other firm standpoint is possible.[13] Fichte's starting point, more exactly, is explicitly moral: the self's recognition of an inner freedom that transcends the influence of the world of sense. This freedom is not indeterminate; it is directed to an end. But the end is supplied entirely by the self. "I myself and my nec-essary goal are the supersensible. I cannot doubt this freedom and its de-termination without renouncing myself." The inner voice doesn't have to be authorized or established *(begründet)* by anything else, nor can it be any further explained: it is "the absolutely positive and categorical." This is why Fichte finds it appropriate to speak of *belief* in the moral world order — because our persuasion of our moral constitution *(Bestimmung)* is the immediate utterance of the moral sense. This does not make it doubtful or insecure; on the contrary, Fichte like Jacobi,

---

12. Cf. the summary statement given later: "Wenn ihr . . . euer eignes Inneres befragen werdet, werdet ihr finden, daß jene Weltordnung das absolut erste aller objektiven Erkenntnis ist, gleichwie eure Freiheit und moralische Bestimmung das absolut erste aller subjektiven; daß alle übrige objektive Erkenntnis durch sie begründet und bestimmt werden muß, sie aber schlechthin durch kein anderes bestimmt werden kann, weil es über sie hinaus nichts gibt" (p. 19).

13. According to Vaihinger, Fichte's approach can be summed up in the formula "I can't act morally if there is no moral world order," whereas Forberg's approach is: "I can act morally even if there *isn't* a moral order" *(Philosophie des Als Ob,* p. 751). But that, it seems to me, moves Fichte uncomfortably close to the anxious father. Fichte wants to say, "Because I *can* and *do* act morally, therefore there certainly *is* a moral order."

holds that faith or belief is the base *(das Element)* of all certainty.[14] If we cannot go behind the moral sense to anything else, neither do we need to. Nor does Fichte, like Forberg, permit a gap between what we will to be and what is possible: in setting my goal before me, I declare that it is possible. The sequence is not "I ought because I can," but "I can because I ought" (pp. 15-17).

Without pretending that everything in this intriguing line of argument is crystal clear, we can surely say this much: Instead of seeking to combine moral obligation with metaphysical skepticism, as Forberg had done, Fichte has here taken the moral imperative itself as the point of departure for a sound metaphysics. Forberg recognized the possibility of such "speculation," even its inevitability to the reflective intellect, but thought it open to doubt and irrelevant to his practical interest in morality. To the question "Does God exist?" Forberg answered that it is uncertain, but the question arises purely out of speculative curiosity.[15] For Fichte, by contrast, the moral constitution of humanity is the Archimedean point from which he can move the earth. He has already said that from the transcendental viewpoint there is no self-existent world, since all we see is the reflection of our own mental activity. He now proceeds to interpret the world of sense strictly from the standpoint of the moral consciousness. Not only my own existence and the existence of other moral beings, but the world of sense, too, as the stage or theater *(Schauplatz)* of our activity, acquires a relation to morality. It goes serenely on its way, according to its eternal laws, in order to establish a sphere for freedom. It has not the slightest influence on morality, nor the slightest power over free beings, who soar autonomous over nature. "The whole world," Fichte concludes, "has acquired a totally changed aspect for us." And indeed it has. The only reality that exists for us is constituted by the structured activity of our own selves. Our world can accordingly be defined simply as "the material of our duty made visi-

14. Also like Jacobi, Fichte can describe as "revelation" the manner in which faith in the reality of the world of sense occurs: "So, als das Resultat einer moralischen Weltordnung angesehen, kann man das Prinzip dieses Glaubens an die Realität der Sinnenwelt gar wohl Offenbarung nennen. Unsre Pflicht ist's, die in ihr sich offenbart" (p. 18). On Jacobi, see my essay "Faith and Existence in the Philosophy of F. H. Jacobi" (1989), reprinted in *Continuing the Reformation,* chap. 4.

15. Forberg, "Entwickelung des Begriffs der Religion," p. 35. See further Chap. 4 below.

ble": *that* is the real "stuff" of all phenomena. People are not to be blamed, Fichte admits, if the transcendental theory — which takes the solid ground from under them — makes them feel strange (pp. 17-18).

The final step in the argument is to assert that the moral order, the reality of which we know for certain in free moral action, is divine. The only article of belief is that we should do our duty cheerfully on every occasion; unbelief — real atheism — is unwillingness to obey the voice of conscience until one thinks one foresees a good result. We need no other God than the moral order itself, nor can we conceive of any other. There is no reason to pass in thought beyond the moral order to a particular being inferred as its cause; and if we did, no coherent concept of such a being could be formed. It would have to be endowed with personality and consciousness, properties that you cannot conceive of apart from limitation and finitude. And so, in the end you will not have thought God, as you wanted to, but will only have duplicated yourself in thought: the moral order will remain unexplained and absolute as before, and belief will still be immediately given (pp. 18-20).

In his concluding statement, Fichte sets out the worship we owe to his deity:

> It is therefore a misunderstanding to say it is doubtful whether there is a God or not. It is not at all doubtful but the most certain thing there is — indeed, the foundation of all other certainty, the sole absolutely valid objective truth *(Objektive)* — that there is a moral world order; that in this order every rational individual is assigned his appointed place and is expected to do his work; that every item of his destiny, except insofar as it may be brought about by his own conduct, is the result of this plan; that without this plan not a hair falls from his head, and in its sphere of operation no sparrow falls from the roof; that every truly good deed succeeds, every evil one surely fails; and that to those who only love the good aright all things must serve the best.
>
> On the other hand, to anyone who reflects for but a moment and is willing to avow the result of this reflection honestly, it can just as little remain doubtful that the idea of God as a separate entity *(Substanz)* is impossible and contradictory. And it is permissible to say this candidly and to suppress all the school prattle, so that the true religion of gladly doing what is right may rise [p. 21].

Fichte clinches this eloquent confession of faith by quoting poems of Goethe and Schiller. Whether it was really "permissible" to announce such an unorthodox faith was one of the questions that the Atheism Controversy was about. I would have thought, however, that anyone reading this remarkable passage at the end of his article would have immediately grasped Fichte's point when he said later, in reply to an opponent: "Let him perhaps call me an *acosmist;* only let him not call me an *atheist.*"[16] What Fichte denied was not God, but the existence of a God beside the world. But his sin, of course, was that the God he believed in was not the church's God. And in his apologetic writings he developed the thesis of his article into a prophetic critique of popular piety, branding as idolatry all service of the God who is supposed to hand out rewards for good deeds and punishment for bad.

Fichte's article "On the Foundation of Our Belief in a Divine Government of the World" is by no means an adequate source for understanding his views on religion and theology. After the move to Berlin, his thought entered a new phase, and he could no longer reduce religious faith to moral reason. Even as a statement of his views in the Jena period, the article hardly stood by itself. Fichte's own commentaries on it were given in his two apologetic writings of 1799: his *Appeal to the Public* and his *Judicial Defense (Verantwortungsschrift)* addressed to the prorector of the university. In the *Appeal* he insisted that the article only hinted at his tenets on religion: it was an occasional piece, he said, which he felt obliged to write as accompaniment to another author's writing.[17] Still, Fichte's companion piece to Forberg's article is interesting as an attempt to interpret religion by analysis of the structure of human consciousness. Schleiermacher followed a similar method, though with very different results: he had no sympathy for the reduction of religion to morality. In the following two chapters I want to explore further the significance of a moral interpretation of religion both for theological construction (Chap. 4) and for criticism of an anti-theologian (Chap. 5).

16. *J. G. Fichtes als Verfassers des ersten angeklagten Aufsatzes und Mitherausgebers des philosophischen Journals gerichtliche Verantwortungsschrift* (1799); Röhr, p. 207.

17. *J. G. Fichtes, des philosophischen Doktors und ordentlichen Professors zu Jena, Appellation an das Publikum über die ... ihm beigemessenen atheistischen Äusserungen* (1799); Röhr, p. 90. The long-winded title, here abbreviated, ends with the charming plea: "A writing one is asked to read before confiscating it."

But I will conclude the present chapter by remarking on Fichte's explicitly revisionist understanding of the theological task, which was not simply to defend the inherited idea of God but to adapt it to fundamental changes in the way the world had come to be perceived.

The Atheism Controversy followed the Pantheism Controversy by more than a dozen years.[18] At first glance, they seem to belong to different worlds. The philosophical contrast between Fichte's article and, say, Herder's conversations on God makes it impossible to conclude that they held a common conception of the deity. Herder's perspective was cosmological, scientific, aesthetic: he looked out on the harmonious order of nature disclosed by the science of his day, and he delighted in it. Fichte's approach was introspective and austerely moral: he found the real world within, and it spoke to him of duty. Inevitably, their perceptions of God differed accordingly. And yet it has been rightly said: "That Fichte's Atheism Controversy was in truth a pantheism controversy cannot be doubted according to modern categories."[19]

Herder and Fichte had in common a loss of faith in the personal God who sits above the circle of the earth and intervenes at will in human history. *Fichte* looks within and discovers a God that is not a "separate substance" beside the world: the world, as moral order, has its divinity in itself. *Herder* looks outward and sees a God that does not interrupt the course of nature: God's activity, he thinks, completely coincides with the movement of the law-governed system uncovered by scientific inquiry. But, for all their differences, both display what we might call the "nisus to monism" characteristic of some of the most creative thinking of the day. And one is struck by the fact that, by consequence, they both conceived of the religious quest as essentially, if not entirely, the search for a proper orientation of oneself in the system of nature, taking one's place in the grand scheme of things — in "the plan," as Fichte puts it.

This may strike us as an obvious enough religious quest, but it is, I think, distinctively modern — the effect of the changed perception of hu-

18. See Chap. 1, pp. 32-33, above; further, my essay "The Secret Religion of Germany: Christian Piety and the Pantheism Controversy" (1987), reprinted in *Continuing the Reformation,* chap. 5.

19. Heinrich Scholz, ed., *Die Hauptschriften zum Pantheismusstreit zwischen Jacobi und Mendelssohn,* Neudrucke seltener philosophischer Werke, vol. 6 (Berlin: Reuther & Reichard, 1916), p. lxxiv, n. 4.

manity's place in the vast, law-governed cosmos. It was certainly not the quest of the Protestant pietism out of which both Herder and Fichte came, and which was dominated by a longing for the personal deity's word of favor and forgiveness. It must be remembered that Herder was by vocation a churchman, superintendent of the Lutheran clergy in Weimar.[20] But it is hardly surprising that Herder's "thinking with the church," as well as Fichte's, could only be judged deviant. We are not obliged to follow them, only to hear them and to recognize that their heterodox views pose questions and furnish insights that are still with us.

20. Even Forberg (perhaps tongue-in-cheek) claimed to be rescuing religion, and he recognized that this required continuity with the old, untenable way of understanding it ("Entwickelung des Begriffs der Religion," p. 37; *Apologie,* p. 329).

CHAPTER 4

Toward a Moral Theology:
Forberg and Practical Belief

Belief in a deity cannot possibly be the foundation of morality but rather, conversely, morality must be the foundation of belief in a deity.

Friedrich Karl Forberg, *Apology*

Forberg was a very minor figure in the history of German philosophy. True, the article he published in 1798 on the concept of religion sparked the famous "Atheism Controversy." But once the initial deed was done, he was totally eclipsed by his older friend and colleague, J. G. Fichte. His philosophical writings have been neglected ever since, and one of them has been hard to come by. But, in my opinion, he posed particularly well a set of problems that arise out of Immanuel Kant's thoughts on religion and morals.[1]

When I made my first attempt to write about the Atheism Controversy, for a lecture I gave a very long time ago (in 1980), I had read only the one notorious article by Forberg on the concept of religion. All I knew of his *Apology,* published in 1799, came to me second-hand from Hans Vaihinger, who saw in Forberg a forerunner of the fictionalist view of religious language.[2] With the confidence of a little knowledge, I

1. The present chapter began as a brief, informal address in which I sought to show the relation of my offbeat interest in Forberg (see *Continuing the Reformation,* chap. 6) to my work in systematic theology.

2. See Chap. 3 n. 11, above. In a reply to Hugo Bund, Vaihinger asserts his independence of Forberg, whom he says he mentioned in his book not as an authority, but rather

ventured to end my remarks on Forberg with a criticism. I commended him for freeing moral obligation from dependence on theistic speculation, then added: "But the weakness of his argument . . . , it seems to me, [is] that it does not occur to him to wonder: What does it say about the world we live in if we perceive the categorical imperative as unconditional despite what he regarded as the death of the old gods? He sets one kind of speculation aside in favor of practical belief, but he does not ask whether practical belief — the remarkable deliverances of the moral consciousness — may have implications for speculation of another kind. And here Fichte was perhaps the better philosopher."

It took me over a year to obtain a workable photocopy of his *Apology*.[3] The task of construing its argument proved unexpectedly difficult, and I had to struggle to get a straight line out of the text. Finally, I reached the conclusion that Forberg was probably not a fictionalist at all, and that what I missed in his controversial article was taken up in some detail in the later work. Happily, I never published my lecture, so that a public retraction might seem affected, and in any case it would not make for a very good discussion if I gave a minute analysis of an obscure text with which few are likely to be familiar. Instead, I want to show how my interest in Forberg linked up with my dogmatics project, more particularly with the doctrine of creation. Then I'll make some comments on moral theology, moral argument, and practical belief, as Forberg understood them. My intention is a modest one: to spell out the agenda with which this leaves me for further reflection. Briefly, my case is that the doctrine of creation and "moral theology" (in Kant's and Forberg's sense) converge in the concept of practical belief in a moral order, and that this calls for reconsideration of some arguments that have recently gone out of style. However, I think we have to take "practical belief" in a different sense than Forberg gave it.

---

as a curiosity ("Die Philosophie des Als Ob und das Kantische System gegenüber einem Erneuerer des Atheismusstreits," *Kant-Studien* 21 (1917): 1-25; p. 21.

3. Forberg's *Apologie* is now readily available in Werner Röhr, ed., *Appellation an das Publikum: Dokumente zum Atheismusstreit um Fichte, Forberg, Niethammer — Jena 1798/99* (Leipzig: Philipp Reclam, 1987), pp. 272-358. I had not seen Röhr's volume when the present address was given, but I have conformed my references to the pagination in his edition.

I. Creation as Moral Order

In modern dogmatics, belief in creation is not about the way the world got started, but about the way the devout mind *perceives* the world. The theologian can leave cosmic beginnings to the friends of Fred Hoyle because "creation," as Schleiermacher taught us to understand it, thematizes the creature-consciousness that all Christians have here and now — that is, their sense of being part of a single system of finite being that is absolutely dependent on the creative causality of God. Christian faith entails total confidence in the reliability of the "law-governed" order that God sustains and the natural scientist investigates. This is not, of course, the actual content of faith in Christ; it is the perception of the world that faith in Christ as Redeemer presupposes. The world can become the theater of redemption only if it is not chaos but order.

But is it sufficient to view the created order as one-sidedly as Schleiermacher did, in terms of *the causal nexus of nature?* He was addressing a problem that was urgent in his own day, and still is: the problem of religion and natural science. But it cannot be allowed to circumscribe or dominate the doctrine of creation. If the Christian consciousness presupposes a stable world order at all, it surely presupposes its *moral* character — or at least the moral character of the order we experience in our tiny corner of nature. It entails, in other words, the recognition that humans are bound together in *a nexus of mutual obligations.* Something like a concept of moral order is essential to the Christian doctrine of creation. The violation of this order is one good reason why Christians find it necessary to move on from creation to redemption.

Let's try bringing these somewhat abstract reflections into the domain of practical Christian existence. The devout Christian's sense of moral order is likely to be awakened, not by following the dogmatic theologian's analysis, but by going to church and listening to sermons — let's say a sermon on Matthew 25:42: "I was hungry and you gave me no food, I was thirsty and you gave me nothing to drink." If Jesus' words sting the Christian's conscience, it is, I suppose, possible to maintain that this is because she is frightened by the threat of eternal punishment (vv. 41, 46), or simply compelled by the Lord's authority. But would it not be correct to say that Jesus' words stir an innate sense of moral community, which, fortunately, is not peculiar to Christians, so that others may find it awakened in other ways? If so, then to this extent we have our doctrine of creation right.

But, of course, "right" here can only mean descriptively right. It is entirely appropriate to ask next: Is such a very practical belief in a moral order rationally defensible? Indeed, can it even stand up to a close conceptual analysis? And that's where Forberg enters. In the one cooperative enterprise that we call "Christian theology" there is room for what Forberg (following Kant) terms "moral theology." *Dogmatic* theology is largely descriptive, insofar as it seeks to give a coherent account of how, as a matter of fact, the Christian way of believing functions. The dogmatician does not have to prove by arguments that there *is* a moral order, but only to show that Christian belief assumes one. Nor would arguments, however elegant, be the way to generate practical belief in a moral order — or, better, to arouse it. That belongs to the task of the preacher who has studied dogmatics. Nevertheless, just because we are rational beings, we are bound to ask, as part of the reflective theological task, whether we are within our epistemic rights (as the philosophers say) in holding this belief, and that calls for something like a *moral* theology.

II. Moral Theology

At first blush, Forberg doesn't seem to contribute anything very reassuring to the dogmatic theologian. Consider his use of the expression "practical belief" in his essay on the concept of religion. When I myself just invoked the expression, at the end of my remarks on creation, I used it in what was intended to be a standard, dictionary sense simply to mean a belief that "is suited to use or action," and I took it for granted that by a "belief" we mean a conviction that something is the case. A practical belief is accordingly a conviction which, things being as they are, prompts the believer to action. Later, I want to expand this provisional definition, but for now it will do. When the sermon on Matthew 25:42 stirs belief in a moral order, what it stirs is the conviction that one really is, as a matter of fact, entangled in a network of moral obligations, and that one ought to do something about it.

Forberg's entire argument, by contrast, turns around a sharp distinction between "practical" and "theoretical" or (as we would say) "factual" belief. A practical belief, for him, is not a factual belief that has, should have, or is likely to have, practical consequences; it asserts nothing at all but simply expresses moral commitment in the grammatical guise of a factual claim. To have practical belief in a moral order, or a kingdom of God that will triumph on earth, is not to assert or suppose that there *is* a moral order, or that it will eventually prevail, but only to act *as if there were* a moral order. Whether or not there is in fact a moral order or a kingdom of God remains, for Forberg, wholly irrelevant to practical belief, so construed, and practical belief is all we mean, or ought to mean, by religion.[4] Clever, sophisticated skeptics can go on using religious language and can presumably even go to church, if they have a mind to. But religious language, as they use it, has no factual meaning whatever.

It is easy to see why, with only the essay on the concept of religion to go by, I took Vaihinger to be right about Forberg and agreed that he must have been a fictionalist. A fiction, as Vaihinger describes it, is a mode of thought known to be false but retained for the time being because of its practical utility. Forberg's essay can be read that way, and much of what he says in his *Apology* seems to reinforce the main point of the essay.[5] Duty is something absolute, unconditioned, grounded wholly in itself. One ought because one ought, not because one expects something for it, nor because there is a God who requires it of us. Forberg denies that he is an atheist, but he ventures the opinion that an

4. Friedrich Karl Forberg, "Entwickelung des Begriffs der Religion" (1798); reprinted in Röhr, *Appellation an das Publikum*, pp. 23-38.

5. He writes, for example: "Hence religion is not (theoretical) belief that a kingdom of God is coming. Striving for its coming, even if one believes that it will never come — this and this alone is religion . . ." (Forberg, *Apologie*, pp. 349-50). Vaihinger drew attention to passages in Forberg that seemed to affirm an agnostic rather than an atheistic viewpoint, but he took this to be a lingering inconsistency that Forberg gradually overcame. He found a similar inconsistency in Kant himself, who sometimes confused a fiction (known to be false) with a hypothesis (possibly true, open to testing). Vaihinger proposes that there are, in fact, two forms of *as if* religion: one weaker (agnostic), the other radical (atheist). Hans Vaihinger, *Die Philosophie des Als Ob,* 9th and 10th eds. (Leipzig: Felix Meiner, 1927), pp. 747-51. (Unfortunately, this suggestion is not reflected in C. K. Ogden's English version.) It should be noted that, in Vaihinger's view, to assert "It is *as if* X were so" grammatically implies that X is *not* so. But it seems to me that, sometimes at least, the tacit implication is: " — and, for all I know, X *may be* so." In any case, Vaihinger's argument that the real Kant was a fictionalist hasn't persuaded all Kant scholars. See, for instance, J. N. Findlay, *Kant and the Transcendental Object: A Hermeneutic Study* (Oxford: Clarendon, 1981), pp. 272-75.

attack of atheism could help you get his point clear: "A mild attack of theoretical atheism is accordingly something everyone should actually wish to have at least once in his lifetime, to make an experiment on his own heart: to see whether it wills the good for its own sake, as it should, or solely for the sake of some advantage to be expected — if not in this world, then in another."[6]

This, however, is not all Forberg has to say in his *Apology*. In effect, he takes up precisely the question I wanted to address to him in my lecture: Granted that the moral imperative needs no speculative support from theism, does it perhaps have speculative implications that the theist should be very interested in? Admittedly, Forberg's utterances on this score are often slippery. Take this, for instance:

> I do not understand how I would have to express myself to escape the reproach of atheism. I teach that at a certain point of speculation the moral disposition unavoidably appears as a belief in a moral world order, hence also as a belief in a *principle* of this moral world order. I conceive of this principle as a *supreme intelligence,* as an almighty, omniscient, holy being. My God is the God of the Christians.[7]

There are questions one would like to put to the author of this interesting passage, not least about the expressions "appears as" and "conceive of." But I can only construe the passage to mean that reflection on the moral disposition, or on *practical* belief, inescapably generates *theoretical* belief. And this is not just a matter of the good person's wish, but rather of the moral theologian's strict conceptual analysis. Religion is not theoretical belief, but it does give rise to theoretical belief: that is, to a theology that analyzes the concept of morality and asks about the principle of its possibility, or God: if it didn't, there would be no reason to speak of religion at all, only of morality.[8]

Having blocked the route from factual to practical belief, then, Forberg concedes that there is a path in the other direction.[9] Nowhere

---

6. Forberg, *Apologie,* p. 289.

7. Forberg, *Apologie,* pp. 346-47 (emphasis Forberg's).

8. Forberg, *Apologie,* pp. 335-36; cf. p. 350.

9. "Unless everything that has been said and written on this point for almost two decades is to be considered said and written in vain, then one can accept it as agreed that belief in a deity cannot possibly be the foundation of morality but rather, conversely, moral-

have I been able to discover evidence for Vaihinger's blunt assertion that Forberg "unequivocally denies the existence of a moral world order."[10] Forberg's remarks on moral theology make very little sense unless he thought "moral order" and "God" to be *possible* concepts. True, he has his doubts, and he hints that what he teaches in school may not be what he thinks in his heart.[11] But that is something other than unequivocally denying the existence of a moral world order. His main point, many times repeated, is that a moral theology that reflects on moral order, though possible, is irrelevant to religion as practical belief.

In short, Forberg may not have been either an atheist or a fictionalist (in Vaihinger's sense): most likely, he was a Kantian agnostic. Like Kant,[12] he thought a moral theology to be at least possible — not, that is, a casuistic theology that tells us *what* we ought to do, but a philosophical theology that reflects on the fact that to be human is, among other things, to be aware *that* one ought. Moral theology (or "ethico-theology") seeks to draw out the speculative implications of the moral disposition and to find appropriate ways of representing them. Again like Kant, Forberg will not admit that we can properly be said to *know* God by this procedure: we can, however, by an *analogia relationis*, propose suitable symbols not for picturing God, but for representing the relation of the Unknown to the moral order it effects. And this is what we are doing when, for example, we speak of the unknown principle of moral order as an intelligent creator; for "*man* is the sole known principle of moral achievement on earth."[13]

---

ity must be the foundation of belief in a deity" (*Apologie*, p. 276, the source of my epigraph to the present chapter).

10. Vaihinger, *Philosophie des Als Ob*, p. 751.

11. Forberg, *Apologie*, p. 305. There are other complications besides Forberg's hint that he conceals the thoughts of his heart. (1) He asserts that, strictly speaking *(strengenommen!)*, it is not the task of theology to deduce from the moral consciousness the existence of the kingdom of God, but only the existence of the *idea* of the kingdom of God (p. 338). (2) He expressly distinguishes logical and real possibility (pp. 339-42). But when he speaks of the possibility of "moral order," he surely means a concept that is really possible (i.e., *may* have a real object), not just a concept that is free from internal contradiction.

12. See Chap. 1, pp. 29-32, above.

13. The analogy is between the *relation* of the Unknown to its given effect (i.e., moral order) and the *relation* of a known principle (human intelligence) to *its* effect, which is moral achievement. Forberg, *Apologie*, pp. 343-47.

III. Moral Argument

The content of the Kantian moral theology used to be considered under
some such rubric as "Moral Arguments for the Existence of God," and a
wonderful succession of Gifford Lecturers spoke and wrote eloquently
on this theme: W. R. Sorley, W. G. DeBurgh, A. E. Taylor, and others.[14]
Such arguments, once perhaps the dominant type of theistic proof in
British religious thought, have become, as Robert Adams remarks, "one
of philosophy's abandoned farms."[15] Confessing his own taste for
Victoriana, Adams is nevertheless one philosopher who wants to see the
old field cultivated again. And I agree with him — though I take to heart
Schleiermacher's warning against an exclusive or one-sided (i.e.,
Kantian!) association of religion with morality.[16]

If we take our point of departure from Forberg, it seems that we will
have to distinguish three steps in a moral argument for theism. He
moves from moral obligation, through moral order, to God as the principle of moral order. Let's explore these three steps without claiming to
be actually marshaling the requisite argument.

First, concerning moral obligation. Forberg spoke with great confidence about the assured conclusions of the recent (that is, Kantian) philosophy, and we may be inclined to respond that today the moral imperative doesn't sound as absolute as it used to. Kantian talk about "the moral
law" is likely to encounter the retort that "conscience is society's censor."
The first item on the agenda, then, will be to go back to the drawing
board, which means back to the moral strand in our everyday discourse.
And while the Kantian rhetoric may sound inflated, at least it points to
the fundamental — and intriguing — fact that humans do habitually say,
or imply, or assume, that there are some things they ought to do and
other things they ought not to do. They make a distinction between right

14. DeBurgh admitted, however, that the moral argument for theism is "beset with
graver difficulties than either the cosmological or the teleological arguments." W. G.
DeBurgh, *From Morality to Religion*, Gifford Lectures 1938 (London: Macdonald & Ev-
ans, 1938), p. 155. For his part, Forberg denied that he was presenting a new *proof* for the
existence of God (*Apologie*, p. 315).

15. Robert Merrihew Adams, *The Virtue of Faith and Other Essays in Philosophical
Theology* (Oxford: Oxford University Press, 1987), p. 144.

16. "Religion knows nothing of such partisan preference; for it the moral world is
not the universe. . . ." Schleiermacher, *Über die Religion*, KGA I, 2:236; Crouter, p. 128.

and wrong, and this appears to be a universal human characteristic — not to be obscured by the equally plain facts that humans differ over *what* they ought and ought not to do, and how to tell the difference.[17]

I tried out these reflections on a friend. The reply I received was that to speak of moral obligation as though it were universally human is absurd: consider, for instance, the behavior of cannibals. But cannibalism, I think, confirms my point. The cannibal has good reasons for thinking he *ought* to eat his fallen enemy; and when he returns home, he won't eat his mother-in-law. The conflict between codes of behavior doesn't invalidate Step 1 in the moral argument. The *ought* is still there — it's there even when the amoralist tells us that moral standards are fictions, so we *ought* to be more tolerant. In actual fact, moral codes may not be so utterly unlike one another as we commonly suppose, and ethicists often manage to come up with imperatives that win general consent. "You ought to keep a promise." "It's wrong to torture a child for fun." And so on.[18] Of course, there are times when we don't keep our promises. But when that happens, we confirm the "ought" by making excuses: "Well, I had to because . . . and, anyway, you don't have to keep a promise to a communist, a terrorist, a criminal," etc. The implication is that, as a rule, I ought to keep my promises.

But what exactly does the ubiquitous "ought" prove? That brings us to Steps 2 and 3. I don't see that moral obligation directly implies the existence of a universal norm of right, a law of nature, or a teleological kingdom of ends, though it may very well be possible to arrive at any of these notions by filling in some missing steps. Hence the next item on the agenda — Step 2 — will be so to formulate the concept of moral order that it doesn't claim too much. This I have tried to do by using the expression "a nexus of mutual obligations." As I intend it, the move from Step 1 to Step 2 is a very modest one, although it is a real move and not a tautology. I am not claiming that there must be a world govern-

17. It is the *what* question that requires us to speak of *communities* of obligation (plural). The thought of one human *community* (singular) arises with particular force when a natural disaster in some distant land is perceived as a call for international aid.

18. Ongoing discussion of the possibility of a basic ethic, common to the human species, was encouraged by the "Declaration of Universal Human Rights" of the General Assembly of the United Nations (1948) and the declaration "Towards a Global Ethic" endorsed by many religious leaders at the Parliament of the World's Religions in Chicago (1993).

ment (a *Weltregierung,* as the Kantians liked to say). I am simply asserting that if not only I but others, too, are aware of moral obligation, then
we can and must be said to constitute a nexus or community of mutual
obligations. That is all I can get into the concept of moral order — at this
stage.

As for Step 3, by which Forberg produced the idea of God as moral
World Ruler, this is the most important point at which Fichte differed
with him. Fichte held that the existence of a moral world order is precisely what we *mean* by the existence of God, and that to think of God as
a "separate entity" is to entertain an impossible and self-contradictory
notion. Here, obviously, is another item that has to go on the agenda.
The moral argument for theism cannot be successfully executed without opening up the entire question of the *concept* of God. I don't mean
to say that no philosophical case can be made for a transcendent principle of the possibility of moral order. It is just that the revival of the moral
argument I would like to see will have to take account of developments
in the concept of God that lie outside the Kantian orbit. It is hardly too
much to say that Kant simply took over the concept of God in
eighteenth-century rational theism, but gave it a new and different logical status. Important efforts to rethink the inherited concept, including
Fichte's, came after him. So, of course, do the attempts of evolutionary
biologists to account for the development of human morality without
transgressing into metaphysics.

IV. Practical Belief

As a short postscript, I want to end by suggesting a better use for
Forberg's expression "practical belief." To equate "practical belief" with
"acting as if" seems to me an indefensible proposal, bound to give rise
to confusion. As far as I can see, the only kind of belief the dictionary
knows is what Kant and Forberg call "theoretical" belief — that is, a
Fürwahrhalten, taking something to be true. Factual claims cannot be
detached from the concept of belief. Even when "belief" means "trust"
or "confidence," factual beliefs are always implied, if not asserted. But if
doing (or "acting as if") is not believing, there is surely a kind of believing that *arises out of* doing, or at least out of willing. Forberg wanted religious belief to be no more and no less than moral commitment. But he

recognized that, by way of reflection, moral commitment appears as factual belief. Would it not have been better had he reserved the term "practical belief" for beliefs that arise in this fashion out of practice or out of the concern for practice? As Jacobi put it, "Out of man's *willing* springs his truest *knowing.*"[19]

Naturally, one would not wish to deny that practical belief, in this sense, also has moral consequences. I'm not retracting my earlier definition of practical belief as a conviction that *calls for* action: I'm completing it by the recognition that practical belief also *arises from* action, or a concern for action. Irenically, we might appropriate both the Lutheran formula "faith active in love" (practical belief that calls for action: cf. Gal. 5:6) and the Thomistic "faith formed by love" (practical belief that arises from action). You may gleefully object that now I am hoist with my own petard, since I have just rebuked Forberg for using language in a nonstandard way. But I am proposing to take the words "faith formed by love" not in an off-dictionary sense, only in a non-Thomistic sense. If one may understand "love" *(caritas)* as the most inclusive word for moral concern, then there surely is a belief that is formed by love: not a finished and self-contained belief that then, only subsequently to its formation, is expressed and applied in good works, but a belief that actually takes shape out of the self's struggle with its awareness of moral obligation. It is, I think, precisely in this struggle that many religious persons have the most immediate assurance of making contact with reality. To weigh the concepts that *fides caritate formata* generates is the task of a moral theology.

---

19. *David Hume über den Glauben, oder Idealismus und Realismus: Ein Gespräch,* 2nd ed., *Friedrich Heinrich Jacobi's Werke,* ed. Jacobi, Friedrich Köppen, and Friedrich Roth, 6 vols., vol. 4 in 3 pts. (1812-25; reprinted, Darmstadt: Wissenschaftliche Buchgesellschaft, 1980), 2:44 (from the preface). Cf. p. 120, where Jacobi includes goodness among the things that make a stronger impression on the heart *(Gemüth)* than any sensible object can. An interesting argument, though not entirely persuasive. See my essay cited in Chap. 3 n. 14, above.

CHAPTER 5

Feuerbach's Religious Illusion

> The pious mind does not dream up for itself any god it pleases, but contemplates the one and only true God. . . . The pious mind also deems it meet and right to observe his authority in all things, reverence his majesty, take care to advance his glory, and obey his commandments.
>
> John Calvin, *Institutes*

According to the Hebrew Scriptures, humans were made in the image and likeness of God. But the perceived kinship between deity and humanity lends itself only too readily to the possibility of inversion. What if the gods are human creations, fashioned after the image and likeness of humanity? Around 500 BCE, the Greek philosopher Xenophanes noticed that the gods of the Ethiopians were black and had flat noses, whereas the gods of the Thracians were blond and blue-eyed. He suggested that oxen, lions, and horses, if they could make gods, would make them like oxen, lions, and horses. Not that he found no use for the notion of deity. But his own God resembled mortals, he said, neither in shape nor in thought. He mocked the all-too-human gods around him for the sake of a better, purer concept of God. And so did the Hebrews, though a philosopher like Xenophanes might think that they had less success.

The God of the Hebrews, in whose likeness humanity was created, insists, "I am God and not man, the Holy One in your midst" (Hosea 11:9 RSV). The Hebrew Scriptures are replete with scorn for the idolatry that makes gods in the likeness of humans. Isaiah would certainly not have allowed that the God of Israel, "who sits above the circle of the earth . . . [and] stretches out the heavens like a curtain" (Isa. 40:22), might exhibit the same idolatrous principle as the heathen gods he despised, only in the milder form of a *mental* image. What he proclaimed was a busy, active God rather than an idol that did not move. And yet, he could only represent the divine activity as very like human activity.

The Hebrew persuasion that the gods of the heathen are idols (Ps. 96:5), while the true God is God and not human, was carried over into the Christian community to affirm the sovereign uniqueness of the Christian deity. The Protestant reformers, it is true, discovered the worst idolatries of all within the Roman Catholic church (much as the Hebrew prophets of old accused the children of Israel of whoring after other, pagan gods), but they did not doubt that Christianity — and Christianity alone — worshiped the true God without taint of idolatry. Throughout the history of the church, risky anthropomorphisms in Christian discourse were excused by appeal to the accommodated, analogical, symbolic, or poetic form of the scriptural revelation.

Modern critical thought about religion arose when the privileging of Christian discourse was finally challenged. In the seventeenth and eighteenth centuries, a distinction familiar in classical antiquity was revived: the dividing line was drawn not between Christianity and other religions, but between popular religion, including Christianity, and a purely rational theism. The rational theists were content to marvel at the orderly course of nature without worshiping it or supposing it to be the activity of a cosmic Thou, open to the influence of sacrifice and prayer. This left the way clear for such early pioneers of religious psychology as John Trenchard to uncover the supposedly pathological origins of bad religion in the soul, while appearing to remain on the side of "God" (properly understood as cosmic order). But in the German philosopher Ludwig Feuerbach (1804-1872) the privileging of Christian discourse and the promotion of rational theism both dissolve, and all talk of God is unmasked as the product of human invention. "Some day," he predicted, "it will be universally recognized that the objects of Christian religion, like the pagan gods, were mere imagination."[1] And he had no in-

---

1. Ludwig Feuerbach, *Vorlesungen über das Wesen der Religion* (1848), FSW 8:245; *Lectures on the Essence of Religion,* trans. Ralph Manheim (New York: Harper & Row, 1967), p. 195, hereafter cited as "Manheim."

terest in saving the "utterly superfluous, unnecessary God," whose activity adds nothing to the law-governed processes of nature.[2]

I. Two Theories of Religion

Van Harvey's book on Feuerbach was the first volume in a new series: Cambridge Studies in Religion and Critical Thought.[3] The timeliness — the urgency even — of its central question is plain from the first chapter to the last: Can religion be plausibly explained without the assumption that "God" denotes a being of a higher ontological rank than the mundane objects of our daily experience? More than fourteen years' labor went into the writing of the book, and the author tells us that his preoccupation with Feuerbach goes back further still — to the time when he first encountered him in a graduate seminar at Yale Divinity School and found himself "strangely disturbed" (p. viii).

Feuerbach is well known as the author of *The Essence of Christianity,* which first appeared in 1841.[4] Harvey's thesis is that fascination with this one work, interesting and important though it is, has obscured a shift in Feuerbach's understanding of religion that is most evident in his *Lectures on the Essence of Religion,* published seven years later. We ought to read Feuerbach for two theories of religion, not just one, and in Harvey's judgment the later, neglected theory is more interesting and persuasive. Not that an absolute break occurs. Rather, the passage from the earlier to the later writing is largely a shift of dominance: subordinate themes in *The Essence of Christianity* become dominant in *The Essence of Religion.*

The central thought in *The Essence of Christianity* is that the suppos-

---

2. Feuerbach, *Wesen der Religion,* FSW 8:187; Manheim, p. 149.

3. Van A. Harvey, *Feuerbach and the Interpretation of Religion,* Cambridge Studies in Religion and Critical Thought, vol. 1 (Cambridge: Cambridge University Press, 1995).

4. Ludwig Feuerbach, *Das Wesen des Christentums,* FSW vol. 6. The translation of the second edition (1843) by the Victorian novelist George Eliot (1854) was reprinted as a Harper Torchbook: *The Essence of Christianity* (New York: Harper & Brothers, 1957), hereafter cited as "Eliot." It was furnished with a foreword by H. Richard Niebuhr and an introductory essay by Karl Barth, translated by James Luther Adams from Barth's *Die Theologie und die Kirche: Gesammelte Vorträge II* (Zollikon-Zürich: Evangelischer Verlag, 1928), pp. 212-39.

edly superhuman deities of religion are actually the involuntary projec-
tions of the essential attributes of human nature. In Feuerbach's own
words: "Man — this is the mystery of religion — projects his being into
objectivity, and then again makes himself an object to this projected image of himself thus converted into a subject."[5] What the devout mind
worships as God is accordingly nothing but the idea of the human species imagined as a perfect individual. Once they are unmasked, shown
for what they really are, religious belief and the idea of God can be useful instruments of human self-understanding, revealing to us our essential nature and worth. But taken at face value, they are alienating insofar
as they betray us into placing our own possibilities outside of us as attributes of God and not of humanity, viewing ourselves as unworthy objects of a projected image of our own essential nature. Theology, as
Feuerbach sees it, only reinforces the state of alienation by taking the
objectifications of religion for real objects, and the theologians end up
with dogmas that are self-contradictory and absurd.

Very differently, *The Essence of Religion* locates the subjective
source of religion in human dependence on nature. The forces of nature
on which our existence wholly depends are made less mysterious and
more pliable by perceiving them as personal beings like ourselves. And
this, we are now told, is the meaning of religion, which is not so much
encoded truth as pure illusion. "[N]ature, in reality, is not a personal being; it has no heart, it is blind and deaf to the desires and complaints of
man."[6] In short, religion is superstition, and science must eventually
supplant it.

For all the striking differences between Feuerbach's two theories of
religion, there are strands that tie them together. One such strand, obviously, is the theme of anthropomorphism, picturing God or the gods as
personal like us. Another, closely connected with it in Feuerbach's
mind, is the conviction that religion is wishful thinking. Feuerbach's "felicity principle," as Harvey calls it, assumes that the point of being religious is to secure one's well-being both here and hereafter. Hence the
emphasis in the later work on the *Glückseligkeitstrieb* (the "drive after

---

5. Feuerbach, *Wesen des Christentums,* FSW 6:37; Eliot, pp. 29-30. Feuerbach echoes
Xenophanes when he writes: "If God were an object to the bird, he would be a winged being" (FSW 6:21; Eliot, p. 17).

6. Feuerbach, *Wesen der Religion,* FSW 8:253; Manheim, p. 202.

happiness") that motivates the entire business of religion. The God we imagine is the God we want, who can give us what we want, and this means a personal God who takes notice of us and guarantees us a blessedness that transcends the limits of nature. But that, according to Feuerbach, is the religious illusion. We are inescapably bounded by the limits of nature, and even what we take for the goodness of God is nothing more than the utility of nature personified.

Small wonder if a budding theologian finds good reason in all this to be "strangely disturbed"! The unreflective believer may dismiss Feuerbach as a charlatan who trivializes religion. But Harvey fully vindicates his opinion that in any critical scrutiny of religion we must grant Feuerbach a place alongside Paul Ricoeur's "masters of suspicion" — Nietzsche, Marx, and Freud — and judge him worthy to be brought into the present-day discussion. The last two chapters of the book set the later Feuerbach's interpretation in the forum of more recent views of projection (Freud, Sierksma, Berger), anthropomorphism (Stewart Guthrie), and the need for illusion (Ernest Becker). Harvey concludes: "It is extraordinary how well Feuerbach's later views stand up when compared with those of contemporary theorists; so much so that one can, by adopting his position, mount important criticisms of these theories" (p. 292).

His book's aim, Harvey tells us, is "constructive," at least in part. This is why he brings Feuerbach into the company of recent religious theorists. He doesn't venture a systematic statement of his own views on religion; he writes as if listening in to the conversation and notes the points at which Feuerbach, if present, might speak up. Historians who insist on keeping past thinkers strictly in their own historical, social, and intellectual contexts may raise their eyebrows at such a hazardous procedure. I, for one, welcome it. Of course it cannot, and in this book it does not, replace historical description and painstaking analysis of the sources. If a constructive conversation is to be an honest conversation, it has to respect historical understanding and take to heart the historian's warnings against anachronistic misreading of the texts. But a constructive interest in the past ("rational reconstruction," as Richard Rorty calls it) adds something to the sober exercise of setting the record straight and may even, on occasion, alert the historian to patterns and pieces in the record that she had overlooked.

Harvey's main thesis is in fact both historical and constructive. That a shift occurred in Feuerbach's thoughts on religion, and what it was — these are factual matters. The book seems to me to have settled them (though I should defer to the Feuerbach specialists). But why does Harvey think the shift marked an improvement over the more familiar projection theory in *The Essence of Christianity?* Why is the later theory to be preferred? Chiefly for two reasons: first, it is unencumbered by the arcane Hegelian speculation on which the analysis of consciousness rests in the earlier work; second, it does greater justice to the religious sense of encounter with an "other." The second reason will bring less comfort to the believer than the first. It is one thing to be liberated from Hegel, another to be told that the other encountered in religion is nature.

At first glance, Feuerbach's later theory looks like an elaboration of a view that goes back at least to the Roman poet Statius and was revived by Spinoza, Hobbes, Hume, and others: that fear of the terrifying forces of nature first created the gods — "in the ignorance of causes," as Hobbes explains.[7] In actual fact, Feuerbach made himself the critic of this view. The human encounter with nature is far too ambiguous and complex to be subsumed under the single emotion of fear. It includes joy, gratitude, and love, all of which, Feuerbach inferred, must also be makers of divinity. And he believed that if we seek one all-embracing term for the full range of religious emotions, we will find it only in the "feeling of dependence," of which each religious response to nature is, so to say, a concrete individuation: fear of death, gloom when the weather is bad, joy when it is good, and so on.[8] The merit of this account in Feuerbach's own eyes, and clearly also in Harvey's, was that it put a determinate concept, nature, in place of the vague, mystical word "God." But does that make his later theory of religion successful?

II. A Defect in the Later Theory

Shortly after publication of *The Essence of Christianity*, Feuerbach, as we have seen (in Chap. 2), followed a venerable German custom and under-

---

7. See Chap. 1, p. 9, above. Even Feuerbach's *Glückseligkeitstrieb* seems to echo Hume's "anxious concern for happiness" in *The Natural History of Religion*. See David Hume, *Writings on Religion*, ed. Anthony Flew (LaSalle: Open Court, 1992), p. 115.

8. Feuerbach, *Wesen der Religion*, FSW 8:36-39; Manheim, pp. 29-31.

took to demonstrate that he was only saying what Martin Luther had already said. In *The Essence of Faith according to Luther* (1844), it turns out that the felicity principle is nothing other than Luther's celebrated *pro me* ("for me"). For a man must believe that God is God only for the sake of his blessedness, and it is the trust and faith of his heart that create both God and an idol. With dozens of quotations from Luther, Feuerbach demonstrates to his own satisfaction that self-love — egoism, narcissism — motivates Protestant piety, and that the piety itself creates the God it needs and wants.[9]

To be sure, a serious Luther scholar will wish to say a bit more about the function of the *pro me* in Luther's theology and will point to some complicating counterevidence. In particular, the young Luther departed from the Augustinian tradition in taking the words "You shall love your neighbor as yourself" not as a command for "ordered love" of yourself and others, but as a *prohibition* of self-love, which he identified as the root of sin.[10] And the mature Luther asserted that he knew his theology to be true because it takes us out of ourselves.[11] But when all is said and done, is it possible that Feuerbach had a point?

It is, of course, not Luther but Schleiermacher who comes to mind when Feuerbach speaks of religion as the feeling of dependence. Feuerbach himself makes the connection. But Schleiermacher anticipated the naturalistic reduction of the religious feeling of dependence and rejected it as a misunderstanding. Our awareness of God is a feeling of *absolute* dependence, whereas our dependence on nature is relative, qualified by our ability to influence the way the world goes. Dependence on nature and dependence on God are not the same thing.[12] A highly controversial way of explaining the distinction, as the process theologians like to remind us. But the conversation is not yet closed.

Karl Barth doubted whether Schleiermacher had, in fact, *any* de-

---

9. Ludwig Feuerbach, *Das Wesen des Glaubens im Sinne Luther's* (1844), FSW 7:311-75; *The Essence of Faith according to Luther,* trans. Melvin Cherno (New York: Harper & Row, 1967).

10. Martin Luther, *Vorlesung über den Römerbrief* (1515-16), WA 56:482-83, 516-18; LW 25:475-76, 512-14.

11. "Haec est ratio, cur nostra Theologia certa sit: Quia rapit nos a nobis et ponit nos extra nos. . . ." Martin Luther, *In epistolam S. Pauli ad Galatas commentarius* (1531/35), WA 40/1:589; LW 26:387.

12. Friedrich Schleiermacher, *CG,* §32.2 (p. 132).

fense against a Feuerbachian reduction of theology to anthropology: he believed that Feuerbach merely showed the world what Schleiermacher had already done to the queen of the sciences.[13] In his own way, Barth liked Feuerbach. (Many of us first learned of him from Barth.) But Barth drew Feuerbach's fangs by treating *The Essence of Christianity* simply as a critique of bad religion. For Barth the word "bad," strictly speaking, is redundant: all religion is the fruitless human quest for God. The Christian theologian is concerned not with religion, but rather with revelation — the Word of God. From Barth's viewpoint, then, Feuerbach gave us no cause for worry. From Feuerbach's point of view, however, Barth's countermove was a relapse into premodern privileging of Christian discourse. For why should we presuppose at the outset that the one Word of God is Jesus Christ?

For myself, I think Christian theology must face Feuerbach's relentless exposure of the subjective roots of religion — even worry a little about it. True, the unmasking of narcissistic motives for being religious, though it may weaken the structures of plausibility, affords no logical grounds for an inference about the reality of the religious object. The God one would like to exist may actually exist, even if the fact that one wishes it invites suspicion. Nonetheless, in our consumer society, in which success in the church, as elsewhere, is supposed to require market analysis of what people want, and to supply what they demand, the mechanism of wishful thinking is something the theologian needs to keep in mind. So does the preacher, who is under pressure not to prophesy what is right but to speak smooth things, to prophesy illusions (Isa. 30:10). The question remains whether illusions are all the theologian and the preacher are able to offer.

Feuerbach was a good listener, and Harvey is a powerful spokesman for him. But, as I have suggested (Chap. 2), his later theory works better with some kinds of religious experience than with others. There are *religions of adjustment,* as we might call them, that begin not with the felicity principle but with the reality principle, and admonish us to adjust our lives to the brute fact that things are not as we would like them to be. Feuerbach was too good an interpreter of religion to overlook the phenomenon of self-abnegation, but he read it as a subtle form of self-love. It is no doubt true that in adjustment to reality a person may find peace,

---

13. See Barth's introductory essay to Feuerbach, *Essence of Christianity,* pp. x-xxxii.

99

but surely the felicity principle here is being stretched too far: it does not cover the data but looks suspiciously like a procrustean bed. In his remarks on Ernest Becker, Harvey himself hints that Feuerbach does not do justice to "participatory religions" of self-surrender.

Feuerbach's later theory also seems to me to work badly with *religions of moral demand*. (We will have to leave for another day the question whether Émile Durkheim's theory works any better.) Feuerbach was convinced that religious belief corrupts morality as well as truthfulness, and he had said already in *The Essence of Christianity:* "[I]t lies in the nature of faith that it is indifferent to moral duties. . . ."[14] Well, *some* faith perhaps! But the function of religion has sometimes been to counter moral indifference with a stern moral demand. It might perhaps be just possible to outdo the ingenuity of the theologians and show how the life of Mother Teresa, say, which has every appearance of being motivated by an astonishing compassion rooted in religious conviction, was actually driven by a subtle but irresistible *Glückseligkeitstrieb.* But it strains our credulity less to acknowledge the evidence in her life of a close bond between (some) religion and (some) morality.[15]

It would be too cheap to conclude that Feuerbach's religious illusion was to take one kind of Protestant piety for religion itself. Still, unless there's more to be said than Harvey has told us, Feuerbach's account must strike us as lopsided and incomplete. An explanation of religion need not be ruled out just because it does not take religion at face value or keep to the first-order language of the believer. That would disqualify not only the masters of suspicion but a lot of theologians as well, myself included. The test is whether the explanation is adequate to the full range of the utterances (or phenomena) it intends to explain. Feuerbach claimed with some justice that, unlike the speculative philosophers, he let religion speak for itself. However, it is hardly surprising that he heard

---

14. Feuerbach, *Wesen des Christentums,* FSW 6:315; Eliot, p. 261.

15. The surprising revelation, made recently, of Mother Teresa's doubts doesn't incline me to choose another witness. It is in fact remarkable that the moral imperative remained so powerful in her faith even when she agonized over the apparent absence of her God. See Mother Teresa, *Come Be My Light: The Private Writings of the "Saint of Calcutta,"* ed. Brian Kolodiejchuk (New York: Doubleday, 2007). I should add that my epigraph from Calvin for this chapter seems to me to convey aptly the religious sense of confronting a reality that is simply *given* and calls for adjustment and obedience (Calvin, *ICR* I, ii.2 [1:42]).

best what came closest to home. Stung by the criticism that he offered an interpretation of Christianity as an interpretation of religion, he moved from *The Essence of Christianity* to *The Essence of Religion* and, later, to his *Theogony according to the Sources of Classical, Hebraic, and Christian Antiquity* (1857). And yet, throughout all these major works there seems to linger the influence of a strong dislike for the self-centered individualism of Lutheran pietism, evident already in his *Thoughts on Death and Immortality* (1830).

This is by no means to conclude that I am done with Feuerbach because, like the rest of us, he heard selectively. Rather, as Harvey asserts, "he still has the power to compel us to define our own positions" (p. 24). Without qualifying as a Feuerbach scholar, I have found myself returning again and again, like Harvey, to this "devout atheist" (as Max Stirner called him), fascinated by the richness, tenacity, and nettling style of his thoughts on religion. The options, at any rate, have become clearer to me. To return to our point of departure: Christian anthropomorphism could be wholly fictional, the reification of mere abstractions; or a misconstrual of purely natural phenomena; or an imperfect symbolization of encounter with a transcendent reality. Feuerbach himself moved from the first to the second option. What I take to be the gap in his later view gives me some leverage on the third option. That the transcendent reality is experienced by the religious imagination as a commanding will may be conceptually problematic. But there is surely more to it than personification of some aspect of physical nature. A more nearly adequate theory of religion, or at any rate of the Christian religion, will have to give a better account of it.

PART THREE

The Calvinist Tradition

CHAPTER 6

The Place of Calvin in Christian Theology

> God has never seen fit to bestow such favor on his servants that
> each individually should be endowed with full and perfect knowl-
> edge on every point. No doubt, his design was to keep us both
> humble and eager for brotherly communication.
>
> John Calvin, *Commentary on Romans*

Anyone, whether historian or theologian, who writes on John Calvin is likely to venture judgments concerning his place in Christian theology. Over the years the judgments have varied widely. Calvin's admirer Benjamin B. Warfield argued that the man the Roman Catholic Church judged a heretic actually marked a fresh epoch in the history of the catholic dogma of the Trinity. A less generous opinion, made from another ecclesiastical corner, is that Calvin was at best a mere epigone of Martin Luther, at worst a debaser of pure Reformation doctrine. At the end of the nineteenth century, it was said that Calvin represented a certain "atrophy" or "degeneration" of the idea of Protestantism (Ferdinand Kattenbusch), and in the mid-twentieth century one of the most widely used textbooks of church history in Germany could still present Calvin's theology in the form of six "deviations" from the theology of Luther (Kurt Dietrich Schmidt). Yet another well-known estimate from the last century judged Calvinism a more creative intellectual force in the modern world than Lutheranism but placed Calvin himself, with Luther, on the side of the "old Protestantism," which only tried to give a new answer to an old medieval question, "What must I do to be saved?" (Ernst Troeltsch).

105

These sample judgments could be multiplied indefinitely. But they suffice to forewarn us that Calvin's place in Christian theology is a wide-ranging and controversial question. It could be asked with respect to every topic of Christian theology on which he voiced an opinion, and the evidence goes to show that the answer given may betray the theological location of the person asking the question. The present chapter addresses the *historical* question of Calvin's place in the story of Christian theology, only indirectly the *theological* question what he might have to say in the current theological conversation. The task certainly calls for critical insight, even theological insight, not merely for juxtaposing statements Calvin made with statements others have made, before and since, and the author of this chapter may not be any more successful in hiding his own theological leanings than others have been in curbing theirs. The very selection of topics and material, as always in studies of the past, already says something about an author's standpoint. Nevertheless, the criterion of a defensible historical assertion is the historical evidence advanced, not norms appropriate to systematic theology. And the conclusions reached here are not intended to promote Calvin unduly even in the context of historical theology, but rather, as he himself would wish, to note some of the contributions he made, sound or not, to the "brotherly" [add "sisterly"!] communication on which theological progress depends.[1]

A suitable point of entry is Calvin's relation to the Augustinian tradition, especially on the Christian understanding of grace. In Augustine's struggle with Pelagianism a profound gratitude for the grace of God led him inexorably to the thorny question of predestination or *the election of grace* (sec. I). The Augustinian piety of gratitude for divine grace shines through the theology of Calvin, but "Calvinism" became virtually synonymous in the minds of its critics with the enigma of predestination and the bondage of the will. Questions of *free will and merit* (sec. II), bequeathed by the Pelagian controversy, continued to exercise the theologians of the Middle Ages; among them Calvin had a special regard for Bernard of Clairvaux, in whom he found the witness of a kindred spirit to the cardinal theme of God's grace. In Calvin's own day, the

---

1. The quotation that serves as my epigraph for this Chapter comes from the dedicatory letter to Simon Grynaeus (18 October 1539) that serves as foreword to Calvin's *Commentary on Romans* (1540); CO 10/2:405.

Augustinian heritage remained a major reference point in the Reformation debates on other questions as well. Partly inherited from Augustine were two issues on which Calvin thought differently than Luther: *spirituality and sacramental signs* (sec. III). After the Protestant Reformation, a good deal of theological attention turned to *the task of Christian theology* itself, and a few reflections will be added in conclusion (sec. IV) on Calvin in relation to Friedrich Schleiermacher and Karl Barth, the two most influential theologians of the Reformed or Calvinist family in modern times. All these themes have generated complex, controversial discussions. Exploration of them here can do little more than open the door to further "brotherly communication."

I. The Election of Grace: Calvin and Augustine

In the address to the King of France that served as a preface to the first edition of the *Institutes* (March 1536) and to every subsequent edition, Calvin defended the evangelical cause against the charge of novelty. The defense expressed his twofold persuasion that while patristic authority mostly favored the evangelicals, the patristic consensus from which they allegedly deviated was a fiction. His adversaries, as he put it in the acerbic style of the time, were bent on gathering dung amid the gold. Calvin's facility for marshaling citations from the Fathers, demonstrated in the address to Francis I, stood him in good stead at the Lausanne Disputation (October 1536), where he made his first public appearance as a reformer. Being the newcomer in the Genevan party, he was silent until the Roman Catholics charged the Reformed with rejecting the "the holy doctors of antiquity." He then rose and delivered from memory a discourse on the eucharistic opinions of Tertullian, pseudo-Chrysostom, and especially Augustine, five of whose writings he cited. With a touch of vanity, he regretted that he could not recall whether his quotation from one of Augustine's homilies on John came from the eighth or the ninth section.[2]

These early statements from 1536 set a pattern for Calvin's subsequent writing. As he explained at Lausanne, we listen to the Word of God with the Fathers, but the highest authority belongs to the Word itself.

2. John Calvin, "Two Discourses on the [Lausanne] Articles," trans. J. K. S. Reid, first discourse, LCC 22:38-45.

Scholarly tabulation has shown that in the *Opera omnia* Calvin's explicit references to the early church fathers number more than 3,200; some 1,700 of them are references, often with extended quotations, to Augustine. The numbers are greatly increased when echoes and allusions are taken into account.[3] But the principle Calvin laid down at the Lausanne Disputation is never in doubt: we use the help of the Fathers' teaching as it serves and as occasion offers. When his teaching on the bondage of the will and predestination was challenged by the Roman Catholic theologian Albert Pighius, Augustine's anti-Pelagian writings served Calvin well. In reply, he made his forthright claim, "Augustine is wholly ours," borrowed recently as the title for a major study of Calvin and Augustine.[4]

For Augustine (354-430), the doctrine of predestination grew out of a passionate celebration of divine grace. He testified that, even before the Pelagian controversy, a crucial change of mind came to him as he reflected on Paul's words, "What do you have that you did not receive? And if you received it, why do you boast as if it were not a gift?" (1 Cor. 4:7). He had long believed that conversion to God is a work of God's grace, which alone, by an "infusion" of love for God, can bring about a radical reorientation from the fault of seeking life in one's own self to receiving life in faith from the true Fountain of life. And he had understood that the ability to accept the gospel in faith must itself be the gift of grace, or it would not be true that we have nothing we did not receive. But why is it that one person comes to faith, while another does not?

In one of his last writings, the anti-Pelagian treatise *On the Predestination of the Saints* (428 or 429), Augustine recalls his change of mind. He once supposed that at least our consent to the gospel, when it is preached to us, must be our own doing and come from ourselves. This, he now realizes, was a mistake: he had not yet grasped *the election of grace.* Everyone has the ability to believe, just as everyone has the ability to love; but it does not follow that everyone has faith, any more than everyone loves. If a person comes to faith, it is because the Lord prepares the wills of those he has chosen for himself. The ability to have faith

---

3. A useful guide in English, furthering the earlier work of R. J. Mooi and Luchesius Smits, is Anthony N. S. Lane, *John Calvin: Student of the Church Fathers* (Edinburgh: T&T Clark, 1999); see p. 28 n. 96, p. 41 n. 198.

4. J[an] Marius J. Lange van Ravenswaay, *Augustinus totus noster: Das Augustin-verständnis bei Johannes Calvin,* Forschungen zur Kirchen- und Dogmengeschichte, 45 (Göttingen: Vandenhoeck & Ruprecht, 1990).

(fidem posse habere), then, is the gift of nature; actually to have faith *(fidem habere)* is the gift of a special grace, given only to God's elect.[5]

For Calvin, too, the divine election was the final proof that everything is of grace, including the division between those who come to faith and those who do not. "We shall never be clearly persuaded, as we ought to be, that our salvation flows from the wellspring of God's free mercy until we come to know his eternal election, which illumines God's grace by this contrast: that he does not indiscriminately adopt all into the hope of salvation but gives to some what he denies to others."[6] Here, clearly, the Augustinian concern to maintain the utter gratuitousness of God's grace or mercy is fundamental, and the eternal election of grace explains the observed fact that some accept the gospel while others don't.[7] Calvin further agrees with Augustine that while the division between the elect and the non-elect is inescapably the teaching of Scripture, the reason for it is hidden in God's inscrutable justice.[8] It could surely be said that in this doctrine, if not in others, the proper placement of Calvin's theology will see in it "a great revival of Augustinianism."[9] But this need not exclude differences between them even on grace and election.

It is often asserted, for instance, that what is distinctive of Calvin is the doctrine of a *double* predestination, to eternal life or to eternal damnation,[10] whereas Augustine wrote of a *single* predestination of the saints that simply passes by the rest of humanity. The assertion is not entirely true. Their emphasis may differ, but Calvin often used the language of "passing by" the non-elect, and Augustine occasionally wrote of predestination to death, or eternal death.[11] The reason for the two

---

5. Augustine, *praed. sanct.,* chaps. 7-10 (iii-v); NPNF 5:500-503. A key to MPL and other editions of Augustine's works, along with standard abbreviations of individual titles, will be found in *Augustine through the Ages: An Encyclopedia,* ed. Allan D. Fitzgerald et al. (Grand Rapids: Eerdmans, 1999), pp. xxv-xlii.

6. John Calvin, *ICR* III, xxi.1 (2:921).

7. Calvin, *ICR* III, xxi.1 (2:920-21).

8. Calvin, *ICR* III, xxiii.4-5 (2:951-52).

9. Benjamin Breckinridge Warfield, *Calvin and Augustine,* ed. Samuel G. Craig (Philadelphia: Presbyterian and Reformed Publishing Co., 1956), p. 22.

10. Calvin gives his definition in *ICR* III, xxi.5 (2:926): "We call predestination God's eternal decree, by which he determined with himself what he willed to become of each man. For all are not created in equal condition; rather, eternal life is foreordained for some, eternal damnation for others."

11. E.g., Augustine, *an. et or.* (419/420), 16 [xi]; NPNF 5:361.

ways of speaking is that both are found in Scripture: the Fourth Gospel represents Jesus as calling his chosen disciples out of the world (e.g., John 15:19; 17:6), whereas Paul contrasts "the vessels of mercy" with "the vessels of wrath made for destruction" (Rom. 9:22-23). In any case, the supposedly milder language of "preterition" (passing by) is no comfort to the non-elect, who will be damned either way.

Connected with election and predestination is a point on which Calvin expressly rejects an opinion of Augustine's. Baptism was so essential to salvation in Augustine's view that he felt constrained to draw the logical inference: unbaptized infants who die in infancy cannot be numbered among the predestined but are condemned to hell. Their penalty is by no means unjust; though they have not yet committed actual sins, they inherit the guilt of Adam. Augustine took no pleasure in this terrible inference. The best he could find to say by way of mitigation, however, was that such infants would suffer only the mildest of pains.[12] Calvin, too, believed infants are tainted by original sin, but he could reject the Augustinian opinion on their fate, if they die without baptism, because for him election trumps the sacrament of baptism. To the insistence that any who die unbaptized will be in danger of forfeiting the grace of regeneration, Calvin retorts: "Not at all. God declares that he adopts our babies as his own before they are born [that is, the babies of the elect, the people of the covenant], when he promises that he will be our God and the God of our descendants after us."[13] God can call those who are his without the ordinary means even of preaching, and sometimes he certainly does.[14]

A third difference between Augustine and Calvin on election has less to do with the content of the doctrine than with the use to which they put it. They were agreed that only the doctrine of election can safeguard the sovereign freedom of grace. But Calvin had also a secondary use for it: to establish assurance of salvation.[15] Augustine, by contrast, held that none can know whether or not they are elect; the doctrine accordingly in-

---

12. Augustine, *pecc. mer.* (411), I, 15 [xii], 21 [xvi], NPNF 5:20-23; *gr. et pecc. or.* (418), II, 17-19 [xv-xvii], NPNF 5:242-43.

13. Calvin, *ICR* IV, xv.20 (2:1321); cf. xvi.26 (2:1349).

14. Calvin, *ICR* IV, xvi.19 (2:1342).

15. Against the opinion of Gregory the Great, Calvin asserts that "predestination, rightly understood, brings no shaking of faith but rather its best confirmation" (*ICR* III, xxiv.9 [2:975-76]). But he admits that in 1 Cor. 10:12 "Paul himself dissuades us from over-assurance" about our future state (xxiv.6 [2:972]).

spires fear rather than confidence.[16] And this is a point on which Roman Catholics and Calvinists took opposing sides at the time of the Reformation. For the followers of Calvin, assurance of election was a duty and a privilege (they appealed to 2 Pet. 1:10); for the Council of Trent, Calvinist assurance was only "the vain confidence of heretics."[17]

II. Free Will and Merit: Calvin and Bernard

Predestination was not, in Calvin's eyes, a useless topic, good only for contentious arguments. As he wrote in his second treatise against Pighius, the doctrine "lifts us up into an admiration of the unbounded goodness of God towards us [i.e., the elect!]."[18] Like Augustine, Calvin contended for an awareness of total dependence on the free grace of God, an awareness that would nurture in believers a piety of humility and thankfulness. But the witness to grace that inspired them has again and again been buried under a mountain of indignant objections to the determinism they inferred from it.[19] After Augustine's death, the Pelagian controversy led to the so-called semi-Pelagian controversy, which the Second Council of Orange (529) calmed by a compromise, affirming the prevenience of grace without Augustine's election of grace. Controversy reawakened in the ninth century (Gottschalk), and throughout the Middle Ages predestination remained a *quaestio disputata* in the schools. The fourteenth century saw a revival of Augustinianism, partly in reaction against the alleged Pelagianizing of the times (Thomas Bradwardine, Gregory of Rimini), partly in defense of an inward definition of the church as "the number of the elect" (John Wycliffe, followed in the fifteenth century by John Hus).

16. Augustine, *corrept.* (426/427), 40 [xiii]; NPNF 5:488. The reception of baptismal grace is therefore no guarantee that one will receive the grace of perseverance (*persev.* [428/429], 33 [xiii]; NPNF 5:538).

17. H. J. Schroeder, *Canons and Decrees of the Council of Trent: Original Text with English Translation* (St. Louis: B. Herder, 1941), sess. VI, chaps. ix, xii; pp. 35, 38 (English), pp. 314, 316 (Latin).

18. John Calvin, *De aeterna Dei praedestinatione* (1552), CO 8:260; trans. Henry Cole in *Calvin's Calvinism* (first published in two vols., 1856-57; reprinted in one vol., Grand Rapids: Eerdmans, 1956), p. 29.

19. See further Chap. 12 below.

In contrast to his abundant references to the Fathers, Calvin rarely cited the medieval doctors by name: Anselm and Bonaventure only once each, Duns Scotus and William of Ockham twice each, Thomas Aquinas four times. Peter Lombard, the "master of the sentences," who gave the medieval schools their textbook of theology, fared better with thirty-nine citations.[20] Attempts to trace the medieval influences on Calvin's theology have naturally foundered on the paucity of his references to medieval authors, which has given rise to doubts about the extent of his reading. His place in Christian theology cannot, of course, be settled by gathering his references to his predecessors, nor by speculation about possible influences on his intellectual development from predecessors he seldom or never mentions.[21] The question of his "place" has more to do with affinities and dissimilarities. But, as it happens, how Calvin saw the implications of grace for *free will and merit* is admirably reflected in explicit references to his favorite medieval theologian: Bernard of Clairvaux, whom he cites forty-one times.[22] He thought Bernard's use of the two controverted terms "free will" and "merit" invited misunderstanding, but he could not bring himself to believe there was any material difference between him and the medieval monk whom he honored among "the ancient doctors" of the church.

1. Free Will

In his influential treatise *On Grace and Free Choice,* Bernard (1090-1153) followed Augustine in holding that the first man fell into servitude to sin

20. Lane, *Student of the Fathers,* p. 44 n. 231, pp. 61-66.

21. On Calvin's relation to the various streams of medieval thought, see Heiko A. Oberman, "*Initia Calvini:* The Matrix of Calvin's Reformation," in *Calvinus sacrae scripturae professor: Calvin as Confessor of Holy Scripture,* Papers from the International Congress on Calvin Research 1990, ed. Wilhelm H. Neuser (Grand Rapids: Eerdmans, 1994), pp. 113-54. Oberman sees "a close proximity to Scotus" in Calvin's theological vocabulary (pp. 124-27).

22. Lane, *Student of the Fathers,* pp. 101-14. See also Dennis E. Tamburello, *Union with Christ: John Calvin and the Mysticism of St. Bernard,* Columbia Series in Reformed Theology (Louisville: Westminster John Knox, 1994), and Lane, *Calvin and Bernard of Clairvaux,* Studies in Reformed Theology and History, new series, 1 (Princeton: Princeton Theological Seminary, 1996).

and took the entire human race into slavery with him. Once he had fallen, Adam lacked the ability to get up again. Sinners cannot *not* sin, for it is not so easy to climb out of a pit as to fall into one.[23] Nevertheless, Bernard could still affirm that the sinner has an inalienable *free will*,[24] and to Calvin this was a misuse of language. *Liberum arbitrium* properly means "free choice" and is commonly taken to imply that the agent is poised between two equally possible courses of action. But this could not have been what Bernard meant by an inalienable human freedom, because, in agreement with Augustine, he spoke expressly of the agent's powerlessness to do anything but sin until the Holy Spirit liberates the will. By "free," Calvin infers, Bernard meant "voluntary." Sinners remain free in the sense that they are *voluntary* slaves of sin: that is, although they cannot will not to sin, they are not *forced* to sin against their will. Bernard invites misunderstanding when he defines the inalienable freedom of the will as freedom from *necessity:* rather, it is freedom from *coercion.* Sinners sin necessarily because that is what they are, sinners; they are not compelled to sin against their will by some external force.[25]

Still, Calvin professes himself reluctant to quibble over words. With a modest caveat, he is content to accept the distinction Bernard made between three freedoms: from necessity, from sin, and from misery, the first inalienable and the other two lost through sin. Calvin comments: "I willingly accept this distinction, except in so far as necessity is falsely confused with compulsion."[26] Likewise, he thinks the expression

23. Bernard, *De gratia et libero arbitrio* (ca. 1128), vii.23; Eng. trans., "On Grace and Free Choice," trans. by Daniel O'Donovan, with an introduction by Bernard McGinn, in Bernard of Clairvaux, *Treatises III,* Cistercian Fathers Series, no. 19 (Kalamazoo: Cistercian Publications, 1977), p. 80.

24. Bernard, *De gratia,* viii.24; O'Donovan, p. 81.

25. Calvin, *ICR* II, ii.6-7 (1:263-64), iii.5 (1:294-96). Calvin's most careful discussion of the term "free will" appears in his reply to Pighius: *Defensio sanae et orthodoxae doctrinae de servitute et liberatione humani arbitrii adversus calumnias Alberti Pighii Campensis* (1543), CO 6:225-403. Trans. as *The Bondage and Liberation of the Will,* etc., ed. A[nthony] N. S. Lane, trans. G. I. Davies, Texts and Studies in Reformation and Post-Reformation Thought, vol. 2 (Grand Rapids: Baker, 1996); see pp. 103, 114, 122, 140, 146. The translation is based on the 1543 original but keyed (in the margins) to CO 6.

26. Calvin, *ICR* II, ii.5 (1:262). Cf. ii.7 (1:264): "I abhor contentions about words." Calvin uses the Greek word *logomachia.*

liberum arbitrium could be used without misunderstanding, but he prefers not to use it himself and recommends others also to avoid it.[27] For Calvin, as (he thinks) for Augustine and Bernard, the condition for moral responsibility is not free choice but voluntary action — doing what, in fact, one wills to do. He makes no claim to originality; he only suggests greater care in the use of language.[28]

2. Merit

The other controverted term *merit* leads to a similar conclusion. Luther had agonized over the Nominalist belief that God gives grace to those who merit grace by first doing the best they can without it — a belief he finally dismissed as crassly Pelagian. But even Augustine and Bernard, though they denied that any human merit can *precede* the gift of justifying grace, held that merit should *follow* grace, which, once it is given, frees the will from the necessity of sinning. Calvin could write: "[O]n the beginning of justification there is no quarrel between us and the sounder Schoolmen."[29] However, he located a continuing problem in the universal scholastic teaching that after the reception of grace the acquisition of merit is a possibility and a duty, and he had to face the difficulty that the Schoolmen had his two favorite theologians on their side. Once again, he took the line that, as far as Augustine and Bernard were concerned, the problem was semantic. "Merit" is a prideful term foreign to Scripture, mistakenly defended by appeal to biblical talk of "reward." For the kingdom of heaven is not servants' pay; the reward is the inheritance of God's children.[30] Though he did speak of "merit," Bernard, like Augustine, acknowledged that all our merits are gifts of God, and he pointed us away from our good works to the gracious Giver, who forgives what is still lacking in them.[31] Accordingly, "the fact that he uses the term 'merits' freely for good works, we must excuse as the custom of the time."[32]

27. Calvin, *ICR* II, ii.8 (1:266).
28. Calvin, *ICR* II, iii.5 (1:296).
29. Calvin, *ICR* III, xiv.11 (1:778).
30. Calvin, *ICR* III, xv.2 (1:789), xviii.2 (1:822).
31. Calvin, *ICR* III, ii.25 (1:571-72), xi.22 (1:752), xii.3 (1:757), xii.8 (1:762).
32. Calvin, *ICR* III, xii.3 (1:758).

No one is likely to suspect Calvin of belittling the demand for good works. Some may be willing to commend him for his criticism that talk of "merit" puts the good works of the Christian life under the wrong metaphor — hired service instead of filial obedience. One might even venture to conclude that, although he didn't invent the distinction between necessity and coercion, his use of it introduced greater conceptual clarity and consistency into the understanding of free will in the Augustinian tradition. Not everyone will applaud him for so doing. The bondage of the will remains an obstinately problematic idea, and too much clarity about it may seem suspicious. But it is worth noting that in our time philosophers, to say nothing of behavioral scientists, often take the limitations of human freedom more earnestly than Calvin's theological critics. His reply to Pighius was what we would call these days a species of "compatibilism": he sought to show "how self-determination and necessity can be combined together."[33] Calvin's case resembles the well-known argument of G. E. Moore, for instance, that right and wrong depend not on what we absolutely *can* do, but on what we can do *if* we choose. We have free will if we do what we will to do. Moore remained doubtful whether it is also true that we could sometimes have willed differently than we did. But, be that as it may, moral responsibility does not require us to assert that acts of will are uncaused.[34]

III. Spirituality and Sacramental Signs: Calvin and Luther

Within the overall theme of Calvin's place in Christian theology, his relation to Martin Luther (1483-1546) deserves more generous attention than can be given here.[35] The German reformer displayed a respect for Calvin that he was notoriously unwilling to extend to Ulrich Zwingli,

33. Calvin, *Bondage and Liberation,* p. 70. Cf. the rhetorical question concerning Augustine's talk of *liberum arbitrium:* "But does it therefore follow that nothing is at the same time both voluntary and necessary?" (p. 101).

34. G[eorge] E. Moore, *Ethics,* Home University Library (London: Oxford University Press, 1912; reprinted 1952), chap. 6.

35. I have dealt with the question somewhat more fully elsewhere: see, in particular, "John Calvin on Luther" (1968), reprinted as "The Pathfinder: Calvin's Image of Martin Luther" in Gerrish, *The Old Protestantism and the New: Essays on the Reformation Heritage* (1982; reprinted, London: T&T Clark International, 2004), chap. 2.

the reformer of Zurich, and his generosity won an answering generosity from Calvin. In 1539, when it was pointed out to Luther that the younger man had apparently criticized his teaching on Christ's presence in the Eucharist, he still refused to think ill of him. Calvin, in turn, steadfastly defended his "most respected father" throughout the later eucharistic controversies that embittered Luther against the Swiss and, after Luther's death, turned many Lutherans against Calvin. Even on the sacraments Calvin sensed a greater kinship with Luther than with Zwingli. But it by no means followed that he could agree with all Luther's opinions: rather, he did not permit their disagreements to annul the essential harmony between them. Among their differences, Calvin did not endorse Luther's assertion, in refutation of free choice, that "to purpose anything either evil or good is in no one's control, but . . . everything happens by absolute necessity" (an assertion borrowed from John Wycliffe).[36] That, we might say, was to confuse a psychological with a metaphysical necessity. Calvin, of course, could not escape the metaphysical problem, but when he turned to it, in his doctrine of providence, he was willing to make use of careful scholastic distinctions that Luther had dismissed.[37] Two further differences between them had to do with *spirituality* and *sacramental signs*.

1. Spirituality

A common stereotype contrasts "Calvinist activism" with "Lutheran quietism," and sometimes the explanation is added that Lutheranism nurtures an intensely inward and individual religiousness. The question of Lutheran and Calvinist social ethics is much too complicated to be brought under such simple formulas. But a difference of *spirituality* (as we call it these days), whether or not it can account for their different programs for reform, has been well-nigh universally detected in the respective utterances of Luther and Calvin on the Christian life. It is reflected, in particular, in the way they spoke of grace and law in the life of the Christian.

36. Calvin, *Bondage and Liberation*, pp. 28, 35-36.
37. Calvin, *ICR* I, xvi.9 (1:210); but see xvii.2 (1:214), where Calvin rejects the notion of God's absolute *will*.

For Luther, "grace" was nothing but the favor or good will of God in freely justifying the sinner. Not that he was uninterested in "sanctification": appealing to Romans 5:15, he maintained that besides the *grace* that forgives the sinner there is the *gift* that little by little heals the sin.[38] But Luther's great boon to the church was his profile of the Christian as one who lives in the liberating joy of unconditional forgiveness, and he was ever watchful for the least trace of a resurgent works-righteousness. Calvin, on the other hand, taught a "double grace" that both justifies and sanctifies, and his thinking was marked by a concern to balance these two gifts of participation in Christ.[39] In a sense, he even gave preeminence to sanctification, or the cultivation of purity of life, since he could say that the Lord freely justifies his own *in order that* he may restore them to true righteousness by sanctification.[40] True piety, its loss and restoration, was the subject of his *Institutes* from beginning to end: the title page of the first edition fittingly described the work as a "summary of piety" *(pietatis summa).* To be sure, Calvin could call justification "the sum of all piety."[41] But it was more characteristic of him to describe justification as the main *hinge* on which religion turns, or the *foundation* on which to build piety toward God.[42] The Calvinist profile of the Christian portrays a dutiful son, pledged to willing obedience, although it is not filial obedience but fatherly indulgence alone that secures the relationship.[43]

Consistent with this image of the Christian as called to the obedience of the children of God is a distinctive perception of God's "law." Luther spoke of two uses of law: a civil use, to restrain wrongdoing, and a theological use, to bring about conviction of sin and drive the sinner to Christ. Calvin, following Luther's colleague Philip Melanchthon, spoke of a threefold use: "The third and principal use, which pertains more closely to the proper purpose of the law, finds its place among believers in whose hearts the Spirit of God already lives and reigns."[44] There it

---

38. Martin Luther, *Rationis Latomianae confutatio* (1521), WA 8:105-8, 113-15; LW 32:226-30, 238-41.

39. Calvin, *ICR* III, xi.1 (1:725); cf. iii.1 (1:592-93), xi.6 (1:732).

40. Calvin, *ICR* III, iii.19 (1:613).

41. Calvin, *ICR* III, xv.7 (1:794).

42. Calvin, *ICR* III, xi.1 (1:726).

43. Calvin, *ICR* III, xix.5 (1:837).

44. Calvin, *ICR* II, vii.12 (1:360).

serves both as instruction in God's will and as a stimulus to obey it. The nature of God's law is misinterpreted, in Calvin's view, when seen only in the context of Paul's struggle against the *legalism* of false religion.[45] The "proper purpose of law" is to be understood from the *covenant* context, in which the law is seen as God's gracious gift to his people.[46]

2. Sacramental Signs

A trace of anti-Lutheran polemic can perhaps be detected in Calvin's remark about "those who always erroneously compare the law with the gospel by contrasting the merit of works with the free imputation of righteousness."[47] On our other theme, *sacramental signs,* he saw himself unambiguously as Luther's champion and was indignant that, after Luther's death, not all the German reformers were able to see him in the same light.[48] Before the controversy with the Swiss, Luther had freely used the notion of a sacramental sign in the Eucharist, though sometimes in a peculiar sense. In his *Treatise on the New Testament, that is, the Holy Mass* (1520), he identified the sign not with the elements, but with the actual presence of Christ's body and blood *under* the bread and wine to confirm the promise of forgiveness. Zwingli and the Swiss Reformers also used the notion of a sign and claimed the support of Augustine. In their view, when Jesus said "This is my body," he must have meant that the bread signified, or was a sign of, his body, and they thought that the primary reference of sacramental signs was to the past: they signal the fact that something has taken place. The Eucharist, then, was a *remembrance* of the crucifixion — of the body slain for our salvation — not a celebration of the real bodily *presence.* Luther was appalled.

45. Calvin, *ICR* II, ix.4 (1:426-27).

46. Calvin, *ICR* II, vii.1 (1:348); cf. *ICR* III, xi.20 (1:750). It may be noted that, in this respect, Calvin anticipates those present-day Old Testament scholars who describe the religion of Israel as "covenantal nomism."

47. Calvin, *ICR* II, ix.4 (1:426).

48. For documentation and details on sacramental signs in Calvin and Luther, see B. A. Gerrish, *Grace and Gratitude: The Eucharistic Theology of John Calvin* (1993; reprinted, Eugene, OR: Wipf & Stock, 2002), pp. 62-86, 160-73, 182 n. 78, and *Continuing the Reformation: Essays on Modern Religious Thought* (Chicago: University of Chicago Press, 1993), chap. 3. See also Chap. 11 below.

The "fanatics," he scoffed, were stupidly misinterpreting Augustine, for whom a sacrament was not a sign of something absent but of something invisibly present. And yet Luther did not counter the Swiss blunder with a more authentically Augustinian understanding of sacramental signs: he sought to exclude sign talk from the interpretation of the words of institution.

A third option — neither Luther's nor Zwingli's — was obviously open: to interpret the sacramental signs as bearers of the reality they signify. This was the option that Calvin, among others, tirelessly commended as the only way to reconcile the parties in the dispute. When Paul says that the bread we break in the Lord's Supper is "a participation in the body of Christ" (1 Cor. 10:16 RSV), there is no reason to protest that the language is figurative. "I indeed admit that the breaking of the bread is a symbol; it is not the thing itself. But, having admitted this, we shall nevertheless duly infer that by the showing of the symbol the thing itself is also shown. . . . [T]here ought not to be the least doubt that [the Lord] truly presents and shows [*vere praestet atque exhibeat*] his body."[49] In Calvin's opinion, it was the notion of "exhibitive signs" that provided the basis for settling the eucharistic debate. And by *exhibere,* as is plain from the tandem expression "presents and shows," he meant more than the English word "show" might seem to imply. Christ once gave his body to be crucified: he *gives* it to us daily, and in the Supper he inwardly fulfills what he outwardly signifies.[50]

In his understanding of both the "graced" life and the function of sacramental signs, Calvin stood closer than Luther to Augustine. But he remained uneasy with Augustine's failure to distinguish the grace of justification sharply enough from sanctification, or at any rate with his manner of putting it;[51] and he was convinced that Luther, though he made no use of the Augustinian notion of signs in interpreting the words of institution, would have been content with the view "that what the sacraments figure is truly presented to us."[52] Much more could be said. But it hardly seems appropriate to assign Calvin a place in the sixteenth century either as a mere epigone of Luther or as a debaser of pure

49. Calvin, *ICR* IV, xvii.10 (2:1371).
50. Calvin, *ICR* IV, xvii.5 (2:1364).
51. Calvin, *ICR* III, xi.15 (1:746).
52. Calvin to John Marbach, 24 August 1554, CO 15:212-13.

Lutheran doctrine. They represent, rather, two interesting and perhaps complementary variants of a common evangelical witness, rooted in the New Testament and the Augustinian tradition.

IV. The Task of Theology: Calvin, Schleiermacher, Barth

Like every other great intellectual of the past, Calvin left a legacy that his heirs have received in more ways than one. The uses to which his thought has been put, partisan though they may have been, have served to highlight aspects of it that certainly belong to the assessment of his place in Christian theology. Much discussion has turned around the question whether Reformed scholasticism developed or distorted his legacy. Very little serious reflection has been given to Schleiermacher's thoughts on Calvin, though he was the most eminent theologian of the Reformed family between Calvin and Barth.[53] The neglect is largely due to uncritical echoing of Barth's verdict that Schleiermacher's theology marked a break with the Reformation heritage. Our interest is in Calvin's place in Christian theology, not Schleiermacher's or Barth's. But the remarks made on Calvin by these two Reformed theologians of modern times may draw attention to some features of *the task of Christian theology* as Calvin understood and practiced it.

Schleiermacher commended Calvin's masterwork, the 1559 *Institutes,* for two main reasons: because it never loses touch with the religious affections, and because it is distinguished by sharpness of method and *systematic* compass. Evidently, he admired most in the *Institutes* what he himself strove for in his own dogmatic work, *The Christian Faith.*[54] To be sure, during the twentieth century it was sometimes denied that Calvin could properly be seen as a systematic theologian. The denial appears to have arisen out of a limited notion of a "system" as a deductive construct in which everything is derived with logical precision from a first principle. The *Institutes* is certainly not a deductive system. Neither was Calvin interested in contriving an intellectual edifice for its own sake.

---

53. In several essays, I have attempted to narrow the gap in the literature, and I may refer to them for details and documentation: Gerrish, *The Old Protestantism,* pp. 196-207, and *Continuing the Reformation,* pp. 178-216; also the essay reprinted in Chap. 8 below.

54. See Chap. 8, nn. 22, 23, below.

From Desiderius Erasmus and Martin Bucer he learned that genuine theology, unlike the "sophistry" of the late medieval schoolmen, is eminently practical: its aim is piety or, as Bucer said, "a godlike life."[55]

Calvin nonetheless earns a special place among the sixteenth-century Protestant Reformers not least because, in the final Latin edition of his *Institutes*, he produced a comprehensive and organized whole in which he took care to establish the interconnections between one doctrine and another. His *pietatis summa* was a true systematic theology. Schleiermacher's theme also was Christian piety, though he intended *The Christian Faith* to be a "scientific" rather than a directly edifying work, and he clearly stated the nature of a systematic theology when he wrote that the meaning of a dogmatic proposition is partly determined by its place (its "definite context") in the work as a whole.[56] To take the *Institutes* as a systematic theology in *this* sense is always to ask, not just what Calvin said on any topic, but where the topic fits in. Though this is not, of course, all that needs to be said about the design of the *Institutes*, neglect of it is bound to give rise to misunderstandings: for example, the misunderstanding that predestination was Calvin's central dogma.

For his part, Karl Barth warned against any theological system that might prejudge what is heard when God speaks. He didn't direct this warning at Calvin. But he did think that the title of the *Institutes* — "instruction in the Christian *religion*" — was unfortunate if taken (erroneously) as comfort to those who want a "theology of religious consciousness." God's activity, not human activity, is the proper theme of the theologian. In his early Göttingen lectures on the theology of John Calvin (1922), Barth found in Calvin's dominant concern for living out evangelical faith in the real world his special place in the Protestant Reformation. Calvin's understanding of faith as obedience and his preoccupation with Christian ethics was a "second turn" of the Reformation that completed Luther's achievement — but also, Barth thought, jeopardized it (a judgment with which many Lutherans would agree).[57] Later,

---

55. Quoted in Wilhelm Pauck, *The Heritage of the Reformation*, rev. ed. (Glencoe: Free Press, 1961), p. 97.

56. Schleiermacher, *CG*, §28.2 (p. 120). He goes on to reject the assimilation of dogmatics to the kind of deductive science that works from a single first principle *(einen Grundsatz)*.

57. Karl Barth, *The Theology of John Calvin*, trans. Geoffrey W. Bromiley (Grand Rapids: Eerdmans, 1995).

in *The Holy Spirit and the Christian Life* (1929), Barth showed himself less inclined than Calvin to excuse Augustine's shortcomings or to interpret him *in optimam partem*. Barthian grace comes to us moment by moment as a totally free act of the Holy Spirit in the word of promise: Augustine, by his concept of infused grace and his mixing of justification with sanctification, made man's own actions a condition of fellowship with God. The Reformers (this time Luther is included!) held firmly to Augustine's anti-Pelagian polemics but "neglected to warn, with sufficient clearness and force, against the sweet poison that is meant when Augustine speaks of 'grace.'"[58]

In principle, Calvin could not complain about this attempt to open a greater distance between Augustine and the Protestant Reformers: he held the task of theology to be not only systematic, but also open-ended or *progressive*. In his reply to Albert Pighius on free will, he pointed out that not even Augustine arrived at the truth all at once. One could hardly expect more from Luther. If Luther's language was sometimes unguarded and exaggerated, it was justified by the needs of the day. But we are not obliged to repeat his every word, since we do not merely echo him but honor him as the one who opened up a path for us. "If Pighius does not know it, I want to make this plain to him: our constant endeavor, day and night, is to *form* in the manner we think will be best whatever is faithfully *handed on* by us."[59] As Calvin sees it, *fideliter tradere* is always *formare;* or, as he sometimes puts it less technically, there is a difference between a disciple and an ape.[60]

The determination of Calvin's place in Christian theology must surely include recognition of his insistence on the development of Christian doctrine. Many of his heirs have claimed, in turn, a similar right to wrestle with *his* teaching and propose revisions of it. Particularly interesting is the way Schleiermacher and Barth both felt bound to acknowledge the importance of Calvin's doctrine of election, but free to re-form it. Schleiermacher astonished his contemporaries by coming to

58. Karl Barth, *The Holy Spirit and the Christian Life: The Theological Basis of Ethics,* trans. R. Birch Hoyle (1938; reprinted in the Library of Theological Ethics, Louisville: Westminster John Knox, 1993), p. 22. Cf. Barth's expression "the subtle works righteousness of infused love" (p. 26).

59. Calvin, *De servitute et liberatione,* CO 6:250 (my trans. and emphasis); cf. Lane, *Bondage and Liberation,* p. 29.

60. See, e.g., Calvin to Martin Seidemann, 14 March 1555, CO 15:502.

Calvin's defense in a long article on election (1819). His argument was carried over into *The Christian Faith*. He grants that there is indeed an antithesis between those who do, and those who don't, belong to the fellowship of redemption. We must agree with Calvin that the antithesis is grounded solely in the divine good pleasure. But the reason for the antithesis is that Christ established the kingdom of God as a phenomenon of history: it spreads slowly from its beginning at a single historical point, so that not everyone can be taken up into the kingdom at one time. However, it is a *vanishing* antithesis; it is not, as Calvin supposed, unalterably fixed by an irrevocable foreordination of some to blessedness and others to damnation.[61] There is but one divine foreordination — the decree to assume the human race into fellowship with Christ. It is *humanity* that is elect in Christ.[62] In this fundamental assertion Schleiermacher was followed (without explicit acknowledgments) by Barth.[63] The only antithesis, then, that we are entitled to draw is not between the elect and the non-elect, but between the regenerate and the not yet regenerate (Schleiermacher), or between those who live as God's elect and those who don't (Barth).

There is, of course, a great deal more to the theme of election in Schleiermacher and Barth, but even this much raises the question of *legitimate* development. There is no foothold in Calvin's theology for the idea of a single divine decree, which in fact resembles what he dismissed as the "absurd invention" of Pighius: that the whole human race was chosen in Christ but some deprive themselves of the benefit of universal election.[64] We can only conclude that Calvin's powerful argument for the election of grace has gripped even disciples, or heirs, who have no wish to be "apes": his place in the history of Christian theology is partly given by his ability to set an agenda and incite dissent.

Many pertinent issues have been left untouched, or touched on only obliquely, in this chapter: Calvin's "Scripture principle" and correlation of Word and Spirit, for example, or his thoughts on such diverse matters as the person and "threefold office" of Christ, the organization and dis-

---

61. Schleiermacher, *CG*, §§117-18 (pp. 536-45). See further Chap. 8, pp. 167-68, below.

62. Schleiermacher, *CG*, §119.3 (p. 549); cf. §109.3 (p. 501).

63. Karl Barth, *KD* 3/2, §§32-35.

64. Calvin, *De praedestinatione*, CO 8:259, 270, 285-86; Cole, pp. 27-28, 45, 71.

cipline of the church, and the cause of unity among the evangelical churches. It would be unwise to reduce even the themes explored here to a single formula descriptive of Calvin's place in Christian theology. No doubt, his relation to the Augustinian heritage is pivotal. But it hardly locates him in relation to others of whom one might wish to say the same. Warfield pointed out that Calvin's Augustinianism was not peculiar to him but common to all the Protestant Reformers. Calvin learned it from Luther and especially from Bucer, "into whose practical, ethical point of view he perfectly entered," only adding clearness and religious depth to what he learned. Bucer "was above all others . . . Calvin's master in theology."[65] Moreover, Protestant Augustinianism, as Warfield conceded, was highly selective; hence his famous aphorism, "[T]he Reformation, inwardly considered, was just the ultimate triumph of Augustine's doctrine of grace over Augustine's doctrine of the Church."[66]

Calvin cared about continuity of doctrine. But he was not interested in a repristination of the whole Augustine, and he was no mere echo of Luther — or of Bucer either. Any such characterization of him and his work would go against his explicit theological principles. Lange van Ravenswaay's suggestion is that, instead of always looking back on Calvin's debts to Augustine, we might think of him as "the initiator of a *distinctive* 'Schola Augustiniana' [Augustinian school] whose program goes far beyond the Wittenberg program."[67] Whatever Calvin learned from the Fathers, the medieval Schoolmen, and his fellow Reformers he made his own and integrated into his comprehensive interpretation of the Christian faith, establishing a Reformed theological tradition which, insofar as it is true to his understanding of the theological enterprise, does not merely repristinate *his* teaching either but remains open to further "brotherly communication" and development.

---

65. Warfield, *Calvin and Augustine,* p. 22. In an essay on Calvin and Bucer, Pauck concludes that Bucer "was the father of Calvinism" (*Heritage of the Reformation,* p. 99).

66. Warfield, *Calvin and Augustine,* p. 322.

67. Lange van Ravenswaay, *Augustinus totus noster,* p. 181 (emphasis his; translation mine).

CHAPTER 7

Charles Hodge and the Europeans

The taste for German writers on dogmatic theology is factitious,
alien to the genius of the Anglo-American mind.

Charles Hodge, "Neander's History"

By way of a preface, two disclaimers are perhaps in order, though they
may later seem to have been too obvious to mention. In the first place, I
am not a Charles Hodge scholar, or even a specialist in American church
history. You might say that I speak for "the Europeans"; at any rate, my
competence is mainly in European religious thought from the time of
the Protestant Reformation. But I have had a long-term interest in
Hodge: he was the first theologian I ever became acquainted with by
more than name. Even before I attended seminary, my circle of student
friends in London and Cambridge used to pore over a worn set of
Hodge's three-volume *Systematic Theology,* and our quest for theological wisdom led us as well to his *Commentary on the Epistle to the Romans.*
As I recall, our liveliest interest was not in the Princeton doctrine of plenary inspiration (though we talked about that, too), but in the great
soteriological themes at the beginning of volume three. We were all
staunch Calvinists, worried that the Arminians were dictating the methods of evangelism; and we nodded approvingly when we found in
Hodge, the foremost American Calvinist, that conversion is the effect of
regeneration, which is an act of God alone and therefore not to be credited to the evangelist's powers of persuasion or the sinner's own

choice.[1] But I don't believe I have ever "dismissed" Hodge on *any* theme, and my subsequent attraction to his Mercersburg adversary John Williamson Nevin, who stood for an alternative brand of Calvinism, only quickened my old interest in him.[2]

My second disclaimer follows from the first: I can't address my assigned topic out of the full range of the Hodge sources and secondary literature, as a specialist would. This certainly makes for a high-risk contribution to the critical appraisal of his life and work, but still, I hope, a contribution even where it may prove to require additions or qualifications. A pattern repeatedly appears in the sources I have used; it is not likely to need radical revision in the light of other sources that I have *not* used. With the theme of "Charles Hodge and the Europeans" in mind, I have gone through the *Systematic Theology* once more and the biography by his son, A. A. Hodge,[3] and I have picked out what sound like pertinent titles from the *Biblical Repertory and Princeton Review.*[4] It is possible that I have missed some other interesting material. I am told, for instance, that archival sources for Hodge's European tour in 1826-1828 still remain insufficiently explored, particularly letters to his wife that were not reproduced in the biography.[5] As for the secondary litera-

---

1. See Charles Hodge, *Systematic Theology* (hereafter *ST*), 3 vols. (1871-72; reprint, Grand Rapids: Eerdmans, 1981), 3:3-40; cf. 2:684-89. My frequent references to *ST* are mostly inserted in the main body of this chapter. The pagination has remained the same in all the various printings of this work. In my own copy (the 1981 reprint) the eighty-one page index, paginated separately, is placed at the beginning of volume one.

2. This is meant as a (very mild) protest against John Stewart's statement that "Brian A. Gerrish dismissed Hodge as being uninteresting, except in Hodge's controversy with John Nevin and the Mercersburg theology." John W. Stewart, *Mediating the Center: Charles Hodge on American Science, Language, Literature, and Politics* (Princeton: Princeton Theological Seminary, 1995), p. 2 n. 5.

3. Archibald Alexander Hodge, *The Life of Charles Hodge, D.D., LL.D., Professor in the Theological Seminary, Princeton, N.J.* (New York: Charles Scribner's Sons, 1880); hereafter *LCH*, with page references mostly in the body of the text.

4. Hereafter *BRPR*. Wherever possible, I give references to the reprints in Charles Hodge, *Essays and Reviews* (New York: Robert Carter & Brothers, 1857), hereafter *ER*, or to the extracts in Mark A. Noll, ed., *The Princeton Theology, 1812-1921: Scripture, Science, and Theological Method from Archibald Alexander to Benjamin Breckinridge Warfield* (Grand Rapids: Baker, 1983).

5. Stewart reports, presumably on the basis of the archival evidence, that Hodge "actually attended Schleiermacher's *seminars* [plural] and preaching in Berlin in 1828"

ture, as far as I have been able to ascertain, it is thin at just the point where my own interest is strongest: Hodge's attitude to Schleiermacher, very different as it was from the attitude of the recent graduate, Nevin, who stood in for him during his European tour.

We must not make too much of the European tour, fascinating though his reports of it may be. They tell us about Hodge's impressions of the Europeans during two years at the very beginning of his career, and they tell us a good deal about how his impressions were formed. But the time span between his sojourn in Berlin and publication of the *Systematic Theology* was more than forty years. It cannot be presumed that between the earliest sources and the last he did not have any second thoughts about the Germans, though it cannot be presumed that he *did* either. The point to note is that in 1827-28 he was a novice instructor in Bible (Professor of Oriental and Biblical Literature since 1822) and in 1871-72 had become one of America's foremost systematic theologians (Professor of Exegetical and Didactic Theology since 1840, of Polemic Theology since Archibald Alexander's death in 1852).[6] Might he, one wonders, even have spent his time in Berlin differently had he been already a systematician?

Be that as it may, in what follows a brief word on the theological traffic between Britain, America, and continental Europe, and the spectacles through which Hodge viewed it (sec. I), will be amplified by noting the remarkable breadth of his explicit references to British and Continental authors (sec. II). This sets the stage for examining more closely his comments on the theological situation in Germany (secs. III-IV). We can then see where he placed Schleiermacher in this setting and where he found Schleiermacher's thought perilously wanting (sec. V). My next chapter (Chap. 8) will consider Hodge and Schleiermacher as intellectual heirs of John Calvin.

I. The Theological World Through Hodge's Spectacles

The triangular relationship between theologies in Britain, America, and continental Europe is still less thoroughly researched than one might

---

(*Mediating the Center,* p. 4 n. 10 [emphasis mine]; cf. p. 11) and "apparently conversed at length with the famed Berlin theologian" (p. 12).

6. Hodge was born 28 December 1797. He was twenty-eight when he left for Europe.

expect. Claude Welch reminded us in 1972 that studies of nineteenth-century religious thought have been written as regional histories even when their titles have seemed to offer something more. Karl Barth's *Protestant Theology in the Nineteenth Century,* for example (German 1946), was in fact concerned exclusively with the Germans. "A general history of nineteenth-century Protestant theology," Welch said, "has not yet appeared." His own two-volume work sought to narrow the gap. While granting that nineteenth-century theology was not as obviously international as the religious thought of the Enlightenment, he argued that national or linguistic boundaries are not the primary grids for interpreting it. He looked for a measure of international unity in "concerns, tendencies, and problems" shared by Protestant theologians everywhere.[7]

Claude Welch's project was not, of course, identical with an inquiry into the actual exchange of critical appraisals and constructive proposals between Britain, America, and the Continent. Throughout the nineteenth century, a traffic in theological ideas went on, often couched in chauvinistic talk about "the Teutonic mind," "the Anglo-Saxon character," or some other ethnological watchword; and this invites interesting questions about what Stephen Sykes calls "theological diplomacy." Sykes hopes to see eventually a "thorough and detailed history of the theological relations between England and Germany," a history that will take account of the manner in which the interpretation and reception of "foreign" ideas simultaneously transforms them.[8] Such a history, now lacking, could be very illuminating. How much more intriguing, albeit more complicated, it might be if Scotland and North America were allowed their place among the English-speaking theologians!

Whatever issues of diplomacy between England and Germany remain mooted or unexplained, it is commonly agreed that by the end of the eighteenth century the dominant flow of the intellectual traffic among the Europeans had been reversed: no longer from Britain to

---

7. Claude Welch, *Protestant Thought in the Nineteenth Century,* 2 vols. (New Haven: Yale University Press, 1972-85), 1:1, 4, 15-16. If the approach is by examining responses to common problems, one might question Welch's assertion that "it would be too much to ask for a combined study of Protestant and Roman Catholic thought" (1:1).

8. Stephen W. Sykes, ed., *England and Germany: Studies in Theological Diplomacy,* Studies in the Intellectual History of Christianity, vol. 25 (Frankfurt am Main: Peter D. Lang, 1982), p. 1.

France and Germany, it was now from Germany to France and Britain. An interesting testimony to the change of direction can be found in the editorial introduction to a brief English translation from Johann Gottfried von Herder that appeared in a Boston journal in 1820: "The language and literature of the Germans have not till lately been much attended to by foreigners. It is a singular fact, that while scarcely a work of note, either in letters or the sciences, appears in English, without soon issuing in translation from the German press; our own language has been put in possession of little in return. . . ." The editor then adds, however, that "men are beginning to believe that there is not science in the whole circle, which does not owe great obligations to German genius and research."[9]

When the tide turned, English churchmen greeted the theological scholarship of Germany with horror as something alien to the native good sense of Englishmen, although the Germans might be said to have been repaying with interest a debt they owed to England. Against the common assumption that biblical criticism began in Germany in the late eighteenth and early nineteenth centuries, Henning Reventlow has shown that it actually began earlier in England, in the period between the Reformation and the Enlightenment, and was occasioned by the effort to harmonize the Scriptures with the new scientific and moral outlook that seemed to undermine their veracity. Reventlow traces the story to its climax in the subversive writings of the English Deists.[10] In the nineteenth century, the hostility of English divines to German theology in general and German biblical criticism in particular showed no trace of penitence for the stimulus Germany had formerly received from England: the evil was assumed to be foreign. It is amusing to find Connop Thirlwall, Schleiermacher's first English translator, remarking defensively: "It would almost seem as if at Oxford the knowledge of German subjected a divine to the same suspicion of heterodoxy which we know was attached some centuries back to the knowledge of Greek."[11] Admittedly, Thirlwall was a Cambridge man, as was his

9. *The Christian Disciple*, n.s. 10 (1820): 233.

10. Henning Graf Reventlow, *The Authority of the Bible and the Rise of the Modern World*, trans. John Bowden (Philadephia: Fortress, 1985).

11. Friedrich Schleiermacher, *Luke: A Critical Study*, trans. Connop Thirlwall (1825; reprinted, with further essays and emendations by Terrence N. Tice, Schleiermacher Studies and Translations, vol. 13, Lewiston: Edwin Mellen, 1993), translator's intro., p. ix.

friend Julius Hare, who tried harder than anyone to help his countrymen understand Martin Luther as well as the more recent German theologians.[12] But Thirlwall and Hare were lonely prophets even in their alma mater. Only a few weeks after publication of Thirlwall's translation, H. J. Rose delivered his notorious four "sermons" at Cambridge attacking German rationalistic theologies, including Schleiermacher's.[13]

Charles Hodge, an almost exact contemporary of Thirlwall, maintained a lively interest in the progress of theology in France, Britain, and Germany throughout his career. He found himself thrust into the bitter controversy over the new German theology and German biblical criticism. Unlike some, he took pains to master the dreaded German language;[14] but, like most, he was inclined to lard his observations on the theological situation with conventional wisdom (not to say prejudice) about the French, the English, and the German "minds." In general, he sided with the English mind against the German mind; and he aligned the French with the Germans, and the Americans with the English. The English are clear and sensible; the Germans, obscure and speculative. German writers are seldom intelligible: they cannot discern the limits of knowledge and so are unable to distinguish between truth and "the phantoms of their creative imaginations," whereas the English mind rests content within the sphere God has assigned to it.[15] Germans of the Transcendental School may find the Anglo-Saxon race "dull, terrestrial,

12. See N. Merrill Distad, *Guessing at Truth: The Life of Julius Charles Hare (1795-1855)* (Shepherdstown: Patmos, 1979).

13. Hugh James Rose, *The State of the Protestant Religion in Germany* (Cambridge, 1825; 2d ed., titled *The State of Protestantism in Germany, Described*, London, 1829). Hodge quotes Rose in *ST* 1:45-46 on "Wolf" (i.e., Christian Wolff). Rose was a high churchman, a precursor of the Oxford Tractarians. It is interesting that E. B. Pusey, then studying biblical literature in Bonn, undertook to correct Rose's distortions of German theology. Pusey could not help admiring Schleiermacher, even though he was not to become an advocate of German theology: in 1845 he assumed leadership of the Oxford Movement when John Henry Newman defected to Rome. See Sykes, *England and Germany*, pp. 149, 156.

14. He found German difficult to get into. During his stay in Germany, he was not always sure he understood what was said to him (*LCH*, pp. 115, 119-21). Later, however, he was more likely to blame the author than himself when he failed to comprehend a German text.

15. Hodge, "Schaf's Protestantism," BRPR 17 (1845): 626-36; see pp. 626, 634-35 (Noll, *Princeton Theology*, pp. 157, 163).

and shallow," but their own defect is equally unfortunate: they lack the faculty for recognizing nonsense when they see it.[16] And so on. The English writers reminded Hodge of those admirable qualities that made Francis Turretin and other orthodox divines highly favored at Princeton:

> After all the alleged improvements in theological research, we never feel so much disposed to take down one of the old Latin dogmatic writers of the seventeenth century, as immediately on closing a fresh work from Germany. . . . They have one obvious claim upon our preference, that they accord in their chief peculiarities with the characteristic of the American, or what is the same thing, the British mind.[17]

II. Judgments on British and French Authors

But now, to sharpen the focus a little: Of whom was Hodge talking when he pronounced his global verdicts on the British and the Germans? And where do the French fit in? My concern is only with European thinkers of the eighteenth and nineteenth centuries who were Hodge's immediate predecessors or contemporaries. He died in 1878, and this must obviously be my cut-off date. The victorious advance of the Ritschlians in and beyond Germany had barely started: the great, three-volume system of Albrecht Ritschl, *Justification and Reconciliation* (German 1870-74), came off the press at about the same time as Hodge's *Systematic Theology*. In the Netherlands, the revival of Dutch Reformed

---

16. Hodge, "Transcendentalism," BRPR 11 (1839): 87.

17. Hodge, "Neander's History," BRPR 16 (1844): 155-83; see pp. 182-83 (Noll, *Princeton Theology,* p. 116). My epigraph at the head of this chapter is taken from the same source. Hodge's negative perception of the German mind, it should be added, never blinded him either to the excellence of German learning or to the warmth of the German character (see, e.g., *LCH,* pp. 117, 131, 188, 207). Moreover, some of his German friends saw the national mind much as he did. August Neander spoke appreciatively to Hodge of "the wonderful contrast between the practical common sense of the English, and the speculative spirit of the Germans" (*LCH,* p. 184; see also the letters to Hodge from Ludwig and Otto von Gerlach in *LCH,* pp. 213, 221). Ernst Wilhelm Hengstenberg was convinced that if Strauss's *Life of Jesus* (see n. 22 below) had been published in England, it would have been forgotten in a couple of months. See Hodge, "The Latest Form of Infidelity" (BRPR 1840), *ER,* p. 110. All further references to this article follow the pagination in *ER.*

theology under Abraham Kuyper and Herman Bavinck was also just beginning: it was left to Warfield to represent Princeton in engagement with the Dutch theologians, notably on the question of apologetics and a scientific theology.[18] But a large field remains, and the extent of Hodge's acquaintance with it is remarkable.

As we would expect, the *Systematic Theology* has plenty of references to the Scottish philosophers: David Hume, Thomas Reid, Dugald Stewart, Thomas Brown, William Hamilton, James McCosh. Hodge refers also to Scottish churchmen and theologians such as Thomas Chalmers and John Tulloch. The index to the *Systematic Theology* is by no means exhaustive: some names mentioned by Hodge, such as Tulloch's, are not included at all, and some others that are included are mentioned more often than the index records. But it is not my intention to supply missing references, only (at this stage) to give some indication of which Scots and other Europeans Hodge had chiefly in mind, and of this the index is usually a reliable guide.[19]

When we note Hodge's references to men of learning south of the border, in England, it again comes as no surprise to discover a host of exact references to writers on scientific subjects. He was immensely interested in developments in the natural sciences and the ways in which they impinged on Christian beliefs. His confidence in the authority of Scripture never wavered, but he admitted that "it is unwise for theologians to insist on an interpretation of Scripture which brings it into collision with the facts of science" (*ST* 1:56; cf. 1:170-71). Darwinism was the main problem. Hodge took it seriously, but only as a *theory* that could not be endorsed by anyone who was even more serious about the facts of the Bible.[20] Besides Charles Darwin himself, he engaged Charles Lyell, William Benjamin Carpenter, A. R. Wallace, T. H.

---

18. See Noll, *Princeton Theology*, pp. 302-7. Close in thought to Kuyper and Bavinck was the neglected reviver of Calvinism in Calvin's own native country, Auguste Lecerf, but his contributions lay even further in the future.

19. Princeton's attraction to the Scottish "common sense" school has been the subject of considerable scholarly research. For a brief guide to the literature, see Noll, *Princeton Theology*, pp. 30-33. Hodge was particularly interested in William Hamilton, who tried to combine the common sense tradition with the critical philosophy of Immanuel Kant. See, for example, the excursus in *ST* 1:346-65 and Hodge's critical essay "Philosophy of the Conditioned," BRPR 32 (1860): 472-510.

20. See especially *ST* 2, chap. 1.

Huxley, and others.[21] But I must move on to some of the more properly theological developments in England that caught his attention.

He was particularly attentive to English writers on natural theology. Indeed, it should not be overlooked that the necessity for systematic theology, argued so forcefully by Hodge (*ST* 1:2-3, 18-19), is something that on the whole eluded the English, who were preoccupied with preliminary questions of religious epistemology. Hodge mentions the famous Bridgewater Treatises, Paley's *Natural Theology,* the doubts of philosopher John Stuart Mill concerning the need for an ultimate explanation of natural sequences. What catches his eye in the controversial *Essays and Reviews* is the protest Baden Powell leveled "in behalf of men of science" against belief in miracles as interruptions of natural law (1:619).[22] These are all issues in philosophical theology that border on Hodge's scientific interests. More strictly philosophical were the Bampton Lectures of 1858, in which H. L. Mansel relentlessly dismantled every claim to *theoretical* knowledge of God's nature and then commended the Scriptures as our only source of *regulative* knowledge concerning the way we ought to conduct ourselves in relation to the unknown Absolute.[23] Hodge devotes one of his longest excursuses to Mansel; indeed, the chapter on "The Knowledge of God" in volume one of the *Systematic Theology* (part 1, chapter 4) is a running debate with the kindred views of Mansel and Hamilton. Hodge's acute criticisms show him at his argumentative best. But if the theory of Hamilton and Mansel is "suicidal . . . an incongruous combination of sceptical principles with orthodox faith" (1:363), and if Darwin's theory is as incredible as "the Hindu mythology and cosmology" (2:20), Hodge surely risks shattering our faith in British good sense.[24]

---

21. Hodge and the natural sciences is another theme that has been well explored in the secondary literature. See Stewart, *Mediating the Center,* chap. 2.

22. Publication of the *Essays and Reviews* in England (London, 1860) has sometimes been compared to the appearance of David Friedrich Strauss's *Life of Jesus* (1835) in Germany as the pivotal event that forced the problem of faith and secular learning to the forefront of theological discussion. See Ieuan Ellis, *Seven Against Christ: A Study of "Essays and Reviews,"* Studies in the History of Christian Thought, vol. 23 (Leiden: E. J. Brill, 1980).

23. Henry Longueville Mansel, *The Limits of Religious Thought Examined* (London, 1858).

24. Hodge considered the strand in British religious thought represented by Samuel Taylor Coleridge to be largely derivative. He did not have much to say about him in the

We shall not expect him to have thought any more highly of the theologians of the "Oxford School." The contexts in which he would have occasion to refer to the Tractarians in the *Systematic Theology* are predictable. Tract 85 is mentioned on tradition and authority (1:106, 127). John Henry Newman, "one of the richest prizes gained by the Romanists from the Church of England in this generation" (3:454), is quoted by name on the teaching authority of the church (1:124, 126-27), ecclesiastical miracles (3:454), relics (3:459-61), and the Protestant identification of the pope with the Antichrist (3:818-19, 822). E. B. Pusey is quoted for his objections to "the cruel invention of purgatory" (3:752-53, 756). The doctrine of baptism provides the occasion for mentioning William Palmer on the church (3:543). Presumably, we would hear much more about the Tractarians if Hodge had reached the fifth part of his grand system, which was to have been devoted to ecclesiology — oddly located after the Last Things. (The inclusion of baptism and the Lord's Supper in part three, on Soteriology, is also, to say the least, unusual.) Hodge thought the *Tracts for the Times* could be regarded as "among the most important ephemerical [*sic*] productions of the day." He judged their content to be a case for popery without the pope. The "second reformation" that the Tracts called for would be a step back to the system against which the sixteenth-century Reformers, not least the English Reformers, had struggled and protested: that is, the church understood as the storehouse of grace and the sacraments, dispensed by episcopally ordained clergy, as the instruments for conveying it to individuals.[25] "The Reformed churches have ever considered Christ and justification by faith in his merits, as the great center of the Christian system. The Oxford Tract writers make the church the main point: the church as an ordinance for conveying life to all its members by means of the sacraments."[26]

Systematic Theology, though he mentioned (1:180) the views on inspiration held by Coleridge and his "friends and followers": Arnold, Hare, and F. D. Maurice. By "Dr. Arnold" Hodge meant Thomas Arnold, who was one of the broad churchmen, better known as the headmaster of Rugby.

25. Charles Hodge, "Oxford Tracts," BRPR 10 (1838): 84-119, a review of *Tracts for the Times,* by members of the University of Oxford, 2d ed., 3 vols. (London, 1837); see pp. 84, 93, 99, 116, 118. Also pertinent are "Bishop Doane and the Oxford Tracts," BRPR 13 (1841): 450-62, and "Theories of the Church," BRPR 18 (1846): 137-58, reprinted in *ER,* pp. 201-20.

26. Hodge, "Oxford Tracts," p. 88.

The virtues of the British mind notwithstanding, Hodge found much to criticize in its characteristic theological products. But he retained his respect even in disagreement. A noticeable difference of tone pervaded his observations on French religious thought, and I can consider them much more briefly before turning to the Germans. The two French thinkers of whom he had most to say were Victor Cousin and Auguste Comte. Cousin he saw as an unoriginal pantheist (*ST* 1:63, 301), and he was plainly piqued by his Gallic personality. He did not believe Cousin had done much more than transmit German pantheism to France, and he thought the French language ill suited to the task. In his *Introduction to the History of Philosophy* (French 1828; English 1832), Cousin had found no reason to consider England or Scotland, Germany and France being taken for the only countries worthy of notice. Hodge quoted him as saying: "England, gentlemen, is a very considerable island; in England *everything stops at certain limits,* nothing is there developed on a great scale." The remark needed no refutation; it was sufficient to describe it as a "truly French statement."[27]

Comte's Positivism earned a long excursus in the *Systematic Theology* (1:245-62) with copious quotations from the condensed English version of the *Philosophie positive* by Harriet Martineau (2 vols., London, 1835; New York, 1855). Naturally, Hodge alluded to Comte's "religion of humanity," in which the object of public worship was to be humanity itself, and he supposed that merely to state its leading features was sufficient to establish its absurdity. He gave rather more space, albeit not one bit more credence, to Comte's law of human development. Comte believed that the human race as a whole and each individual pass through three distinct stages, in which events are respectively attributed to supernatural causes (the theological stage), referred to invisible forces (the metaphysical stage), or simply connected with one another in relations of resemblance and sequence (the positive stage). Theories of development seem always to have made Hodge nervous. Comte's theory he dismissed partly by enlisting the aid of the infidel T. H. Huxley, who had exposed it as unscientific. Of Comte's system, then, Hodge concluded triumphantly: "Among the

27. Hodge, "Transcendentalism," BRPR 11 (1839): 37-101; see p. 54n. And yet Hodge himself began this article with the admission that "metaphysical research" in Britain was at a standstill and had been so longer in England than in Scotland (pp. 37-38).

advanced men of science in England, there is scarcely one so poor as to do it reverence" (1:262).[28]

III. The Germans and Hodge's European Journey

References to the contemporary German theologians are scattered with a generous hand throughout Hodge's *Systematic Theology*, and they cover the entire range of the Protestant "schools": rationalist, right-wing Hegelian and left-wing Hegelian, confessionalist, and mediating schools as well as the schools of Tübingen and Erlangen. There is no need to call the entire roll.[29] Hodge didn't merely drop names but often gave exact quotations. Some of his favorites may at first glance seem surprising. There are several references to D. F. Strauss's dogmatics, for instance — more than the index lists.[30] The explanation lies partly in Hodge's characterization of him as "the most candid of the recent philosophical theologians" (1:414). Strauss made no effort to conceal the departure of much German theology from traditional Christian be-

---

28. Charles Cashdollar has shown that Positivism reached its peak relatively late, in the 1870s and early 1880s — that is, after Comte's death — and that it was perceived in both Britain and America as the most serious challenge of the time to religious belief. See Charles D. Cashdollar, *The Transformation of Theology, 1830-1890: Positivism and Protestant Thought in Britain and America* (Princeton: Princeton University Press, 1989). Cashdollar's book is an outstanding historical achievement, and it proves that Hodge underestimated Positivism. But it is a bit unfair to him to give the impression that he opposed Comte only with the Book of Genesis (p. 278). He thought Positivism had been discredited as bogus science.

29. He also read the Roman Catholics, particularly Johann Adam Moehler (1796-1838), "the ablest and most plausible of the modern defenders of Romanism" (*ST* 3:718). Some of the weightier German Protestants with whom he entered into conversation were F. C. Baur, K. G. Bretschneider, Karl Daub, Wilhelm DeWette, I. A. Dorner, J. H. A. Ebrard, E. W. Hengstenberg, J. C. K. von Hofmann, Philipp Marheineke, Julius Müller, F. A. Philippi, Alexander Schweizer, F. J. Stahl, D. F. Strauss, August Tholuck, August Twesten, Karl Ullmann, J. A. L. Wegscheider — and, of course, Friedrich Schleiermacher. The list could be extended, especially if it included biblical scholars such as Franz Delitzsch and church historians such as August Neander and Karl August von Hase. It is a list that would stand up well in a history of theology; it is astonishing in an English-language work of systematic theology.

30. Hodge usually quotes Strauss's dogmatic work as *Dogmatik*. The German title is *Die christliche Glaubenslehre*, etc. (2 vols., 1840-41).

liefs, and Hodge loved to marshal the troops of honest antitheologians and unbelievers against theological positions he considered pretentious but unstable (3:77).

The foundation of Hodge's extensive knowledge of the German theologians was laid during the European journey. His travels took him from France to Germany, and on the way home he stopped in Switzerland, France, and Britain. The visit to "old England" evoked some deep emotions from him. He wrote to his wife (27 June 1828): "You may suppose it was with a swelling heart I trod upon the soil of the mother country, which, with all her faults, is the most wonderful and admirable the world has ever seen" (*LCH*, p. 200). But it was vacation time. The visits to London, Cambridge, Oxford, and Edinburgh were without opportunity for theological exchange, though Hodge was delighted to hear the leader of the Cambridge evangelicals, Charles Simeon, preach a sermon. Only the stay in Germany can be considered an important influence on Hodge's intellectual formation.[31]

Hodge did not go to Europe to learn about theology. In Paris he worked on his French, Arabic, and Syriac. He moved on to Halle because he heard it was the outstanding university for the study of biblical literature. The main attraction was the reputation of orientalist Wilhelm Gesenius. Hodge had also been drawn by reports of August Tholuck's ability to combine learning and piety, and he took Tholuck's introduction to theology, "principally," as he said, "to gain an acquaintance with the theological literature" (*LCH*, p. 117). This, however, was not the sort of course we would call today "Introduction to Theology," meaning contemporary systematic or constructive theology. It was a course in so-called theological encyclopedia: the aim, he wrote to his mentor Archibald Alexander, was "to give the character of the most important works belonging to each department" (*LCH*, p. 117; cf. p. 119). Hodge kept his focus on Scripture and languages — now including German.

In Berlin, as in Halle, he sought out classes pertinent to his interest in the Scriptures, regularly attending lectures by August Neander,[32] oc-

---

31. He stayed in Halle for a little over seven months (28 February–10 October 1827) and in Berlin for about a month less (12 October 1827–30 April 1828). The principal sources for information on his sojourn in Germany are his journal and letters home. His son used the letters selectively in his biography (chap. 6), on which I depend.

32. The notes he took down on Neander's lectures on the Corinthian letters have survived (*LCH*, p. 153n.).

casionally lectures by E. W. Hengstenberg and the philologist August Böckh. Entirely in keeping with what we know of him, he also obtained permission to sit in on the instruction Alexander von Humboldt was then giving on physical science.[33] But A. A. Hodge gives no indication that his father might have seized the opportunity to sit at the feet of G. W. F. Hegel or Schleiermacher, whom he had met briefly while still in Halle.[34] (And Schleiermacher, it should be remembered, lectured regularly on the New Testament.) He did hear Schleiermacher read a short paper before the Royal Academy of Sciences on "Kings as Authors" (*LCH,* pp. 170-71), and the biography gives a journal extract recording a visit to the Trinity Church — apparently because he couldn't think of anywhere better to go. "I went to hear Schleiermacher, not knowing of any more evangelical preacher who had service in the morning" (*LCH,* p. 152). Hodge found the sermon, on the first and great commandment, "peculiar" and the ideas "vague and indefinite." He was not too sure that he managed to follow it, but his outline of the "drift" sounds plain enough: in brief, Schleiermacher said that the commandment is fulfilled with a willing heart through the work of Christ in renewing our nature. The visit, to be sure, came at the start of his Berlin residence (14 October 1827). In an aside in the *Systematic Theology* (2:440, n. 1), Hodge later tells us that he "often attended Schleiermacher's church." The biography gives no account of other visits; it doesn't say whether they may have proved more edifying than the first, but it does document Hodge's preference for the "evangelical" preachers G. F. A. Strauss (the court preacher) and Emil Gustaf Lisco (pastor of the Marienkirche).

His understanding of the German theological situation did not come, however, from lectures and sermons so much as from the personal friendships he formed with Tholuck in Halle and with the circles of Hengstenberg and the von Gerlach family in Berlin. August Tholuck (1799-1877), who was frequently with Hodge also in Berlin, was especially important.[35] He warned Hodge that the variety of German theological opinions defied classification (*LCH,* p. 121). The influence of the old "Neologists" had given way not only to a new philosophy but to a

33. The biography reports that Hodge kept full notes on these lectures, too, but does not say if they survived (*LCH,* p. 162).

34. The meeting appears to have been casual and without significance. It is reported in Hodge's journal entry for 18 April 1827 (*LCH,* p. 128).

35. See the tribute to Tholuck in *ST* 2:451-52n.

spiritual awakening as well.[36] Professors and students alike were being identified as "pious" or "religious" if they had experienced awakening, and the awakened frequently reaffirmed traditional beliefs that had long been under assault.[37] "Pious" and "orthodox" were not necessarily identical terms. Tholuck certainly believed that "very few of those not religious were orthodox," but apparently the connection was not entirely reversible: he reported that converted Neologists could not shake off their old skepticism, especially with regard to the Old Testament (*LCH*, pp. 121-22).

Tholuck's remarks about the role of "vital religion" in German theology are very interesting, and Hodge later echoed them (as we will see), extending Tholuck's reflections beyond the German context. It has often been pointed out that what was sometimes called "the new pietism" departed from the old (the Pietism of Philip Jakob Spener [1635-1705]) in making itself the guardian of correct belief rather than the critic of orthodox formalism. Always one of the *Herrnhuter* at heart, Schleiermacher found the new pietists *(unsere neuen Frommen)* very different: in an uncharacteristic show of anger, he described them as uncharitable to the point of defaming others, painfully addicted to a handful of formu-

---

36. By the "Neologists" Tholuck presumably meant those among the theologians of the eighteenth-century *Aufklärung* who held that revelation could confirm but not add to the truths of reason, and who understood the task of biblical interpretation in this light (see pp. 27-28 above). It is not entirely clear to me from Hodge's reports how Tholuck perceived the relationships between "Neologists," "Deists," and "Rationalists." The affinity of the Neologists with such English Deists as Matthew Tindal is evident. By the German "Rationalist School" is usually meant Bretschneider, Wegscheider, H. E. G. Paulus, and their friends. Their dominance could certainly be assigned to the period 1790-1815 or 1817, in which Tholuck placed "the prevalence of Rationalism in Germany" (*LCH*, p. 137), whereas the heyday of Neology was earlier. I think Hodge uses the terms more broadly, or less precisely, than most historians would. See Horst Stephan, *Geschichte der deutschen evangelischen Theologie seit dem deutschen Idealismus*, 2d ed., revised by Martin Schmidt (Berlin: Alfred Töpelmann, 1960), pp. 9-13. Tholuck credited the 1817 theses of Claus Harms with initiating the revolt against the Rationalists, but they hardly played dead; Schleiermacher attended lectures by Wegscheider at Halle (*LCH*, p. 178).

37. Other terms used to designate evangelical ministers were "positive" and "believing." By now "evangelical," once the banner of the Protestant churches in general (both Lutheran and Reformed), had been hijacked as the name for a party within Protestantism. In one passage in his journal (23 March 1828), Hodge even distinguished "Christians" from "liberals" and assigned Schleiermacher to the liberals (*LCH*, p. 178).

las by which they divided everyone into black or white, and resistant to open-minded enquiry.[38] But the religious awakening was by no means confined to one party. Tholuck told Hodge that even the new philosophy had nurtured a "deep religious feeling" in contrast to the system it displaced (*LCH,* p. 120). What, then, are we to understand by the new German philosophy?

From Tholuck Hodge learned that Hegelian speculation had eclipsed not only Kant's critical idealism but the systems of Fichte and Schelling as well. The speculative spirit seduced even the biblical theologians, unless the influence of religion on their hearts restrained them. A journal entry for 6 March 1827 shows Hodge still struggling a bit to understand his new friend and teacher, but beginning to grasp the main point: German religious thought had become pantheistic.

> The reigning philosopher of the day is Hegel. Schleiermacher has a system of his own. The present systems are all Pantheistic. Hegel and Schleiermacher both deny the personality of the Deity and the individuality of the soul of man. The universal principle with them is God, and, according to Hegel, the world itself is the Realität of the Deity, and all it contains, the different races of men, and the animals in their various orders, are all modes of existence of this one universal principle. This, at least, is the idea I got from Tholuck's description [*LCH,* p. 119].

The catchword from then on, whenever Hodge considered German religious thought, was "pantheism," represented not by the Hegelians alone but also by Schleiermacher. Indeed, Hodge felt that even Tholuck himself, who denied the dualism of matter and spirit, was not unaffected by the new philosophy (*LCH,* p. 119; cf. p. 140).

The next day (8 March 1827), Tholuck put in a good word for Schleiermacher: "His authority stands so high," he said, "that the respect which he manifests for the Bible, and the reverence with which he speaks of Jesus Christ, has [*sic*] great influence." Tholuck testified that Schleiermacher had been the "means of awakening the attention to religion of many young men," including Neander, and that he himself owed

---

38. Friedrich Schleiermacher, *On Religion: Speeches to its Cultured Despisers,* trans. John Oman from the 3rd German ed. of 1821 (1894; reprinted Louisville: Westminster John Knox, 1994), speech III, explanation 4, pp. 144-45 (German in KGA I/12:178).

"much of his religious feeling to Schleiermacher's influence" (*LCH,* p. 120).[39] On a subsequent occasion (14 March 1827), Tholuck informed Hodge that Schleiermacher in fact rejected "the appellation of Panthe- ist" (p. 122), and he read him some passages from Schleiermacher's *The Christian Faith.* "But," says Hodge, "they seemed to me to darken coun- sel by words without wisdom" (p. 123). Just a few days later (20 March), Tholuck mentioned that Schleiermacher, who belonged to the Re- formed Church, was an outspoken champion of some of the distinc- tively Reformed doctrines (p. 123).

In sum, Tholuck gave Hodge a warning about the complexities of the German theological situation in general and painted a complex por- trait for him of Schleiermacher in particular. Upon his return to Prince- ton, however, Hodge felt himself equipped by his journey to present his students with a simple classification of German theologians into three main parties: orthodox, rationalist, and pantheist. And he echoed Tholuck's sentiments on the connection between vital piety and ortho- doxy.[40] On the whole, then, he seems to have fulfilled Archibald Alexan- der's prayer and wish for him: "I pray God to keep you from the poison of Neology! I wish you to come home enriched with Biblical learning, but abhorring German philosophy and theology."[41] We must ask next whether the increasing complexity — indeed, the fragmentation — of the German scene, with which he tried to remain in touch, moved Hodge to make some later adjustments to his classification scheme for the German theologians, or to think again about Schleiermacher's place in it.[42]

---

39. Later, in Berlin, Neander pointed out to Hodge the shift in Schleiermacher's thinking from *Über die Religion* to *Der christliche Glaube,* evident in his later affirmation of the personal existence of the soul after death (*LCH,* p. 184). As the religious parties be- came increasingly polarized, Neander himself moved closer to Schleiermacher's side (see Otto von Gerlach to Hodge, 28 February 1834, *LCH,* p. 184). It is also worth noting that even Neander was willing to defend the expression that worried Hodge, "Alles Seyn ist das Seyn Gottes" (*LCH,* p. 181).

40. Hodge, "Lecture Addressed to the Students of the Theological Seminary" (BRPR 1829), in Noll, *Princeton Theology,* p. 111.

41. Alexander to Hodge, 27 July 1827, in *LCH,* p. 161. No doubt, the "poison of Neology" refers to the skeptical approach of the Neologists to Scripture, noted by Tholuck. But Alexander's use of the term "Neology" seems anachronistic.

42. One indication of problems in Hodge's scheme is that, whereas he saw Schleiermacher as pantheist, he classified his disciple Twesten (who eventually suc-

IV. Pantheism and the Fragmentation of German Theology

A decade after the European trip, Hodge knew well that Schleier-macher's prestige had waned. His was no longer the most influential voice in German theology, and his followers were no longer the leading school. The prevalent system was Hegel's, and it had "diffused itself" to a remarkable degree among the educated of all classes: not reclusive professors and speculative theologians only, but also statesmen, poets, scientists, and journalists. It had become, as Hodge nicely put it, the form in which the German mind then existed and exhibited itself to other nations. The Hegelian school had divided into the right and the left, and the left had divided again into center left and extreme left. At the extreme Hodge perceived a breakdown not only of truth, but of public decency, too (that is, a flaunting of the embodied, sensual side of human nature). Still, Hegelianism remained one school: in a word, it was "pantheism."[43]

Relying on the authority of some of Hegelianism's most vociferous critics — Hengstenberg, Tholuck, and Heinrich Leo — Hodge piled his own scorn on top of theirs. D. F. Strauss's *Life of Jesus* (1835) was now the focus of theological contention, creating a sensation "almost without parallel" in Germany. Strauss denied the existence of a personal God: the Infinite Spirit had reality only in the finite spirits of humanity, in whom it attained self-consciousness; and they in turn found their reality — and their only immortality — in the Infinite Spirit. The incarnation of God did not occur once and for all in Christ; it was occurring constantly in the endless succession of individuals in the human race. Christ's person and fate were simply the occasion of awakening the consciousness of humanity to the truth of its identity with God, and the gospel "history" was in the main a mythological byproduct of the consciousness of this truth. Patent surrender of fundamental Christian

---

ceeded to his chair at the University of Berlin) as orthodox (*LCH,* pp. 142-43). This surely presumed a fundamental opposition between them that neither one would have acknowledged, whatever their differences.

43. Hodge, "Latest Form of Infidelity," pp. 101-3. In this article (p. 126), Hodge asserted that the Germans managed to isolate their philosophy, so that when the Hegelian Philipp Marheineke turned his hand to writing on the German Reformation, the result was good, plain history. How this observation is to be harmonized with the alleged Hegelianizing of every aspect of German culture, Hodge did not explain.

truths was covered up by the argument that there was no dishonesty in freely using the language of the imagination *(Vorstellung)*; the unsophisticated believer was reassured to hear the conventional religious language, and the philosopher knew what it really meant.[44]

> Such, then, is this Latest Form of Infidelity. It knows no intelligent or conscious God but man; it admits no incarnation, but the eternal incarnation of the universal spirit in the human race; the personality of men ceases with their present existence, they are but momentary manifestations of the infinite and unending; there is neither sin nor holiness; neither heaven nor hell. Such are the results to which the proud philosophy of the nineteenth century has brought its followers.[45]

Hodge conceded that the overthrow of deism had given pantheism a semblance of truth: in place of an absentee deity, pantheism affirmed a God who is ever present and ever active. And it was winning its advocates beyond Germany — in France, England, even America. Samuel Taylor Coleridge was an Englishman, preserved from excess by his native disposition and his familiarity with the Bible. Cousin, on the other hand, was a vain Frenchman, on whose mind the Scriptures had left no strong impression. In America, Hodge expected the progress of pantheism to be stemmed by the power of true religion and the national character inherited from the English: "A sanity of intellect, an incapacity to see wonders in nonsense, is the leading trait of the English mind. The Germans can believe anything." It is this "want of adaptation" — this happy inability of the Anglo-American mind to adapt to German ways of thinking — that made Hodge find Ralph Waldo Emerson's transcendentalism ludicrous and profane.[46]

In 1846, only a few years after his scornful reflections on the latest German infidelity, Hodge described a Hegelian empire that was not just divided but crumbling, and he could see no new cultural force taking its place. Pantheism or self-deification was still "the prevailing form of

44. Hodge, "Latest Form of Infidelity," pp. 110, 108. Hodge's summary clearly had D. F. Strauss chiefly in mind, though not exclusively. Even though he could make use of Strauss to unmask the duplicity of others, he thought Strauss himself guilty of duplicity in his adoption of the Hegelian contrast between *Vorstellung* and *Begriff.*

45. Hodge, "Latest Form of Infidelity," p. 119.

46. Hodge, "Latest Form of Infidelity," pp. 20-26; quotation on p. 125.

German infidelity," but the centrifugal forces had thrown everything into confusion. The simple, threefold classification of German theologians had begun to dissolve in what Hodge called "a state of active fermentation." Alongside the rationalists and the confessionalists, he now wrote of "the German Catholics." These were the three he now identified as the leading parties, "or the principal elements in the struggling mass." But their subdivisions were almost endless.[47] Greeted initially as advocates of reform within the "Romish" Church, the German Catholics quickly proved that they did not want emancipation from the errors and oppressions of Rome, but from the gospel. They believed that the church's day — the day of doctrinal Christianity — was over and that the state "should set forth the vaguest possible confession of faith, and require all to submit to it."[48]

Among the Protestants, Hodge reported, the extreme left of the rationalists was styled "Protestant Friends" or "Friends of Light." There was nothing novel in their attack on church dogma, but they generated a good deal of excitement because they pitched their appeal directly to the masses. Academic rationalism, in fact, was now represented in the theological faculties only by a few old men, except at Giessen. The ranks of the Friends of Light actually included advocates of pantheism, who had similarly moved philosophy out of the classroom into the pulpit and the popular press. A determined reaction from the growing number of the friends of evangelical doctrine followed: in their opinion, pastors who popularized "atheism" should not be tolerated in the church; they should be deposed.[49]

Clearly, Hodge was no longer talking only about theological disagreement. As the old boundaries between "schools" eroded in the

47. Hodge, "Religious State of Germany," BRPR 18 (1846): 514-46; see pp. 527, 545, 514. The article is a review of the 1845 volume of Hengstenberg's *Evangelische Kirchenzeitung,* the organ of the evangelical party.

48. Hodge, "Religious State of Germany," p. 522. Hengstenberg also took account of a more conservative group calling itself "the Protestant or Christian Catholics," which was itself split into two (pp. 524-25).

49. Hodge, "Religious State of Germany," pp. 525-58. Strauss is credited in part with bringing the Hegelian philosophy down from the ivory tower of the universities (p. 527). "Feuerback" (i.e., Ludwig Feuerbach) is also named in a quotation (p. 528), but Hodge does not pursue Feuerbach's declaration that theology is anthropology, and religion illusion.

flood, *parties* became determinative: that is, coalitions formed to win the populace and influence the ecclesiastical and civil authorities. Declarations in the *Evangelische Kirchenzeitung,* signed by hundreds of clergymen of the evangelical party, denounced other, unbelieving clergy by name. Moderates and even many of the evangelicals themselves were appalled and protested against the declarations. This suggested to Hodge yet another threefold division: "Thus, three parties were formed": Hengstenberg's confessionalists, the Friends of Light, and "this middle party composed chiefly of the followers of Schleiermacher."[50] The painful record of fragmentation and polarization continued as Hodge noted that the Schleiermacherian center itself fell into two divisions. One was "composed of those who by his [Schleiermacher's] influence were brought to Christ, and then from Him, the only true Master, learned the truth." The other consisted of "mere disciples," committed to Schleiermacher's hopeless program of harmonizing church doctrine and rationalism, but without the inspiration of his personality.[51]

I cannot delay over Hodge's summary of Hengstenberg's case against the theology of Schleiermacher's school.[52] (I shall come back to Hodge's own case shortly, which echoes Hengstenberg's.) Nor is there any point in looking into the acrimonious trading of insults between Schleiermacher's party and Hengstenberg's.[53] Fourteen years later, in

50. Hodge, "Religious State of Germany," pp. 528-30. Hodge described Hengstenberg's party as "the advocates of the standards of the church" (p. 514). The opposition called them "pietists," "strict orthodox," or — less politely — "the church magazine party." They called themselves "church minded" or "friends of the confession" (p. 531n.).

51. Hodge, "Religious State of Germany," pp. 530-31. Hodge used "Rationalism" loosely with reference to Schleiermacher's program: he knew that the champions of the Rationalist School were among the most vigorous adversaries of Schleiermacher ("Latest Form of Infidelity," p. 98). Among the "personal friends and pupils of Schleiermacher" he elsewhere named Friedrich Lücke, Ullmann, and Twesten ("Latest Form of Infidelity," p. 101). In his journal, he said of Lücke that he "appears to be a great friend of Schleiermacher, although reckoned as belonging to the orthodox party" (*LCH,* p. 191), and in a later article he singled out Twesten as belonging to "the most moderate and orthodox class of Schleiermacher's disciples": "The Theology of the Intellect and That of the Feelings, II" (BRPR 1851), in *ER,* p. 99 n. 1. See further *ST* 2:532-33, where Hodge suggested that if Schleiermacher did not strictly found a school, he did introduce an influential method.

52. Hodge, "Religious State of Germany," pp. 531-41.

53. Schleiermacher's friends have always seen him as gentle and irenic, never speaking a harsh word unless provoked beyond human endurance. Hengstenberg insisted that

an interesting essay titled "What is Christianity?" (1860), Hodge offered a further glimpse of the picture he entertained of the theological situation in Germany and beyond, and I turn to it for my final testimony on the subject. The breakup of Schleiermacher's school, we learn, continued. The numerous divisions all "depart[ed] more or less from the great master whose authority they recognize[d]." Though Hodge might have continued to speak of "the Schleiermacher system" from its acknowledged author, the designation had really become too restrictive in view of the modifications it had undergone. He now, in fact, distinguished three groups *within* the school of Schleiermacher: those who like him were pantheists at heart; those who were theists but not trinitarians; and "those who sincerely endeavour[ed] to bring their theory into harmony with the doctrine of the Bible, and especially with the doctrine of the Trinity." It was not possible anymore to hold one disciple responsible for the teaching of another. Most of them were theists, even though "the substratum of Schleiermacher's system was Pantheism."[54]

From Tholuck Hodge had learned that Schleiermacher repudiated the charge of pantheism. Over the years, however, he had evidently become increasingly convinced that a pantheistic philosophy underlay Schleiermacher's theological program, even if some of his disciples had managed to overcome it. Hodge had nothing against philosophy: "Every theology is in one sense a form of philosophy. To understand any theological system, therefore, we must understand the philosophy which underlies it, and gives it its peculiar form."[55] The trouble was that Schleiermacher picked a bad philosophy — a philosophy "almost entirely foreign to the ordinary modes of thought among Americans and Englishmen." The conclusion at which German speculation had arrived in the hands of Hegel and Schelling was "the unity of the divine and human, of God and man," and Schleiermacher's philosophy, in Hodge's

---

the first provocation actually came when Schleiermacher announced (with Hengstenberg's party in mind): "The ground is heaving beneath our feet, and miserable worms are crawling out from religious crevices, who regard all speculation, beyond the circumvallation of the ancient letter, as satanic" (quoted by Hodge, "Religious State of Germany," p. 531). This outburst Hengstenberg judged worth an article in reply.

54. Hodge, "What is Christianity?" BRPR 32 (1860): 118-61, ostensibly a review of books by William Cunningham, Ullmann, and Robert Wilberforce, but largely directed against Nevin; see pp. 121, 131n, 138.

55. Hodge, "What is Christianity?" p. 121.

opinion, "was scarcely less avowedly pantheistic than that of Spinoza or Hegel." Schleiermacher's Moravian training had induced him to try presenting philosophical ideas alien to the church in a Christian garb. But he had failed, bequeathing to his more orthodox successors the problem of bringing the deification of man, which is the worst form of atheism, into harmony with theism and the gospel. Hodge did not believe that the disciples had any better success than their teacher.[56]

In sum, Hodge was fascinated by German theology, but what he said of it seems always to have sounded a note of warning. "Few parts of the world present so much to interest the Christian," he said, "as Germany in its present state. Its elements of power for good or evil are immense."[57] As he surveyed the entire world of European theology at the end of the second third of the nineteenth century, he saw the Germans bewitched by a pantheistic philosophy that was extending its pernicious influence to the French and Anglo-Saxon peoples. Actually, he thought, the doctrine of Schelling and Hegel had by then been recognized in Germany, by friends and foes alike, as irreconcilable with Christianity.[58] As for Schleiermacher's followers, they had become hopelessly divided, though they were all frantically engaged in the same impossible task of mediation: they were "reduced to the sad necessity of either holding a philosophy in conflict with their theology, or of explaining away the plainest teachings of the Bible." In the eyes of the Germans themselves, the mediating theology *(Vermittelungstheologie)* had already passed away. Sadly, it survived elsewhere as an item of export. "It is unfortunate," Hodge complained in his best Olympian tone, "that the sun does not rise on America until it begins to set on Germany.... [The mediating theology] served for a while to occupy the German mind, and then was shipped to America."[59]

56. Hodge, "What is Christianity?" pp. 121-23.

57. Hodge, "Religious State of Germany," p. 545. I recall only one issue on which Hodge drew attention to an influence going the other way: in this same essay, he said it was obvious that the German controversy over church polity ("the church question") drew on the Free Church controversy in Scotland (p. 543).

58. Hodge, "What is Christianity?" p. 122. In his *Systematic Theology* he observed that for a new generation in Germany, the philosophy of Schelling, Hegel, and Schleiermacher had become a thing of the past. A new materialism had taken its place: "The German mind has swung round from making spirit everything, to making it nothing" (*ST* 1:533 n. 1).

59. "What is Christianity?" pp. 135, 157. See also *ST* 2:452-54. The journal *Theologische Studien und Kritiken* was founded in 1828 as the organ of the mediating program,

V. Schleiermacher Found Wanting

Schleiermacher was something of an enigma to Hodge. He did not question the man's stature. "Schleiermacher," he wrote, "is regarded as the most interesting as well as the most influential theologian of modern times" (ST 2:440). However, "he was not and could not be self-consistent." Hodge's point was that Schleiermacher could not be consistent as he went about the attempt to reconcile contradictory doctrines. But he immediately went on to state the inconsistency as a disharmony between Schleiermacher's personal religion and his theological speculations, not between one doctrine and another. From the Moravians he learned a "reverence for Christ" that he retained all his life. In a footnote Hodge offered this warm testimony:

> When in Berlin the writer often attended Schleiermacher's church. The hymns to be sung were printed on slips of paper and distributed at the doors. They were always evangelical and spiritual in an eminent degree, filled with praise and gratitude to our Redeemer. Tholuck said that Schleiermacher, when sitting in the evening with his family, would often say, "Hush, children; let us sing a hymn of praise to Christ." Can we doubt that he is singing those praises now? To whomsoever Christ is God, St. John assures us, Christ is a Saviour.[60]

Sadly, in Hodge's opinion, the Moravian piety never found an adequate expression in the doctrines of this "very extraordinary man": his theol-

---

which sought to accommodate biblical faith to modern thought. Its advocates looked to Schleiermacher's dogmatics as the model of the mediating ideal. But in their ranks are usually included, besides such Schleiermacherians as Twesten and Schweizer, some of the "awakened" or "pectoral" theologians (Tholuck, Neander, Müller) and the more speculative Dorner and Richard Rothe, who were as much indebted to Hegel as to Schleiermacher. Hodge believed that Schleiermacher's mediating program was inherently unstable: those who thought to further it were bound either to move on to something worse (Hegelian "atheism") or else to turn back to the Bible ("Latest Form of Infidelity," p. 125).

60. ST 1:440, n. 1. A passage in "Latest Form of Infidelity" also mentions Schleiermacher's fondness, both at home and in church, for hymns that Hodge could endorse as "of correct sentiment" (pp. 98-99). He describes Schleiermacher as "a very extraordinary man," who "made Christ the centre of his mystical system" and was, in fact, "a worshipper of Christ." Later in this same article, he writes approvingly of Schleiermacher's contempt for Pelagians as well as for rationalists (pp. 124-25).

ogy and his religion were two very different things (*ST* 1:452, 534). Perhaps Hodge had Schleiermacher in mind when he remarked in general: "It is a great mercy that, at least in some cases, those whose philosophy forbids their believing in the personality of God, believe in the personality of Christ, whom they regard as a man invested with all the attributes of the Godhead, and whom they love and worship accordingly" (1:439).[61]

Recall Tholuck's belief that spiritual awakening promotes correct doctrine. Hodge echoed it in the lecture he gave to his Princeton students after his return from Germany: reverence for the Redeemer, he assured them, is the vital piety that preserves the soul from infidelity when all else has failed.[62] If reverence for the Redeemer did *not* keep Schleiermacher from holding incorrect beliefs, he must, after all, have been an exception. "As a general rule, a man's faith is the expression of his inward life" (*ST* 2:443). Hodge could exercise a judgment of charity when *vital piety* was made the measure of a theologian — that is, finding in Christ the object of highest devotion. "Every true worshipper of Christ," he asserted, "must in his heart recognize as a Christian brother, wherever he may be found, any one who loves, worships, and trusts the Lord Jesus Christ as God manifest in the flesh and the only Saviour of men" (3:136). But Hodge found dogmatic security in the old ecclesiastical formulas, which in his view were to be resolutely repeated, not examined critically and revised as needed. Hence he warned: "The man should tremble, who ventures to say: I believe in Jesus Christ our Saviour, unless he believes in his true and perfect Godhead. For only on that assumption is he a Saviour or an object of faith."[63] Here the relation between piety and theology seems to be reversed: the measure of the theologian — indeed, the test of piety — is *correct belief.* And where does that leave Schleiermacher? Hodge found his doctrine of Christ's person seriously flawed.

The theological points at issue between Hodge and Schleiermacher are often subtle, not to be disposed of with a simple formula or two.

---

61. On one traditional doctrine, the soul's survival of death, Hodge observes: "There is good reason to believe that . . . Schleiermacher sacrificed his philosophy, *as he certainly did in other points,* to his religion" (*ST* 1:303; my emphasis).

62. Hodge, "Lecture to the Students," in Noll, *Princeton Theology*, pp. 111, 113 (cf. *LCH*, p. 204).

63. Hodge, "Religious State of Germany," p. 520.

They are also important and fascinating, and they deserve much more detail than I can offer here. Hodge rightly insisted: "His [Schleiermacher's] doctrine concerning Christ is so implicated with his peculiar views on anthropology, on theology, and on the relation of God to the world, that it can neither be fully presented nor properly appreciated except as an integral part of his whole system" (ST 2:442). My modest purpose is only to note the main points at which Hodge introduced criticisms of Schleiermacher in the Systematic Theology and at least to open the question, Do the criticisms appear to rest on a sound understanding of him? This, of course, will leave the historical agenda open and will postpone to another day entirely the more properly theological question, Which of the two, if either, was right on the disputed issues — Hodge or Schleiermacher?

The index to the Systematic Theology lists twenty-nine references to Schleiermacher, one more than the references to Calvin. (Augustine earns still more, Turretin fewer.) I would not wish to infer too much from this perhaps surprisingly generous number of references to Schleiermacher — beyond noting that they afford solid evidence of a continuing preoccupation with this "very extraordinary man." They vary in length; some of them overlap; and in any case the index is selective. But what are the theological issues that led Hodge to refer to Schleiermacher's views, whether the references were included in the index or not? A closer look discloses, first of all, four excursuses that appraise Schleiermacher's theories on the dogmatic themes under discussion: three shorter ones, on the "mystical" theory of religion (ST 1:65-66), revelation and inspiration (1:173-79), and sin (2:138-40); and a much longer one (already referred to) on the person and work of Christ (2:440-54; cf. 3:211-12). Second, there are a number of scattered allusions to Schleiermacher's understanding of the divine attributes (1:370, 376, 395, 398, 401-2, 411, 417, 428),[64] secondary causation in relation to the feeling of absolute dependence (1:592-94, 604), and the doctrine of the

---

64. Hodge conceded that for the seventeenth-century divines, both Lutherans and Reformed, the divine "simplicity" made it impossible to allow any real distinctions between one attribute and another; and he evidently recognized that this put Schleiermacher on the side of orthodoxy, whereas he himself wanted to take the distinctions among the various divine attributes in Scripture at face value (ST 1:394-96). It does not seem to have occurred to him that this might call for second thoughts on Schleiermacher's — and his own — relation to the dogmatic tradition.

Trinity (1:481, 534; 2:445).[65] Third, reference is made in passing to his thoughts on theological method (1:9; cf. 2:532), historical development (1:118-19), the soul's survival of death (1:302-3; 2:57), miracles (2:448), grace (2:731-32), the unity of body and soul (3:19), the unity of God and the world (3:20), and humanity as the existence form of God on earth (3:20; cf. 1:176).

Each of the points at issue deserves more careful attention than I can offer here. In any case, simply to locate Hodge's references to Schleiermacher under their several dogmatic rubrics, which often overlap, does not in itself determine the springs from which his criticisms came. I think it can safely be said that he traced all Schleiermacher's mistakes to two sources: a defective method and commitment to a pantheistic philosophy. The two were closely connected in Hodge's mind. It would not be mistaken to say, more simply, that he discovered but one source of error in Schleiermacher's theology: the imposition of a pantheistic idea of God on everything else in the system.[66] But I will comment first on the question of method.

Hodge's objection to Schleiermacher's theological method was that it allegedly negated biblical authority by deriving doctrines from the religious consciousness, whereas we ought rather to "find in the Bible the norm and standard of all genuine religious experience" (*ST* 1:11, 16). Sometimes the warmth of Hodge's convictions led him to state the accusation incautiously: he was simply wrong to assert that Schleiermacher allowed the Scriptures no authority as a rule of faith (1:66); or

---

65. Cf. Hodge, "What is Christianity?" p. 160. Though he admitted that the ecclesiastical doctrine of the Trinity could not be "adequately proved by any citation of biblical passages" (*ST* 1:446), Hodge thought it well enough established by construction from the several constituent elements attested in Scripture that the church "has always refused to recognize as Christians those who reject this doctrine" (1:443). The Trinity was important to him because, he believed, it provided a foothold for belief in God's personality (2:392). Schleiermacher's approach to the Trinity and every other church dogma was entirely different and, in Hodge's eyes, put his credentials as a Christian theologian in doubt. See Schleiermacher, *CG*, §§170-72 (pp. 738-51); cf. §96 (pp. 391-98).

66. The connection between the two sources of error becomes plain in Hodge's remarks on revelation and inspiration: for the mystic or pantheist, revelation cannot be "the communication of new truth" (*ST* 1:65-66), and "if the supernatural be impossible, inspiration is impossible" (1:168). Revelation and inspiration, as Hodge understood them, require a personal, extramundane God who may act directly, not only mediately through fixed laws (1:173).

that he made all theology consist in what the sense of dependence teaches us (1:376); or that he wove a whole system of theology "out of the materials furnished by *his own* religious consciousness" (2:441; my emphasis).[67] It may not be wrong, but it misses the point to say that Schleiermacher's "appeals to the Scriptures in support of his peculiar doctrines are extremely rare, and merely incidental" (2:443). The point, which wholly eluded Hodge, is that in Schleiermacher's view it falls to *exegetical* theology to judge whether doctrinal positions are genuinely Christian, whereas the task of *dogmatic* theology is to present Christian doctrines systematically in their distinctively evangelical (that is, Protestant) form. Hence the proximate court of appeal in *The Christian Faith* is of necessity provided by the Protestant confessions of faith — another point that Hodge seems never to have noticed.[68] And this carries with it the obligation always to formulate a doctrine in relation to the official teachings *(Lehrsätze)* of the church, although they must always be tested and not merely parroted.[69] What is certainly true of Schleiermacher's theological method is that he thought it always needful to ask whether there were better ways than the old ecclesiastical dogmas had devised to bring the church's language into conformity with actual Christian (not just religious!) experience. Any suggestion that he simply set aside Scripture and church doctrine flies in the face of what he actually does, chapter by chapter, in his entire dogmatic masterwork.

In his more circumspect moments, however, Hodge (following Hengstenberg) put his finger on precisely the real issue: it is about the *nature* of the Bible's canonical authority (*ST* 2:443).[70] For Hodge, the Scrip-

---

67. Like so many of the critics, Hodge seems to confuse what Schleiermacher says about the abstract essence of religion with what he says about the concrete essence of Christian faith, which is the actual subject of *The Christian Faith*. See my response to Emil Brunner in B. A. Gerrish, *Tradition and the Modern World: Reformed Theology in the Nineteenth Century* (1978; reprint, Eugene, OR: Wipf & Stock, 2007), chap. 1.

68. See Schleiermacher, *CG*, §27. Given the fact that *The Christian Faith* is intended as a work of dogmatic, not exegetical, theology, the index of Scripture references might even be considered surprisingly bountiful.

69. Hodge therefore misses the mark once more, at least as far as Schleiermacher himself is concerned, when he says that the mediating theology does not "pretend to be founded on the Bible" or "profess allegiance to the Church doctrine" (*ST* 1:453). See also Hodge, "Religious State of Germany," pp. 533-34, and "What is Christianity?" pp. 121, 131.

70. Cf. Hodge, "Religious State of Germany," p. 532, where he states Hengstenberg's criticisms of the school of Schleiermacher.

tures have their authority as a "storehouse of facts" (1:10), or of truths and doctrines, supernaturally communicated (by revelation) and preserved from error (by inspiration) — except for a few minor mistakes that the Christian shouldn't worry about (1:56, 155, 170, 176-77; 2:441). For Schleiermacher, the Scriptures of the New Testament both mediate and norm Christian faith in the present insofar as they contain Christ's self-testimony and the original preaching of Christ by his first disciples.[71] To be sure, Hodge's statement even of the real issue is hostile. He identified the *experience* of the apostles and early Christians as Schleiermacher's theological norm and added: "He denies that the interpretation which they gave of their experience has normal [i.e., normative] authority for us, that is, he says that we are not bound to believe what the Apostles believed" (2:443). In fact, as I have indicated in his own words, Schleiermacher spoke of the apostolic *preaching* as the norm; but he held that the way Christians think today need not be restricted to the actual language of the apostolic norm.[72] Still, Hodge evidently recognized the issue: not whether, but why the Scriptures are authoritative.

As for the pantheistic philosophy, Hodge believed that it had brought about a revolution in theology (*ST* 2:730; 3:650). He was convinced that it was the foundation of everything else in Schleiermacher's dogmatics: his thoughts on revelation, historical development, Christ, humanity, miracles, sin and grace, prayer (3:695), the Lord's Supper (3:656-57), and the afterlife (3:715). Hodge took pains to say what he understood by "pantheism" or "monism": not a naive identification of the world and God, but the affirmation of their essential unity (2:444), in particular the essential unity of God and humanity (2:731).[73] God and world are correlative concepts: one of the most familiar aphorisms of

---

71. Schleiermacher, *CG*, §§128-29.

72. The difference between Hodge and Schleiermacher on what makes Scripture authoritative entailed divergent estimates of the Old Testament, to which Schleiermacher allowed no dogmatic authority (*CG*, §27.3 [p. 115]). A further consequence is that although both claimed scientific status for their methods, Schleiermacher's "facts" were empirical (open to direct experience), while Hodge's were contained in reports that had to be taken on faith (*ST* 1:9, 11, 20-21). See further my essay "Friedrich Schleiermacher" (1985), reprinted in *Continuing the Reformation*, pp. 147-77, especially pp. 152-54.

73. The main discussion in *ST* 1:299-334 presents in some detail a characterization, a history, and a critique of pantheism. My other references will be mostly supplementary. Hodge expressly indicated that in his account of pantheism he was thinking chiefly of Fichte, Schelling, and Hegel (1:331).

the German philosophers is, "Without the world there would be no God; and without God there would be no world" (3:301).[74] According to pantheism, "in its most rational form, all power, activity, and life, are the power, activity, and life of the one universal mind" (1:276).[75] Humanity is accordingly a mode of the divine existence (2:441, 449, 453, 731), the impersonal God come to consciousness (1:176, 393; 2:444).[76] Consequently, it matters little that Christ is said to be divine: that is not meant to set him apart from other men. The divine is human, the human divine (2:445). Against all these monstrous speculations, as he took them to be, Hodge affirmed his theistic belief in an extramundane, personal God — "God" in the only legitimate sense of the word (1:204, 242, 284). The incarnation of God the Son in Jesus Christ was a unique union of the divine and the human natures — without confusion — for the sake of our redemption (2:389, 455).

So, was Schleiermacher a pantheist? Hodge knew that Schleiermacher defined the concept of "pantheism" with care,[77] and from Tholuck he had learned that Schleiermacher rejected the name. Nevertheless, one half of Germany thought him pantheistic;[78] and though Hodge sometimes professed himself willing to leave the question open,[79] his entire critique of Schleiermacher's doctrines presupposes that he had made up his mind.[80] The metaphysical issues are, if anything, even more difficult to sort out than the methodological ones. But two brief comments are in order. First, it is hard to suppose that Schleiermacher confused God and the world, or failed to distinguish them adequately, as long as critics from the other side, so to speak, saw his God as so "wholly other" that no contact between God and the

74. Cf. Hodge, "What is Christianity?" p. 125.

75. It is this line of thought that made pantheism, in Hodge's judgment, inevitably deterministic (ST 1:327; 2:281) and therefore anti-supernaturalist: the continuous divine activity admits no interruption. This certainly posed a difficulty for Schleiermacher, who, as Hodge pointed out, wanted to make the appearance of the Redeemer supernatural (1:173; 2:448, 453). See Chap. 2, pp. 54-56 above.

76. Cf. Hodge, "What is Christianity?" p. 126.

77. Hodge, "What is Christianity?" p. 126. The "avowed Pantheists" in ST 1:481-82 are presumably the Hegelians.

78. Hodge, "What is Christianity?" p. 123.

79. Hodge, "Latest Form of Infidelity," p. 98.

80. Hengstenberg, by contrast, deliberately avoided this presupposition in his critique of Schleiermacher. See Hodge, "Religious State of Germany," p. 542.

world was thinkable.[81] Second, Schleiermacher surely avoided any talk of deifying humanity precisely by asserting that the distinctive presence of God to humans is through consciousness of God, which in Christ was a perfect — and therefore unique — consciousness.[82] Though Hodge wrote that in that case "the only difference between Christ and other men was that the *Gottesbewusstseyn* ... determined in him all his activity from beginning to end," it must be noted that the *only* is his, not Schleiermacher's.[83] Schleiermacher believed that he was offering a way to reconceptualize nothing less than the church's belief in the union of God and humanity in the incarnation.

What happened, it seems to me, is that Hodge did not adequately distinguish Schleiermacher's philosophy from Hegelianism. He acknowledged that within the one new philosophy was a great diversity of individual systems, some closer to pantheism, others to theism (*ST* 3:650). But they melted together in his mind as "the modern German theology" (3:651). He was grieved to learn, he said, that Nevin, his friend of more than forty years, had taken offense when he read the first volume of the *Systematic Theology* and found his position confused with Hegel's, whose system he abhorred. Hodge's solution in volume three leaves much to be desired: to avoid any further danger of misrepresentation, he said, he had described the principles of the modern theology as far as possible in the language of its advocates, but he added: "No reference to names is given, so that no one is made responsible for the views expressed" (3:655, n. 1). Obviously, this won't do unless the generaliza-

---

81. More precisely, the question concerns the relationship between divine and natural *causality*. While Schleiermacher described them as coextensive, he insisted that they are wholly antithetical in kind (*CG*, §51), as must clearly be the case if, as he says, the divine causality is absolutely timeless (§52) and spaceless (§53). For him, "No God without the world" certainly cannot denote an ontological relationship of mutual dependence any more than an identity of substance. It is rather an epistemological assertion that the dogmatic theologian cannot *say* anything about God apart from God's relation to the world: "We have only to do with the God-consciousness given in our self-consciousness *along with* our consciousness of the world; hence we have no formula for the being of God in Himself as distinct from the being of God in the world" (§172.1 [p. 748]; my emphasis). The point is, of course, commonplace in the tradition, which teaches that *in se* God is not known. Calvin gives the point a practical turn: we should ask not what God is in himself, but what he is like, or how he is disposed, to us (*ICR* I, ii.2 [1:41]); x.2 [1:97]); III, ii.6 [1:549]).

82. Schleiermacher, *CG*, §94.2 (p. 387).

83. Hodge, "What is Christianity?" p. 130. Cf. *ST* 2:447.

tions are followed by a close reading of individual texts when individual theologians are under discussion. I have not found persuasive evidence that Hodge ever worked through Schleiermacher's *Glaubenslehre* as carefully as he appears to have read D. F. Strauss. He tended to fall back on books about Schleiermacher or publications critical of him. On one of the interpreters of German religious thought, J. D. Morrell, he remarks: "[T]hose who wish to understand the theory which he presents, would do well to study it in the writings of its authors."[84] Good advice, which all of us should take to heart.

Charles Hodge stood for a way of doing theology that is in danger of extinction. He saw himself as a participant, along with others, in a grand enterprise that had a history of nearly two thousand years behind it and deserved the best intellectual resources he could bring to it. The reader is constantly amazed at the wealth of quotations and exact references that Hodge's erudition could marshal on every one of his dogmatic themes. They range over the history of theology, the (then) contemporary theological discussions, and the systematic theologian's continuing dialogue with conversation partners in philosophy and the sciences. His intention to bring the advocates of alternative positions into the discussion and to deal fairly and honestly with them is evident in the painstaking descriptions of their positions and the forthright enumeration of his objections. If I, as at least in part what Hodge calls a "naturalized German" (see *ST* 2:731 n. 2), complain that his usual learning and fairness came short in his treatment of Schleiermacher, that is only to say that I don't think the enterprise he engaged in is finished. A part of Hodge's legacy may be the comfort he brings to anyone who fails to take Schleiermacher seriously as an evangelical theologian. But he has left, in addition, a powerful testimony for those who continue to regard his style of systematic theology as a serious intellectual enterprise, which ought still to have its institutional home in both the seminary and the university.

84. Hodge, "The Theology of the Intellect and That of the Feelings, I" (BRPR 1850) in *ER,* pp. 540-41n. Among Hodge's favorite interpreters of Schleiermacher were C. J. Braniss and F. W. Gess in Germany, Morell in England, and Nevin in America. He also relied heavily on Dorner for Schleiermacher's christology and Müller for Schleiermacher on sin. When he did offer quotations from Schleiermacher, they sometimes came to him secondhand (e.g., *ST* 1:302; "What is Christianity?" pp. 124, 126). More often he simply referred to what others said about Schleiermacher (e.g., *ST* 2:446-47).

CHAPTER 8

Constructing Tradition:
Calvin, Schleiermacher, and Hodge

I have offspring by thousands all over Christendom.

John Calvin, *Reply to the Calumnies of Baudouin*

On 25 April 1564, shortly before his death, Calvin dictated his last will and testament to a Genevan notary, who certified that the reformer, though sick in body, was of a sound mind. Calvin first reaffirmed his faith in the gospel: he had no other refuge, he said, than God's gratuitous adoption, on which alone his salvation depended. He then went on to specify how his slender patrimony was to be assigned. The boys' school, the fund for impoverished aliens, and the daughter of Calvin's half-sister, Marie, were each to receive ten crowns *(escus)*. Next, Calvin designated unequal sums of money for the children born from his brother Antoine's two marriages: for two of the boys forty crowns each, for the three girls thirty each, and for their brother David only twenty-five, to chastise him for his frivolousness. Calvin added the proviso that should the sale of his books and other personal effects raise a larger amount than he expected, the surplus was to be distributed equally among the children — including David, if through the goodness of God he had returned to good behavior.[1] The testator thus exercised full control over his legacy, discriminating as he saw fit among his several bene-

---

1. Calvin's will is reproduced in French in CO 20:298-302. It is also given in Latin in the third version of Theodore Beza's life of Calvin (1575), CO 21:162-64; Eng. trans. in TT 1:lxxxv-lxxxix.

ficiaries: the girls received less than two of the boys, but David received less than the girls. Though Calvin would not be in a position to supervise the way the children spent their inheritance, he alone determined what each of them had to spend.

Quite different from a monetary bequest is a theological legacy. It is not only possible for Calvin's theological heirs to spend their inheritance in ways he might not approve: even what they receive is pretty much what they decide to take. In this sense, a Calvinist "tradition" is not simply a bequest but a construct — something we make rather than passively receive.[2] This is all the more so when, as usually happens, the word "tradition" carries normative overtones. Bickering over the inheritance is likely. Not that everyone will want the same things from the treasure chest; the argument will be over the value of the things chosen.

Historical inquiry certainly limits what one may reasonably claim as Calvin's theological legacy. It is always possible to protest, "Calvin never said that," or, "That's not what he meant," or, "Well, he did say that, but it's not *all* he said." Still, appropriating Calvin's theological legacy — making out of it a normative tradition — is not the same as getting him right, or setting the historical record straight: the difference between his time and ours makes it impossible to take him just as he was, and we are deluding ourselves if we think otherwise. An appeal to Calvin's legacy *as a theological warrant,* even if it presupposes historical knowledge, is not a historical procedure. What he said may have a certain *prima facie* weight among those who profess to stand in the Calvinist tradition. For the systematic theologian, however, the appeal to Calvin must be subjected to the same theological norms as everything else. The preeminent norm will naturally be the one to which he himself pointed his readers in the preface to the 1541 French *Institutes:* "Above all, they will be well advised to resort to Scripture, in order to ponder the testimonies I advance from it."[3] And precisely because our time is not his time, most systematic theologians will recognize in the present state of knowledge *outside* the Scriptures a second norm, whether as part of a full-blown method of correlation or simply in recognition of the need to adapt and apply whatever we receive from the past.

2. Strictly speaking perhaps, Calvin's theological "legacy" is the *Opera omnia.* It is what is taken from this legacy that constitutes a theological "tradition."

3. *Institution de la religion chrestienne* (1541), "argument du présent livre," OS 3:8.

It is not my intention in this essay to make a case either for or against Calvin's legacy, or any part of it. For now, I am interested in a third task that falls between determining what his theology was and appropriating his theology today: I mean the quest for examples of how Calvin's theological legacy has, as a matter of fact, been perceived or assimilated by others in other times. The quest may well be undertaken for the sake of the properly systematic task, and the historical theologian will not exclude the task of critical reflection; but the quest calls, in the first instance, for historical description. Obviously, there is more than enough material out there to fill an entire book on the reception of Calvin's theological legacy from the sixteenth to the twentieth century. I am not aware of any attempt to write such a comprehensive study. If the attempt were made, the result would not be just a history of Calvin scholarship, and it would not be a book quite like McNeill's classic *History and Character of Calvinism,* in which the precise connection of Calvinism with Calvin is not the focus of inquiry.[4] Neither, incidentally, would it be a book like Bornkamm's fascinating study that traces the changing images of Martin Luther reflected in the successive phases of German intellectual history.[5] The eagerness of the Germans to claim Luther's authority for their various programs has made him the patron of an astonishing number of contradictory causes. The Reformed, on the other hand, despite one or two attempts at hagiography, have not discovered in John Calvin good material for a personality cult, and in modern times they have not always turned instinctively to his theology as the touchstone of "pure doctrine." But at no time has he been without his beneficiaries, and for now I want to think about just two of them: Friedrich Schleiermacher and Charles Hodge. Then I will offer one or two concluding comments about Calvin's theological legacy. To anticipate: I want to show, first, that Schleiermacher and Hodge exemplify two quite different views of faithfulness to a tradition and, second, that Schleiermacher's view bears a striking resemblance to Calvin's progressive understanding of Luther and the Reformation tradition.

---

4. John T. McNeill, *The History and Character of Calvinism* (New York: Oxford University Press, 1954).

5. Heinrich Bornkamm, *Luther im Spiegel der deutschen Geistesgeschichte, mit ausgewählten Texten von Lessing bis zur Gegenwart* (Heidelberg: Quelle & Meyer, 1955).

I. Schleiermacher and the Theological Legacy of Calvin

Schleiermacher was the greatest theologian of the Reformed church between Calvin and Barth. Only Jonathan Edwards comes close. I have
made more than one previous attempt to explore the question of
Schleiermacher's relation to Luther, the Reformation, and especially
Calvin, always concluding that much more needs to be done.[6] The most
obvious reason for neglect of the question is that since the 1920s the canonical narrative of Protestant history has represented Schleiermacher's thought as a disastrous break with the heritage of the Reformation. Barth's famous declaration of 1922 set the pattern. Speaking of
the line that runs back through Kierkegaard to Luther and Calvin, and
so to Paul and Jeremiah, Barth added: "And to be absolutely clear, I
would like to point out expressly that in the ancestral line I am com-
mending the name *Schleiermacher does not appear.*"[7] The most detailed
and comprehensive critique of Schleiermacher from what we commonly call the "neo-orthodox" camp was written not by Barth, but by
his associate Emil Brunner. In *Mysticism and the Word* (German 1924),
Brunner passionately accused his adversary of replacing biblical-
Reformation faith with a mystical religion. Taking this hermeneutic key
in hand, he exposed the alleged flaws in a wide range of Schleiermacher's doctrines.[8] A few years later, an article by Wilhelm Niesel
dealt specifically with Schleiermacher's relation to the Reformed tradition. His negative conclusion was stated as an ironical question: Did
Schleiermacher's supposedly Reformed makeup consist only in the fact
that he possessed a Reformed certificate of baptism?[9]

Brunner and Niesel considered the matter closed; Barth was never

---

6. See especially "Schleiermacher and the Reformation: A Question of Doctrinal
Development" (1980), reprinted in *The Old Protestantism*, chap. 11, and "From Calvin to
Schleiermacher: The Theme and the Shape of Christian Dogmatics" (1985), reprinted in
Continuing the Reformation, chap. 8.

7. Karl Barth, "Das Wort Gottes als Aufgabe der Theologie" (1922), *Karl Barth
Gesamtausgabe* III, 19 (Zurich: Theologischer Verlag, 1990), p. 158 (Barth's emphasis).

8. [H.] Emil Brunner, *Die Mystik und das Wort: Der Gegensatz zwischen moderner
Religionsauffassung und christlichem Glauben, dargestellt an der Theologie Schleiermachers*
(Tübingen: J. C. B. Mohr [Paul Siebeck], 1924[1]; 2nd ed., 1928).

9. Wilhelm Niesel, "Schleiermachers Verhältnis zur reformierten Tradition,"
Zwischen den Zeiten 8 (1930): 511-25.

quite so sure.[10] But it must be added that the way the neo-orthodox theologians construed the story found some support from German historians, who professed disappointment with Schleiermacher's strange failure to display much warmth in speaking of Martin Luther.[11] And here one must note another reason for the state of the secondary literature: in Germany the assumption — sometimes tacit, sometimes spoken — has always been that the Reformation means Luther. Hence the question of Schleiermacher's connection with the Reformation is presumed to have been answered when his rare and somewhat restrained remarks about Luther have been duly noted and lamented. But the obvious next step would be to see if he spoke more approvingly either of the Reformation in general or of John Calvin in particular, the reformer most esteemed in Schleiermacher's own church. Though German, Schleiermacher was not a Lutheran, and even after the union of the Lutherans and the Reformed in 1817, which he supported, he continued to profess his allegiance to what he called the Reformed "school."[12]

It must be said that one should not expect much more warmth in Schleiermacher's references to Calvin than in his references to Luther. He understood history to be everywhere the collective work of a "common spirit" and was unwilling to attribute too much to individuals.[13] He hoped that when the dividing names "Lutheran" and "Reformed" disappeared in the Church of the Union, it would no longer seem as if the Reformed were less respectful than the Lutherans of the man after whom the Lutherans were named, nor yet as if the Lutherans were less concerned than the Reformed to avoid glorifying any one man too

---

10. Karl Barth, "Brunners Schleiermacherbuch," *Zwischen den Zeiten* 2 (1924): 49-64; see p. 60. The apparent uncertainty — despite some heady rhetoric — continued to the year of Barth's death, when he admitted he was not so sure of his own cause (*Sache*) that his *yes* entailed a *no* to Schleiermacher's cause. "Postscript" to Heinz Bolli, ed., *Schleiermacher-Auswahl,* p. 307; trans. George Hunsinger in *Karl Barth: The Theology of Schleiermacher,* ed. Dietrich Ritschl, trans. Geoffrey W. Bromiley (Grand Rapids: Eerdmans, 1982), pp. 274-75.

11. I mentioned some of the pertinent literature in the articles referred to in n. 6 above.

12. See, for example, Schleiermacher, *An Herrn Oberhofprediger Dr. Ammon über seine Prüfung der Harmsischen Säze* (1818), SW I, 5:341.

13. He applied this view of history expressly to the Reformation in his lectures on church history. *Geschichte der christlichen Kirche, aus Schleiermachers handschriftlichem Nachlasse und nachgeschriebenen Vorlesungen herausgegeben* (1840), SW I, 11:576.

much.[14] He viewed Luther's achievement as part of a larger, unfinished Reformation that could not be the work of any single individual, but in which several individuals — Erasmus, Luther, Zwingli, Calvin, and others — all played their essential roles.[15] No belittling of any one of them, nor of the Reformation itself, was intended. Schleiermacher believed that he still lived and did his theology in the period of the Reformation, which was likely to endure for a good many more years: no comparable epoch separated him from the first generation of Protestants.[16] For the Reformation was not merely a correction of abuses; much less was it simply the restitution of the apostolic age. It brought into existence a new and distinctive formation of the Christian spirit, which for the foreseeable future will stand over against the Catholic type of Christianity.[17]

Although he was certain that the work of theology, or more exactly the work of dogmatic theology, had to be determined by the antithesis of Catholic and Protestant, Schleiermacher had some hesitation defining the exact nature of the antithesis. Sometimes he located it in the contrast between symbolic action and the spoken word; sometimes in the different ways the two communions represent the relation of the individual to the church.[18] But there is no need to pursue the problem here. The point is simply that if we are to understand his references to Calvin, we have to read them in the context of what he made of the Protestant Reformation. Then we will not be disappointed if we find little inclination to venerate Calvin, or even to elevate him above the other evangelical Reformers.

This leads me to a second contextual point, closely related to the first. If the Reformation is the collective work of a common spirit, collective expressions of the Reformation will naturally be assigned dogmatic precedence over the opinions of individual theologians. With this

---

14. Schleiermacher, *An Ammon,* pp. 396-97.

15. Schleiermacher, *Gespräch zweier selbst überlegender evangelischer Christen,* etc. (1827), SW I, 5:542-48, 625; *Geschichte der Kirche,* pp. 582-83 (on the role of Erasmus).

16. Schleiermacher, *KD,* §§71-93, 186, 212. Cf. *Geschichte der Kirche,* pp. 36, 612.

17. Schleiermacher, *CG,* §24.1 (p. 104).

18. The ecclesiological contrast appears in *CG,* §24.2-4 (pp. 105-7). For the contrast between word and symbolic action in worship, see *Die christliche Sittenlehre, nach den Grundsätzen der evangelischen Kirche im Zusammenhange dargestellt* (1884), SW I,12:212. Cf. *Geschichte der Kirche,* pp. 45-46.

in mind, no one need be surprised that Schleiermacher's great dogmatic work, *The Christian Faith,* especially the second part, bristles with quotations from the Protestant confessions; often, he introduces a new theme with a long catena of passages. At the time of his writing, the authority of so-called symbolic books was the center of a heated theological controversy, in which he was obliged more than once to take a public stand. Ironically, the formation of the united church coincided with the rise of Lutheran confessionalism and even intensified it. Many Lutherans feared that association with the Reformed might further dilute the purity of Lutheranism, already threatened by rationalism, and they called for strict adherence to their Reformation creeds.

In response, Schleiermacher pointed to a middle way between rationalism and inflexible confessionalism. He professed astonishment that there were those who would have erased so many years of church history, demanding subscription to a document from the sixteenth century. But if this set him firmly against the Lutheran confessionalists, it did not align him with the opposing rationalist party, which held that precisely because the Reformation confessions were written for their own time, they were *mere* historical documents and had no claim to present-day attention. In its own way, he argued, this view also betrayed a lack of historical sense. For there is always a difference between the first decisive moments and the subsequent course of a historical phenomenon, and between a merely personal statement and one that represents a widespread conviction. Although we are not forever bound to the letter, Schleiermacher held that the confessions have their unique worth as the first public expressions of the Protestant spirit, which is identical in both the Lutheran and the Reformed churches.[19] The difference between the two communions that trace their lineage back to the Reformation is only a difference of "school": not, that is, a divergence in the religious affections, but in the way they are represented.[20]

It is against the background of these fundamental principles that

19. Schleiermacher, *Über den eigenthümlichen Wert und das bindende Ansehen symbolischer Bücher* (1819), KS 2:143-44, 159-62. Nevertheless, against any temptation to exaggerate the perfection of the old confessions, he points out that their authors were, after all, men and theologians like us (*An die Herren D. D. D. von Cölln und D. Schulz, Ein Sendschreiben* [1831], KS 2:237-38).

20. Schleiermacher, *CG,* §24, postscript (pp. 107-8). The English translators misconstrue *Sache der Schule* as "an academic matter."

Schleiermacher's attitude to Calvin and his theological legacy is to be understood. He could not confer on Calvin the value reserved for the Reformation confessions, both Lutheran and Reformed, and he was not tempted to make him a denominational hero. Within these limits, his judgments on Calvin are generous. He did not claim to be a Calvin scholar with a broad knowledge of the *Opera omnia,* but he was well acquainted with the *Institutes.* When a theological opponent attributed a dubious sentiment to Calvin, Schleiermacher's reaction was confident: "I cannot find this principle anywhere in my Calvin; rather, as I consider the matter more closely, I find grounds enough in my slight knowledge of Calvin to assert that he cannot have written that." The expression "my Calvin" is intriguing. By his "slight knowledge of Calvin" he evidently meant his limited acquaintance with other works of Calvin besides the *Institutes.* For when the opponent supplied a reference, it turned out that he had misrepresented a passage on election from the third book of the *Institutes,* with which Schleiermacher was perfectly well acquainted. "And I thought the proof would come," he remarks, "from who knows what more seldom read commentary of Calvin!"[21] We can safely infer that he had not spent much time reading Calvin's commentaries. But he seems to have been at home in the *Institutes.*

He admired Calvin's *Institutes* for two main reasons, as we have already noted (in Chap. 6). First, he judged it a priceless work because it never loses touch with the religious affections, not even in the most intricate material. Second, it is distinguished by sharpness of method and systematic compass.[22] Though he regretted the fact that in Calvin the systematic impulse was hindered by a polemical tendency, it is obvious that Schleiermacher admired most in the *Institutes* exactly what he himself strove for in his own systematic work, *The Christian Faith.*[23] But it does not necessarily follow that he actually *owed* his methodological ideals to Calvin's theological legacy. The next question is whether he was indebted to Calvin for the content he gave to some of his dogmatic themes.

There are a number of points at which a comparison between the 1559 *Institutes* and the second edition of *The Christian Faith* proves very

21. Schleiermacher, *Zugabe zu meinem Schreiben an Herrn Ammon* (1818), SW I, 5:409-10.

22. Schleiermacher, *An Ammon,* p. 345; *Geschichte der Kirche,* p. 602.

23. Schleiermacher, *Geschichte der Kirche,* pp. 615-16. Cf. *CG,* §§17 (pp. 83-85), 20.1 (p. 94), 27 (p. 112), 28.2 (p. 120).

interesting. Some of them I have taken up elsewhere.[24] But resemblances, if and when they emerge, do not necessarily establish debts; and the comparison just as often uncovers differences, whether or not they reflect conscious modifications or corrections of the Calvinist heritage. For this reason, I want to confine my attention to the passages in *The Christian Faith* in which Calvin is expressly named. There are sixteen references to Calvin[25] — more than to Zwingli (7) or Luther (13), but fewer than the references to Johann Gerhard (19), Melanchthon (21), Reinhard (25), or Augustine (33). Obviously, I cannot take a close look at all Schleiermacher's Calvin citations, but I can at least make a start. All the references, without exception, are to the *Institutes:* six to book one, two to book two, five to book three, and three to book four.

It is not always certain whether Calvin is being cited to confirm Schleiermacher's argument, or to exemplify a position he is criticizing. He tells us, for instance, it is questionable *(bedenklich)* to teach that angels bring outside protection to us, and he adds a footnote reference to the *Institutes.*[26] Now, in the passage cited Calvin does assert that angels are our protectors, but he hesitates to say that each of us has a personal guardian angel and warns us against transferring to the angels what belongs to God and Christ.[27] So, is Calvin cited disapprovingly for his as-

24. In addition to the essays cited in n. 6 above, see "Theology Within the Limits of Piety Alone: Schleiermacher and Calvin's Notion of God" (1981), reprinted in *The Old Protestantism,* chap. 12, and "Nature and the Theater of Redemption: Schleiermacher on Christian Dogmatics and the Creation Story" (1987), reprinted in *Continuing the Reformation,* chap. 9.

25. Sixteen is the number of references given under "Calvin" in the authors and sources index to the English translation. The index to Martin Redeker's edition of the German (Berlin: Walter de Gruyter, 1960) lists fifteen, but that is because he takes as one reference the citations from Calvin in *CG,* §119.3. (Neither index includes the third mention of Calvin, without quotation, in this same section.) In Redeker's first reference "§37" is apparently a slip for §38. There are also slips — presumably errors of transmission — in the references in *The Christian Faith* itself to Calvin's *Institutes:* in *CG,* §108.4 (p. 490 n. 2), the footnote reference should be to book four, chapter sixteen, section twenty (IV, xvi.20, not ix.16.20); the second Calvin quotation in §119.3 (p. 550 n. 1) is from chap. xxi of the third book, not chap. xxiii; and the quotation at the head of §141 (p. 651) is from book four, chap. xvii, not chap. vii. The index to KGA I, 13 adds a reference to the "Calvinistic" *(kalvinische)* understanding of the Lord's Supper in *CG,* §143.3, where there is no explicit reference to Calvin.

26. Schleiermacher, *CG,* §43.1 (p. 159).

27. Calvin, *ICR* I, xiv.6-11 (1:166-71).

sertion, or approvingly for his warning? Perhaps both, since Schleiermacher thinks the hazard is great enough to warrant the complete exclusion of angel talk from dogmatics, allowing it only a limited private and liturgical use.[28] Similarly ambivalent is a passage in which Calvin is described as acute *(scharfsinnig)*, but unable to put together a consistent account of the Devil's activity from the different strands in the biblical allusions to him.[29]

Schleiermacher can of course quote what Calvin says without either endorsing or criticizing it, simply as one of the views held on the theme under discussion. This is the point of his quotations from Calvin on the Lord's Supper: We have to distinguish the Lutheran, the Zwinglian, and the Calvinistic views, but none of them is free from difficulties.[30] Mostly, however, he refers to Calvin to indicate their agreement. The list of approving references is interesting. (1) Calvin's reading of the Mosaic creation narrative rules out the use of Genesis to construct an actual theory of creation. (2) Calvin asserted that God foresees future events because he decreed them. A good point, Schleiermacher thinks, but John Scotus Erigena put it better when he said "God sees," not "God foresees," what he willed to make. Again, (3) Calvin refused to say that the contagion of original sin is transmitted through the substance of either the flesh or the soul. (4) He rightly distinguished God's *will* from his *precept:* that is, the efficient from the commanding will of God. (5) Whereas some deny the necessity for the baptized to be converted, Calvin represented baptism precisely as the "seed" of future repentance and faith. And (6) he held it to be beyond controversy that no one is loved by God outside of Christ.[31] On all of these six points Calvin gives expression to thoughts that Schleiermacher shares with him. He is

28. Schleiermacher, *CG*, §43.2 (p. 160).

29. *CG*, §45.2 (p. 167). The footnote cites Calvin, *ICR* I, xiv.17 (1:175), 18 (1:177), but the actual quotations don't all fit; the first is not verbatim from Calvin at all. Schleiermacher used the Leiden edition of the *Institutes* (1654) and here he evidently paraphrased the marginal summary in that edition. See KGA I, 13:260 n.

30. *CG*, §140.4 (pp. 648-51). At the beginning of the following section (§141), Schleiermacher quotes Calvin — among others — on the effects of the Lord's Supper, but without comment.

31. *CG*, §§40.2 (p. 151); 55.1, n. 1 (p. 220); 72.4, n. 3 (pp. 299-300); 81.1, n. 3 (p. 332); 108.4 (p. 490); 109.4, n. 2 (p. 503). Calvin is also cited (with implicit approval) for his assertion that belief in providence, no less than creation, distinguishes Christians from unbelievers (§38 [p. 146]).

drawing on the theological legacy of Calvin — whether to confirm his own thoughts, or to acknowledge a formative influence on them, is hard to say. But I have saved until last (7) the most instructive of his attempts to see himself in Calvin's lineage: his adherence to the doctrine of election, which led his contemporaries to characterize him as a "bold and resolute disciple of Calvin."

Schleiermacher defended election in the long, 119-page article that launched the *Theologische Zeitschrift* in 1819.[32] He stated expressly that he wished to take up the doctrine in its original presentation in Calvin's *Institutes,* avoiding the later Canons of Dort (1618-19). The argument of the article is carried over into *The Christian Faith,* only there, as one would expect, in the form not of an apology for Calvin but of a constructive statement, followed as usual by an assessment of the official church teachings *(kirchliche Lehrsätze).* Schleiermacher's key thought is very simple: The kingdom of God established by Christ is a phenomenon of history, and it is therefore impossible that the whole of humanity should be taken into it at one time. What proceeds from a single point can spread only gradually. This "law" is so plainly a part of the divine governance of the world that we must judge the antithesis between those who are, and those who are not, members of the church to be grounded solely in the divine good-pleasure. But it is a *vanishing* antithesis as Christianity spreads, and the Christian consciousness cannot suppose that because some die outside the kingdom, a part of the human race is intended to be finally excluded. In other words, we hope for the antithesis to continue diminishing even after death.[33]

It is when he turns to the ecclesiastical doctrine that Schleiermacher refers to Calvin. Like him, he has been wrestling with the evident inequality in the operations of grace; and like him he can attribute it only to the divine good-pleasure. Now he quotes Calvin directly three times, but each time with a critical comment, or in a context that in part runs counter to Calvin's views. (1) Calvin says that election could not stand unless set over against reprobation. Schleiermacher agrees, but only in the limited sense that those who at any particular time are passed over

32. Schleiermacher, "Über die Lehre von der Erwählung," etc., reproduced in SW I, 2:393-484. It is in this article that he mentions the description of him as a "bold and resolute disciple of Calvin," adding, "I do not know with what justice" (p. 399).

33. Schleiermacher, *CG,* §§117-18 (pp. 536-45). For the notion of a *verschwindender Gegensatz,* see §118.1 (p. 540).

or rejected are *not yet* chosen. We have no warrant for concluding that they never will be.[34] (2) Calvin speaks of a twofold foreordination, either to blessedness or to damnation. Schleiermacher argues that there is but *one* divine foreordination — the decree to assume the human race into fellowship with Christ.[35] (3) Calvin defines predestination as the eternal decree of God by which he determined what he willed to become of each individual. Schleiermacher protests against any atomistic view of the work of redemption and understands the operations of grace on the individual strictly in relation to the one eternal decree to redeem *humanity* in Christ.[36] So, was Schleiermacher a "bold and resolute disciple of Calvin" or not? I shall come back to the question in my conclusion. But first some reflections on Hodge. They will need to be briefer.

II. Charles Hodge and the Theological Legacy of Calvin

Hodge was not an original thinker of Schleiermacher's caliber, but he was surely the greatest American Calvinist since Jonathan Edwards.[37] Not a Calvin scholar, as B. B. Warfield was a little later at Princeton, he was a learned advocate of the Calvinist theological legacy — or, as he of-

34. *CG*, §119.2 (p. 548). Schleiermacher recognizes that the qualification he introduces resembles the view Calvin rejects as childish: that the idea of election is unobjectionable if no one is actually condemned (*ICR* III, xxiii.1 [2:947]).

35. *CG*, §119.3 (p. 549).

36. *CG*, §§109.3 (p. 501); 119.3 (pp. 550-51); 120.2 (p. 554). Schleiermacher finds Calvin's formula for a twofold predestination logical enough, and he clearly sympathizes with Calvin's refusal to accept the attempts often made to soften the doctrine. If the operations of grace end at death, then the logical conclusion can only be that some are predestined to blessedness, others to damnation; and it does not help to argue that the latter are "passed over" (not foreordained to damnation), or that God merely "foreknows" their fate. For Schleiermacher, however, the doctrine of election is made tolerable — i.e., consistent with the Christian consciousness — by denying the premiss that death ends the work of grace. Hence §119 concludes (p. 551) with a pointer to the eschatological doctrines he will take up later. See, in particular, the appendix and postscript to §163 (pp. 720-22).

37. Concerning the relation of Edwards himself to the theological legacy of Calvin, we have his own direct testimony in the preface to his *Freedom of the Will* (1754). He accepts the party label "Calvinist" (in distinction from "Arminian") but disclaims dependence on Calvin: he neither holds his doctrines simply because Calvin taught them nor believes everything exactly as Calvin taught.

ten said, "the Augustinian system." He was appalled at the direction German theology had taken, partly under the lead of Schleiermacher's charismatic personality. In a way, his critical estimate of Schleiermacher anticipated Brunner's, since it ended in a perplexing conflict between the two sides of the father of modern theology: his devout faith in Christ and his allegedly pagan philosophy.[38] Hodge reached back into the seventeenth century for sounder and safer theological models.[39] Our question must be, then, whether by way of Francis Turretin and the other orthodox divines Hodge received a larger bequest from Calvin than Schleiermacher did. Different it was certain to be. Schleiermacher held that theological progress, though it cannot be heretical, is bound to be heterodox and must include an honest critique of the official dogmas of the church.[40] Hodge, by contrast, liked to commend his opinions as biblical and orthodox — nothing more than the church had always taught.[41] Interestingly, there was at least one topic on which he had to locate Schleiermacher closer than himself to Johann Gerhard and Johann Heinrich Heidegger. He conceded that for the seventeenth-century theologians, both Lutheran and Reformed, the divine "simplicity" made it impossible to allow any real distinctions between one divine attribute and another, and he recognized that this put Schleiermacher in the succession of the orthodox divines, whereas he himself wanted to take the distinctions between God's various attributes in Scripture at face value.[42] But this odd change of dancing partners did not lead him to have second thoughts about Schleiermacher's relation to the dogmatic tradition.

When it comes to direct references to Calvin, Hodge easily outquotes Schleiermacher. The index to the three-volume *Systematic Theology* directs us to twenty-eight places where Calvin is named or quoted, in one of which multiple pages in the third volume are indicated.[43] In

---

38. See, for instance, the remarks in Hodge, *ST* 2:440-41.

39. See the quotation in Chap. 7, p. 131.

40. Schleiermacher, *CG*, §§21 (p. 95); 25, postscript (p. 110); 27.2 (pp. 114-15); 95.2 (p. 390); etc. Cf. *KD*, §§60, 203-8.

41. For example, Hodge, *ST* 2:479. To preserve his claim that he presents simply what "has always been the faith of the Church," Hodge is sometimes obliged to unchurch not only the rationalists (as here), but even Roman Catholics, Lutherans, and (implicitly) the Eastern Orthodox (2:367, 373, 418, 450-51, 621).

42. Hodge, *ST* 1:394-97.

43. *ST* 3:131-34 (on justification).

some of the places mentioned, more than one actual citation from Calvin is given; in two, there are excursuses headed "Calvin's Doctrine" (on justification and the Lord's Supper). The total number of citations also needs to be adjusted to allow for the fact that Hodge quotes the Geneva Catechism (1545) without assigning it to Calvin's authorship and, conversely, cites the Zurich Consensus (*Consensus Tigurinus,* 1549; published 1551) as though Calvin were its sole author. Further, the index is not complete.[44] But I am not anxious to determine Hodge's exact score, so to say. The point is to discern, if possible, the pattern in his references to Calvin. Three observations are warranted.

First, most of the references are to the 1559 *Institutes,* but not all. Hodge also quotes from Calvin's *Harmony of the Gospels* (on Matt. 19:10-11); from the commentaries on Romans, 1 Timothy, and Titus; and from the Geneva Catechism, the Scholars Confession (1559), the treatise against Tileman Heshusius (1561), and two of Calvin's letters.[45] Three quotations from Calvin are given without identification of their sources.[46] Clearly, Hodge had some acquaintance with the commentaries and other "who knows what more seldom read" writings of Calvin.

Second, as we would expect, nearly all the discussions of Calvin serve as corroboration for Hodge's own views, but again not all. Aside from the place where Hodge simply notes that Calvin used the word "regeneration" more inclusively than we do, to denote the entire Christian life and not just its beginning,[47] he differs with Calvin on two topics: on virginity and on what he calls "the peculiar views of Calvin" on the Lord's Supper.[48] I will come back to the Lord's Supper in a moment. Hodge is surprisingly vehement in his critique of the views on virginity and marriage in book two of the *Institutes* (II, viii.41-42 [1:405-6]), the only passage he refers to in the second book. He comments: "[Calvin says that] virginity is a virtue. Celibacy is a higher state than marriage. Those who cannot live in that state, should descend to the lower platform of married life. With such dregs of Manichean philosophy was the

---

44. In the long section on the Lord's Supper (*ST* 3, chap. 20, §§15-19), the index omits some of the pages on which Calvin is named (pp. 639, 645, 656, 676 n. 3), or named and quoted (pp. 641, 646). There may well be other omissions that I haven't noticed.

45. *ST* 3:373; 3:90, 369 n. 1, 389, 596; 3:487, 501, 580; 2:209; 3:629-30; 1:467; 3:631.

46. *ST* 2:209.

47. *ST* 3:3-5.

48. *ST* 3:630.

pure truth of the Bible contaminated even as held by the most illustrious Reformers."[49] Hodge does not mention that Calvin was attempting an honest interpretation of the Lord's saying about men who castrate themselves for the sake of the kingdom (Matt. 19:12) and Paul's unsentimental view of marriage as a divine remedy for lust (1 Cor. 7:2). Calvin's assertion that nature and the fall combine to make us "doubly subject to women's society" does make you wonder about him, but it may not be necessary to explain it by "the dregs of Manichean philosophy."

This brings me to my third observation: Though he quotes Calvin often, Hodge's use of Calvin, whether approving or disapproving, is not always fair. On the whole, I think, he is honest enough. But (like everyone else's, it may well be) he sometimes selects only what he wants, and sometimes bends what he selects. It is remarkable that in his long argument against baptismal regeneration Hodge's only quotation from Calvin is a bland remark retrieved from his Commentary on Titus 3:5, "Partam a Christo salutem baptismus nobis obsignat."[50] Hodge says nothing of Calvin's argument in the *Institutes* that God can, and sometimes certainly does, effect the regeneration of baptized infants.[51]

On the other evangelical sacrament, Hodge seems in one place clearly to misuse the sources. He concedes that Calvin spoke of receiving a supernatural power that flows from Christ's life-giving flesh in heaven. But he repudiates this "peculiar" notion and tries to show that it was only a minor strand, not only in Reformed theology generally, but even in Calvin's own thoughts on the Lord's Supper. Calvin, he says, "avowed his agreement with Zwingle [*sic*] and Oecolampadius on all questions related to the sacraments." However, "at times" he did teach the peculiar notion of an influence from the glorified body of Christ. As evidence of Calvin's occasional lapse, Hodge quotes from Calvin's exposition of the Zurich Consensus. "Unless," he goes on, "we are willing to accuse the illustrious Calvin of inconsistency, his meaning must be made to harmo-

---

49. *ST* 3:371.

50. *ST* 3:596. That is, "Baptism seals for us the salvation procured by Christ."

51. Calvin, *ICR* IV, xvi.17-26 (2:1339-49). By the end of this segment of book IV, chapter xvi, Calvin can speak confidently of the *dogma* he has established concerning the regeneration of infants (xvi.26 [2:1349]). Though Hodge does not cite Calvin's teaching on infant baptism, as he does Calvin's teaching on the Lord's Supper, the conclusion to his section on baptism as a means of grace (*ST* 3:590) is actually in close agreement with Calvin.

nize with what he says elsewhere." And to prove his point, Hodge quotes from the Consensus itself.[52] But this, surely, is to get things exactly the wrong way around. Calvin wrote the exposition as a fuller explanation of the Consensus, fearing that its brevity might leave it vulnerable to quibbling. And if there is some tension between the explanation and the document itself, we should attribute it not only to the brevity of the Consensus, but also to its character as a compromise document, in which Calvin did not say all he liked to say about the Lord's Supper. His exposition is where we must look to find out what was in *his* mind during the negotiations. An exposition by the coauthor of the Consensus, Heinrich Bullinger, would no doubt look very different.[53]

Hodge's fascinating debate on the Lord's Supper with John Williamson Nevin was an immensely instructive chapter in the history of Calvin's theological legacy. I have written about it elsewhere and don't want to delay too much over it here, other than to reaffirm its importance for our present topic.[54] It was a clash between two varieties of Calvinism, the one predestinarian and the other sacramental. Hodge had no antenna for Calvin's strange talk about the life-giving flesh of Christ. He could not deny that Calvin did talk that way ("at times"!), but he explained that this was an "uncongenial foreign element" in Reformed theology, partly derived from Lutheran influence, and he did not wish to be troubled with the "private authority of Calvin."[55]

---

52. Hodge, *ST* 3:646-47.

53. The pertinent documents, including the articles of the Consensus and Calvin's exposition of them (i.e., his *Defensio sanae et orthodoxae doctrinae de sacramentis*, etc., 1555), will be found in OS 2:241-87. On Calvin's intention in writing the exposition, see p. 267. The Consensus is translated with the title *Mutual Consent as to the Sacraments* in TT 2:199-204. Calvin's defense, translated as *Exposition of the Heads of Agreement*, will be found in TT 2:221-44.

54. See Gerrish, *Tradition and the Modern World*, pp. 57-65.

55. Hodge, "Doctrine of the Reformed Church on the Lord's Supper," *Princeton Review* 1848, reprinted in Charles Hodge, *Essays and Reviews* (New York: Robert Carter & Brothers, 1857), pp. 341-92; see p. 365. Hodge dismissed the distinction, crucial to Calvin's doctrine, between "believing" and "eating" as a "distinction without a difference" (*ST* 3:644-45). He thought the distinction could only arise if one were to restrict the idea of faith to knowledge and assent, not including "the real appropriation of Christ" ("Doctrine of the Reformed Church," p. 361). It should also be noted that Hodge was more interested than Zwingli in maintaining the notion of union with Christ, but without Calvin's talk of a mysterious influence from Christ's body in heaven ("Doctrine of the Reformed Church," pp. 342-43, 368-70, 380-81).

For his part, Nevin was convinced that Calvin's talk of Christ's life-giving flesh was all-important, not least because it excluded the Zwinglian alternative. Nevin admitted, however, that much of Calvin's language was fantastic and tried to reclothe the substance of it in modern categories — leaving him open to Hodge's accusation that he had fallen victim to the dreaded German philosophy.[56] Moreover, Nevin was convinced that there is a fundamental disharmony between Calvin's predestinarianism and his sacramentalism, and that increasing obsession with the divine decrees was responsible for the decline of the authentic Calvinistic view of the Eucharist.[57] If Hodge ceded Calvin's eucharistic theology to Mercersburg, then Nevin gladly let Princeton keep the Calvin of the "horrible decree."

Nevin was a learned adversary. James Hastings Nichols, the historian of the Mercersburg theology, suspected that Hodge's Calvin citations were actually gleaned from Nevin's copious footnotes, and he concluded that Hodge was "beyond his depth. . . . He made the mistake of challenging a man whose command of the field was vastly greater than his own."[58] Personally, I would distribute the honors a bit more evenly. Hodge rightly challenged Nevin's belief that in the Calvinistic Eucharist there is "an altogether extraordinary power," quite different from what is available in the preached word. Nevin (like Schleiermacher) understood the Calvinistic doctrine to assert a real presence of Christ's body and blood in the Supper not available anywhere else. Hodge had no difficulty showing that, as an interpretation of Calvin, this was a mistake.[59]

---

56. John W. Nevin, *The Mystical Presence: A Vindication of the Reformed or Calvinistic Doctrine of the Holy Eucharist* (Philadelphia, 1846); reprinted, with some modernization and corrections, in Nevin, *The Mystical Presence and Other Writings on the Eucharist,* ed. Bard Thompson and George H. Bricker, Lancaster Series on the Mercersburg Theology, vol. 4 (Philadelphia and Boston: United Church, 1966), to which my pagination refers. See pp. 150-200. Nevin traced the difficulties under which Calvin's theory labored to a false psychology, and he believed that his proposed revisions rested on a scientific psychology.

57. Nevin, "Doctrine of the Reformed Church on the Lord's Supper," *Mercersburg Review* 1850; reprinted in Thompson and Bricker, *The Mystical Presence,* pp. 267-401. See p. 373.

58. James Hastings Nichols, *Romanticism in American Theology: Nevin and Schaff at Mercersburg* (Chicago: University of Chicago Press, 1961), pp. 89-91.

59. Hodge, "Doctrine of the Reformed Church," pp. 387-88. It must be added, however, that if Nevin, in this respect, overestimated the significance of Calvin's doctrine of the Lord's Supper, Hodge's refutation of Nevin underestimates Calvin's doctrine of the

Hodge's debate with Nevin was partly a difference over the interpretation of Calvin, partly a difference over what there is in his legacy that is worth preserving. In short, it was consciously, directly, and expressly an *argument* about the theology of Calvin: what it was and where it was sound. I want to end my remarks on Hodge and the Calvinist tradition by commenting briefly on a paradigmatic issue of another kind, in which the question is not directly about Calvin, but about an uncontroverted theological concept whose prominence in Reformed theology goes back to him. After Calvin, the schema of the *munus triplex* — Christ's three offices as prophet, priest, and king — became a commonly accepted resource in the theologian's equipment for interpreting the work of Christ. Calvin is credited with introducing it into Protestant dogmatics, though he himself did not make as much use of it as he leads us to expect.[60] In book two of the *Institutes,* the fifteenth chapter sets up the framework. We are to look at three things in Christ: his "offices" as prophet, king, and priest. Calvin takes the offices to denote not only a work of Christ accomplished *extra nos,* but also an activity into which believers are drawn along with him. But chapter 16 appears to leave the threefold office behind and to concentrate heavily, if not exclusively, on the priestly work of Christ, understood as a work carried out in our place.

Similarly, Hodge begins his discussion of the work of Christ with the threefold office of the Mediator, and he stresses its dogmatic importance.[61] But he develops the *munus triplex* even less than Calvin did, and his rearrangement of the sequence — now prophet, priest, and king — makes the imbalance in his treatment of the offices very obvious. The presentation of the priestly office is so long that the reader has probably forgotten the kingly office by the time it receives its short chapter. Hodge's discussion of the work of Christ runs to 184 pages. He needs

---

preached word (see Gerrish, *Tradition and the Modern World,* pp. 62-63). In his *Mystical Presence* (p. 56) Nevin cited Schleiermacher in his support, who understood the Calvinist Lord's Supper to affirm "die nirgend sonst zu habende wirkliche Gegenwart seines Leibes und Blutes" (*CG,* §140.4 [p. 649]).

60. See J[ohn] F. Jansen, *Calvin's Doctrine of the Work of Christ* (London: James Clarke, 1956), pp. 51-58. For a different estimate of the role of the *munus triplex* in the 1559 *Institutes,* see Klauspeter Blaser, *Calvins Lehre von den drei Ämtern Christi,* Theologische Studien, no. 105 (Zurich: EVZ-Verlag, 1970).

61. Hodge, *ST* 2:461. See further Chap. 9.

but two pages to dispose of the prophetic office, and only a slightly more generous fourteen to explain the kingly office. In between he lingers for no fewer than 132 pages over Christ's priestly work, most of them on the idea of satisfaction for sin (128 pages), but with a short addition (four pages) on Christ's priestly intercession. Further, Hodge takes the work of the Mediator to be a work performed strictly *extra nos* — outside of ourselves, in our place, in our stead. Calvin's notion of a threefold work of Christ performed both *for* us and *in* us is conspicuously absent.

Now, the striking absence of balance in Hodge's treatment of the three offices and his one-sided emphasis on the work of Christ in our place could, of course, reflect a sound grasp of dogmatic priorities. It would require a move from the historical to the dogmatic mode if I wished to pronounce a *theological* verdict on what Hodge does here — or does not do — with the heritage of John Calvin. I am certainly not shy about making such a move in the proper place. But let me, for now, simply conclude my remarks on Hodge with a comparison. When Schleiermacher comes to speak of the ecclesiastical doctrine of the Redeemer's threefold office, he commends it precisely because it prevents undue emphasis on a single aspect of Christ's redeeming and reconciling activity, and he is closer than Hodge to Calvin's understanding of the entire work of Christ as, at least in part, an activity into which Christians are drawn by and with Christ.[62] Schleiermacher makes no reference to Calvin's treatment of the threefold office. Neither does Hodge; had he done so, he might have had second thoughts about both his and Schleiermacher's interpretations of the work of Christ. Evidently, one of the ways in which Calvin's offspring may relate to his legacy is by way of oversight or neglect — unwitting failure to explore further what Calvin left simply in the form of hints and possibilities.

When a mean-spirited adversary, François Baudouin, made a joke of Calvin's childlessness, Calvin replied that he had offspring by thou-

---

62. See Schleiermacher, *CG*, §§100-102, especially §102.3 (pp. 440-41). The *Zusammenstimmung* of which Schleiermacher writes in this passage is surely the harmony between (or among) the three offices, not "between the old covenant and the new," as in the English translation (p. 440); there is nothing in the German corresponding to this phrase.

sands all over Christendom.[63] So he did — and still does. But his heirs have not all used his legacy in the same measure or the same way. Sometimes they seem to have drawn unconsciously on their heritage, or equally unconsciously to have neglected it. But they have also argued over what Calvin said, what he meant, and what he left that is worth preserving. From the two examples I have given it is, I think, plain that the way the legacy is used is determined in part by fundamental dogmatic principles. Hodge, on the whole, held a static view of past sources and norms. True, I was able to point to one place in which he notes that a dogmatic term, "regeneration," is differently employed by us today than in his day by Calvin. But he does not stop to ask if the change of term reflects a change of thought. In this instance, it probably doesn't. And in general the question did not arise at all for Hodge, who understood the language of the theological tradition, like the language of Scripture, to be immobile. Hence, when reading Calvin, he could agree with what he read, or (less often) he could disagree; there was no third option. And the criterion of "orthodoxy," by which he judged even Calvin, meant firm adherence to what the church had always believed and taught as the sense of Scripture.[64]

Schleiermacher held a quite different, developmental understanding of tradition. This is nowhere more clear than in his doctrine of election. He did not quote passages from Calvin on the subject simply in order to agree with some, disagree with others. Rather, he wrestled with the *idea* of election, thought he saw what was important in Calvin's treatment of it, and tried to formulate it anew. As for Calvin's actual language, he could appropriate some of his terms, limit the application of others, and quietly set yet others aside. Had he persuaded his church to follow him in his admittedly heterodox moves, then the single divine decree that creates only a vanishing, temporal division in the human race would have become orthodox; for orthodoxy, as Schleiermacher understood it, is not what the church has always and everywhere taught, but

63. *Responsio ad Balduini convicia* (1562), CO 9:576. The one child of Calvin's marriage to Idelette de Bure lived only a few days.

64. In ST 2:166, Hodge mentions without comment the "celebrated formula" of the semi-Pelagian Vincent of Lérins: "Quod ubique, quod semper, quod ab omnibus creditum est." Though he does not expressly endorse the formula here, he comes close to it in his characteristic appeal to what has always been the faith of "the Church" (see n. 41 above).

what has become the prevailing doctrine in a particular church at a particular time.[65]

So was Schleiermacher a "bold and resolute disciple of Calvin"? If we think of the disciple as one who simply echoes the words of the master, our answer will be "No." But an interesting fact is worth mentioning when Calvin's theological legacy is under discussion. To one of his correspondents he wrote: "If I was not permitted at any point to depart from the opinion of Luther, it was utterly ridiculous of me to undertake the office of interpretation *(munus interpretandi)*."[66] To those who refused to move beyond the details of Luther's eucharistic teaching Calvin remarked, as we have seen, that there is a difference between a disciple and an ape; and when accused by Albert Pighius of diverging from Luther's opinions on free will, he replied that *fideliter tradere* is also *formare*.[67] There is an affinity between Schleiermacher's use of Calvin and Calvin's use of Luther. We might even venture to say that we find in them both something like the old motto *Ecclesia reformata, semper reformanda*. But it is not an easy conception of the theological task to put into practice. If the obvious difficulty with Hodge's appeal to two thirds of the Vincentian canon *(Quod semper, quod ubique)* is that it is only a pious fantasy, the idea of a developing tradition poses acutely the problem of continuity. For did Calvin leave the substance of Luther's opinions unchanged, as he believed, merely expressing them more judiciously? Ask any Lutheran! And was Schleiermacher really the champion of Calvin and his doctrine of election, or was he proposing a new doctrine? If

65. "[T]he interpretation of Christian faith which validates itself in each age as having been evoked by Scripture is the development, suited to that moment, of the genuine original interpretation of Christ and His work, and constitutes the common Christian orthodoxy *(Rechtgläubigkeit)* for that time and place" *(CG,* §131.2 [p. 606]). Schleiermacher understood the development of doctrine not simply as an observed historical phenomenon, but as a theological task (see, e.g., *KD,* §§177-82), which, by definition, both holds the theologian accountable to authorized ecclesiastical doctrines and frees him from being *nur ein Träger der Überlieferung (KD,* §19). In *KD,* §29, he writes of "mindless tradition" *(geistlose Überlieferung)*. But the implicit contrast between *Überlieferung* and *Fortentwicklung* does not mean that "tradition" always carried negative connotations for Schleiermacher. See for instance *CG,* §127.2 [p. 587]; *KD,* §47; and the references on orthodoxy and heresy in n. 40 above.

66. Calvin to Francis Burkhardt, 27 February 1555, CO 15:454.

67. Chap. 6, p. 123, above. Calvin thought of Luther as the pathfinder, who opened up the path on which we progress.

his doctrine of election was something new, shall we call it a development or apostasy?[68] I hope I may have taken a small step toward answering these questions by showing that traditions are not simply given but constructed; and that when we look for continuity, we need to ask ourselves what kind of continuity we are looking for — Hodge's or Schleiermacher's, the preservation of past doctrines or development of them.

68. Continuity may, of course, be located in the questions asked rather than in the answers given, and of this the doctrine of election is a prime example. Preoccupation with the divine decrees and efficacious grace has been characteristic of Reformed theology from Calvin to Barth; but it has largely taken the form of agreeing with Calvin on the importance of the doctrine of election while attempting to revise what he said about it. Elsewhere, I have suggested that the continuity of Reformed theology might also be sought less in the preservation of a short list of distinctive doctrines than in the "habit of mind" that generates them. See B. A. Gerrish, "Tradition in the Modern World: The Reformed Habit of Mind," in *Toward the Future of Reformed Theology: Tasks, Topics, Traditions,* ed. David Willis and Michael Welker (Grand Rapids: Eerdmans, 1999), pp. 3-20.

PART FOUR

Atonement

CHAPTER 9

Charles Hodge on the Death of Christ

Christ died for our sins.

1 Corinthians 15:3

Charles Hodge stands out as the best known and most respected Presbyterian theologian in nineteenth-century America. He may have had his equals in theological wisdom and learning, but no one in the Reformed family of the time exercised a broader or deeper influence. Through the pages of the *Biblical Repertory and Princeton Review,* he made his voice heard on the full range of current issues in church, academy, and society; and the best-known theological publication of his later years, the three-volume *Systematic Theology,* brought together in 2,260 dense pages his mature thoughts on nearly every item of Christian doctrine. His labors as an essayist and a systematic theologian, to say nothing of his immediate personal influence in his classroom at Princeton Theological Seminary, add up to a formidable intellectual achievement. His reputation was well deserved: he earned it.

And yet, in the twentieth century his star lost some of its brightness, not least because of his stand on two of the most controversial issues of his day, Darwinism and the inerrancy of Scripture. The other major publication of his final decade, *What Is Darwinism?* (1874), is sometimes dismissed as quaintly obscurantist. This is not at all fair to Hodge. His views on scientific matters, as on everything else, were buttressed by extensive reading and reflection, and he may have understood what was at stake in the Darwinian controversy better than the Christian naturalists who cheerfully embraced Darwinism as an account of the way divine providence governs the world of nature. To Hodge, Darwinism, as the exclusion of teleology from nature, was atheism. But a theologian wins no points in the world of learning if she concludes that *therefore* Darwin's theory must be mistaken. It is a question of scientific evidence, not theological convenience, and Hodge did not help his cause when he concluded that Mr. Darwin's theory was incompatible with the "facts" of the Bible and deserved no more credence than Hindu mythology (*ST* 2:20). The weight even of theological opinion lay increasingly on the side of those who found mythology precisely where Hodge saw biblical facts. It is true that his own church endorsed the Princeton doctrine of plenary inspiration long enough to drive out some of its best scholars. Then it changed its mind. It is, of course, still possible to be a Presbyterian *and* a believer in the plenary inspiration and inerrancy of Scripture, but that is no longer the exclusive or official position of Hodge's church — or its heir, the Presbyterian Church (USA). Plenary inspiration is not what Hodge liked all his opinions to be: the *orthodox* doctrine. The Confession of 1967 moved the church toward the *neo-orthodox,* or neo-Reformation, understanding of the Bible as human words that witness to the Word of God in Jesus Christ.[1]

The conference on Charles Hodge held at Princeton (22-24 October 1997), in celebration of the two hundredth anniversary of his birth, showed little eagerness to put him back on his old pedestal, and none at all to reinstate the Princeton theology. Still, hardly anyone yielded to the temptation to dance on Hodge's grave — though it *is* a temptation whenever one is irked by his lofty tone of perfect assurance or his caustic dismissal of theologians at least as eminent as himself. The accent of the conference fell on critical assessment of Hodge in his own historical context. "Charles Hodge Revisited: A Critical Appraisal of His Life and Work — A Symposium of Historians and Theologians" was what it announced itself to be: a revisit, not a resurrection. And yet, when all of that is said and granted, there are those, myself among them, who don't

1. Originally a product of the United Presbyterian Church in the United States of America, with the union of 1983 the Confession of 1967 became part of the *Book of Confessions* of the Presbyterian Church (USA): *The Constitution of the Presbyterian Church (U.S.A.), Part I: Book of Confessions,* published by the Office of the General Assembly, Louisville.

think Hodge can be left entirely to the history books — without a voice in the present-day theological discussion.

Interest in Hodge, even if it has become regional, has never disappeared. In some, if not all, evangelical circles, his *Systematic Theology* and commentaries on the New Testament have always been read with respect, or even reverence, and his continuing influence is attested by the abridged, one-volume edition of his systematics (in a mere 585 pages).[2] The principles by which the abridgement was made are understandable. But it is with sadness that a historical theologian will note the ruthless excision of Hodge's conscientious, if sometimes tendentious, discussions on the history of Christian doctrine and the rival opinions of other churches and other theologians. Naturally, it is chiefly by admirers who share his conservatism that Hodge's work is circulated: the conservative standpoint is what they want to keep in print. But even those who disagree with him must feel that he is on the side of Christian theology as a serious academic discipline with a long history, and as a continuing conversation in which every voice must be heard — not once and for all, but again and again. Hodge's own voice deserves to be heard not least on the doctrine of atonement.

I. The Atonement in Hodge's Systematic Theology, Volume Two

The treatment of the work of Christ in Hodge's *Systematic Theology*, volume two,[3] is among the most carefully honed segments of the entire work, and its center is one of the most sophisticated defenses of the satisfaction theory of atonement (or of one version of it) in English-language theological literature. There is no mistaking Hodge's passionate conviction that here he has arrived at the heart of the religion of the Bible (pp. 492, 573). As so often, the reader may be irritated by his self-confident tone, expressed in his customary persuasion that he is merely presenting the biblical faith and the orthodox doctrine of the church in all ages, so that those who question him must have been seduced by a

---

2. Charles Hodge, *Systematic Theology*, abridged edition, ed. Edward N. Gross (Grand Rapids: Baker, 1988; revised paperback edition, 1992).

3. All the parenthetic references to Hodge in this and the following section are to *ST* 2.

vain philosophy that puts them beyond the pale (p. 479). One is astonished to find steps in the argument at which he opposes Roman Catholic
teaching on the covenant of grace with "the common doctrine of the
Church" (p. 367; cf. p. 373), or rejects Lutheran teaching on the person of
Christ as forming "no part of Catholic Christianity" (p. 418; cf. p. 621),
or judges it alien to "the Catholic faith" to speak of Christ's infusing a
new principle of life into the church and humanity (pp. 450-51). There
ought to be a better, more modest way to commend one's theological
convictions than by unchurching Lutherans, Roman Catholics, and the
Eastern Orthodox. And so there is! The main line of the argument carries Hodge through a massive accumulation of biblical texts, painstaking definition of terms, and a genuine engagement with views he finds
flawed and inadequate. And as a matter of fact, he can make a strong
case for his insistence that in the notion of Christ's satisfaction for sin
the churches have spoken with one voice (pp. 482, 563; cf. p. 566 —
"even Origen"!).

1. The Threefold Office

Hodge presents his satisfaction theory with a great deal of repetition,
and there is no need to trace the entire presentation in detail. Some of
the questions he investigates with his usual thoroughness we can
quickly set aside. For instance, as a good Augustinian, he asks: For
whom did Christ die — for all, or for the elect only? He answers: Christ
gave himself for his people and their redemption, but his death brings
incidental benefits to all humankind and should be offered to all, just as
a man may rescue his shipwrecked wife and children in a boat big
enough to save the whole ship's company (p. 556). But Hodge notes that
the question does not concern the *nature* of Christ's work: it concerns
only the *extent*. And we may take this as our warrant for not considering
it any further. Similarly, I need not add much more about Hodge's exposition of Christ's threefold office — a subject already touched on in as-
sessing his place in the Calvinist tradition (Chapter 8) — since he himself makes less use of it than he leads us to expect. But his neglect of two
of the offices is certainly germane to the interpretation of his views on
the work of Christ.

Hodge does begin his discussion of the work of Christ, like Calvin, with the threefold office of the Mediator as prophet, priest, and king. But it soon becomes apparent where, for him, the heart of Christ's saving work is to be located. The design of the incarnation was to reconcile us to God, and reconciliation requires satisfaction for sin. Christ was born to die (p. 612): the emphasis therefore falls on his priestly office and sacrifice for sin. Of the 184 pages he devotes to the work of Christ, Hodge assigns 132, as we have seen, to Christ's priestly work, most of them on the idea of satisfaction for sin, but with a short appendage on Christ's priestly intercession.[4] As for the other two offices, he needs but two pages for the prophetic office, fourteen for the kingly office. The remarkable imbalance in this treatment of the work of Christ may leave readers wondering if the use of the traditional threefold office is a good idea: Does the old scheme mislead them into false expectations? Is it a mistake to begin by inviting the assumption that the work of Christ can be divided into equal thirds? Well, Hodge might answer that no such assumption is intended. But his insistence on the *three* offices is firm:

> We as fallen men, ignorant, guilty, polluted, and helpless, need a Saviour who is a prophet to instruct us; a priest to atone and to make intercession for us; and a king to rule over and protect us. . . . This is not, therefore, simply a convenient classification of the contents of his mission and work, but it enters into its very nature, and must be retained in our theology if we would take the truth as it is revealed in the Word of God [p. 461].

Hodge decides, then, to retain the threefold office, and he quotes with approval Francis Turretin's remark that a single action of the Mediator may be an exercise of more than one office: the cross, for example, is at once a priestly sacrifice and a prophetic lesson. And yet Hodge leaves us in no doubt that of the three offices one so excels the other two in importance that, in practice, we can set it apart as the proper rubric for the Christian understanding of reconciliation with God. That, surely, is the first thing that strikes the reader in Hodge's exposition.

---

4. "As to the nature of Christ's intercession," Hodge explains, "little can be said. There is error in pressing the representations of Scripture too far, and there is error in explaining them away" (p. 593). He ends his presentation of the work of Christ with two chapters on the traditional dogmatic themes of Christ's humiliation and exaltation (pp. 610-38).

Notice, secondly, that Hodge takes the work of the Mediator to be a work performed strictly *extra nos,* "outside of ourselves," in our place or in our stead. Consider again the quotation just given: we need a prophet to instruct us, a priest to atone for us, a king to protect us. Calvin, by contrast, spoke of Christ's offices as exercised both *for* us and *in* us. Christ received his anointing as *prophet,* Calvin explained, "not only for himself that he might carry out the office of teaching, but for his whole body that the power of the Spirit might be present in the continuing preaching of the gospel." The anointing "was diffused from the Head to the members, as Joel had foretold: 'Your sons shall prophesy and your daughters . . . shall see visions,' etc." (Joel 2:28). Similarly, by Christ's office as *king* he "equips us with his power," so that "believers stand unconquered through the strength of their king." And, most explicitly, Calvin saw a twofold benefit in the office of *priest:* "Christ plays the priestly role, not only to render the Father favorable and propitious toward us . . . but also to receive us as his companions in this great office *(in societatem tanti honoris)."*[5]

The tiniest trace of Calvin's twofold emphasis is left in Hodge's very brief remarks on the prophetic office. Since the ascension, he says, Christ continues to reveal the will of God "in the institution of the ministry . . . and by the influence of the Holy Ghost, who cooperates with the truth in every human heart" (p. 463). But this does not mean, Hodge hastens to add, that ministers are prophets (p. 462), and he insists that the very definition of a priest in the Scriptures (Heb. 5:1) is that he is one who acts for others, "for their benefit and in their place" (p. 465). The distinction between a work of Christ performed wholly outside of us and a work into which we are drawn as Christ's "companions" invites further reflection. But Hodge is no more interested in presenting a balance between Christ's work *pro nobis* and his work *in nobis* than he is in striking a balance between one office and another. He pushes off to the future Luther's notion that Christians are kings and priests with Christ (cf. Rev. 1:6) — to a time when the redeemed shall reign with Christ in glory (p. 608), a topic which, as Hodge says, "belongs to the head of Eschatology" (p. 609).

---

5. Calvin, *ICR* II, xv.2 (1:496), 4-5 (1:499-500), 6 (1:502).

2. *Christ's Satisfaction for Sin*

How, then, according to Hodge, does Christ execute the all-important priestly office on behalf of humanity and in their place? Answer: "In his once offering up Himself a sacrifice to satisfy divine justice, and reconcile us to God, and in making continual intercession for us" (p. 468). "Satisfaction" is the heart of the matter, and it refers to "all He has done to satisfy the demands of the law and justice of God, in the place and in behalf of sinners" (p. 470). That sounds comprehensive enough, reminding us of Calvin's assertion that Christ has reconciled us to God "by the whole course of his obedience."[6] But it is immediately obvious that what Hodge has almost exclusively in mind when he speaks of Christ's satisfaction is his vicarious suffering and death.[7] However, he avoids saying, as Calvin had said, that the price paid for redemption was Christ's "suffering in his soul the terrible torments of a condemned and forsaken man." Hodge insists: "He did not suffer either in kind or degree what sinners would have suffered" (p. 471).[8] Why is that so important to Hodge? The answer turns on a distinction.

Hodge explains that there are two kinds of satisfaction, which are not to be confused: "The one is pecuniary or commercial; the other penal or forensic" (p. 470; cf. pp. 487, 554). A monetary *debt* is satisfied when the precise sum due is paid, neither more nor less. But the penalty for a *crime* is seldom of the same kind as the injury done. "All that is required is that it should be a just equivalent. For an assault, it may be a fine; for theft, imprisonment; for treason, banishment, or death"

---

6. Calvin, *ICR* II, xvi.5 (1:507).

7. That is, what the dogmatic tradition called the *passive* obedience of Christ. Hodge's references to Christ's *active* obedience are incidental and perfunctory (see, e.g., *ST* 2:494, 613). On the meaning of "vicarious," see 2:475-76, where Hodge explains that the word "includes the idea of substitution." "Vicarious suffering is suffering endured by one person in the stead of another, *i.e.,* in his place. . . . What a substitute does for the person whose place he fills, is vicarious, and absolves that person from the necessity of doing or suffering the same thing."

8. See Calvin, *ICR* II, xvi.10 (1:516). Hodge doesn't refer to Calvin but clearly denies what Calvin asserts. Note that the denial doesn't hinder him from saying — inconsistently? — that Christ "endured the wrath of God": the words of dereliction ("Why have you forsaken me?" Mark 15:34) "show that He was suffering under the hiding of His Father's face"; indeed, "He suffered all that a holy being could suffer that was enduring the divinely appointed penalty for sin" (*ST* 2:614-15).

(p. 490). Penal satisfaction must, to be sure, be a real and adequate satisfaction, not merely something graciously accepted as such (p. 471): it must be proportionate to the crime. But it is not an exact *quid pro quo*.[9] In actual fact, because of his divine-human personality, Christ's sufferings were *more* than enough to effect satisfaction (pp. 482-84; cf. pp. 545, 555); and when we say that the satisfaction was a matter of grace, we mean, not that God assigned it a value it did not inherently have, but that God the Father was by no means bound to provide a substitute for fallen humanity at all, and the Son was not bound to assume the priestly office. Of course, since the demands of justice are met, they cannot be enforced again (p. 472), and in this sense there remains at least an analogy between the work of Christ and the payment of a debt.[10] But, properly speaking, the satisfaction is not the payment of a debt, but a just equivalent for the crime of sin: penal satisfaction "must bear an adequate proportion to the crime committed," but it "may be different in kind" (pp. 470-71; cf. p. 482).

Hodge's contrast between pecuniary and penal satisfaction is an interesting testimony that the satisfaction theory of atonement is not as simple and straightforward as is sometimes supposed. He is not saying what Calvin had said, nor what Anselm said either.[11] However, what I wish to underscore at this stage of the discussion is that penal satisfaction, for Hodge, rests on an agreement, or covenant, or (as he likes to say) a "transaction," between God the Father and God the Son. He traces the notion of atonement as a transaction between two parties

---

9. Cf. *ST* 2:473-75 on the terms "penalty" and "penal." Hodge avoids saying that Christ was *punished* in our stead: the character of his sufferings as penal "depends not on their nature, but on their design" — i.e., to serve as an *equivalent* of the punishment for sin required by God's law.

10. Note, however, Hodge's insistence that whereas the payment of a debt *ipso facto* liberates the debtor the moment it is paid, the benefit of penal substitution, precisely because it is a matter of an agreement or covenant, may be deferred (*ST* 2:470-72; cf. p. 557). This is how Hodge turns aside the objection that if Christ died in my place, I am delivered from the penalties of sin whether I believe it or not.

11. For Anselm (ca. 1033-1109), the satisfaction lay in the fact that by dying Christ, in whom there was no sin, gave more than he owed to God. His work of supererogation compensated for the guilt of humanity, whose sin was the failure to pay God the honor due to him; but it was not vicarious punishment. Anselm's notion is *either* punishment *or* satisfaction. Anselm, *Cur Deus Homo*, I, xi; II, xix; MPL 158:376-77, 428-30; Eng. trans., *Why God Became Man*, LCC 10:118-19, 179-81.

back to the Old Testament idea of a "covenant." "Covenant" has trans-action built into it. "When used of transactions between man and man [the Hebrew word *berith*] means a mutual compact. We have no right to give it any other sense when used of transactions between God and man" (p. 354). Strictly, there are two covenants, not one, for the covenant of *grace* between God and God's people rests on a covenant of *redemption,* formed in eternity and revealed in time, between the Father and the Son. "Of the one Christ is the mediator and surety; of the other He is one of the contracting parties" (pp. 357-58).

All the essential elements of a covenant are present, Hodge assures us, in the covenant of redemption: we have contracting parties, a promise, and a condition. The Son of God was to assume our nature, be made under the law, and bear our sins; his promised reward for performing his work was to include deliverance from the power of death and reception of power as head of the church (pp. 361-62).

> When one person assigns a stipulated work to another person with the promise of a reward upon the condition of the performance of that work, there is a covenant. . . . Such being the representation of Scripture, such must be the truth to which we are bound to adhere. It is not a mere figure, but a real transaction, and should be regarded and treated as such if we would understand aright the plan of salvation. . . . This may appear as an anthropological [i.e., "anthropomorphic"] mode of representing a transaction between the persons of the adorable Trinity. But it must be received as substantial truth [pp. 360-61].

Is there perhaps a slight trace of uneasiness in this passage? Hodge admits that the transaction language may appear anthropomorphic, and in his exposition the language is so elaborated as to be, or seem, oppressive. Is the language of an inner-Trinitarian transaction, we may wonder, the most effective way of developing the various biblical metaphors for what Christ achieved by his suffering and death?

3. The Justice of God

One more word by way of setting out Hodge's view. Perhaps it is obvious, but because it is the lynchpin of the entire argument it needs to be heavily underscored. Take this passage, for instance:

Guilt must, from the nature of God, be visited with punishment, which is the expression of God's disapprobation of sin. Guilt is expiated, in the Scriptural representation, covered, by satisfaction, *i.e.*, by vicarious punishment. God is thereby rendered propitious, *i.e.*, it is now consistent with his nature to pardon and bless the sinner. . . . Satisfaction or expiation does not awaken love in the divine mind. It only renders it consistent with his justice that God should exercise his love towards transgressors of his law. . . . In the Old Testament and in the New, God is declared to be just, in the sense that his nature demands the punishment of sin; that therefore there can be no remission without such punishment, vicarious or personal [p. 478].

Clearly, the entire satisfaction theory rests on the principle: Justice demands punishment. Satisfaction of the divine justice is absolutely necessary if sinners are to be pardoned (pp. 488-89). It follows that the purpose of punishment is not simply to exhibit the moral order that sin violates. Hodge has in mind here the governmental theory of the learned Dutch lawyer-theologian Hugo Grotius, who also claimed that his theology of atonement was the "catholic" one. The purpose of punishment, according to Grotius, is not to appease divine justice for past sins, but so to manifest God's justice that we shall be obedient in the future. We are to think of God as like the father in a family, or a king in the commonwealth. He is not out for retribution, and there is nothing in his nature that makes punishment necessary. But he is bound by his office to maintain order. He is *rector* (literally "governor"), responsible for the preservation of the common good, but perfectly free to inflict or withhold punishment, to enforce or to relax the law, as he sees fit. "[T]he right of punishing does not exist for the sake of him who punishes, but for the sake of the community. For all punishment has as its object the common good, viz. the preservation of order, and giving an example."[12]

---

12. Hugo Grotius (De Groot, 1583-1645), *Defensio fidei catholicæ de satisfactione Christi adversus Faustum Socinum,* chap. II, in *Hugonis Grotii opera omnia theologica,* 3 vols. in 4 (Amsterdam, 1679), 3:308-9; Eng. trans. by Frank Hugh Foster (Andover: Warren F. Draper, 1889), p. 64. From there, Grotius goes on to argue that it is not unjust for one person to be punished for the sins of others (chap. IV), and that the punishment of Christ attests God's love for us as well as his hatred of sin (chap. V). Grotius may have had a deeper understanding of God's justice than Hodge, but it was no easier for him to justify Christ's sufferings and death as a penal *example* (an affirmation of moral order)

Needless to say, Hodge had no sympathy at all for Grotius's under-standing of divine justice (pp. 573-81). The nature of the atonement turns on the nature of God, and God is determined by his own moral excellence to punish all sins (p. 493; cf. p. 489).

> [E]verything depends on what is meant by justice. . . . [I]f justice is that perfection of the divine nature which renders it necessary that the righteous be rewarded and the wicked punished, then the work of Christ must be a satisfaction of justice in that sense of the term. . . . It is not, therefore, this or that declaration of Scripture, or this or that institution which must be explained away if the justice of God be denied, but the whole form and structure of the religion of the Bible. That religion as the religion for sinners rests on the assumption of the necessity of expiation. This is its corner-stone, and the whole fabric falls into ruin if that stone be removed [pp. 490, 492].

Hodge is careful to defend this notion of the divine justice against the objection that it portrays God in an unflattering light as "a vindictive being, thirsting for revenge." "Vindicatory" does not mean "vindictive" (p. 489). On the contrary, Christ's satisfaction for our sins is an expression of the divine love that finds a way to be just in forgiving sins (pp. 508-9, 514-15). God is a righteous judge, not a malicious murderer: his justice belongs to his moral excellence.

II. Toward a Critical Appraisal

We now have before us the main features of the work of Christ, as Charles Hodge understood it. Without attempting an exhaustive critique, or presuming to develop an alternative, I will venture to offer some comments toward the detailed critical appraisal that Hodge's thorough exposition deserves. He himself stated the doctrine of satisfaction by vicarious punishment in quotations from the Lutheran, Reformed, and even Roman Catholic creeds (pp. 480-82). But if we might

---

than for Hodge to justify them as a penal *substitution* (the just equivalent of the punishment due to humanity). Either way, we are left wondering if the objection of Faustus Socinus (Sozzini) has been met: that it cannot be just for God to afflict the innocent instead of the guilty (see below, pp. 193-94).

risk a summary definition on his behalf, which takes into account his particular spin on the approved ecclesiastical formulas, it would go something like this: *The atoning work of Christ in the place of sinners was a transaction between God the Father and God the Son, by which the Father accepted the suffering and death of his Son as the just equivalent for the punishment of their sins; in this sense, Christ's work was vicarious punishment.* This understanding of the way in which Christ achieved reconciliation between God and sinful humanity, though it may still represent the prevailing view among Christians, has been firmly rejected by a vocal minority from Reformation times to the present.

1. Objections to Vicarious Satisfaction

Hodge was well acquainted with the objections to the satisfaction theory of atonement and the alternatives proposed to replace it. He perceived them either as candid denials of biblical authority or as devious attempts to twist the Bible's plain sense (pp. 528-30, 533, 539). Either way, their intent was to substitute human thoughts for God's thoughts (p. 498). The objections, he suggests, are of two kinds: "The one drawn from speculative or philosophical principles, the other from the sentiments or feelings" (p. 527). The latter kind are presumably those Hodge takes up under the heading "popular objections" (pp. 539ff.). I am not sure that the distinction between the two kinds of objections is maintained, but in any case I am more interested to note that Hodge can never bring himself to entertain a third possibility: that some of the objections are neither speculative nor sentimental, but rest on honest exegesis of Scripture.

Among the philosophical kind, Hodge mentions the moral objection that the innocent cannot justly be punished for the guilty. He has already parried this objection in advance by denying that Christ was actually *punished* in our place: what is transferred to him is the obligation to satisfy the demands of God's justice (p. 532). Later, he restates the moral objection in "popular" form and replies that though the transfer of guilt is impossible as a matter of moral character, the transfer of guilt as responsibility to justice is "no more impossible than that one man should pay the debt of another" (p. 540). The defense at this point is purely conceptual and, within limits, astute. Not so convincing are Hodge's tactics when he shifts the debate to biblical grounds and assumes, rather than demonstrates, that his feeble opponents haven't an exegetical leg to stand on.

Under popular objections — those that rest on sentiment or feeling — Hodge returns, for instance, to the concept of retributive or vindicatory justice and dismisses the critics in a couple of lines (pp. 539-40). He knows that the critique of retributive justice was already urged by Faustus Socinus (1539-1604) and his friends at the time of the Protestant Reformation, but he doesn't mention that Socinus rested his case largely on the foundation of Scripture. According to Socinus, the Scriptures provide plentiful instances when God is said to forgive sins freely, without any mention of satisfaction. Indeed, if satisfaction were made, there would be no call for forgiveness: "to forgive" and "to receive satisfaction" are mutually exclusive concepts. The Scriptures invite us to think of God as a sovereign who may waive legal requirements if he wishes, or a creditor who cancels debts, not as a judge who is bound by the law. For Christ to bear our sins is not to bear their punishment but to carry them away, as the scapegoat carried the sins of the Hebrew people into the wilderness. If Christ had died in our stead, he could hardly have told his disciples to take up their cross and follow him. And so on. Socinus should be treated as a much more worthy opponent than Hodge cared to admit: the Socinian case, too, was an astute mixture of conceptual and exegetical arguments. Especially important was the argument of Socinus that the sufferings and death of Christ were the *consequence* of his mission, not the mission itself.[13]

This is not at all to say that the Socinians came up with a better doctrine of atonement than the satisfaction theory they rejected. Criticism comes cheaper than construction; and if Hodge did not always give due weight to the arguments against his own position, he could sometimes (not always) prove himself much more formidable in exposing flaws in the alternatives. He devoted an entire chapter to "Theories of the Atonement" (part three, chapter nine) and found that there are five in

---

13. Faustus Socinus, *De Jesu Christo Servatore* (completed 1578, first published 1594); *Fausti Socini Senensis opera omnia,* 2 vols. (Amsterdam, 1656), 2:115-246. The works of Faustus Socinus were included as the first two volumes in the *Bibliotheca fratrum Polonorum quos Unitarios vocant.* For a thorough examination of his most important work, see John Charles Godbey, "A Study of Faustus Socinus' *De Jesu Christo Servatore*" (Ph.D. diss., 2 vols., University of Chicago, 1968).

all. The first is the "orthodox" satisfaction theory, which he believes he has vindicated (pp. 563-64). Second comes the theory, common among the early Christian fathers, that Christ effected deliverance from Satan, whether by offering himself as a ransom, or by conquering Satan, or by causing Satan to overreach himself and forfeit his claim on humanity (pp. 564-66). Third is the moral theory. It has appeared in various forms, but all of them see Christ's reconciling work not in his satisfaction of divine justice but in the moral effect produced in the sinner's heart by Christ's character, teaching, and acts (pp. 566-73).[14] Fourth is the governmental theory proposed by Grotius. Against the Socinians, Grotius sought to retrieve the idea of satisfaction, but only as an exhibition of God's displeasure with sin, not as a necessary punishment of it (pp. 573-81). The fifth and final theory Hodge calls "mystical" (pp. 581-89). It has had a long and varied history, but the affirmation common to all its varieties is that atonement is effected by the mysterious union of God and humanity in the incarnation.

Naturally, Hodge's strategy is to oppose the alternatives with the satisfaction theory. But his detailed comments are always interesting and sometimes telling. The patristic theory of deliverance from Satan he sets aside as now of merely historical interest (p. 565). What about the remaining three — the moral, governmental, and mystical theories? I think it can be said that, in effect, Hodge views them all as in essence one. The governmental and mystical theories collapse into the moral theory because all three understand atonement not as an objective work performed outside of us, but as a subjective change effected on sinners, or in them. For according to the governmental theory, as Hodge presents it, "the work of Christ was purely didactic . . . designed to teach, by way of an example, God's hatred of sin" (p. 575). And he asserts expressly that the mystical theory could be included under the moral "in that it represents the design of Christ's work to be the production of a subjective effect in the sinner. . . . It produces a change in him" (p. 581). This, then, invites one last question, perhaps the most important question of all: Is there in truth no means to preserve the objectivity of Christ's atoning work if the idea of vicarious satisfaction is abandoned? If they cannot go all the way with

14. In the view of Horace Bushnell (1802-1876), as Hodge points out (*ST* 2:568), the moral transformation of sinners does indeed rescue them from "the retributive consequences provoked by their sins," but not as "the release of penalties by due compensation."

Hodge, are today's theologians left with no choice but to surrender the belief that Christ carried out a work of redemption on behalf of humans and in their place, a work they could never have performed for themselves and without which they would remain in their sins?

2. Atonement and the Norm of Doctrine

To sum up: Our look at Hodge on the atonement has given rise to at least five questions. Do the offices of Christ describe a "work" done exclusively *for* us, in our place? Is the meaning of atonement to be found entirely in his suffering and death? Is God's justice adequately understood as strictly retributive? What is the logical status of (metaphorical?) language about a "transaction" between God the Father and God the Son? And, finally, is vicarious satisfaction or penal substitution the only guarantee of an objective work of Christ? Each of these questions deserves a fuller discussion than I can offer here. In general, I think I have said enough to make one wonder whether the demands of polemic betrayed Hodge into unduly narrowing the norms and content of the doctrine of atonement.

As for the *norms,* he professed himself willing to listen to both "moral intuitions" (p. 531)[15] and "religious experience" (p. 523) as guides to knowledge of the truth. But he could not perceive either one behind the objections persistently urged against penal substitution by theologians as devout and intelligent as himself. Intuition and experience told *him:* "We know that we ought to be punished, and therefore that punishment is inevitable under the government of a just God" (p. 580). This may be a *non sequitur,* but it reinforced Hodge's retreat to *scriptura sola* as the inflexible condition for continuing the argument (pp. 355, 494, 527), whereas he might have been more attentive to the intuitions and experience that led others to read the Scriptures differently than he did. Of course, Reformed theologians will hardly dissent when Hodge insists that we have to test intuition and experience by Scripture.[16] But they may not be so quick to assume that the sense of Scripture is per-

15. See also *ST* 1:10.
16. *ST* 1:15-16. Hodge takes universal moral intuitions, "founded on the constitution of our nature," as a primary revelation: that "sin deserves punishment" is one of them; that "the innocent cannot justly be punished for the guilty" is not (1:10-11; 2:531).

fectly plain (p. 437), or that anyone who finds in it a meaning other than Hodge finds must have been misled by taste and feelings (p. 541), or by vain philosophy (pp. 498, 539, 590-91), and does not qualify for the honorific category of "all true Christians" (p. 437).[17]

Even if Hodge was not wrong in principle, however, to move the discussion into the domain of exegesis, one may well think that his own actual use of Scripture betrays a narrowing of the *content* of Christ's work. He begins broadly enough. He insists on retaining the three offices and concedes that there are elements of truth even in the alternative doctrines that he rejects, since errors are generally half truths (pp. 567, 571; cf. p. 589). He recognizes that Christ's saving work included more than his expiatory sufferings. It had two great objects in view: "We have guilt to be removed, and souls dead in sin to be quickened to life." Both "objects" belong to the biblical doctrine of redemption, though in the history of Christian theology one or other has often been unduly subordinated or even ignored (p. 563). That is very well said. But one is bound to ask: Doesn't Hodge himself succumb to the temptation, if not to ignore the communication of divine life, at least to subordinate it overmuch to the removal of the curse under which humanity labors on account of sin?

Again and again, he excludes later what, on his own initial principle, he ought to include and frames his sentences with an either-or: not this, but that (e.g., pp. 496, 520). He asserts that it is by his priestly sacrifice that Christ saves us (pp. 497-98): therein lies "what is essential to the Scriptural doctrine of atonement" (p. 571). And this means that he saves us as our representative or substitute: *all* he did was vicarious, done for his people and in their place (pp. 496, 521-22). Perhaps Hodge would reply that atonement is not the whole of salvation. But if we hold him strictly to his words, it follows that the prophetic and kingly offices are not essential to Christ's saving work, and that only his satisfaction of God's justice *for* us, not his life *in* us, belongs properly to salvation, or at least to atonement — that is, to the Christian understanding of how the broken relationship of God and humanity is overcome.

Along with Hodge's narrowing of the norms and content of the doctrine of atonement, there goes — naturally enough — an unyielding

---

17. Hodge affirmed that all theology is shaped by the current philosophy (*ST* 2:397-98). It is not very easy to see how this is to be harmonized with his insistence that we should "admit no philosophy . . . except the philosophy of the Bible itself" (2:591; cf. 1:14).

insistence on the exact language of Scripture. If diversity is to be excluded, so also must any latitude in the interpretation of what is included. It would be a caricature of the Princeton doctrine of plenary inspiration to imagine that for Hodge the process of inspiration could only have been mechanical and the individuality of the biblical authors must accordingly have been suppressed. He never denied that the Scriptures reflect the mental characteristics of the individual writers, or that the writers reflected the mental outlook of their time.[18] But he resolutely refused to take the further step of making the kind of distinction between form and substance that enabled his adversaries to question what he himself took to be the substance. He states their wrong-headed viewpoint like this:

> The sacred writers were Jews, and accustomed to a religion which had priests and sacrifices. It was, therefore, natural that they should set forth under figures and in the use of terms, borrowed from their own institutions, the truths that Christ saved sinners, and that in the prosecution of that work He suffered and died. These truths may be retained, but the form in which they are presented in the Bible may be safely discarded [p. 528].

Hodge will brook no such evasion (as he assumed it to be), any more than the similar argument that the Bible contains in popular language, useful for the masses, truths that the theologian is to recast in sound philosophical terms (p. 529; cf. p. 498). The forms of revelation are not unessential and mutable: biblical teaching is not given in mere metaphors, but in doctrines, which faith must accept on pain of losing salvation.[19] While Hodge conceded that we ought not to press the representations of Scripture too far (p. 593), he plainly thought it the duty of the dogmatic theologian, when the language of satisfaction seemed problematic, to refine it further, not to grant that it was, after all, metaphorical. He recognized the diversity of biblical metaphors for atonement and knew there was a risk of dwelling disproportionately on a single mode of scriptural representation (p. 589). But his critics will judge that his defense of vicarious punishment led him into the trap of transforming the wealth of biblical metaphors into an over-refined dogmatic theory.

18. See, e.g., *ST* 1:156-57, 165.
19. See, e.g., *ST* 1:58-59, 3:67.

Still, when it comes right down to it, his appeal to Scripture was not his sole argument: he was also convinced that Christian piety over hundreds of years was on his side (pp. 524-27; cf. p. 522). All Christians trust in Christ for their salvation and look to him obeying and suffering in their stead; they thank and bless him for giving himself as a ransom for their redemption (p. 524).

> After all, apart from the Bible, the best antidote to all these false theories of the person and work of Christ, is such a book as Doctor Schaff's "Christ in Song." The hymns contained in that volume are of all ages and from all churches. They set forth Christ as truly God, as truly man, as one person, as the expiation for our sins, as our intercessor, saviour, and king, as the supreme object of love, as the ultimate ground of confidence, — as the all-sufficient portion of the soul. We want no better theology and no better religion than are set forth in these hymns [p. 591].

Not many theologians, if any, would disagree. The faithfulness demanded of them is faithfulness to the language of Scripture *and* to the language of the believing, singing, worshiping community. The question, then, must be: Can justice be done to the devout Christian's confidence in a work of Christ in her place without reducing the biblical metaphors of atonement to a transaction between God the Father and God the Son — a transaction that requires us even to say that Jesus the Beloved Son "endured the wrath of God"? Might it be possible to move in exactly the opposite direction from Hodge, not digging in tenaciously in response to the critics but learning from them how to modify the theory, making it a support rather than a problem for the church's songs of praise to the Redeemer? John Williamson Nevin, for one, certainly thought so.

CHAPTER 10

John Williamson Nevin
on the Life of Christ

In him was life.

John 1:4

John Williamson Nevin, Charles Hodge's one-time pupil, has never won as much fame or influence as his teacher. Not exactly an outsider, he was a maverick in American Protestantism and became one of Hodge's most determined theological opponents. He threw himself into controversy fully as energetically as Hodge, and his irony could be devastating: he could be just as acidly self-assured. But his style was less complacent, less Olympian. He voiced the protest of a small minority against more powerful parties in the American churches, including the Presbyterian church in which he grew up. His voice was heard in the German Reformed Church, which called him in 1840 to a chair in theology and biblical literature at its seminary in Mercersburg, Pennsylvania, but even in his adopted church his theological progress landed him in heated controversies.

A widely used volume titled *Reformed Theology in America*[1] distinguishes five major schools or traditions in American Reformed theology. Nevin's "Mercersburg theology" is not one of them. The winners are identified as the Princeton theology, the Westminster school, the Dutch schools, the Southern traditions, and neo-orthodoxy. Why is

---

1. David F. Wells, ed., *Reformed Theology in America: A History of Its Modern Development* (Grand Rapids: Eerdmans, 1985).

199

Mercersburg shut out? True, the emphasis in the book falls on the twentieth century. But Hodge and R. L. Dabney have sections to themselves on the grounds that "the school or tradition in which we find them could not be understood without taking account of their work."[2] Nevin, by contrast, earns but one entry in the index. The solitary reference is to a passing judgment by Mark Noll that schools of theology that did not, like Princeton, adopt the intellectual conventions of the day "are of considerable interest to twentieth-century scholars, but they were close to nullities in their own day."[3] Among the near nullities is the Mercersburg theology. That is not intended to deny that there has been, and is, a slender Mercersburg tradition that goes back to the association of Nevin and Philip Schaff (1819-1893), formed in 1844 when the young Swiss scholar came to America from Berlin. Fierce controversy made Mercersburg rather more than a "nullity" in its day, and it has been said that "a faithful school of supporters kept the Mercersburg theology alive for at least one generation."[4] But then it languished, and its revival in the 1980s was indeed due to the academic interest of scholars. Mercersburg has never been in the mainstream of American Protestantism; its initial importance lay partly in its introducing to America the exotic ideas of modern German theology.

For our present purpose, Nevin's contribution lies simply in the fact that he offered an interpretation of the work of Christ that seems diametrically opposed to Hodge's theory. Hodge consistently points to the *death* of Christ as the means of reconciliation with God; Nevin just as consistently points to Christ's *life*. We must inquire into the nature of this contrast and the reasons for it. Hodge always saw his wayward student as a purveyor of German speculative fantasies, for which (in Hodge's eyes) Nevin sold his Reformed birthright. But Nevin's thoughts on the work of Christ were steeped in ancient patristic theology and (so he argued) in the Reformation theology of none other than John Calvin. The quarrel with Hodge had its antecedent in the differences between Calvin and Zwingli, the two original creators of the Reformed tradition.

2. Wells, *Reformed Theology,* p. xiv.
3. Mark Noll in Wells, *Reformed Theology,* pp. 27-28.
4. Sam Hamstra and Arie J. Griffioen, ed., *Reformed Confessionalism in Nineteenth-Century America: Essays on the Thought of John Williamson Nevin* (Lanham: Scarecrow, 1995), p. xxi n.

I. Nevin and the Mercersburg Theology

There can be no possibility of mistaking the center of the Mercersburg theology. Nevin declares tirelessly, with a hundred repetitions, that the main point in Christianity, the heart of the gospel, is the incarnation, and that the merit of Mercersburg has been to insist upon this point more than any other variety of Protestant theology in America.[5] He made himself the relentless critic of American Protestantism, seldom, if ever, echoing the sentiments of any of its leading parties. In his emphasis on the mystery of the incarnation he looked, rather, to the old Greek fathers. As James Hastings Nichols said, Nevin "made himself at home with Irenaeus, Athanasius, Basil, and the two Gregories. With some justification Dorner called Nevin Eastern Orthodox in his orientation."[6] But if this orientation made him something of an oddity among American theologians, that merely showed, in Nevin's opinion, how far Americans who professed to stand in the Reformed tradition had fallen from the wisdom of their assumed master, John Calvin, who could write so passionately on the life-giving flesh of the Son of Man. Nevin's defense of the Mercersburg theology was at the same time an accusation of apostasy in the supposedly Calvinistic churches. Our agenda, then, will require us, within the obvious limits, to consider what the Mercersburg theologians meant by the incarnation, what place they found in the incarnation for the atonement, and how Nevin could justify the Mercersburg theology as "a vindication of the Reformed or Calvinist doctrine of the Holy Eucharist." Then we can conclude with some critical reflections concerning the disagreements between Nevin and Hodge on the atonement.

---

5. Nevin provided a very brief sketch of "the Mercersburg System of Theology" in a communication of uncertain date to Henry Harbaugh, reproduced in *Catholic and Reformed: Selected Theological Writings of John Williamson Nevin*, ed. Charles Yrigoyan, Jr., and George H. Bricker, Pittsburgh Original Texts and Translations, vol. 3 (Pittsburgh: Pickwick, 1978), pp. 407-11. "Its cardinal principle," he says, "is the fact of the Incarnation" (p. 408).

6. James Hastings Nichols, *Romanticism in American Theology: Nevin and Schaff at Mercersburg* (Chicago: University of Chicago Press, 1961), p. 159. On Dorner see n. 15 below.

1. The Incarnation and the New Liturgy

A useful statement of the Mercersburg theology was occasioned by efforts to embody a sound incarnational theology in a new Reformed liturgy. In 1861, the General Synod of the German Reformed Church sent a provisional liturgy (drafted in 1857) back to the liturgical committee for revision. (Nevin had been the original chairman of the committee, but since he never convened it, the honor had passed to Philip Schaff.) Not until the Synod met in Dayton in 1866 was the committee's work completed, too late for the tricentennial celebration of the Heidelberg Catechism in 1863. "The Order of Worship for the Reformed Church in the United States," as it was titled, was adopted for use at the discretion of individual pastors and congregations, not imposed on the church as a liturgical rule. But so bitter had been the opposition from the anti-liturgical party, that twenty-one elders of the church petitioned Nevin to furnish a history of the committee's work and a critical review of the liturgy's merits. Nevin's response, *Vindication of the Revised Liturgy, Historical and Theological,* appeared the following year (1867).[7] The narrative of the liturgical committee's work, the historical part of Nevin's vindication, is an interesting testimony (for anyone who needs it) to the chicanery of ecclesiastical politics. The theological part represents the revised liturgy not as a mere arrangement of liturgical fragments, but as the embodiment of a total theological outlook, at variance with the total outlook of its critics. The liturgical controversy was about two gospels, Nevin believed, two different versions of the meaning of Christianity. "The Liturgy," he says, "represented one system of religious thought; the opposition to it represented another; the two constitutionally different, and mutually repellant" (p. 362).

Nevin assumes that the theological opposition suffers from "want of sympathy with the true idea of the Gospel" (p. 362). They are committed to views that are unevangelical and heretical (p. 363). (If this sounds harsh and extreme, we should bear in mind that he is throwing back at the critics their own charges against the committee.) Opposition to the liturgy, he continues, is opposition to the system of theological belief "from whose inspiration it draws its life and power." Nevin

7. Reprinted in Yrigoyen and Bricker, *Catholic and Reformed,* pp. 313-403. Page numbers, given in parentheses, are to this edition.

means, of course, what came to be called "the Mercersburg theology"; and he characterizes it in three summary points: "it is Christological, or more properly perhaps Christocentric; . . . moves in the bosom of the Apostles' Creed; . . . is Objective and Historical, involving thus the idea of the Church as a perennial article of faith" (p. 365). Nevin is more than a little tendentious in his appeal to the creed. But all three points, as he develops them, are fundamental to his understanding of the work of Christ and his distaste for the atonement theory defended by Charles Hodge. At bottom, the three points are one.

First: To put Christ at the center is to reject both a merely *anthropological* divinity, or humanitarian theology, which starts from the idea of humanity, and a merely *theological* divinity, which starts from some general idea of God. Everything depends on surveying things from the right point of view: what the heliocentric standpoint is for astronomy, the Christocentric standpoint is for theology, which, if it is sound theology, "revolves around Christ as a centre, and is irradiated at all points by the light that flows upon it from his presence" (p. 366). "Presence" is the operative word here. Nevin is not talking about the centrality of a doctrine, but about a fact and a reality — "the mystery of godliness: God was manifest in the flesh" (1 Tim. 3:16).[8]

> As an object of faith and knowledge, and in the only form in which it can be regarded as having reality in the world, Christianity has been brought to pass through the mystery of the Incarnation, and stands perpetually in the presence and power of that fact. . . . [A]s regards Christianity itself, strictly taken, what is it, we may well ask, in difference from all else pretending to call itself religion, if it be not the product and outgrowth of the new order of life, which first became actual in the world by the assumption of our human nature into union with the Divine Word (John i.14, 17), having in this view its beginning, middle, and end in Christ, and in Christ only? [pp. 365, 369]

Christocentric theology is not a theology of the *cross*: it is incarnational, placing at the center the *person* of Christ, the mystery of the Word made flesh.

8. Here, as elsewhere in my account of Nevin's thought, I give his Scripture texts in the KJV, as he does. I also reproduce (in quotations) his inconsistent capitalizing of such words as "incarnation."

Second, one sure guarantee that we do not go astray in our understanding of Christianity, Nevin thinks, is the old rule of faith, the Apostles' Creed. He may be right when he boasts that no other theology has held the banner of the creed so high as Mercersburg. But he is mistaken when he claims that the creed has been formally accepted in every age by all branches of the church, both Eastern and Western. The Eastern Orthodox churches in fact recognize only the Nicene Creed, the sole "ecumenical" creed properly so-called.[9] And perhaps Nevin claims too much for the content of the Apostles' Creed when he appeals to it to authorize the right sequence for unfolding Christian truths, everything "growing forth from the mystery of the Incarnation" (p. 372). That, surely, would require us to start with the second article, which actually begins as an added topic, not the first: ". . . *and* in Jesus Christ, his only Son our Lord. . . ." However, we can understand Nevin's point that the creed does sketch in articles two and three an orderly, progressive framework, within which every doctrine, including the doctrine of the atonement, may have its proper place. It is a framework of what Nevin calls "fundamental facts . . . growing forth from the mystery of the Incarnation." This order is not optional, but "bound to its own principle" (p. 372). Everything flows, as it must, from the conception and birth of God's Son — the manifestation of God in the flesh.

Nevin's third point is simply that the objective historical manifestation of God in Christ leads us necessarily to the third article of the creed: "I believe in the Holy Ghost, the holy catholic *Church.* . . ." The revelation of God through Jesus Christ was not an oracle, but an act in history: it "has entered permanently into the stream of the world's life, not just as the memory of a past wonder, but as the continued working of the power it carried with it in the beginning" (p. 377). Accordingly, we are not called on merely to remember what was once a real presence in the world. The "once for all" of the gospel does not point us to something concluded and left behind, but rather to something that, "having once entered into the life of the world, has become so incorporated with it as to be part of its historical being to the end of time" (p. 378). And here, Nevin says, we have the true idea of the holy catholic church: the "church," in the sense

9. The ecumenical claims even of the Nicene Creed are of course jeopardized by the Western church's insertion of the word *filioque,* which affirms that the Holy Spirit "proceeds from the Father *and the Son.*"

of the creed, means "the organ through which Christ works in the world (His body), the medium of His presence among men, the home of His Spirit, the sphere of His grace" (p. 389). The church is not a merely human organization: it is also superhuman "in virtue of its organic outflow from the fountain head of all grace and truth in the world, the union of the divine and human in the Person of our Lord and Saviour Jesus Christ, through the mystery of the Incarnation" (p. 391). In a word, the church is the objective, historical form of the order of grace "flowing" from Christ. Not the way most Presbyterians speak of the church, and we can appreciate the outcry Nevin's language evoked.

It is easy to anticipate where his idea of the holy, catholic church must lead Nevin when he turns to the Eucharist. He says expressly: "Such a churchly theology, we feel at once, can never be otherwise than sacramental," and "sacraments cannot possibly be regarded as outward signs only of what they represent": they are seals of a present reality (p. 380). The real presence defines the church; this must therefore be what the sacrament of the Supper is about and what a "true altar Liturgy" (as Nevin calls it: p. 361) seeks to embody.[10] But let's ask first, before turning to the Sacrament, What now becomes of the kind of atonement theory we found in Hodge?

2. Incarnation and Atonement: Nevin's Concio ad clerum

Some of Nevin's writings might lead us to suppose that if Hodge could never do justice to what he called "the mystical theory of atonement," Nevin had as much difficulty finding room for the motifs of sacrifice and satisfaction. One fascinating testimony is the sermon Nevin preached at the opening of the first general synod of the German Reformed Church in America (1863). He calls it a *concio ad clerum*, "an address to the clergy." The published version describes the address as "preached," and Nevin had a text, 1 Corinthians 1:21-24, which includes the assertion, "We preach Christ crucified" (v. 23).[11] Considering that

---

10. The *Vindication* concludes with Nevin's response to criticism of the liturgy's "Office for the *Holy Communion*" (pp. 400-403).

11. J[ohn] W. Nevin, *Christ, and Him Crucified: A concio ad clerum, Preached in Grace Church, Pittsburgh, November 18, 1863, at the Opening of the First General Synod of the Ger-*

the sermon was clearly intended to celebrate the Mercersburg theology, we can only marvel at Nevin's choice of what must strike us as an unpromising text for this purpose, since Mercersburg made so much of the *incarnation*. Nevin mentions the fact that the German Reformed Church has been attacked by those who make the idea of *atonement* the principle of Christianity. Perhaps a little defiance lies behind his announcing what might be considered the perfect text for his critics. Be that as it may, I think it must be said, in all honesty, that the address proves to be a tour de force rather than plain exegesis.

The great problem of religion, Nevin begins, is the restoration of man's being to its original dignity, and this is to be found only in union with the Fountain of life. Paganism — even in its highest form, the philosophy and religion of Greece — is the vain, titanic endeavor to solve the problem with the world's own resources. "The world by wisdom knew not God" (1 Cor. 1:21). Judaism, though it had the promise of a deliverance to come, could not rise above the deistic idea of a God outside the world who works on it from beyond, "without any real entrance, after all, into its actual life and history" (p. 6). That is why, when the Word was made flesh, the Jews still asked for a sign from heaven, "not content with the evidence of his divinity, which shined through his own person" (p. 7). "For the Jews require a sign" (1 Cor. 1:22). But in the person of Jesus Christ God became man, and man was exalted to living union with God.

And so, as we hear so many times from Nevin, the advent of Christ brought supernatural powers into the world, or a "principle" that was not there before: namely, his own theanthropic life. "In him, the world received into lasting union with its fallen constitution the power of God's own life" (p. 11). Consequently, any representation of Christ's work as a merely external deed falls short of the truth. Nevin doesn't mince words: he is warning us against a "heresy."

> The doctrine of the atonement is true, regarded as the power of a permanent fact [i.e., the incarnation] comprehended in the death of Christ, followed by his resurrection; but, considered as something of force through his death alone, a sort of outward work which he came

---

man *Reformed Church in America* (Pittsburgh: J. McMillin, 1863). Page references to this address are given in parentheses.

into the world to perform in this way, and for which his incarnation was contrived and designed in the relation of means to end, the whole imagination becomes magical, and so visionary and false [pp. 15-16].

As so often, Nevin's meaning is less than perspicuous. What he denies is plainer than what he wants to affirm. We are cautioned not to make of the atonement an outward work connected exclusively with Christ's death, much less to suppose that this outward work is what he came into the world to perform. Such a misconception would be "magical" — in the sense, I take it, of being discontinuous with what came before and what came afterwards. That this is Nevin's meaning appears from his description of the "magical" way in which Judaism thought of the presence of the supernatural in the world: namely, as "a sort of apparition, or unearthly oracle, breaking in upon the settled order of things, and passing away again in the character of a mere outward miracle or sign" (pp. 6-7).[12] Atonement as an isolated event, a transaction outside of our history — that is what Nevin is *against,* and it goes with "a doctrinal orthodoxy, which works disastrously to the interests of practical piety, substituting a mere dry theory of religion for its life" (p. 19).[13] Very well. But what is Nevin *for?* The *truth* of the doctrine of the atonement is left unexplained.

All he tells us in the *Concio ad clerum,* when it comes right down to it, is that we must view Christ's atoning death strictly in the frame of the incarnation. The point is made repeatedly. "[Christ's] incarnation drew after it, with necessary consequence, and in the way of sure historical development, the whole work of redemption, as it was wrought out subsequently through his death and resurrection" (p. 9). All the words and works of Christ rest on "the absolute fullness and sufficiency of what he was, and still is, in his own person and life" (p. 10). All Christian doctrines "grow" or "flow" from the mystery of the incarnation (pp. 13, 21). "Torn from their living, organic union with this divine constitution, they become no better than hollow abstractions" (p. 15). "All Christian truths . . . branch forth from this fundamental mystery" (p. 21). But none

12. In the *Vindication* "magical" is contrasted with "abiding, historical" (p. 388).

13. In the *Concio ad clerum,* as elsewhere, Nevin stresses that he is speaking of a fact, not a theory or dogma. The incarnation was "a simple historical fact" (p. 12), "the great living and historical fact" (p. 13). But note that even the Trinity is taken for "a divine fact," not a mere dogma (p. 14).

of this leads Nevin to explain the meaning the death of Christ has, when placed in due perspective.

To his text from 1 Corinthians 1:21-24 he does not hesitate to add 2:2, Paul's insistence: "I determined not to know any thing among you, save Jesus Christ, and him crucified." Nevin comments that "this is sometimes taken to mean simply ringing changes on the death of Christ, the atonement, and justification by faith, viewed in a mechanical and separate way" (p. 22). Against this unfortunate error he insists that the doctrine of the cross is "the living centre, we may say, of the universal movement of Christ's life, having its significance wholly in its antecedents and consequents embraced in this life" (p. 22). And again we wonder: What *is* this significance? A mere hint of an answer is given in the assertion that only through humiliation and death could Christ enter into his glory. The allusion is to Christ's words on the Emmaus road (Luke 24:26). But what is going on in this intriguing address is more obvious in Nevin's suggestion that, by preaching Christ and him crucified, Paul means "nothing more nor less than the simple proclamation of the Gospel, as comprehended in the real, and not merely imaginary, coming of Christ into the world, *in the sense of St. John*" (p. 22; my emphasis).

What Nevin is doing becomes immediately obvious: he is incorporating the gospel of Paul into the gospel of John, and he is so confident of the soundness of this procedure that it scarcely occurs to him to ask whether it is a fair exegesis of his text. He even finds a warrant of sorts in the Johannine rule for testing whether or not the spirits are of God (p. 21): "Every spirit that confesseth that Jesus Christ is come in the flesh is of God" (1 John 4:2).[14] To Nevin, it follows that anything any of us, including the apostle Paul, can say truthfully about Jesus Christ and his work must be said under the inclusive rubric of the incarnation: it must be a confession that Jesus Christ is come in the flesh. In Acts, he points out, Paul and the other apostles preach Jesus and the *resurrection,* and here too the lesson we are to learn is the same: "The Gospel is assumed to be, throughout [in Acts], the stupendous fact of the Incarnation, drawing after it the leading results of Christ's life: his death, his resurrection, his glorification," etc. (p. 23). In short, Nevin's claim is this: "As a Church [the German Reformed Church] we have endeavored to bear witness to the truth that Jesus Christ is come in the flesh,

14. A favorite text, he appealed to it also in the *Vindication* (p. 387).

and to follow out this great mystery of godliness to its necessary historico-theological consequences and results . . ." (p. 29). The death of Christ is one such consequence. Once it is correctly identified as such, Nevin has very little — in this address — to say about it. His Pauline text notwithstanding, he seems more interested in having us view the death of Christ as a consequence of the incarnation than in telling us what atoning significance the death may have had.

The cross does, of course, have its place in others of Nevin's writings. But it seldom moves to the center for very long. Inevitably, the Mercersburg approach met with fierce opposition, and the eminent German theologian Isaak Dorner thought Nevin emphasized the incarnation and the life of Christ at the expense of his death and the atonement.[15] But from Nevin's viewpoint, justice is done to the atonement precisely when we see it in the context of the incarnation. As soon as the context was secured, he believed he could use the language so dear to his opponents. Hodge may not have been reassured when Nevin insisted that his case was compatible with *any* theory of atonement. (Hodge wanted only one.) In his theology lectures, Nevin could even tell his students that God's justice must be satisfied, and that either the sinner or the sinner's surrogate must be punished.[16]

On those rare occasions when Nevin gives a clear signal of his thoughts on the atonement, he takes exactly the direction we would expect: back to the *Christus Victor* motif of the Greek fathers, which viewed Christ's death and resurrection as a triumph over sin, death, and hell — the powers that held humanity in bondage. In a word, the atonement was the victory of life over death. "Conceived by the Holy Ghost and born of

15. Isaak August Dorner (1809-1884) published a critical account of the liturgical controversy in the German Reformed Church in America (1867), and Nevin replied with a series of rebuttals in *The Weekly Messenger,* brought together in a single long article, "Answer to Professor Dorner," in *The Mercersburg Review* 20 (1868): 534-646. Selections from this article will be found in James Hastings Nichols, ed., *The Mercersburg Theology,* Library of Protestant Thought (New York: Oxford University Press, 1966). Nevin expressly repudiates Dorner's "persistence in the strange opinion that to lay emphasis on the Incarnation and to magnify the life of Christ is necessarily to wrong the claims of the Atonement, and to make small account of the death of Christ" (Nichols, *Mercersburg Theology,* p. 193).

16. See W. H. Erb, ed., *Dr. Nevin's Theology, Based on Manuscript Class-room Lectures* (Reading, 1913), p. 94. I owe this reference to Nichols, *Romanticism in American Theology,* p. 146.

the Virgin Mary," Nevin says, "Jesus Christ must necessarily suffer also and die, but only that by doing so he might conquer death, and bring in everlasting righteousness and immortal life for the nature he came to redeem and save."[17] The direction of Nevin's thoughts on the atonement is especially clear in *The Mystical Presence* (1846), his study of the Reformed or Calvinist doctrine of the Holy Eucharist. Probably his best-known work, it led him into direct controversy with his former teacher.

3. The Mystical Presence: Nevin's Appeal to John Calvin

Nevin was persuaded that everything in Christianity flows from the mystery of God made manifest in the flesh. The cause he fought for so energetically was a better understanding of the church as a historical organism brought into existence by the incarnation and continually nurtured by the life of the Son of Man. But he also believed that the best *access* to a sound incarnational theology is through the sacrament of the Lord's Supper. In the doctrine of Christ's real presence in the Eucharist both his personal piety and his theological insight came to their sharpest focus. "To my own mind," he wrote, "all that is great and precious in the gospel may be said to center in this doctrine. . . . Both for my understanding and my heart, theology finds here all its interest and attraction."[18] In the introduction to *The Mystical Presence,* he declared that our view of the Lord's Supper must finally govern our thoughts on both Christ and the church, and must materially influence our whole system of theology (p. 23).[19] One can well imagine the astonishment with which Reformed and Presbyterian churchgoers would have read this declaration. For most of them, the Sacrament was an occasional feature of their church's practice — one item among others, perhaps even marginal to the church's life

---

17. Nevin, "Wilberforce on the Incarnation," *Mercersburg Review* 1850, in Nichols, *Mercersburg Theology,* p. 80.

18. Nevin, "The Mystical Union," *Weekly Messenger* 1845, in Nichols, *Mercersburg Theology,* p. 197.

19. My references to *The Mystical Presence* (1846), mostly given in parentheses in the main body of this section, provide the page numbers in John W. Nevin, *The Mystical Presence and Other Writings on the Eucharist,* ed. Bard Thompson and George H. Bricker, Lancaster Series on the Mercersburg Theology, vol. 4 (Philadelphia and Boston: United Church, 1966).

and thought. Nevin assigned it a *regulative* importance that defied the prevailing mentality of American Protestantism. And what he discovered in the Sacrament must have seemed more astonishing still.

In Nevin's view, the Eucharist has its place in the church as a unique source of the life that flows to us from the flesh of the Lord. Receiving the Sacrament, believers do not merely receive Christ's benefits: they participate in his true and proper life, and the participation is real, substantial, and essential (p. 36). Further, the life-giving virtue of the Sacrament is not put into it by the faith of the communicant: it is there, objectively, and the signs attest its presence (pp. 39-40). Nevin freely used the Johannine language of feeding on the flesh of the Son of Man, and he believed that he was simply reproducing the eucharistic faith of "nearly the whole Christian world from the beginning" (p. 116). (American Protestantism was a minor aberration.) But his main appeal was to John Calvin, and his pages bristle with direct citations from the Genevan Reformer, who, among other things, had assured one of his Lutheran opponents: "I do not teach that Christ simply dwells in us by his Spirit, but that he so raises us to himself as to transfuse into us the life-giving vigor of his flesh" (p. 35n).

In Princeton, Charles Hodge was appalled. He determined to review Nevin's *Mystical Presence* for the *Princeton Review,* but for two years the book just sat on his table, so painful was it for him to read it. Nevin's talk of apostasy in the Reformed church, which (he believed) had abandoned and forgotten Calvin's eucharistic ideas, stung Hodge, the presumed spokesman for American Calvinism. He tried to discredit Nevin's view by attributing it to the same German mysticism that had spoiled Friedrich Schleiermacher. But then there were all those quotations from John Calvin! What was Hodge to do with them? He grandly dismissed all talk of Christ's life-giving flesh as a merely private opinion of Calvin's, an "uncongenial foreign element" in Reformed theology, derived in part from Lutheran influence. Calvin's opinion, he said, received no endorsement from the most important Reformed confessions and soon died out.[20] Where Nevin saw apostasy, Hodge saw progress.

Nevin did not permit his old teacher to have the last word. He launched an entire series of detailed rebuttals in the *Weekly Messenger* of

20. Charles Hodge, "Doctrine of the Reformed Church on the Lord's Supper," *Princeton Review* 1848; reprinted in Hodge, *Essays and Reviews* (New York: Robert Carter & Brothers, 1857), pp. 341-92; see pp. 341-42; 373n, 376n, 378-81, 389-92.

the German Reformed Church, then collected and expanded them in his new theological journal, the *Mercersburg Review,* in a massive article that ran to 128 pages. It was overkill, as we say these days. Hodge did not venture to reply. Neither did he change his mind. In the sections on the Lord's Supper in his *Systematic Theology,* he again alludes to "the peculiar views of Calvin" (*ST* 3:630) and goes on to attribute Nevin's eucharistic theology to philosophical infiltration from Germany. "[A]nd philosophy we know from an infallible authority, is a vain deceit. It is vain (κενή) empty; void of truth, weightless and worthless" (*ST* 3:660-61). If, as James Hastings Nichols thought, Hodge lost the argument with Nevin,[21] he seems not to have noticed.

It is another question what exactly Nevin might have meant by his talk of Christ's life-giving flesh. As he pointed out in *The Mystical Presence,* Calvin denied that he took the language of "eating the flesh of the Son of Man" in a crude, literal sense (pp. 37-38), and he thought it possible to restate Calvin's doctrine without the serious difficulties under which it labored (pp. 150-51). Nevin's efforts to recast the Calvinist doctrine in an improved, "scientific" form may strike us as laboring under difficulties of their own. What mattered to him, however, was the fundamental contrast Calvin drew between two ways of coming at the expression "life-giving flesh."

The one approach, Zwingli's, assumed that the flesh of Christ could give life only in the sense that it was once crucified for our salvation. The other approach, Calvin's, wanted to say more: that the flesh of Christ gives life to believers daily because — somehow, they are not sure how — they are united with Christ in a sacred union that the sacrament of the Supper nurtures and increases in them. This, for Nevin, was the *substance* of Calvin's stand in the eucharistic controversy, and he was determined not to let the problematic *form* of Calvin's doctrine open the door to surrender of the substance (p. 158). For the alternative, into which the Reformed and Presbyterian churches had fallen wholesale, was a theory that reduced the mystery of communion with Christ to a mere recollection of what he once did — a devotional exercise that has in it, Nevin caustically remarked, as little mystery as a common Fourth of July celebration (p. 107). Of what he calls "the modern Puritan doctrine" he could say only this:

21. See Chap. 8 above, at n. 58.

The entire interest of communion with Christ's human *life,* it deliberately rejects as an antiquated superstition. It will hear only of communion with his *death;* by which it means, not the abiding force of this as a real quality or property of the still living Savior, but the thought or memory of it only as something past and gone. The bond thus between sign and thing signified is completely severed.[22]

Against this desacralized ritual, which Hodge supposed to be an improvement on Calvin's private opinion, Nevin argued that the original Reformed confession, no less than the Lutheran, insisted on participation in Christ's life as the essential thing in the sacramental mystery. Not, however, to the exclusion of an interest in Christ's death![23]

It would hardly be possible to ignore the connection of the Lord's Supper with Christ's death — and, therefore, with the atonement. Nevin noted that the words of institution speak of the body broken, the blood shed: that is, of Christ as sacrifice for the sins of the world. Not that the Sacrament is itself a sacrifice, as the Church of Rome imagines, but it serves to "ratify and advance" the interest believers have in the new covenant established through Christ's blood (pp. 178-79). And for this reason, Nevin had no qualms about describing the "altar feeling" that pervaded the liturgy, in which the people present to God Christ's passion and their own selves on the eucharistic altar.[24] But what does this imply for the *meaning* of the atonement? Here too, as elsewhere, Nevin interprets atonement by the incarnation and returns to the ancient *Christus Victor* motif of the Greek fathers. The purpose of the incarnation was not merely to provide the necessary basis for atonement by Christ's suffering and death.

> The object of the incarnation was to couple the human nature in real union with the Logos, as a permanent source of life. It resulted from the presence of sin only . . . that the union thus formed called the Saviour to suffer. As the bearer of a fallen humanity he must descend with it to the lowest depths of sorrow and pain, in order that he might

---

22. Nevin, "Doctrine of the Reformed Church on the Lord's Supper," *Mercersburg Review* 1850, reprinted in Thompson and Bricker, *Mystical Presence,* pp. 267-401; see p. 395.

23. Nevin, "Doctrine of the Reformed Church," p. 394.

24. Nevin, "Answer to Dorner," in Nichols, *Mercersburg Theology,* p. 186.

triumph with it again in the power of his own imperishable life. . . . The passion of the Son of God was the world's spiritual *crisis,* in which the principle of health came to its last struggle with the principle of disease, and burst forth from the very bosom of the grave itself in the form of immortality. This was the atonement, Christ's victory over sin and hell [pp. 162-63].[25]

This, then, is what Nevin makes of Christ's atoning death, once it is incorporated into the fact of the incarnation. He does not appeal directly to Calvin for the *Christus Victor* motif, though he could have.[26] Calvin's name is invoked rather as a warrant for the determinative idea of the life — "theanthropic life," as Nevin liked to say — that streams from the humanity of Christ. Calvin himself found support for his understanding of Christ's life-giving flesh in one of the Greek fathers, Cyril of Alexandria.[27] Even in his regard for the patristic sources, Nevin was a good Calvinist.

II. Hodge and Nevin: An Appraisal

Now it would perhaps be possible to take a further step and simply identify the *at one*-ment with the incarnation: the manifestation of God in the flesh of Jesus could itself be taken for the divine activity that mends the broken relationship of humanity with God. But Nevin was not, as far as I can see, tempted to take this step. He reserved the word "atonement" for what was accomplished by the death and resurrection of Christ, and he was concerned only to set the atoning death of Christ in the frame of his life, not to diminish it. We might accordingly suggest for Nevin a summary, parallel to our summary of Hodge's theology of atonement, that goes something like this: *The atoning work of Christ's death and resurrection on behalf of sinners was the final engagement be-*

---

25. This passage appears in Nevin's explication of his third and fourth constructive ("scientific") theses on the mystical union. The fourth thesis itself is given in italics: *"The value of Christ's sufferings and death, as well as of his entire life, in relation to men, springs wholly from the view of the incarnation now presented"* (p. 162). Cf. the "biblical argument" from John 6:51-58 (pp. 243-52).

26. See Calvin, *ICR* II, xvi.6 (1:511), 11 (1:517), 13 (1:521).

27. Calvin, *ICR* IV, xvii.9 (2:1369).

tween the forces of evil and God incarnate, in which the divine life of the Word made flesh was victorious over sin and death. For Hodge, the key motif was satisfaction; for Nevin, it was victory. The two motifs are not exclusive, but the contrast is obvious; and the differences are profound, affecting the entire conception one entertains of the Christian faith.

1. Two Reformed Traditions?

Hodge and Nevin agreed that the division over which they argued, with vehemence on both sides, was not new but had its roots in the earliest beginnings of the Reformed tradition. As Nevin said:

> Two phases of thought, it is admitted, come together to a certain extent in the early history of the Reformed doctrine — one which lays all stress on the *sacrifice* of Christ, as an atonement for sin [Zwingli's view]; and another, specially insisted upon by Calvin, which carries back our salvation to the idea of Christ's *life,* as its necessary perpetual source and ground.[28]

Where Hodge and Nevin disagreed was not only in their respective preferences (Hodge liked Zwingli, Nevin liked Calvin), but also in the way they read the historical progress of the two types of Reformed doctrine. Neither of them was willing to conclude that there are two Reformed traditions; each had his own way of resolving the opposition. Hodge thought Calvin's opinion was *replaced* by the other view and deservedly carried no weight in the Reformed church. Nevin, on the other hand, pointed out that the Reformed doctrine actually began in Switzerland "under the first aspect," emphasis on Christ's sacrifice, and that Calvin's view, which came later, *subsumed* the first aspect under his characteristic emphasis on the life of Christ. It was this union of the two views that became the actual creed of the Reformed church. The misery of our modern divinity, Nevin concludes, is that it has fallen from this "divine synthesis" of Calvin and sundered the atonement from its necessary ground.[29]

As far as Hodge himself is concerned, Nevin's severe indictment is

28. Nevin, "Doctrine of the Reformed Church," p. 288.
29. Nevin, "Doctrine of the Reformed Church," p. 295.

not entirely fair. Hodge, too, believed that Christ's work of atonement required him to be the God-Man (*ST* 2:395-96, 457-58); he, too, liked to speak of Christ's "theanthropic" person (e.g., 2:389), and, in harmony with this expression, he was even willing to call Mary "the Mother of God" (2:393). Still, there *are* differences between the two systems, as I have tried to show. They deserve a more thorough critical reflection than I can give them here, and the systematic or constructive theological task is, of course, another matter.[30] It would be interesting to look closely at each of the individual criticisms Hodge fires at Nevin and Nevin at Hodge (or, more generally, at what Nevin takes to be the wrong kind of Calvinism, represented by Hodge). But I must leave the details for another day and, in conclusion, suggest just four points on which I think the systematic theologians might learn from Nevin's opposition to Hodge, and two on which they may have some lingering doubts. The four points on which I commend Nevin's contribution are closely interwoven, as will become clear.

2. *Some Positive Gains of Nevin's Approach*

On the credit side, Nevin reminds us, first of all, that there have always been *diversity and development* in the Reformed tradition. Hodge could not deny it, but, for his part, he liked to see variety and movement eventually brought to an end in a fixed, exclusive formula. He stood, as we have seen, for a static and monolithic understanding of Reformed theol-

---

30. Among other things, we would need to consider whether the antithesis "Zwingli *versus* Calvin" excludes a mediating alternative. In his *Systematic Theology,* which came after the controversy with Nevin, Hodge himself took the view that besides the Zwinglian and Calvinist types of doctrine there was "an intermediate form, which ultimately became symbolical [i.e., came to be incorporated in the Reformed confessions]" (3:626). There is much to be said for distinguishing a third alternative, if the issue is the relation of *sign and reality* in the Eucharist. (See B. A. Gerrish, "The Lord's Supper in the Reformed Confessions" [1966], reprinted in *The Old Protestantism,* chap. 7.) *Mystical union* is another issue that lends itself to mediation. In his review of Nevin's *The Mystical Presence,* Hodge actually began with an affirmation of our real, vital, and mysterious union with Christ that seems to me to go well beyond Zwingli: his citations from Zwingli say nothing about it! Is it possible that reading Nevin's book moved Hodge to affirm an "intermediate" doctrine that is not characteristic of Zwingli and not much emphasized elsewhere by Hodge himself?

ogy, which he identified with "the Augustinian system." And, as always happens with such idealized concepts of the past, his Reformed tradition was largely a construct of his own selective making: whatever he could not approve he winnowed out. Intrusive thoughts or thinkers that might have made the tradition broader or more flexible were disqualified — not only Schleiermacher and Nevin, who were spoiled by vain philosophy (*ST* 2:532), but even John Calvin insofar as he let the Lutherans lead him astray. Even Hodge's appeal to the "Augustinian system" was specious. Augustine stood as much for a view of the church that Hodge deplored as for the doctrine of grace that Hodge applauded.

Not that Nevin was above some pruning of the tradition to fit *his* perspective: he asserted that "the doctrine of the decrees, as held by Calvin, never belonged at all to the constitution of the Reformed Church as such; whereas the sacramental doctrine entered in truth into its distinctive character as a confession."[31] As it stands, the assertion is indefensible. And yet, we must surely concede that Nevin was a faithful and powerful witness to a neglected side of the Reformed heritage, a heritage that ought to include John Calvin even when his opinions strike us as "peculiar." Nevin also understood perfectly well that Calvin and his theology are not fixed and final criteria of dogmatic truth any more than any other Reformed theologian, confession, or doctrine. Hence he undertook, as he said, to revise the *form* of Calvin's eucharistic theology while trying to preserve its *substance*. Fundamental differences over the idea of historical development divided Princeton from Mercersburg.[32] Nevin was never more faithful to the Reformed tradition than when he presented it as richer than we realized, yet open to correction *(ecclesia reformata semper reformanda!)*.

Secondly, what Nevin retrieved from Calvin was, above all, the pivotal idea of *union with Christ.* "For Christianity is grounded," he says, "in the living union of the believer with the person of Christ; and this great fact is emphatically concentrated in the mystery of the Lord's Sup-

31. Nevin, "Doctrine of the Reformed Church," p. 373. That the assertion appears in Nevin's description of theology in the *German* Reformed Church does not seem to limit the expression "Reformed Church as such." His repudiation of Calvin's doctrine of God's absolute decree is severe: it "is in plain contradiction to the entire idea of Christianity."

32. For Hodge's thoughts on development see *ST* 1:116-19, where the adversary is Philip Schaff.

per. . . ."[33] Hodge was quite capable of talking about union with Christ, but he saw everything founded on the work of Christ *extra nos* ("outside of us") as our substitute or representative. Although he could speak of the *mystical* union (*ST* 3:104-6), it was a concept that clearly made him uneasy. He was suspicious of a theological scheme that might call on us "to exchange a hope founded upon what Christ is and has done in our behalf . . . for a hope founded on the glimmer of divine life which we find within ourselves" (2:537). The objectivity of the gospel plan of salvation would thereby be subverted, and the sinner turned in upon himself. Hodge could even protest that the "modern" view of the Lord's Supper advocated by Nevin took away a personal Savior and gave Christians nothing in return but "a new invisible law in their members" (3:660). He laid all his emphasis on Christ's work in our stead, and was more at ease with the notion of a *federal* or covenantal union of Christ with his people: what Christ does as representative, in this view, he does for his covenant people, as Adam acted for humanity under the original covenant of works (2:521, 551).[34] True, there has to be a "subjective application" of Christ's work, an application to the individual (2:581, 3:213). But the sinner's justification is purely by imputation, and even sanctification is founded on substitution (2:522).[35] And, anyway, to be in Christ is simply to believe in him (3:104).[36]

In all these ways, Hodge attempted to make the mystical union

33. Nevin, *The Mystical Presence*, p. 27.

34. Hodge occasionally tries to be more inclusive: in one place he says that the union is "partly federal established in the councils of eternity; partly vital by the indwelling of the Holy Spirit; and partly voluntary and conscious by faith" (*ST* 2:396). But the burden of his complaint against the "modern" view weighs against such inclusiveness.

35. Nevin, by contrast, states that a "real life union with Christ . . . is the only basis on which there can be any true imputation to us of what [Christ] has done and suffered on our behalf" (*The Mystical Presence*, pp. 179-80). Cf. Calvin's statement that reconciliation as well as sanctification is the gift of participation in Christ (*ICR* III, xi.1 [1:725]).

36. Hodge notes Calvin's distinction between "believing" and "eating" (i.e., between believing in Christ and an actual "participation" in Christ), but he thinks it a distinction without a difference if faith includes "appropriating" (*ST* 3:644-45). He goes on to discuss Calvin's distinction between the benefits and the life of Christ (pp. 646-47). For Calvin, "eating" was not faith, but the *effect* of faith — "a small difference indeed in words, but no slight one in the matter itself" (*ICR* IV, xvii.5 [2:1365]) — and he understood union with the living Christ to have priority over the reception of his benefits (xvii.11 [2:1372]).

harmless. No wonder Nevin was as much repelled by Hodge's entire scheme as Hodge by Nevin's! Besides, Hodge's efforts were strained and led him into confusion: in the Pauline metaphor of the body and its members, the body of Christ becomes for him more a political than an organic metaphor (*ST* 2:521), and Paul's language about Christ living in him (Gal. 2:20) is oddly used to buttress the quite different idea of substitution (2:523). Nevin's thoughts on union with Christ make better sense of Pauline language, are certainly more faithful to Calvin, and are probably more true to Christian experience — including Hodge's Christian experience. Nevin says:

> The relation of believers to Christ, then, is more again than that of a simply *legal* union. . . . [E]xternal imputation rests at last on an inward, real unity of life, without which it could have no reason or force. Our interest in Christ's merits and benefits can be based only upon a previous interest in his person; so in the Lord's Supper, we are made to participate, not merely in the advantages secured by his mediatorial work . . . but also in his true and proper life itself. We partake of his merits and benefits only so far as we partake of his substance.[37]

This is surely a perceptive account of Christian experience: there is more to a devout believer's relationship with Christ than a purely legal arrangement. But what about the odd talk of participation in Christ's substance, to say nothing of Nevin's talk elsewhere about an "efflux" from Christ that lodges itself in the inmost core of our personality, where it becomes the principle or seed of our sanctification?[38] This brings me to point three.

Thirdly, I think we can learn something from Nevin about *the use of metaphorical language,* even if we decline to borrow his own metaphors. Here there is unquestionably another profound difference between Mercersburg and Princeton, and it is closely connected with other differences. Because Nevin understood Christianity to be about a life that

---

37. *The Mystical Presence,* p. 34. The point is confirmed with a string of verbatim quotations from Calvin (cf. pp. 188-89). In *Christ, and Him Crucified* (his *Concio ad clerum*) Nevin asserts that justification "deserves no confidence, except as it is made to include always the idea of a living apprehension of the Saviour himself, in his whole human divine life" (p. 16).

38. *The Mystical Presence,* pp. 164-65.

came into the world when the Word was made flesh, he was willing to acknowledge that the gospel is a mystery that eludes our comprehension and that doctrines are always secondary to life itself.[39] His theology was more rhetorical and pliable, even vaguer, than Hodge's, who wanted cool precision in Christian doctrine (hymn singing was another genre). Nevin felt Hodge's brand of Calvinism to be too dry and formal. For his part, Hodge remarked that modern German theories of the Lord's Supper, Nevin's classed among them, "are unintelligible to the majority of educated men, and as to the poor, for whom the gospel is especially designed, they are absolutely meaningless" (ST 3:659). Well, I can sympathize with the judgment and would not wish to take Nevin's side without reservation. Nevin himself once described his personal religion, with its mystical turn, as a "pulse-response to the ineffable."[40] Anyone whose pulse does not beat in time with Nevin's is bound to wonder what it all means.

But did Hodge never recognize that a meaning of sorts can be conveyed even by dark, luxuriant metaphors and arresting symbolic actions, and that such meaning may actually convey more to the "poor" than the most sober and refined dogma? One senses here a difference of Reformed theological temperaments, which also had its original paradigmatic expression in Zwingli and Calvin. Zwingli understood the Eucharist perfectly well, but at the price of taking the mystery out of it. Calvin willingly confessed that the mystery was too sublime for his intelligence to grasp or his words to express: "I rather experience than understand it."[41] What else is Calvin's Calvinism, we may well ask, but a pulse-response to the ineffable? As a good rhetorician, Calvin knew well that it is metaphor that captures the attention and penetrates the heart.[42]

Fourthly, Nevin argued again and again for the connection of atone-

---

39. On Jesus' discourse in John 6 Nevin comments: "It is, of course, in one respect figurative; as in the nature of the case all representations must be, that are borrowed from the sphere of nature to render intelligible what belongs to the sphere of the Spirit.... Here is no oral communication with Christ's flesh and blood. And yet the communication is real" (*The Mystical Presence,* pp. 245, 249).

40. Nevin, *My Own Life: The Earlier Years,* Papers of the Eastern Chapter, Historical Society of the Evangelical and Reformed Church, no. 1 (Lancaster, 1964), p. 124.

41. *ICR* IV, xvii.32 (2:1403).

42. Calvin, *Dilucida explicatio sanae doctrinae de vera participatione carnis et sanguinis Christi in sacra coena, ad discutiendas Heshusii nebulas* (1561), CO 9:514; TT 2:567.

ment with *the historical reality of the church,* and this I consider one of his most important contributions. Like everything else in the Mercersburg theology, the idea of the church is one piece of a consistent whole. The mystery of Christianity, as Nevin puts it, is "the power of a new creation *historically at hand* in the church."[43] While there is certainly a lot of exotic metaphor and queer metaphysics in the Mercersburg theology, it might be best, in the final analysis, to describe its view of Christ's work as thoroughly *historical* rather than speculative. One of the bonds between Nevin and Schaff was their profound admiration for the Berlin church historian, August Neander (1789-1850), whom Nevin began to read avidly when under the necessity to teach history classes at Western Theological Seminary. From Neander he learned, not just a lot of facts and dates from the church's past, but what it means for Christianity to be a historical religion.

No doubt, "a historical religion" is a phrase that suggests different things to different people. For some, like Hodge, the historical deed of God in Jesus Christ meant the carrying out of a once-for-all transaction between the first and second persons of the Trinity — a notion we might better classify as "mythological" rather than "historical." For Nevin and Schaff, it meant that the incarnation introduced into human history a new life, which has worked on human affairs through the church and still does. In this way, the ideas of incarnation and atonement require the idea of the church. Nevin writes:

> There is no opposition, then, between Christ and the Church in the economy of salvation. . . . We deceive ourselves if we imagine that we have faith in his salvation, while we refuse to recognize the actual historical presence of it in his own institution. Without faith in the Church, there can be no proper faith in Christ. If there be no such supernatural constitution in the world as the Idea of the Church implies, the whole fact of the Incarnation is turned into an unreal theophany, and the gospel is subverted to its very foundations. This much, and nothing less, is comprised in the article: *I believe in the holy catholic Church.*[44]

43. Nevin, "The Sect System" (1849), in Yrigoyen and Bricker, *Catholic and Reformed,* p. 160 (my emphasis).

44. Nevin, *The Church* (1847), in Nichols, *Mercersburg Theology,* pp. 66-67 (emphasis in the original).

Nevin must have remembered how closely his words echoed Calvin's Geneva Catechism (Latin, 1545), in which the child is asked whether it is necessary to believe the article of the creed on the holy, catholic church and is expected to answer: "Yes, indeed, unless we want to make the death of Christ and everything that has been rehearsed so far of no effect. For the one effect of it all is that there should be a church."[45] And Nevin knew well Calvin's famous admonition in the *Institutes* that there is no other way to enter into life than for Mother Church to "conceive us in her womb, give us birth, nourish us at her breast, and lastly, unless she keep us under her care and guidance until, putting off mortal flesh, we become like the angels."[46] But that's not how Charles Hodge liked to speak!

Once again, Hodge stood with the other side, which sharply opposed evangelical religion and churchly religion. In Princeton it was assumed that the Reformed churches made justification by faith the center of Christianity, and that it was the Oxford Tractarians who made the church the chief point. A choice had to be made. Hodge knew how Schleiermacher and his friends, including Nevin, sought to hold together the two supposedly antagonistic views (*ST* 1:174; 2:119, 139, 442, 448-51; 3:21, 211-12), but he firmly rejected the attempt: "The life of the believer is not a corporate life, conditioned on union with any outward organization, called the Church..." (2:397). Hodge had bought into the notion, which has little or nothing to do with the original Reformation witness, that Protestantism is about the *free access* of the solitary believer to God, without the intervention or ministration of others (2:468), or the right of *private judgment* without the testimony of the church (1:183).[47] Nevin's reply to this errant variety of Protestantism, presumed to be "evangelical," is that in fact the church "does indeed stand between Christ and the believer, but only as the body of a living man is between one of his limbs and the living soul by which it is quickened and moved."[48] For Nevin, as for Calvin, the metaphor of the be-

---

45. *Catechismus Ecclesiae Genevensis* (1545), q. 94; OS 2:89 (trans. mine; cf. *TT* 2:50).

46. *ICR* IV, i.4 (2:1016); cf. i.1 (2:1012).

47. On "free access" and "private judgment," see B. A. Gerrish, *The Old Protestantism,* chaps. 3 and 5. Nevin's frequent excoriation of the principle of private judgment is well represented in "The Sect System," pp. 140, 145, 164-65.

48. Nevin, "Wilberforce on the Incarnation," in Nichols, *Mercersburg Theology,* p. 90. See also *Vindication,* pp. 386-87, 393.

liever's organic union with Christ passes over naturally into the idea of the church, which is Christ's body.[49] The objectivity that Hodge sought in the substitutionary theory of atonement Nevin found in the historical reality of the church, and he reserved his sharpest arrows for the rampant individualism he saw everywhere in American church life.

3. Two Questions to Nevin

In all four of the points raised so far, I hardly need to confess that I lean more to Nevin's side than to Hodge's. But I hope I have not been unfair to Princeton. Theological issues are never simple, and the truth is seldom, if ever, all on one side. Differences need not be mutually exclusive, even when there is more to them than variations of emphasis. It is mainly for heuristic reasons that I have highlighted the antagonism between Princeton and Mercersburg, hoping that this will prove instructive as the transition is made from historical theology to the dogmatic task of presenting an informed and responsible account of God's reconciling work in Jesus Christ. Whether we could advance from Hodge's thesis and Nevin's antithesis to a genuine dogmatic synthesis must be left to dogmatics. For now, I conclude with two questions to Nevin, the first of which is asked partly on Hodge's behalf; the second is directed simultaneously to Hodge, too, and even to John Calvin.

I ended the previous chapter by wondering if the demands of theological polemic drove Hodge into one-sidedness in his interpretation of atonement. The question is not so much what he denied or rejected as what he didn't affirm strongly enough. "Satisfaction" was so important to him that, when challenged, he emphasized it all the more — to the relative neglect of other pieces that belong in the total picture. He introduced his chapter on theories of atonement by noting expressly that the doctrine of redemption provides for *two* objects: the removal of guilt and the quickening of souls dead in sin "with a new principle of divine life." The Latin church was more preoccupied with the first object, the Greek church with the second. "In the opposing theories devised by

---

49. Nevin, sermon on "Catholic Unity" (8 August 1844, published with the English version of Philip Schaff's *The Principle of Protestantism* in 1845), in Nichols, *Mercersburg Theology*, pp. 35-55; see especially p. 40.

theologians," Hodge observed, "either one of these objects is ignored or one is unduly subordinated to the other" (*ST* 2:563). But one is bound to ask if Hodge himself did not fall into this error, of which he was so plainly aware.

But then my first question to Nevin is this: Is it possible that he, too, failed to achieve a balance between the two "objects" of redemption? Was he also, as much as Hodge, guilty of one-sidedness in his thoughts on atonement? Nevin subsumed the atoning death of Christ under his cardinal idea of Christ's salvific life; and while this makes for systematic coherence, it seems to neglect, or at least to subordinate, the language of guilt, curse, wrath, punishment, satisfaction, sacrifice, expiation — all of which are embedded in the Scriptures and the traditions of the churches. There is a range of significant themes here that Hodge pursued with characteristic thoroughness, and theological construction must work through them as tenaciously as Hodge did. Not everything can be taken up into the idea of Christ's divine-human life. And that leads me to my second question, which concerns the *meaning* Nevin gives to the "life" of Christ.

In his address on Christ and him crucified, the *Concio ad clerum,* Nevin asserts that the root of all evangelical thinking is the incarnation, and he protests that those who like to monopolize the name "evangelical" think it un-evangelical "to make much of the historical facts and realities of Christ's life."[50] The polemical edge of this assertion needs to be smoothed a little. The culprits Nevin had in mind did not intend to minimize the facts of Christ's life; rather, they neglected to draw them in when defining the atonement. And this raises an important question for *any* theory of atonement: What significance does it allow to the words and works of Jesus reported in the Gospels?

Though he did not say so in the *Concio ad clerum,* Nevin certainly included Hodge among the evangelicals who neglect the "facts and realities of Christ's life." In his *Systematic Theology* Hodge had surprisingly little to say about the life of Christ, even where one might have expected him to dwell on it at length. The dogmatic tradition distinguished between the active and the passive obedience of the Mediator: his compliance with all the demands of the law *and* his willing submission to undeserved suffering and death. The distinction plays no role in Hodge's

---

50. *Christ, and Him Crucified,* pp. 33-34.

chapters on the work of Christ. He mentions it later, in passing, when he turns to justification by faith, but only to subordinate the active to the passive obedience: "He obeyed in suffering. . . . We are reconciled unto God by his death" (*ST* 3:143). For Hodge, Christ was born to die (2:612). Under the notion of Christ's "humiliation" he does affirm the traditional doctrine that "the whole course of Christ on earth was one of voluntary obedience" (2:613), but he moves on quickly to Christ's suffering and death, in which he discovers the atonement.

Now on *this* issue, at least, Hodge could have appealed against Nevin to Calvin, whose private opinions on the Lord's Supper did not impress him. Calvin does assert that Christ abolished sin and did away with the separation between us and God "by the whole course of his obedience." But he immediately goes on to say that "to define the way of salvation more exactly, Scripture ascribes this as peculiar and proper to Christ's death,"[51] and his Geneva Catechism includes this astonishing exchange on the second article of the Apostles' Creed:

> Q. Why do you jump straight from [Christ's] birth to his death, leaving out the story of his entire life?
> A. Because nothing is dealt with here but what belongs strictly to the substance of our redemption.[52]

So, none of the words and works of Jesus belong to the substance of our redemption? What can we reply in Calvin's defense, except that, after all, he was limited by his material?

Nevin seems at first to do better, though he professed to move "in the bosom of the Apostles' Creed." Everything, for him, turns on the life of Christ. But on reflection we may well ask (my second question to Nevin): Did Nevin also, in his own way commit the offense with which he charges the evangelicals — neglecting the "facts and realities of Christ's life"? For while he never tires of stating that it is the divine-human life of the incarnate Word that restores fallen humanity to God, he himself, as a rule, has little to say about the words and works of Jesus. It is the theanthropic life of Christ — the hypostatic union of two natures — that captivates him. And this is one point in the Mercersburg

---

51. *ICR* II, xvi.5 (1:507).
52. *Catechismus Ecclesiae Genevensis,* q. 55; OS 2:82 (trans. mine; cf. TT 2:45).

theology where we might like to see less metaphysics, more history.[53] In the words of the new Brief Statement of Faith of the Presbyterian Church (USA):

> Jesus proclaimed the reign of God:
>   preaching good news to the poor
>   and release to the captives,
>   teaching by word and deed
>   and blessing the children,
>   healing the sick
>   and binding up the brokenhearted,
>   eating with outcasts,
>   forgiving sinners,
>   and calling all to repent and believe the gospel.[54]

There, surely, was God in Christ reconciling the world to Godself — the theanthropic life, if you like, that brought about an atonement. We shall have to make sure there is room for it in any constructive statement we ourselves venture to make concerning the work of Christ.

---

53. Nevin's third constructive thesis in *The Mystical Presence* reads like this: *"By the hypostatical union of the two natures in the person of* Jesus Christ, *our humanity as fallen in Adam was exalted again to a new and imperishable divine life"* (p. 161). It will be remembered that the atonement theory of the ancient Greek fathers, on which Nevin was dependent, is commonly referred to as "the physical theory": the atonement is achieved by the conjunction of the divine *physis* (nature) and the human *physis* in the incarnation.

54. Added to the *Book of Confessions* (see Chap. 9, n. 1) in 1991.

PART FIVE

The Eucharist and the
Grace of Christ

CHAPTER II

The Reformation and the Eucharist

The bread which we break, is it not a participation in the body of Christ?

1 Corinthians 10:16 (RSV)

No theological theme, not even justification, was more keenly debated in the Reformation era than the meaning of the central Christian rite, variously called "the Eucharist," "the Mass," "the Sacrament of the Altar," "the Breaking of Bread," "Holy Communion," or "the Lord's Supper." The endless debates were distinguished not only by acrimony (and sometimes tedium) but also by exegetical skill, historical erudition, and theological acuteness. The lines of division, however, were seldom made unambiguously clear. While disagreement rested in part on the choice of different warrants and authorities, the division was just as often over the right interpretation of the same biblical texts and the same patristic or medieval authors; and even the selfsame concepts (e.g., substance) or analogies (e.g., the sun and its rays) were invoked in contradictory senses.

It is not surprising that the sixteenth-century controversies are mirrored in scholarly disagreements among their present-day interpreters. No doubt, theological subtleties that are hard to penetrate today already went over the heads of the multitude in Luther's day, and the great eucharistic controversies (Marburg, Poissy, Montbéliard) were as much personal and political encounters as they were theological. Yet because the theoretical divisions had liturgical consequences, no item of reform had a more immediate visual impact than eucharistic reform. Indeed, profound differences of piety or spirituality were expressed in divergent eucharistic theories and practices.

Controversy on the meaning of the Eucharist followed soon after Martin Luther's protest against abuses in the sale of indulgences (1517). His assault on the Roman Mass reached the point of no return by 1520 and called for liturgical reform in Wittenberg (sec. I). By 1523, a parallel critique of the Mass and demand for liturgical reform began in Zurich under the very different theological principles of Ulrich Zwingli (sec. II). Luther accordingly turned his polemical energies against what he considered, in some respects, a worse misunderstanding of the Sacrament than he had exposed in the Roman Mass (sec. III). Attempts to overcome the polarization of Protestant eucharistic theology in Luther and Zwingli led to a third, mediating view of the Eucharist; John Calvin became its most influential spokesman (sec. IV) and Thomas Cranmer its advocate in England (sec. V). But against the Protestant "innovations," the Council of Trent reaffirmed the traditional Roman Catholic teaching on transubstantiation and the sacrificial character of the Mass (sec. VI).

I. The Sacrament of the Body and Christ's Testament

Written for the laity shortly after the outbreak of the indulgences controversy, Luther's first extended discussion of the Eucharist, *The Blessed Sacrament of the Holy and True Body of Christ,* was almost entirely free of polemic against the Church of Rome, even though there were hints of trouble to come.[1] But just one year after *The Blessed Sacrament,* his thoughts on the Sacrament underwent a remarkable change. In *A Treatise on the New Testament, that is, the Holy Mass,* "testament" replaced "incorporation" as the cardinal motif, and the shift brought with it a sharply polemical tone.[2]

---

1. Martin Luther (1483-1546), *Ein Sermon von dem hochwürdigen Sakrament des heiligen wahren Leichnams Christi und von den Brüderschaften* (1519), WA 2:742-58; LW 35:49-73.

2. Luther, *Ein Sermon von dem Neuen Testament, das ist von der heiligen Messe* (1520), WA 6:353-78; LW 35:79-111.

1. The Sacrament of the Body

In *The Blessed Sacrament* Luther already suggests that the laity ought to be given the cup as well as the bread, and he stresses the necessity for faith in using the Sacrament: to receive what the Sacrament signifies, you must *believe* that you receive it. The purpose of the Mass is precisely to strengthen faith, so that it is impossible to accept the medieval view of the Sacrament as an *opus operatum,* a work effective simply as done — provided only that no obstacle is put in the way. These are certainly harbingers of future controversy. But Luther apparently takes the dogma of transubstantiation for granted and simply ignores the sacrificial understanding of the Mass. The critical part of the treatise (at the end) is directed not against Rome but against the "brotherhoods," lay fraternities whose exclusiveness and self-indulgence stand in sharp opposition to the one true brotherhood, the fellowship of all saints, in which everything is shared in mutual love.

The sacramental eating and drinking, Luther explains, signify the fellowship of all saints as members of Christ's spiritual body, which is why the Sacrament is called *synaxis* in Greek and *communio* in Latin. "To receive this sacrament in bread and wine, then, is nothing else than to receive a sure sign of this fellowship and incorporation *(eyn leybung)* with Christ and all saints" (WA 2:743; LW 35:51). By it we are assured that we do not bear our burdens alone — that there is one body (1 Cor. 12:20-26), one loaf (1 Cor. 10:17). Indeed, in the Sacrament we are actually *made* one body *(eyngeleybet)* with all the saints. Luther sees the conversion of the elements into Christ's natural body and blood as an analogue to the conversion of the assembly into his spiritual body (the church). It is the spiritual body that stands at the center of his exposition, and he can state explicitly: "It is more needful that you discern the spiritual than the natural body of Christ" (WA 2:751; LW 35:62). As the apostle Paul says, it is a great "sacrament" *(mustērion)* that Christ and the church are one flesh and blood (Eph. 5:31-32).

2. Christ's Testament

Luther had no need to renounce this conception of the Sacrament in his later writings, and for some of the Reformers incorporation was to remain the central eucharistic motif. But to say that the Mass, rightly understood, is Christ's testament is to deny that it is a priestly sacrifice. Further, in the *Treatise on the New Testament* the dogma of transubstantiation dropped out. Luther's challenge was to rethink the Mass by getting behind all later additions and reexamining the words of institution, since "the nearer our masses are to the first mass of Christ [the Last Supper], the better they undoubtedly are" (WA 6:355; LW 35:81).

By "testament" Luther understands (as we say) "last will and testament": a promise made by someone about to die (cf. Heb. 9:16-17). God's approach to humans is in the form of a promise that evokes the response of faith, and usually he adds a sign as a kind of seal to give greater confidence in his Word, as he gave Noah the rainbow, Abraham circumcision, and so on. In the first Mass, shortly before his death, Christ accordingly promised forgiveness of sins to his disciples (Matt. 26:28) and added to his words a powerful seal and sign. Luther now takes the sign to be not the elements as such, and not eating and drinking (as in the earlier treatise), but Christ's own true body and blood under the bread and wine. But since the sign is to be grasped only in its relation to the promise, which can save without it, everything depends on the words. It is therefore a travesty of the Mass when the priest says the words to himself in Latin and turns Christ's testament into a work and a sacrifice.

Luther carried over these thoughts into his truculent *Prelude on the Babylonian Captivity of the Church*, in which he assailed the three captivities to which the sacrament of the bread had been subjected: the withholding of the cup from the laity, transubstantiation, and the interpretation of the Mass as a good work and a sacrifice.[3] Transubstantiation is only one opinion among others. Pierre d'Ailly, cardinal of Cambray, proposed a better alternative when he suggested that the bread and wine, not just their accidents, might remain on the altar — though he himself was restrained from adopting it by the authority of the church. We should accept God's words in their literal sense and take "bread" to mean "bread," not "accidents of bread." "And why could not Christ include his body in the substance of the bread just as well as in the accidents?" (WA 6:510; LW 36:32). Luther will "firmly believe not only that

---

3. Luther, *De captivitate Babylonica ecclesiae praeludium* (1520), WA 6:497-573; LW 36:11-126.

the body of Christ is in the bread, but that the bread is the body of Christ" (WA 6:511; LW 36:34).

But if transubstantiation is only an opinion, to be held or not as one chooses, the same cannot be said of the Roman Church's teaching on the Mass as a sacrifice: this is simply an abuse, the most wicked of all abuses, and has turned the Sacrament into a profitable business. "[J]ust as distributing a testament or accepting a promise differs diametrically from offering a sacrifice, so it is a contradiction in terms to call the mass a sacrifice, for the former is something that we receive and the latter is something that we give" (WA 6:523-24; LW 36:52). Later reformers were to echo this language, even when they perceived the Sacrament as a sacred meal, not as Christ's last will and testament.

3. Reform of the Mass

Luther had become convinced that the Roman Mass was a fearful perversion of Christ's testament, but he hesitated to initiate liturgical change. Others before him put together revised services in German: notably, Carlstadt, Caspar Kantz, and Thomas Müntzer. In Wittenberg, it was Andreas Bodenstein von Carlstadt (ca. 1480-1541) who first translated theological revision into liturgical reform, when Luther was absent. On Christmas Day 1521, he celebrated the Sacrament in German, wearing plain street clothes. He suppressed virtually the entire canon of the Roman Mass, left out the elevation of the elements, and placed the bread and the chalice in the hands of the communicants.

Reform of the liturgy began for Luther himself after his return from the Wartburg. In *Concerning the Order of Worship in the Church*,[4] he laid down his fundamental principle of reform: "[T]he Word is important and not the mass. . . . We can spare everything except the Word" (WA 12:37; LW 53:13-14). Daily Masses were accordingly to be replaced by services of prayer and preaching, and the Sunday Mass itself was to give due emphasis to the sermon. In his *Order for Mass and Communion*, published by the end of 1523, Luther outlined an evangelical rite in Latin.[5] He

---

4. Luther, *Von Ordnung Gottesdiensts in der Gemeine* (1523), WA 12:35-37; LW 53:11-14.

5. Luther, *Formula missae et communionis pro ecclesia Vuittembergensi* (1523), WA 12:205-20; LW 53:19-40.

did not intend it to be binding on the Lutheran churches; nor did he understand it as a new rite but rather as a purification of the one in use. Though he excised the sacrificial language of the canon, he retained the elevation of the bread and the cup, supposing that the sermon in the vernacular would prevent misinterpretation. The Sacrament was to be administered in both kinds to those who had given notice of their wish to communicate and had provided evidence of their understanding and satisfactory behavior.

More than two further years passed before Luther published a eucharistic service in the language of the people, his *German Mass and Order of Worship*,[6] in which he noted his wish eventually to have the minister stand behind the "altar," facing the people as Christ must have done at the Last Supper. By now, the proliferation of German liturgies threatened to confuse the Protestant congregations, and Luther, though he repeated his warning against coerced uniformity, desired a measure of consistency at least in the form of an exhortation to the communicants. The exhortation ends with the admonition to discern Christ's testament and above all to take to heart the words in which he gives his body and blood to us for the forgiveness of sins. The body and blood are the pledge and guarantee of redemption from God's wrath.

II. Commemoration and Spiritual Eating

New interpretations of the Eucharist followed Luther's in the mid-1520s. In a series of eucharistic tracts launched in 1524, Luther's colleague Carlstadt rejected the bodily presence of Christ in the Lord's Supper, interpreted the rite as an act of recollection or remembrance, and proposed that when the Lord said *"This* is my body," he must have pointed at his body (not at the bread). The next year, Ulrich Zwingli (1484-1531) published Hoen's *Most Christian Letter*,[7] in which he had found the suggestion that "is" in the words "This is my body" could be

6. Luther, *Deutsche Messe und Ordnung Gottesdiensts* (1526), WA 19:72-113; LW 53:61-90.

7. Cornelis Hendricxzoen Hoen (Honius, d. 1524), *Epistola christiana* (1525), ZW 4:512-18; trans. Paul L. Nyhus in Heiko Augustinus Oberman, *Forerunners of the Reformation: The Shape of Late Medieval Thought Illustrated by Key Documents* (New York: Holt, Rinehart & Winston, 1966), pp. 268-78.

taken to mean "signifies." He spelled out his own symbolic interpretation of the Sacrament the same year in his *Commentary on True and False Religion.*[8]

I. Commemoration

Zwingli explains in the *Commentary* that to eat Christ's flesh and drink his blood is simply to commemorate his sacrifice — to proclaim his saving deed on the cross (1 Cor. 11:26). "Eating" is believing, and to believe is to be thankful. "We therefore now understand from the very name what the Eucharist, that is, the Lord's Supper, is: namely, the thanksgiving and common rejoicing of those who declare the death of Christ" (ZW 3:775; LWZ 3:200). Obviously, this makes the subject of the eucharistic action not God but the congregation. Zwingli's eucharistic thought was part of a total sacramental theory, in which a sign is sharply distinguished from what it signifies and the Holy Spirit is held to impart faith directly, without means. Signs are indicative or declaratory, not instrumental: a sacrament is not a means by which *God* imparts grace, but an indication *believers* give that they have already received grace and belong to the church. In the Lord's Supper, the bread and wine declare that our sins were once and for all done away with by the death of Christ; they picture the benefit of Christ's sacrifice as the food and drink of the soul. Zwingli's "Augsburg Confession," his *Account of the Faith,*[9] addressed to the Emperor Charles V at the Diet of Augsburg (1530), bluntly rejects the entire notion of a means of grace. The grace or pardon of God is given solely by the Holy Spirit, who needs no channel or vehicle. A sacrament is a sign of past grace *(factae gratiae signum):* it pictures what the Spirit has already done. Zwingli is willing to say that in the Eucharist Christ's body is *as if* present in the contemplation of faith, but he deplores the error of those who look back to the fleshpots of Egypt and imagine that the natural body is *really* present and chewed with the teeth (ZW 6/2:803, 805, 806; LWZ 2:46, 48, 49).[10]

8. Ulrich Zwingli, *De vera et falsa religione commentarius* (1525), ZW 3:628-911; LWZ 3:43-343.

9. Zwingli, *Ad Carolum, Romanorum imperatorem, ... fidei ratio* (1530), ZW 6/2:790-817; LWZ 2:35-61.

10. Note that Zwingli doesn't say (*pace* the English translator) that "the church cer-

In his *Exposition of the Faith*,[11] written in the year of his death, Zwingli presses his thoughts further and suggests that the outward eating and drinking of the elements indicate the parallel occurrence of an inward "feeding" on Christ by faith, who is not absent but present within. The soul holds Christ in its embrace, and he sustains and cheers it as bread and wine sustain and cheer the body (ZW 6/5:147-50, 157-58; LCC 24:258-59, 263). But Zwingli's understanding of signs and signification cannot permit him to grant that the outward event causes, or gives rise to, the inward. He can go so far as to say (in the last passage cited) that the sacraments *help* faith (not "augment faith," as in the English translation), but they do so only indirectly: by drawing the senses away from distractions and placing them at faith's command.

In his own eyes, Zwingli's eucharistic doctrine had the merit of rejecting the Roman Mass without retaining the crassness of Luther's talk about an actual presence of Christ's body and blood "under" the elements — a presence excluded by Christ's bodily ascension to heaven. If the giving of grace were bound to the sacraments, the clergy would have God at their disposal and could grant or withhold salvation at will.[12] The very notion of sacramental grace implies another way of salvation, in competition with the *sola fide* ("by faith alone") of the Reformation. To eat Christ's flesh, if it saves, cannot mean anything else than to believe in him.[13] It was not clear to Zwingli that even Luther had carried through the Reformation principle consistently enough.

Zwingli had turned his attention to liturgical revision already in 1523 with his *Attack on the Canon of the Mass*.[14] Despite the belligerent title, the canon is not simply amputated (in this respect, Zwingli began more conservatively than Carlstadt); rather, it is reconstructed in four

---

tifies that grace has been given," but rather that in baptism a testimony to grace received is given *to* the church (ZW 6/2:805; LWZ 2:47-48).

11. Zwingli, *Christianae fidei brevis et clara expositio ad regem Christianum* (published posthumously, 1536), ZW 6/5:50-162; LCC 24:245-79.

12. Zwingli, *Illustrissimis Germaniae principibus . . . de convitiis Eckii* (1530), ZW 6/3:265, 272; LWZ 2:113, 118.

13. Zwingli, *Eine klare Unterrichtung vom Nachtmahl Christi* (1526), ZW 4:817; LCC 24:205.

14. Zwingli, *De canone missae epichiresis* (1523), ZW 2:556-608; Eng. trans. in *Prayers of the Eucharist: Early and Reformed,* trans. and ed. R. C. D. Jasper and G. J. Cuming, 3d ed. (Collegeville: Liturgical Press, 1992), pp. 183-86.

Latin prayers of Zwingli's own, which hold together eucharistic motifs — well grounded in Scripture — that controversy was to put asunder. But Zwingli's German rite, *Action or Use of the Lord's Supper*,[15] published in the same year as the *Commentary on True and False Religion*, focuses more narrowly on the motif of remembrance; indeed, he calls the rite "this memorial of Christ's passion and thanksgiving for his death." Remembrance is not construed as private meditation. On the contrary, Zwingli's rite was designed to emphasize the true nature of the celebration as a common feast of the redeemed: the table was set in the nave, the minister (without vestments) took his place behind it, and the elements were served to the people seated in their places. It has been argued that Zwingli understood the people to be "transubstantiated" into the body of Christ (Julius Schweizer, Jacques Courvoisier). The argument is not convincing, but it has drawn attention to Zwingli's powerful sense of the church, the ecclesial body, which makes its offering of praise in the Eucharist.[16]

2. Spiritual Eating

From the fact that Zwingli did not ask for Communion to be available more than four times a year, it need not be inferred that he belittled the practice. Nevertheless, infrequent Communion meant that the Eucharist could not provide the norm of Sunday worship, which usually consisted of a preaching service. Moreover, one is bound to note the possibilities in Zwingli's tendency both to *spiritualize* and to *psychologize* the Christian religion: faith is worked inwardly by the Spirit and exercised outwardly in the Eucharist by recollection. Whether this double tendency is judged theologically good or bad, it does seem to have occasioned a lesser role

---

15. Zwingli, *Aktion oder Brauch des Nachtmahls* (1525), ZW 4:13-24; Eng. trans. in Bard Thompson, *Liturgies of the Western Church,* Meridian Living Age Books (Cleveland and New York: World, 1961), pp. 149-56.

16. It is interesting that Zwingli took Paul's warning against not "discerning the body" (1 Cor. 11:29) to refer to the *ecclesial* body of Christ: the Corinthians would bring judgment on themselves if they lacked a proper sense of the church (ZW 3:802; LWZ 3:232). I offered a critique of Schweizer and Courvoisier in my essay "Discerning the Body: Sign and Reality in Luther's Controversy with the Swiss" (1988), reprinted in Gerrish, *Continuing the Reformation,* chap. 3; see pp. 66-69, 74.

for the Sacrament in other Christian groups that followed one or the other (or both) of the two characteristically Zwinglian tendencies.

Zwingli's thinking had a plain affinity with the views and practices of the evangelical Anabaptists, and the influence by no means went only one way. Although some of the Anabaptists linked the bread of the Lord's Supper with their notion of Christ's celestial flesh, for the most part they stressed the thankful remembrance of his death. In addition, the distinctive nature of their communities gave prominence to the idea of fellowship, symbolized by the image of the one loaf made of many grains. The "ordinance" (not sacrament) of the Lord's Supper nurtured a powerful sense of the brotherhood for which one surrendered self-will and was ready to suffer. It is arguable that among the Anabaptists the Lord's Supper could not have the central place assigned to it by Roman Catholics and Protestants because, to them, it was simply one of Christ's ordinances, and the celebration was usually accompanied by exercise of the ban and the ritual of foot washing. But, like the Protestants, they had no thought of devaluing the Eucharist; they wished only to restore it to its primitive use.

Among other groups on the left wing of the Reformation, the Eucharist did assume diminished importance or was even abandoned. Belief in the inwardness of the Spirit's working led Sebastian Franck (1499-1542) to withdraw from all ecclesiastical rites, and in 1526 another "Spiritualist," Caspar von Schwenckfeld (1489-1561), called for at least a temporary suspension of the Lord's Supper — pending a better understanding of it. In Schwenckfeld's view, the outward Supper could never do more than picture the inward transformation of the soul by a life-giving substance from the glorified Christ, and controversy over the rite had further reduced it, for the time being, to a mere distraction that should be set aside.[17] In seventeenth-century England, the Quakers were to take a similar course: the Breaking of Bread, like foot washing

17. See George Huntston Williams, *The Radical Reformation* (Philadelphia: Westminster, 1962), pp. 106-17, 265. Williams's book is an indication of just how much Reformation research changed in the twentieth century. Darwell Stone's history — rich though it is in source material for many schools of thought — does not mention the radical or "left wing" reformers: Darwell Stone, *A History of the Doctrine of the Holy Eucharist,* 2 vols. (London: Longmans, Green, 1909). A comprehensive study of the eucharistic thought and practice of the various radical reformers remains a desideratum in the secondary literature.

and anointing the sick, had some initial usefulness as the transition was made to an inward and spiritual communion with Christ, but the substance could now stand without the figure.

The same conclusion was reached among the evangelical "Rationalists" (the Antitrinitarians), though by a different route. In their view, Christ's death was not a sacrifice for sin; hence no ecclesiastical rite was needed to communicate his merits. They pointed out that the thief on the cross was saved without the Sacrament (Luke 23:43). It did not necessarily follow that the churches could dispense with the Eucharist, but that is in fact what sometimes happened. In a treatise on the use and purpose of the Lord's Supper, Faustus Socinus agreed that it was instituted by the Lord himself as a perpetual commemoration of his death, by which he proved God's love for us, and that a commemoration is not a mere remembering but a public celebration. Still, though faith may be strengthened during the celebration, the Lord's Supper cannot itself be said to strengthen faith. It is by definition *our* work, and how can something we do ourselves confirm us in faith? Neither unbelievers nor believers receive anything but bread and wine.[18] Despite Socinus's talk of a *perpetual* rite, the Eucharist — emptied of its old sacramental meaning — lost importance in the later Socinian communities. Before the end of the seventeenth century, the English Socinians were being chided for not observing the Lord's Supper at all.[19]

That, however, is far from being the course taken by Zwingli's own church in the years immediately following his death. The purely memorialist interpretation of the Eucharist, with its rejection of sacramental grace, did not survive for long among the Swiss Reformed. The First Helvetic Confession affirms, partly under the influence of Martin Bucer, that the bread and wine of the Lord's Supper are "symbols by which the true communication of his body and blood is presented *(exhibeatur)* by the Lord himself."[20] The notion of "exhibitive signs"

18. Faustus Socinus, *De usu & fine Cœnæ Domini, brevis introductio; Opera omnia,* 1:753-54.

19. See H. John McLachlan, *Socinianism in Seventeenth-Century England* (Oxford: Oxford University Press, 1951), pp. 317-18.

20. *Confessio helvetica prior* (1536), art. 23; BS 3:225 (Latin and German); English in Arthur C. Cochrane, ed., *Reformed Confessions of the 16th Century* (Philadelphia: Westminster, 1966), p. 108. For *exhibeatur* the German version has *gereicht und angeboten werde.* On the concept of "exhibitive signs," see sec. IV/1 below.

held the promise of reconciliation. But it was not Zwingli's notion, and there is no hint of it in the Zurich liturgy. Polarization, not reconciliation, was the dominant mood of the 1520s.

III. Oral Reception of the Body and Blood

The *Babylonian Captivity of the Church* was not Luther's last word against the Roman Mass and its priesthood: he continued to see in the rival interpretations of the Eucharist, evangelical and papist, two diametrically opposed ways of approaching God. But he believed that the new interpretations of the 1520s obliged him to open a second controversial front; and in the writings of the "fanatics," as he called them, he discovered the same demon that had transformed Christ's testament into a sacrifice — the *Werkteufel* ("work-devil"), who makes a good work out of the offer of grace. By 1521 he had become acquainted with Hoen's theory and responded in *The Adoration of the Sacrament*.[21] He realized that an emphasis on Christ's spiritual or ecclesial body in the Sacrament might, in combination with a figurative interpretation of the words of institution, entirely replace belief in the presence of Christ's natural body. But only participation in the natural body, he insisted, can bring about the fellowship of the spiritual body; the fanatics mistake a benefit of the Sacrament for the Sacrament itself. In *Against the Heavenly Prophets,* he then issued a massive critique of Carlstadt's views on the Lord's Supper.[22] Carlstadt believed that John 6 taught a purely inward and spiritual "eating." But this, in Luther's judgment, was a failure to see that God confers the inward only through the outward — the Word and sacraments (WA 18:136-39; LW 40:146-49). Hence Carlstadt transformed a means of grace into a devotional exercise of meditation on Christ's passion: like the monks, he made of the Sacrament a human work (WA 18:95; LW 40:205-6). The remembrance Christ enjoins is not inner motions of the heart, but outward proclamation: "By the words, 'This do in remembrance of me,' Christ meant what Paul meant by his

---

21. Luther, *Von Anbeten des Sakraments des heiligen Leichnams Christi* (1523), WA 11:431-56; LW 36:275-305.

22. Luther, *Wider die himmlischen Propheten, von den Bildern und Sakrament* (1525), WA 18:62-125 (pt. 1), 134-214 (pt. 2); LW 40:79-223.

words [1 Cor. 11:26], 'Proclaim the death of the Lord'" (WA 18:197; LW 40:207-8).

It was "Carlstadt's poison" that Luther detected in the eucharistic theology of Zwingli and his associates. His *Sacrament of the Body and Blood of Christ, against the Fanatics* voices his dismay that whereas the papists have simply failed to affirm the eucharistic gift despite their belief in the presence of Christ's body and blood, a worse error now denies the presence itself.[23] The new preachers don't heed the words "Take, eat; this is my body, which is given for you" (Luther conflates Matt. 26:26 with Luke 22:19) but come together merely to commemorate Christ's death. They take away the entire *raison d'être* of the Sacrament: which is, to individualize the promise of forgiveness, proclaimed generally and to all in the Word. Though the *fruit* of the Sacrament is certainly the union of love symbolized by the one loaf, its correct *use* is to receive the body of Christ and the assurance of forgiveness that it brings (WA 19:501-12; LW 36:346-54).

Luther's next broadside against the Zwinglians, *That These Words of Christ, "This is my body," Still Stand Firm Against the Fanatics*, concentrates on the meaning of the words of institution.[24] The Zwinglians were persuaded that a literal interpretation of "This is my body" was absurd. Zwingli found a figure of speech in the verb "is," which (he held) means "signifies." His friend Oecolampadius pointed out that the little word *is*, over which there was such a commotion, would not have appeared at all in the original "Hebrew" (Aramaic) spoken by Jesus. For his part, he preferred to locate the figure in the pronoun *This* — that is, in the bread, which is a sign of the body.[25] Both Zwingli and Oecolampadius appealed to Augustine's teaching on signs. Luther retorted that

---

23. Luther, *Sermon von dem Sakrament des Leibes und Blutes Christi, wider die Schwärmgeister* (1526), WA 19:482-523; LW 36:335-61.

24. Luther, *Daß diese Wort Christi "Das ist mein Leib" noch fest stehen wider die Schwärmgeister* (1527), WA 23:64-283; LW 37:13-150.

25. Johannes Oecolampadius (1482-1531), *De genuina verborum Domini "Hoc est corpus meum" iuxta vetustissimos authores expositione* (1525). See Ernst Staehelin, *Das theologische Lebenswerk Johannes Oekolampads*, Quellen und Forschungen zur Reformationsgeschichte, vol. 21 (1939; reprint, New York: Johnson Reprints, 1971), pp. 276-84. On Oecolampadius's later dialogue *Quid de eucharistia veteres tum Graeci tum Latini senserint* (1530), written in reply to Melanchthon, see Staehelin, *Das Lebenswerk Oekolampads*, pp. 607-11.

they misunderstood Augustine, for whom a sacrament was not a sign of something absent but of something invisibly present (WA 23:208-13; LW 37:104-5). In his *Confession concerning Christ's Supper,* he argues at length that in fact there is no sign at all in the words "This is my body."[26] A single new entity comes into existence out of the bread and the body, and we can no longer properly speak of either one separately. If we are to say that there is a figure of speech in Christ's words, it can only be synecdoche — naming the part (i.e., either the bread or the body) for the whole, which is "fleshbread" (WA 26:391-401, 443-45; LW 37:262-68, 301-3).

Luther's concern in the great polemical treatises of 1526-1527 was not to explain the mode of Christ's bodily presence in the Sacrament but to insist that, by the power of the Word, the body and blood are in fact present — whether anyone believes it or not. Even the wicked receive the body and blood with their mouths, albeit to their own destruction (WA 23:178-81, 26:353; LW 37:86-87, 238; the allusion is to 1 Cor. 11:29). But to demonstrate to the fanatics that "presence" need not mean a crude, local presence, Luther had recourse to some old scholastic distinctions. Christ's body and blood are not *locally* or *circumscriptively* in the Sacrament, enclosed in the bread and wine. The resurrection appearances prove that his glorified body can be present *definitively,* that is, visibly present when he so chooses, but without being circumscribed or confined to a single place. And, as God, he is present *repletively* in every place, filling all things: his divine nature imparts its supernatural presence to his humanity (WA 26:327-37; LW 37:214-24). What distinguishes the Sacrament is that there, through the Word, he is present *for me* (WA 19:492, 23:150-51; LW 36:342, 37:68). Along with the "literal" interpretation of the words "This is my body," the eating of the body by the wicked *(manducatio impiorum)* and the ubiquity of the body by communication of properties became the watchwords of the Lutheran doctrine on the Lord's Supper.

In his own summary confession, Luther affirms that "in the sacrament of the altar the true body and blood of Christ are orally eaten and drunk. . . . It does not rest on man's belief or unbelief but on the Word and ordinance of God" (WA 26:506; LW 37:367). The Zwinglian suspi-

---

26. Luther, *Vom Abendmahl Christi, Bekenntnis* (1528), WA 26:261-509; LW 37:161-372.

cion that an oral eating of Christ's flesh must mean a crass, carnal, "Capernaitic" eating (John 6:52-60) was not well founded, though Luther's language sometimes invited the misunderstanding. On the other hand, Lutheran suspicion that any talk of the elements as signs or symbols must leave nothing but bread and wine in the Sacrament was not well founded either, although Zwingli invited misunderstanding by his negative emphasis on what one ought *not* to say. The Lutheran Eucharist was not theophagy, and the Zwinglian Eucharist was not a Pelagian workout. Nevertheless, the famous encounter in the Marburg Colloquy at the end of the decade (1529) presented a picture of intransigence on both sides, the Lutherans taking their stand on "This is my body," the Zwinglians countering that "it is the spirit that gives life; the flesh is useless" (John 6:63).

IV. Exhibitive Signs and Christ's Life-Giving Flesh

The uncompromising antagonism between Luther and Zwingli appeared to leave little common ground. But a third party emerged that tried repeatedly to strike a middle path. At first, the chief spokesman of mediation was Martin Bucer (1491-1551); later, the leadership passed to John Calvin (1509-1564). Their interpretation of the Lord's Supper was shared, in essentials, by Peter Martyr Vermigli (1500-1562), who, like Calvin, spent formative years in Bucer's Strasbourg.[27] The English reformer Thomas Cranmer (1489-1556) also belongs in spirit to their company. Among Luther's own closest associates, Philip Melanchthon (1497-1560) developed a cordial relation with Bucer, which bore fruit in the Wittenberg Concord (1536) and the program for reform sponsored by Archbishop Hermann von Wied (1543). On the other side, Zwingli's successor in Zurich, Heinrich Bullinger (1504-1575), was drawn closer to the mediating camp by the negotiations with Calvin that led to the Zurich Consensus (concluded in 1549).

---

27. See Joseph C. McLelland, *The Visible Words of God: An Exposition of the Sacramental Theology of Peter Martyr Vermigli, A.D. 1500-1562* (Edinburgh: Oliver & Boyd, 1957).

1. Exhibitive Signs

The possibility of the mediating position can be understood only if it is recognized that in the Augustinian tradition realism and symbolism are not opposed. Zwingli's characteristic notion was that a sacramental sign is a pointer to an absent reality, a grace that lies in the past, and for this reason Luther was deeply suspicious of the distinction between sign and reality. One alternative was to argue that although a sign is not itself the reality, it nonetheless attests and brings a present reality, which the mediating theologians identified as communion with Christ or participation in his body ("incorporation"). Their concept of "exhibitive signs" was the shared conviction that united them. It was clearly reflected in the language of a groundbreaking conference between Bucer and Melanchthon at Kassel in December 1534.[28] The conference prepared the way for the Wittenberg Concord (1536), which avoids the disputed word "sign" but states the agreement of the signatories that "with the bread and wine the body and blood of Christ are truly and substantially present, proffered *(exhiberi)* and received."[29] *Exhibere* is also the word Melanchthon used in the controversial change he made in article 10 of the Augsburg Confession, which then read: "with the bread and wine the body and blood of Christ are truly proffered *(exhibeantur)* to those who eat in the Lord's Supper."[30] Along with the fundamental con-

---

28. At the Kassel conference, it was agreed "that bread and wine are signs, *signa exhibitiva,* so that when they are proffered and received, the body of Christ is proffered and received at the same time." German quoted in Ernst Bizer, *Studien zur Geschichte des Abendmahlsstreits im 16. Jahrhundert,* Beiträge zur Förderung christlicher Theologie, 2nd series, vol. 46 (Gütersloh: Gerd Mohn, 1940), p. 76n.

29. *Wittenberger Konkordie,* art. 1: BELK, p. 65 (Latin). The original German text is reproduced in Bizer, *Geschichte des Abendamahlsstreits,* pp. 117-19. The signatories to the Concord go on (art. 2) to deny transubstantiation, a local enclosing of the body in the bread, or a permanent union of the body and the bread beyond the use of the Sacrament, but they "grant that by the sacramental union the bread is the body of Christ: that is, they hold that when the bread is presented, the body of Christ is present at the same time and truly proffered *(vere exhiberi).*" Because of the *unio sacramentalis* even the unworthy truly receive the body and blood (art. 3). The idea of a *manducatio indignorum* was widely taken as less controversial than a *manducatio impiorum.*

30. Augsburg Confession, *Versio variata* (1540): BELK, p. 65, lines 45-46. The original *Invariata* (1530) said that the body and blood "are truly present and are distributed to those who eat" and adds an explicit rejection, omitted from the *Variata,* of "those who teach otherwise" (BELK, p. 64; BC, p. 34).

cept of exhibitive signs, other characteristic thoughts were commonly associated: for instance, that Christ is present where his effects are present, and that the sacramental union of the bread with Christ's body persists no longer than the eucharistic celebration. Fundamental agreement did not exclude differences of expression or emphasis; it excluded only a reduction of sacramental signs to mere reminders of an absent or past reality.

Calvin's mature reflections on the Lord's Supper were occasioned by the Zurich Consensus, which achieved harmony between the German and the French Reformed churches in Switzerland but was vehemently attacked by some of the Lutherans.[31] Calvin held Luther in higher esteem than he did Zwingli, and he believed that the cardinal principle of Luther's opposition to Zwingli was that the Eucharist does not consist in *empty* signs.[32] He had no hesitation in using the language of signs or symbols, provided it was clearly understood that they are not empty but present what they represent. "For why should the Lord put in your hand the symbol of his body, except to assure you of a true participation in it?"[33] But he could not agree with the Lutherans that the words "This is my body" must be construed literally, or that Christ's body is ubiquitous, or that even the wicked take the body of Christ in their mouths. For Calvin, as for Zwingli despite their differences, Christ's ascension to heaven marked a decisive break with the manner of his presence during his earthly life. This, he thought, the Lutheran teaching failed to take seriously enough, although he did not naively suppose that heaven is a place on the cosmological map.[34] And yet, if the signs are not empty but efficacious, there must be a communion with Christ's life-giving flesh in the Eucharist. The only question is how.

Calvin was not greatly concerned to explain *how* Christ is present

---

31. *Consensus Tigurinus* (concluded 1549, published 1551), OS 2:247-58; TT 2:212-20.

32. Many Lutherans, from Calvin's day to the present, doubt that he found the true middle way. Sasse maintained that "there is no via media between 'est' and 'significat'" and judged it a "tragic error for Calvin to believe that he had found the solution" to the eucharistic impasse. Hermann Sasse, *This Is My Body: Luther's Contention for the Real Presence in the Sacrament of the Altar* (Minneapolis: Augsburg, 1959), p. 326.

33. Calvin, *ICR* IV, xvii.10 (2:1371).

34. Further discussion of Calvin's eucharistic theology, with additional documentation, will be found in my *Grace and Gratitude*. On the meaning of the ascension, see p. 183, n. 81.

in the Supper, any more than Luther had been. He writes: "I rather experience than understand it. . . . In his Sacred Supper he bids me take, eat, and drink his body and blood under the symbols of bread and wine. I do not doubt that he himself truly presents *(porrigat)* them, and that I receive them."[35] He was prepared to marvel at what he could not comprehend. But from Romans 8:9-11 he did infer that participation in Christ must be the work of the Holy Spirit, who overcomes the distance between heaven and earth.[36] In short, for Calvin the sacramental signs were efficacious as the Spirit's instruments.[37]

2. Christ's Life-giving Flesh

Calvin had no difficulty in asserting that the communion, communication, or participation that results is *real,* if "real" means "true" as opposed to deceptive or imaginary, and *substantial,* provided that "substance" is not taken for sheer physical mass. He does sometimes speak of the eucharistic gift as a life-giving "virtue" that flows from Christ's body, but he does not mean that the communicant receives only the virtue, not the substance, of the body. Drawing life from Christ's flesh *is* a kind of presence: from Calvin's use of the expression "the operation of the flesh," one might say that the true communication, for him, is an operative presence. The body of Christ is in any case only *locally* absent in heaven, for the person of Christ, as God and man, is present everywhere. But for just this reason his body does not have to leave heaven — to change its spatial location — in order for the whole Christ to be in the Sacrament.

At stake in Calvin's eucharistic thought is not simply the mode of Christ's presence in the Sacrament, but a total conception of how the believer is related to Christ and draws life from him. Calvin rejected Zwingli's equation of "eating" with "believing": the vital union with Christ that results from faith is by no means merely a matter of beliefs about him, or of calling to mind the benefits he has won for our salvation.[38] We become, rather, flesh of his flesh and bone of his bone. Be-

---

35. *ICR* IV, xvii.32 (2:1403-4).
36. *ICR* IV, xvii.12 (2:1373); cf. 10 (2:1370), 33 (2:1405).
37. *ICR* IV, xiv.9-12 (2:1284-87), 17 (2:1293); xvii.21 (2:1385-86).
38. "As it is not the seeing but the eating of bread that suffices to feed the body, so

cause the union is wholly mysterious, it can only be represented by images and metaphors. One such image is the marriage bond between husband and wife (Eph. 5:28-33). In John 6:53 Jesus himself uses another, that is, eating in order to live: "[U]nless you eat the flesh of the Son of Man and drink his blood, you have no life in you." This communion certainly takes place also outside the Lord's Supper. But the *raison d'être* of the Sacrament, for Calvin, is to serve as a kind of seal and confirmation of Jesus' discourse on the bread of life. Jesus was not speaking of the Lord's Supper, but of the uninterrupted communion with his flesh that we obtain even apart from the use of the Sacrament. "And yet, at the same time," Calvin comments, "I acknowledge that there is nothing said here that is not figuratively represented, and actually bestowed on believers, in the Lord's Supper."[39] The Sacrament both confirms and imparts anew the nourishment of believers with the bread of life, the life-giving flesh of Christ, and it calls forth the church's ceaseless thanksgiving — not in public worship alone, but also in all the duties of love for others. In the very first edition of his *Institutes,* Calvin pointed out that the Sacrament is called both "the Lord's Supper" and "the Eucharist." As the Supper by which the benevolent Father feeds his children, it is a gift of grace; as the Eucharist, it is a sacrifice of praise, the liturgical enactment of the church's entire existence as a royal priesthood.[40]

3. The Reformed Liturgy

In Reformed services of worship, the pivotal motif of a mysterious union with Christ appears with varying degrees of clarity and felicitousness. Zwinglian ideas shaped the liturgical endeavors of Oecolampadius and William Farel, but the Reformed liturgies of England and Scotland were derived not from Zurich but from Strasbourg — a clear token of theological affinity. The first Protestant Eucharist in Strasbourg (1524), composed in German by Theobald Schwarz (Nigri), went through several revisions before Calvin arrived to assume leader-

---

the soul must truly and deeply become partaker of Christ that it may be quickened to spiritual life by his power" (*ICR* IV, xvii.5 [2:1365]; cf. Comm. John 6:47, CO 47:51; CC 17:260).

39. Calvin, Comm. John 6:54; CO 47:155; CC 17:266.

40. *ICR* IV, xviii.16-17 (2:1443-45), alluding to 1 Pet. 2:9.

ship of the French refugee congregation. In the 1537 version he found a rite that precisely conveyed the mediating view of the Sacrament as no mere memorial but an actual participation in Christ's body and blood, by which he increasingly lives in us and we in him. The presiding minister prays, "He has not only offered to you [the Father] his body and blood on the cross for our sin, but wills also to give the same to us for food and drink unto eternal life."[41] With a friend's help (he knew no German), Calvin put the Strasbourg rite into French, with one or two changes, in his *Form of Prayers,* which became the model for his Geneva liturgy after his return there in 1541.[42] The intention of the eucharistic service is plainly expressed in the slightly simplified Geneva recension and the instruction that introduced it. The Eucharist, as a commemoration of the body and blood of the Lord, brings about an increase of the life of Christ within us. And the life of Christ consists in this: to seek and to save the lost.[43] Later Reformed liturgies introduced an invocation of the Holy Spirit (corresponding to the ancient *epiclesis*), a fitting expression of Calvin's persuasion that it is the Spirit that effects communion with the body of Christ. But no such invocation appears in Calvin's own eucharistic prayer.[44]

The communicants at Geneva, as at Strasbourg, went forward to receive the elements, either standing or kneeling. But the Sacrament was a meal, not a propitiatory sacrifice: the ministers, dressed in plain

41. German of the various recensions in Friedrich Hubert, ed., *Die Straßburger liturgischen Ordnungen im Zeitalter der Reformation* (Göttingen: Vandenhoeck & Ruprecht, 1900), p. 107; cf. p. 112. Christ's twofold self-offering, on the cross (to his Father) and in the Sacrament (to the communicants), is a constant formula in Reformed liturgies: it reappears, with slight variations of wording, in Bucer's 1539 liturgy, Calvin's 1542 Geneva rite, and John Knox's Geneva service book of 1556. See Thompson, *Liturgies,* pp. 176, 202, 304.

42. *La Forme des Prieres et Chantz ecclesiastiques, auec la maniere d'administrer les Sacremens, et consacrer le Mariage: selon la coustume de l'Eglise ancienne* (1542), OS 2:11-58; Thompson, *Liturgies,* pp. 197-210. The first edition of Calvin's Strasbourg service book (1540) has not survived. A later edition, edited by Calvin and printed at Strasbourg in 1545, is given by Thompson along with the 1542 Geneva liturgy.

43. OS 2:42-44; trans. Mary Beaty and Benjamin W. Farley, *Calvin's Ecclesiastical Advice* (Louisville: Westminster John Knox, 1991), pp. 168-70. Calvin concludes: "In sum, the principal thing about the sacrament's mystery is that we might live in Christ and he in us. This the heavenly Father grants us through Christ. Amen."

44. See Ronald P. Byars, *Lift Your Hearts on High: Eucharistic Prayer in the Reformed Tradition* (Louisville: Westminster John Knox, 2005), pp. 72, 80.

black cassocks and gowns, stood beside the table to serve the bread and wine. (In the Church of Scotland, which had its own service derived from Calvin's, the people came forward to sit at a long table placed in the chancel or nave, and they passed the elements from hand to hand.) Calvin blamed the abomination of the Mass for the practice of infrequent Communion. As Luther insisted in 1523 that Christians should not gather without preaching and prayer, so Calvin upheld the ancient rule that no meeting of the church should take place without also partaking of the Lord's Supper (and giving alms).[45] But he could not persuade the authorities to make so startling a break with medieval custom. Quarterly Communion became the norm in Geneva and Scotland.[46] In the liturgical legacy of both Calvin and John Knox, however, the service of worship on non-Communion Sundays was an "ante-Communion," not morning prayer with a sermon, and in Strasbourg and (probably) Geneva the service was conducted from the table. Knox's *Forme of Prayers* may seem less than forthright in affirming the real presence.[47] But it must be read in the light of the Scots Confession, of which Knox was co-author: article 21 asserts that in the right use of the Lord's Supper there takes place a "unioun and conjunction" with the body and blood of Christ Jesus.[48]

V. The True Presence

Debate on the eucharistic standpoint of the English Reformers has focused, as one would expect, on Thomas Cranmer, the chief compiler of both *The Book of Common Prayer* and the Forty-two Articles (the proto-

45. *ICR* IV, xvii.44 (2:1422).

46. On Calvin's failed efforts to establish more frequent Communion, see William D. Maxwell, *An Outline of Christian Worship: Its Development and Forms,* 4th ed. (Oxford: Oxford University Press, 1952), pp. 116-18.

47. *The Forme of Prayers and Ministration of the Sacraments,* etc. (1556); Thompson, *Liturgies,* pp. 295-307. The "true eatinge of his fleshe, and drinkinge of his bloud" is to partake of Christ's merits and benefits (p. 302). Knox's *Forme of Prayers,* first prepared for the English refugees in Geneva, became the prototype for the Church of Scotland's *Book of Common Order.* See William D. Maxwell, *John Knox's Genevan Service Book 1556: The Liturgical Portions of the Genevan Service Book* (Edinburgh: Oliver & Boyd, 1931), pp. 122, 124.

48. BS 3:468.

type of the Thirty-nine Anglican Articles of Religion). He has been variously represented as a Zwinglian or as more akin to Bucer, Calvin, and others of the mediating theologians on the Continent. Allowances must be made for changes in Cranmer's thinking; it has been argued that at one stage of his development he was strongly influenced by the Lutherans. And it is a moot question to what extent he may have permanently shaped the eucharistic thought of Anglicanism after him.

1. Cranmer's Mentors

A new phase of the debate was initiated by Gregory Dix, who found Cranmer's eucharistic thought indistinguishable in substance from Zwingli's; it followed that Cranmer framed the Anglican rite to express a doctrine few Anglicans have ever held. Dix won some influential, if qualified, support: Cyril Richardson, in particular, added formidable evidence that Cranmer's eucharistic theology "moved within the basic framework of Zwingli's opinions." But others pointed to Cranmer's use of key terms and phrases that seemed to separate him from Zwingli and to link him with Bucer, Calvin, and the "dynamic receptionists" (Timms). Similarly, a monograph on Cranmer's doctrine of the Eucharist discovers in it the idea of a "true presence," the common possession of Bucer, Melanchthon, Bullinger, and Calvin (Brooks).[49] The disagreement is unlikely to end there, since ambiguities undeniably appear in Cranmer's utterances on the Lord's Supper, even though he himself believed his words were so simple that a child could understand them.

The attempt has been made to undercut, or at least to depreciate, the argument over Cranmer's Continental affiliations by insisting that

---

49. Gregory Dix, *The Shape of the Liturgy* (1945), reprinted with additional notes by Paul V. Marshall (San Francisco: Harper & Row, 1982), pp. 640-74; Cyril C. Richardson, *Zwingli and Cranmer on the Eucharist: Cranmer dixit et contradixit* (Evanston: Seabury Western Theological Seminary, 1949), p. 48; G. B. Timms, "Dixit Cranmer," *Church Quarterly Review* 143 (Jan.-Mar., 1947): 217-34; 144 (Apr.-June, 1947): 33-51; Peter Newman Brooks, *Thomas Cranmer's Doctrine of the Eucharist: An Essay in Historical Development* (New York: Seabury, 1965). Dix responded to Timms in "Dixit Cranmer et non timuit: A Supplement to Mr. Timms," *Church Quarterly Review* 145 (Jan.-Mar., 1948): 145-76; 146 (Apr.-June, 1948): 44-60.

the English Reformers drew their inspiration directly from the Fathers and Schoolmen. It was Nicholas Ridley, according to Cranmer, who persuaded him to renounce transubstantiation (probably in 1546), and Ridley, as he himself tells us, had been led to his understanding of the Sacrament by the ninth-century book by "Bertram" (Ratramnus) *On the Body and Blood of the Lord.* In C. W. Dugmore's opinion, Ridley and Cranmer recovered the realist-symbolist tradition that had its roots in the theology of Augustine. A "non-papist Catholic" tradition, it provided the English Reformers with an alternative to the conversionist theory of Ambrose, which had been sanctioned by the "papal-catholic" dogma of transubstantiation.[50] Perhaps it does scant justice to the English Reformers to speak as though the historical problem were merely to fit them into a Continental typology. But Cranmer did read the Continenetal Reformers assiduously, not least Oecolampadius on the eucharistic opinions of the Fathers. The treatise of Ratramnus itself reached England in editions published by Protestants on the Continent; and it is, of course, a problem that he has been claimed as the medieval precursor of both Zwingli and Calvin. Not much can be determined about the eucharistic opinions of Ridley or Cranmer from their interest in the controversial monk of Corbie.

Cranmer's alleged Lutheran phase supposedly came when he abandoned transubstantiation. In his translation (1548) of a Lutheran catechism, which he made from the Latin version of Justus Jonas, he appeared to endorse the view that the communicants receive the body and blood of Christ by mouth. But he later insisted that he took this language to be figurative: by figurative speech, we speak of what is done to the signs as done to what they signify. The Lutheran phase, if there was one, did not last. Cranmer arrived at an understanding of the Sacrament that excluded the Lutheran *manducatio impiorum* just as firmly as the Roman Church's transubstantiation. Only faith receives the body and blood of the Lord; the wicked receive the sign, but not the thing signified.

Bucer, Vermigli, and Ochino were all living in England, by Cranmer's invitation, when the first *Book of Common Prayer* (1549) was under revision, and they might be expected to have had some influence on their host. Jan Łaski was there, too, and is sometimes held to have

---

50. C[lifford] W. Dugmore, *The Mass and the English Reformers* (London: Macmillan, 1958).

nudged Cranmer in a Zwinglian direction. It is difficult to determine which of the foreign guests may have won Cranmer's ear. He refused to let his adversary Stephen Gardiner drive a wedge between Bucer and himself, but his reply to Gardiner also shows him reluctant to admit any real difference between Bucer and Zwingli. In a detailed critique of the 1549 prayer book (his *Censura,* which Vermigli read and approved), Bucer urged, among other things, retaining in the Communion service language that implied a true presence and reception of the body and blood of the Lord, but it was dropped from the 1552 liturgy.[51] Cranmer's Forty-two Articles of the same year, published by royal injunction in 1553, expressly denied "the reall, and bodilie presence (as thei terme it) of Christes fleshe and bloude, in the Sacramente of the Lordes supper" (art. 29).[52] There were unquestionably tokens of a shift to a more radical Protestantism in the latter part of Edward VI's reign, including the change of the words of delivery in the Communion service. The earlier prayer book had, "The body of our Lorde Jesus Christ whiche was geuen for thee, preserue thy bodye and soule unto euerlasting lyfe." The revision said, "Take and eate this, in remembraūce that Christe dyed for thee, and feede on him in thy hearte by faythe, with thankes geuinge."[53] In harmony with this evident shift to an explicit memorialism was the appending of the declaration on kneeling (the "black rubric") at the end of the eucharistic rite: to receive the Sacrament on one's knees did not imply "anye reall and essenciall presence," since Christ's natural flesh and blood are in heaven, not here, and cannot be in more places than one at the same time.[54]

2. Cranmer's Defense

It would not be prudent simply to read Cranmer's mind from these changes in his church's official standards. His opinions are presumably to be sought in his major work, *A Defence of the True and Catholic Doc-*

51. G. J. Cuming, *A History of Anglican Liturgy* (London: Macmillan, 1969), pp. 100-101, 108.

52. Charles Hardwick, *A History of the Articles of Religion* (Philadelphia: Herman Hooker, 1852), p. 288.

53. Thompson, *Liturgies,* pp. 261, 281.

54. Thompson, *Liturgies,* p. 284.

trine of the Sacrament of the Body and Blood of Our Saviour Christ (1550), and in his still weightier response to Bishop Gardiner's refutation of it: the *Answer* of 1551.[55] Unfortunately, it is precisely over these two sources that the controversy is liveliest. Zwingli's favorite text (John 6:63) stands like a defiant banner on the front page of the *Defence.* In the *Answer,* Cranmer reiterates that the Eucharist is not a sacrifice for sin, but a memorial of Christ's sacrifice and a sacrifice of laud and praise, by which we testify that we are members of Christ's (ecclesial) body. His natural body is in heaven, not in the bread. Nor is he "corporally" in the communicants either (*Remains* 3:30). Rather, Christ's *benefits* are in the Sacrament, and he himself is *spiritually* present by his divine nature. Most, perhaps all, of what Cranmer says about "eating Christ's body" means no more than "chewing" and "digesting" the fact of his sacrificial death: eating is believing.

And yet, Cranmer seems constantly to press against the limits of the Zwinglian position. He affirms that the signs are "pithy and efficacious," and alongside the motif of remembrance he can set the theme of union with Christ, accompanied by Calvin's favorite expression that we become "flesh of his flesh and bone of his bones." Christ's body is really *exhibited* in the Sacrament (*Remains* 3:201), and we can certainly speak of him as really present if "really" means "in deed and effectually," or "verily and truly" (3:131, 214; cf. 4:12). He uses the sacraments, as he uses the Word, like instruments "whereby he worketh, and therefore is said to be present in them" (3:38). Cranmer's confession before the papal subdelegate in September 1555 was this: "I believe, that whoso eateth and drinketh that sacrament, Christ is within them, whole Christ, his nativity, passion, resurrection, and ascension; but not that corporally sitteth in heaven" (4:85).

Cranmer does not seem to have judged it as important as Calvin did to distinguish between Christ's flesh and his work or benefits, nor between eating and believing. And he thought that the image of the sun's rays excluded the substance talk that Bucer and Calvin supposed it to justify. "Is the light of the candle," he asked, "the substance of the candle?" (3:170; cf. 2:358).[56] But for him, as for Calvin, the *raison d'être* of

---

55. My references to the *Defence* and *Answer* (given in parentheses) follow the pagination in *The Remains of Thomas Cranmer,* ed. Henry Jenkyns, 4 vols. (Oxford, 1833).

56. Contrast Calvin: "For if we see that the sun, shedding its beams upon the earth,

the Eucharist was to represent and increase a feeding on Christ that occurs also outside the Sacrament (3:130, 553-54; 4:37-38). Since it is the Lord himself who feeds his own, Cranmer could and did sometimes assert that the substance of the body, not only its efficacy, is present in the Lord's Supper (4:13). He meant, presumably, that the substance is rightly said to be *present* where it *acts* efficaciously. "The body of Christ is effectually in the sacrament" (4:11) — not, that is, in the elements but in the "ministration" (3:136-37), by which the ascended Lord himself works.

3. The Elizabethan Settlement

After the suppression of Protestantism under Queen Mary, the Elizabethan Settlement both restored Cranmer's work and modified it. The denial of a "reall and bodilie presence" in the Forty-two Articles was removed in the Thirty-nine Articles (1563/71), which affirm instead that "the body of Christe is geuen, taken, and eaten in the Supper only after an heauenly and spirituall maner."[57] Apart from the omission of the black rubric (restored with verbal changes in 1662) and the permission of vestments (albeit the question *which* vestments was left uncertain in the ornaments rubric), only one change in the new *Book of Common Prayer* (1559) affected the understanding of the Eucharist: for the words of delivery, the formula of 1549 was restored and placed amicably before the formula of 1552.[58]

Small though these changes in the articles and prayer book may seem to be, they mark exactly the direction the English divines in general followed after the accession of Elizabeth. During her reign the influence of Calvin reached its height and helped to bring about the "general agreement" of which Hooker wrote in 1597: that there is a "*real*

---

casts its substance in some measure *(quodammodo)* upon it in order to beget, nourish, and give growth to its offspring — why should the radiance of Christ's Spirit be less in order to impart to us the communion of his flesh and blood?" (*ICR* IV, xvii.12 [2:1373]). *Quodammodo* should perhaps be translated "in a way." See further my *Grace and Gratitude*, pp. 177-81.

57. Art. 28; Hardwick, *Articles of Religion*, p. 289.

58. Details in Francis Procter and Walter Howard Frere, *A New History of the Book of Common Prayer, with a Rationale of its Offices* (London: Macmillan, 1941), pp. 101-3.

participation of Christ and of life in his body and blood *by means of this sacrament.*"[59] By this time, the eucharistic thinking of the established church had moved firmly into the *via media* of the Continental Reformed. But in England, as in Switzerland, theological reinterpretation of the Sacrament failed to issue in frequent Communion. The first prayer book required each parishioner to communicate at least once a year; the second, at least three times a year.

VI. Representation of Christ's Sacrifice

Although harmony between the Lutheran and Reformed branches of Protestantism was not achieved, and full agreement was never likely, after Zwingli's death the two lines did converge. The Lutheran Formula of Concord (1577) certainly intended to condemn the Calvinists and crypto-Calvinists along with the Zwinglians,[60] but Calvin's blunt description of Zwingli's early teaching on the sacraments as "profane" (to Pierre Viret, 11 September 1542) makes it hard to consider him merely a "subtle sacramentarian." Nicholas Selnecker, one of the authors of the formula, explained the Lutheran doctrine in words to which Calvin, or even Bullinger, would not have objected: "[Christ], when giving the bread, gives us simultaneously His body to eat."[61] But mutual suspicion persisted, and the division between the Protestants and Rome went even deeper.

The Council of Trent (1545-1563) did urge the faithful to receive the body of the Lord more frequently than once a year, but it remained unmoved by the plea for a vernacular rite and administration of the Sacrament to the laity in both kinds. Moreover, the council took its stand on the traditional beliefs in transubstantiation and the sacrifice of the Mass. The sixteenth-century debates on both these themes were continuous with medieval debates. But the Church of Rome could hardly allow

---

59. Richard Hooker, *Of the Laws of Ecclesiastical Polity*, 8 books (London: 1593-1662), V, lxvii [2]; books I-V reprinted with an introduction by Christopher Morris, 2 vols., Everyman's Library (London: J. M. Dent & Sons, 1954), 2:320. For the development of Anglican eucharistic theology after the Elizabethan Settlement, Darwell Stone remains a helpful guide: see his *History*, vol. II, chaps. xiii, xv, xvi.

60. *Konkordienformel*, art. 7; BELK, pp. 796-97 (Epitome); BC, p. 482.

61. Quoted by Sasse, *This Is My Body*, p. 103.

Luther's claim that transubstantiation was a matter of opinion: the Fourth Lateran Council (1215) had given it dogmatic status. Even the liberal-minded Desiderius Erasmus (ca. 1469-1536), who had no enthusiasm for the dogma and was tempted by Oecolampadius's case against it, refused to depart from the consensus of the church.[62] Trent's Decree Concerning the Most Holy Sacrament of the Eucharist (1551) needed only to reaffirm the Lateran pronouncement that Christ's body and blood are contained in the Sacrament under the appearance *(sub specie)* of bread and wine.[63] Transubstantiation was not negotiable.

Trent accordingly anathematized the view that the substance of bread and wine remains together with the body and blood of the Lord. The Protestant confessions responded by condemning transubstantiation, no longer leaving it as an optional opinion. This is not to say that the Protestants simply ignored the conversionist strand in the patristic sources, but they located the change in the use or signification of the elements, not in their substance. Calvin, for example, who rejected transubstantiation as a novelty, agreed with the ancient writers who spoke of a "conversion" of the bread: they meant not that its substance is annihilated, but that it is no longer common bread intended only to feed the stomach. It becomes precisely a sign of Christ's body, and the signification would be subverted if only the appearance of bread, and not its substance, were left.[64] But this understanding of the eucharistic conversion, though it anticipated twentieth-century Roman Catholic theories of transignification or transfinalization, was foreign to the thinking of the Tridentine fathers.

The council's Decree Concerning the Sacrifice of the Mass followed the session on the Eucharist more than ten years later (1562). The Mass is declared to be a truly propitiatory sacrifice by which the Lord is

62. Whether the wily Erasmus actually affirmed the dogma of transubstantiation is disputed. See the discussion in John B. Payne, *Erasmus: His Theology of the Sacraments* (Richmond: John Knox, 1970), chap. 8. Payne's conclusion is that the authority of the church meant, for Erasmus, acceptance of the bodily presence of Christ in the Eucharist, not acceptance of the doctrine of transubstantiation (p. 154).

63. Session XIII, chaps. i, iv. H. J. Schroeder, *Canons and Decrees of the Council of Trent: Original Text with English Translation* (St. Louis: B. Herder, 1941), pp. 73, 75 (English), pp. 350, 352 (Latin). In Thomas Aquinas's classic formulation, it is the "accidents" that remain, though he also uses the word "appearance" (*ST* III, q. 75, arts. 4-5 [2:2449-51]).

64. *ICR* IV, xvii.14 (2:1375-76).

appeased, the same Christ who once offered himself in a bloody sacrifice being immolated bloodlessly under the visible signs. In this awe-inspiring mystery, the victim by which we are reconciled to God the Father is daily immolated on the altar by the church through the priests. But, strictly, the agent of the bloodless sacrifice is Christ, who is also the one victim, "the same now offering by the ministry of priests who then offered Himself on the cross, the manner alone of offering being different." The Lord's intention in instituting the Mass was that by the visible sacrifice of the Mass the sacrifice of the cross might be "represented" *(repraesentaretur)* and its saving power applied.[65] *Repraesentare* could perhaps be rendered "to make present," though it is noteworthy that the catechism of the Council of Trent (1566) uses a different term, *instaurare,* which suggests rather "to renew" or even "to repeat."[66] In any case, so far from derogating from it in any way, the bloodless sacrifice is the means by which the benefits of the bloody sacrifice are received, and the catechism asserts expressly that the sacrifice of the Mass is one and the same with the sacrifice of the cross.

The Protestant Reformers were well acquainted with the arguments, sanctioned at Trent, by which the Roman Church's apologists tried to show that the Mass was being misrepresented in Protestant polemics — as though it cast doubts on the perfect sufficiency of the death of Christ.[67] It may be that the Protestants failed to take the arguments seriously enough, despite the fact that Luther and Calvin themselves could occasionally use the language of "offering Christ to God" (Luther) or "setting Christ before God" in order to propitiate him (Calvin).[68] But it was a question of the dominant eucharistic image, even when other images were not wholly denied, and the Reformers could state the issue as a stark, inescapable choice: "[The Lord] has therefore given us a Table at which to feast, not an altar upon which to offer a vic-

---

65. Sess. XXII, chaps. i–ii; Schroeder, *Canons and Decrees,* pp. 144-46, 417-19.

66. *Catechismus ex decreto concilii Tridentini ... editus* (1566; Rome: John Bard, 1920), p. 180; Eng. trans., with notes, by John A. McHugh and Charles J. Callan (London: Herder, 1934), p. 256.

67. See, e.g., Calvin, *ICR* IV, xviii.2-5 (2:1430-34). Luther's critique of the Mass is reviewed by Carl F. Wisløff, *The Gift of Communion: Luther's Controversy with Rome on Eucharistic Sacrifice,* trans. Joseph M. Shaw (Minneapolis: Augsburg, 1964).

68. Luther, *Von dem Neuen Testament,* WA 6:371; LW 35:102. Calvin, Comm. Num. 19:2-3, CO 24:333-34; CC 2/2:39.

tim; he has not consecrated priests to offer sacrifice, but ministers to distribute the sacred banquet."[69] The division appeared at the time to be a matter not of practical abuses, popular misconceptions, or misplaced emphasis, but of mutually exclusive doctrines.[70] For this reason, the desire of the Tridentine fathers that Christians might at last be of one heart and mind "in this sign of unity . . . this symbol of concord" proved fruitless.

69. Calvin, *ICR* IV, xviii.12 (2:1440).

70. Francis Clark shows that what the Protestant Reformers rejected were not simply late medieval abuses, but the eucharistic doctrine of the Roman Church: Clark, *Eucharistic Sacrifice and the Reformation* (Westminster, Md.: Newman, 1960).

CHAPTER 12

The Grace of Christ

The *true* treasure of the church is the most holy gospel of the glory and grace of God.

Martin Luther, *Ninety-five Theses*

At Miletus, we are told, the apostle Paul sent for the elders of the church at Ephesus and in his farewell address gave a memorable profession of his calling: "I do not count my life of any value to myself, if only I may finish my course and the ministry that I received from the Lord Jesus, to testify to the good news of God's grace" (Acts 20:24). It was the *gospel* of grace to which Paul bore witness as a servant of Jesus Christ: the *idea* of grace is attested in many religions, some of which have had debates about grace that strikingly parallel the controversies in Western Christianity. In Hinduism, for instance, a grace tradition goes back to the pre-Christian scriptures of the Bhagavad Gita, which knows of a way of salvation not by works, but by the heart's devotion to a saving, gracious deity. The followers of Ramanuja (d. 1137), one of the greatest interpreters of *bhakti* Hinduism, debated which was the better image of the person under grace: the baby monkey that must at least cling to its mother, or the kitten that is wholly passive as the mother cat carries it by the scruff of its neck.[1]

Hinduism also has its special manifestations *(avataras)* of gracious

---

1. See Rudolf Otto, *Die Gnadenreligion Indiens und das Christentum: Vergleich und Unterscheidung* (Gotha: Leopold Klotz, 1930), pp. 37-40.

divinities. But for Paul grace was tied to the good news of the unique manifestation of God in Jesus Christ: it was the grace of the Lord Jesus Christ (Rom. 16:20; 1 Cor. 16:23; Phil. 4:23; 1 Thess. 5:28). More than a divine attribute (such as kindness), it referred to something that had happened, entered into history. Similarly, the prologue to the Fourth Gospel testifies, "Grace and truth *came (egeneto)* through Jesus Christ" (John 1:17, emphasis mine; cf. 2 Tim. 1:9-10; Titus 2:11). The profound sense that "grace" does not simply describe deity but points to an event, both past and continually re-presented, is fundamental to the controversies on grace in the Western church. But why say only "the *Western* church"?

I. Grace and the Catholic Tradition

In his fascinating comparison of Hindu and Christian religions of grace, the distinguished philosopher and historian of religion Rudolf Otto documents some remarkable parallels but ends with a contrast: for the Christian, salvation means deliverance from sin, guilt, and the terrors of conscience before the holiness of God; for the Hindu, it means chiefly release from the cycle of rebirth and the misery of this vagrant life. The contrast is carefully qualified. Otto speaks only of the respective *centers* of the two religious traditions; it is not as though each wholly lacked what the other took to be the main thing. And he grants that there have been times within Christianity when the axis appears to have shifted from guilt and the troubled conscience to corruption and the yearning for immortality.[2] But this seems to take for granted that Western theology is the main line, occasionally interrupted by a diversion. It would be truer to say that Western theology has always had its counterpart in another, self-consciously rival tradition: Eastern Orthodoxy.

The correlation of grace and the guilty conscience has never played the pivotal role in the theology of the Orthodox churches, in which salvation centers more on life-giving participation in the divine nature (cf. 2 Pet. 1:4) and its grounding in the incarnation of the Word. A recent dic-

---

2. Otto, *Die Gnadenreligion Indiens*, pp. 65, 70-71. See also Otto's interesting point that, although the Hindu deity Isvara is said to forgive, the forgiveness is simply overlooking the offense; it does not require, as in Christianity, expiation of the curse of sin (pp. 82-85).

tionary of Orthodox Christianity describes "deification," or participation in Christ's divinity, as a gift of grace, but it has no independent entry on grace, and none on sin. The entry on Adam and Eve affirms the damage inflicted on creation by the primal sin, including loss of the immortality originally conferred on the first human pair, but disavows the Augustinian doctrine "that we inherit Adam's guilt and are born damned."[3] One of the foremost spokesmen for Orthodoxy in the English-speaking world, Timothy Ware, asserts the need for cooperation *(synergeia)* with God, and he notes the suspicion with which the Orthodox idea of "synergy" is viewed by many brought up in the Augustinian tradition, particularly Calvinists. Most Orthodox theologians, he points out, reject the entire Augustinian idea of original sin, which is "still accepted (albeit in a mitigated form) by the Roman Catholic Church." Humans inherit Adam's corruption and mortality, not his guilt: "they are only guilty in so far as by their own free choice they imitate Adam."[4] Where the Lutherans and the Calvinists, then, say *sola gratia* — saved by grace alone — the Orthodox insist that "we humans as well as God must make our contribution to the common work."[5]

The entire history of theology in the Western — Latin or Catholic — tradition is so dominated by the concept of grace that one could reasonably tell it as the story of theological reflection on grace and the means of grace. My purpose is to look at only three main stages, beginning with *Augustine* (sec. II).[6] Although the Orthodox rightly insist that the Augustinian tradition is not the whole of Christian theology, we can certainly say that, by focusing sharply (and introspectively) on the bondage of the will, Augustine was able to plumb the depths of one kind of human predicament — and its resolution — more powerfully than

---

3. Ken Parry et al., eds., *The Blackwell Dictionary of Eastern Christianity* (Oxford: Blackwell, 1999), p. 5.

4. Timothy [Kallistos] Ware, *The Orthodox Church* (1963; new ed., London: Penguin, 1993), p. 224.

5. Ware, *The Orthodox Church*, p. 221. Biblical warrant for synergy is found in 1 Cor. 3:9, which Ware translates, "We are fellow-workers *(synergoi)* with God." The NRSV has: "For we are God's servants, working together."

6. Even restricting the discussion to a few main stages leaves a daunting task. I have thought it best to concentrate, as far as possible, on just one or two sources for each of the theologians considered, and I have made no attempt to review the extensive secondary literature.

any of the Christian fathers before him. At the high point of medieval scholasticism, *Thomas Aquinas* maintained the Augustinian understanding of grace, albeit partly in a different idiom. But on the eve of the Protestant Reformation, the theological school that Luther knew best compromised the absolute priority of grace, as Augustine and Thomas understood it (sec. III). *Martin Luther's* significance for our theme is twofold: he reaffirmed the *priority* of grace, but modified the inherited *concept* of grace by his belief that the proper means of grace is the spoken Word of God (sec. IV).

II. Healing Grace: Augustine

The understanding of grace in the Catholic tradition was decisively shaped by Augustine's controversy with the Pelagians. The fifteen anti-Pelagian treatises, all occasional rather than systematic in character, deal with grace in connection with questions about a host of other Christian doctrines, including original sin, the origin of the human soul, the possibility of sinlessness, infant baptism, the purpose of the law, faith, free will, justification, and predestination.[7] Augustine tells us, as we have seen (Chap. 6), that a crucial change of mind about grace came to him even before the controversy, and it led to an implicit refutation of the Pelagian heresy in advance of its appearance. Soon after he became coadjutor bishop of Hippo (395), he found himself pondering a question about Romans 9:10-29 put to him by Simplician, who was shortly to succeed Ambrose as bishop of Milan (397). A single verse from another Pauline letter brought him sudden illumination: "What do you have that you did not receive? And if you received it, why do you boast as if it were not a gift?" (1 Cor. 4:7). He tried hard, he says, to affirm the free choice of the human will, but the grace of God prevailed.[8] To Simplician he wrote: "If those things delight us which serve our advancement towards God, that is due not to our own whim or industry or meritorious works,

---

7. Thirteen of Augustine's anti-Pelagian writings are translated in NPNF 5; omitted are the two long works (one unfinished) against Julian. For the Latin texts see Chap. 6 n. 5, above. Others of Augustine's writings are of course pertinent to his understanding of grace, including the anti-Donatist treatises, but they are not discussed here.

8. Augustine, *praed. sanct.* (428/429), chap. 8 [iv]; NPNF 5:502. The chapter is quoted in part from his review of his reply to Simplician in the *Retractationes* (426/427).

but to the inspiration of God and to the grace which he bestows."[9] Augustine's discovery was that the God "who commands us to ask, seek and knock, himself gives us the will to obey." Even before the battle commenced, he had discovered the weapon with which to vanquish the Pelagians: unawares, he was "cutting down a future Pelagian heresy."[10] For what do any of us have that we did not receive as a gift from God?

Pelagianism is commonly simplified as the belief that salvation is by "works." It is true that the Pelagians held a more generous view of human abilities than Augustine, and they rejected his understanding of the original sin by which Adam supposedly ensnared his descendants in guilt and servitude. Their mistake, in Augustine's eyes, was not that they doubted the need for grace, but that they misunderstood the nature of grace. The Pelagians were not all of one mind. But when they spoke of "grace," they generally meant God's gifts of free will, the law, the teaching and example of Christ, and the remission of sins in baptism.[11] Augustine meant something more. He saw the human predicament in the disease that infects everyone's will since the fall, and he argued, with Paul, that the law doesn't strengthen a weakness but uncovers a sickness. "For through the law comes the knowledge of sin" (Rom. 3:20). The need for grace is the need for healing — not just a need for help in achieving what one should, in principle, be able to achieve by free will even without further assistance.

This is the argument Augustine develops in connection with the Pauline doctrine of justification in his second anti-Pelagian treatise, *On the Spirit and the Letter* (412). He finds the meaning of grace in Romans 5:5, which he understands to say that "love for God [not, as in the NRSV, "God's love"] has been poured into our hearts by the Holy Spirit that has been given to us."[12] His interpretation of Paul in this verse may

---

9. Augustine, *Simpl.* (396/398), bk. 1, q. 2, sec. 21; Eng. trans., LCC 6:405. Actually, Simplician's question was a request for exegesis of the entire difficult passage on God's right to choose one and reject another.

10. Augustine, *persev.* (428/429), chap. 52 [xx]; NPNF 5:547.

11. Pelagius himself went beyond Caelestius in allowing for special acts of divine aid to the individual. See John Burnaby's introduction to *The Spirit and the Letter* in LCC 8:190-91.

12. *Spir. et litt.*, chaps. 5 [iii], 7 [v], 20 [xii]; NPNF 5:84-85, 91. For the true purpose of the law and the healing grace that came through Jesus Christ, see chaps. 9-10 [vi], 21 [xiii], 35 [xx]; NPNF 5:86-87, 91-92, 97-98. Cf. chap. 47 [xxvii], where Augustine describes grace as the healing of nature (or "repairing," as in NPNF 5:103).

need revision. But in general he gives a powerful reaffirmation of the Pauline gospel, summing up the proper order of law and grace in the memorable epigram, "The law was given that grace might be sought; grace was given that the law might be fulfilled" (chap. 34 [xix]; cf. Rom. 8:3-4). And, as always, the heart of the matter is found in Paul's searching question in 1 Corinthians 4:7, "What do you have that you did not receive? And if you received it, why do you boast as if it were not a gift" (quoted like a refrain in chaps. 15 [ix], 50 [xxix], 54 [xxxi], 57 [xxxiii], and 60 [xxxiv]). For Augustine, the grace that comes from Christ brings about a conversion, a radical reorientation of the self, which turns a person by the infusion of love *(caritas)* in a new direction: away from the fault of seeking life in one's own self, toward the true Fountain of life, from whose fulness we have all received (chap. 11 [vii]; John 1:16). The symptom of the old, sick life is "boasting": the expression of the new, healed life is gratitude. The ungodly, though they have some knowledge of God, do not "honor him as God or give thanks to him" (Rom. 1:21); the true religion of faith is thankfulness to God for our justification (chaps. 18–19 [xi–xii]). And by "the faith of Jesus Christ" in Romans 3:22, Paul must mean the faith that Jesus Christ bestows on us by his bounty (chap. 15 [ix]).

So relentlessly has Augustine pursued his encomium of divine grace that toward the end of the treatise he must entertain the objection, "Do we then by grace make void free will?" He replies with an indignant "God forbid!" but then embarks on a subtle course of argument that ends in uncertainty (chaps. 52–60 [xxx–xxxiv]). In essentials, the argument goes like this: In actual fact, far from *annulling* freedom, grace *effects* freedom (John 8:36, 2 Cor. 3:17). But what about the initial act of faith that seems to be the first step to salvation, before the reception of grace? Is faith "in our power"? Well, we need to define the term "power," distinguishing the will to act from the ability to act. The payoff of the acute analysis that follows is that in the act of believing there is actually *no* gap between will and ability, since the act of believing is an act of the will. No one has faith without willing it; and if one wills it, one has it. Faith, therefore, is in our power — it is voluntary — by definition. Obviously, the power is given us by God, otherwise it would not be true that everything we have is received as a gift. But then we must ask, *Why* does a person will to believe? And why don't *all?* Answer: The rational soul has a natural freedom of choice, given by the Creator: we can *choose* to believe or not to believe, and it is precisely by our choice that we will one day be judged. Of course, our choice is always in response not only to the preaching of the gospel, but also to the inner persuasion of God, whose mercy anticipates us. But to yield to God's call, or to refuse it, belongs to our own will.[13] That sounds like a satisfactory conclusion. In fact, it only changes the terms of the question: for why is God's persuasion effective in some and not others? Here Augustine gives up and ends with Paul's doxology, "O the depth of the riches . . . !" (Rom. 11:33) and Paul's defiant question, "Is there injustice on God's part?" (Rom. 9:14).

In one of his last treatises, *On the Predestination of the Saints* (428 or 429), Augustine gives his clearest statement of what has, perhaps, been implicit all along — or at least since the answers to Simplician. He repeats his insistence that faith is a gift.[14] Then he recalls his change of mind. He had once supposed that to consent to the gospel, when preached to us, is our own doing and comes to us from ourselves. The source of that error was this: "I had not yet very carefully sought, nor had I as yet found, what is the nature of the election of grace."[15] Everyone has the ability to believe, just as everyone has the ability to love; but it does not follow that everyone has faith, any more than everyone loves. If a person does come to faith, it is because "in the elect the will is prepared by the Lord" (Eph. 2:8-10).[16] Even this, of course, relocates the puzzle rather than solving it: we simply cannot say *why* God chooses to give the gift of faith only to some, not to all. "For it is better in this case for us to hear or to say, 'O man, who art thou that repliest against God?' [Rom. 9:20] than to dare to speak as if we could know what He has chosen to be kept secret."[17]

---

13. *Spir. et litt.,* chap. 60 [xxxiv]; NPNF 5:110. It is the notion of *choice* that is the logical problem. The Latin *liberum arbitrium* properly means "free choice" rather than "free will." If, as Augustine says, God's will is invincible (chap. 58 [xxxiii]; NPNF 5:109; cf. *corrept.* [426/427], chap. 45 [xiv]; NPNF 5:489), it is difficult for him to say, in addition, that the human will has a choice. The solution (if it is one) lies in his persuasion that God "turns" the human will as he pleases (see, e.g., *gr. et lib. arb.* [426/427], chaps. 41-43 [xxxxi]; NPNF 5:461-63), which means, I take it, that God maneuvers the human will to the point where it "freely chooses" the option God wills for it.

14. *Praed. sanct.,* chap. 3 [ii]; NPNF 5:499.

15. *Praed. sanct.,* chap. 7 [iii]; NPNF 5:500-501.

16. *Praed. sanct.,* chap. 10 [v]; NPNF 5:503. For the assertion that "predestination is the preparation for grace, while grace is the donation itself" (chap. 19 [x]; NPNF 5:507), Augustine appeals to Eph. 2:10.

17. *Praed. sanct.,* chap. 16 [viii]; NPNF 5:506.

And so, the profound confession that we have nothing we did not receive as a gift from God (1 Cor. 4:7 is liberally cited in this treatise, too!) becomes the harsh dogma of predestination, which we have no right to question. The spirituality of thanksgiving is in danger of being silenced amid the acrimonious objections that have haunted the Augustinian heritage ever since.

III. Grace as "Habit" and Source of Merit: Thomas Aquinas

The greatest of the medieval schoolmen, Thomas Aquinas, included a systematic Treatise on Grace in his magisterial *Summa theologiae,* which was to enjoy special significance in the Roman Catholic response to the Protestant Reformation.[18] A work of scholastic theology is more interested in precision and comprehensiveness than in stimulation, and Thomas's style of acute and orderly dissection of Christian concepts is perhaps out of fashion these days, even among Roman Catholics. That said, however, it must immediately be added that the total dependence of humans on divine grace has seldom, if ever, been affirmed more meticulously than in Thomas's Treatise on Grace, where the passionate Augustinian testimony to grace is coolly articulated in the language of Aristotelian kinetics — and sometimes modified by it.[19]

In an elegant piece of conceptual analysis, which does not go quite so well in English as in Latin, Thomas points out that in our ordinary usage "grace" sometimes means *love* or *favor,* as when we speak of being in someone's "good graces"; sometimes a *gift* freely given, as when we say, "I do you this favor, this act of grace"; and sometimes *thanks,* as

18. *ST* II/1, qq. 109-14. A readily accessible English version of the Treatise on Grace will be found in LCC 11:137-218. But, here as elsewhere, I provide references, when needed, to the complete translation of *ST* by the Fathers of the English Dominican Province (see Abbreviations); the Treatise on Grace is in 1:1123-61.

19. Q. 109 argues that the need for grace is fourfold: to initiate action or movement; to provide the form by which a person, like every other created thing, acts; to elevate human nature by a "superadded light"; and to heal the sickness of sin. That even the first two needs, expressed in technical Aristotelian terms, call for grace — i.e., the wholly gratuitous condescension of God — rests on the principle that God owes his creatures nothing (q. 111, art. 1, ad 2). Thomas's distinction between grace as "divine aid" and grace as "habitual gift" (art. 2) becomes in later Roman Catholic theology the distinction between "actual" and "sanctifying" grace.

when we "say grace," or give thanks for benefits received (q. 110, art. 1). His main interest is in the second sense of "grace," grace as a gift freely given. But he insists that it depends entirely on the first because, unlike human love, which is moved by something appealing in its object, the love or favor of God *creates* goodness in the object of his love.[20] In this sense, grace denotes something in the soul: it is a quality of the soul, an effect of God's gratuitous will (arts. 1-2). Taking a term from Aristotle's *Ethics,* Thomas calls this God-given quality of the soul a "habit" (Greek *hexis*): that is, a new disposition. "[M]an is helped by God's gratuitous will, inasmuch as a habitual gift is infused by God into the soul" (art. 2 [1:1133]). The echo of Romans 5:5 is unmistakable. Obviously, habitual grace and love for God *(caritas)* coincide, and Thomas can sometimes use the terms interchangeably.[21] In essence, if not in terminology, we can say that Thomas is being faithful to Augustine. But the notion of "habitual grace" was one aspect of the medieval heritage that Luther vehemently rejected. Another was the notion of "merit."

Augustine had not disallowed the concept of merit, only the erroneous Pelagian view that the grace of eternal life is acquired by meritorious acts. That would not be mistaken, he says, if the Pelagians had added that it is grace that makes meritorious acts possible. Rightly understood, even our merits are gifts of God (1 Cor. 4:7!); and at the end, when God grants eternal life, he crowns his own gifts.[22] God "operates, therefore, without us, in order that we may will; but when we will, and so will that we may act, He co-operates with us [Phil. 2:13]."[23] In his Treatise on Grace, Thomas takes over these reflections from Augustine, whom he frequently quotes as his authority. Since Scripture promises eternal life as a reward (Matt. 5:12, 19:17), there must be merits; but there cannot be merits without the gift of habitual grace (q. 109, art. 5; q. 114, arts. 1-3), and the first instalment of grace is a gift that cannot be merited (q. 112, art. 2; q. 114, art. 5). For Luther, by contrast, there could be no smuggling in of merit even at the later step. Moreover, the Nominalist

---

20. Cf. the earlier discussion of God's *love* in *ST* I, q. 20, art. 2 (1:115).

21. E.g., *ST* II/1, q. 114, art. 8 (1:1158). Cf. art. 4 (1:1156): Grace is the principle of merit through love.

22. *Gr. et lib. arb.,* chap. 15 [vi]; NPNF 5:450.

23. *Gr. et lib. arb.,* chap. 33 [xvii]; NPNF 5:458. Cf. Thomas on operative and cooperative grace (*ST* II/1, q. 111, art. 2 [1:1137]) and prevenient and subsequent grace (art. 3 [1:1137-38]).

theologians whom Luther knew best, and who he assumed spoke for the Roman Church, tried to get merit in sooner as well as later. They argued that, although grace is necessary for justification, God gives the necessary grace to those who have first done the best they could without it — an opinion that Thomas once held but abandoned by the time he wrote his Treatise on Grace for the *Summa theologiae* (q. 114, art. 5).

The Nominalist understanding of grace and merit is sometimes described as "semi-Pelagian." Against the Pelagians, the Nominalists took "grace" in the Augustinian sense as the infused gift of love for God *(caritas)*; but, unlike Augustine, they thought one should prepare for receiving grace by doing as much as one can with one's natural abilities. (For Augustine the sole preparation for grace was all on God's side: predestination.) To be sure, the Nominalists admitted that doing one's natural best isn't *strictly* meritorious *(de condigno)*, since strictly merit is the gift of grace. But it is *fittingly* judged meritorious *(de congruo)* because God has graciously covenanted to reward it. As the favorite Nominalist watchword put it, "God does not refuse grace to those who do what is in them" — that is, those who have done what they could before receiving the gift of grace.

This apparently sensible scheme enabled such a Nominalist theologian as Gabriel Biel (ca. 1420-1495) to sound the authentic Augustinian note. In a charming sermon preached in Mainz cathedral about 1460, Biel confesses the marvel of grace and draws the inference that the heart of Christian piety is thankfulness. Grace, he says, is like a precious ring given by a king to his subjects — a golden ring, studded with diamonds. "How could one ever praise highly enough the clemency and the preciousness of the gifts of such a king? Behold, such is our King and Savior! The gift is grace, which is bestowed abundantly on us."[24] But Biel knows exactly who will receive the gift of grace: those who have done the best they could do without it. God will then provide the means to do better. Biel's motive, no doubt, was pastoral: he wanted, like Pelagius, (whom he says he rejects), to encourage effort, not complacency. But it didn't work for Martin Luther.

---

24. Gabriel Biel, sermon on Luke 2:21 ("And he was called Jesus"), trans. Paul L. Nyhus in Heiko Augustinus Oberman, *Forerunners of the Reformation: The Shape of Late Medieval Thought Illustrated by Key Documents* (New York: Holt, Rinehart & Winston, 1966), pp. 165-74; quotation from p. 173.

IV. Grace as Unmerited Favor: Luther

Luther tells us in a famous phrase that he fled to a monastery of the Augustinian Eremites in Erfurt "to get a gracious God." The story of his spiritual pilgrimage has been told many times, and it has given rise to endless scholarly disagreement. But there is no doubt that his struggle, on its theological side, came to a focus on the Nominalist watchword, "God does not refuse grace to those who do what is in them" — their best. For how do we know for sure when we have done the best we could? Isn't there always the possibility, in retrospect, that we could have done better? And what *is* our best? Do we have a natural ability, as the Nominalists believed, to love God above everything? Even when he told himself at the end of a day that he had done nothing amiss, Luther wondered if he was falling prey to the sin of pride. A scrupulous conscience tormented him with uncertainty whether he had in fact done all he could — until he decided that the Nominalists were fools and "pig theologians," crypto-Pelagians who had subverted nearly the entire church with their obnoxious formula.[25]

The discovery of Nominalist "folly" did not put Luther at odds with the Catholic tradition of Augustine and Thomas. Many historians and ecumenical theologians these days, both Roman Catholic and Protestant, think he was actually a champion of the Catholic understanding of grace against a semi-Pelagian deviation from it.[26] The conflict with the Roman Church first arose not from Luther's rejection of Nominalist theology, but from his critique of an ecclesiastical practice that had been scandalously abused, as everyone admits: the traffic in indulgences. There was certainly a straight line from Luther's discovery of grace to his attack on indulgences. The Roman Church taught that a treasury of merits had accumulated from the good works of the saints, who did more than was required of them: the surplus was available to compensate for the debts of those who had done less. Luther's sixty-second thesis on indulgences (1517) protested that "the *true* treasure of the church is the most holy gospel of the glory and grace of

25. Martin Luther, *Vorlesung über den Römerbrief* (1515-16), WA 56:274, 502-3; LW 25:261, 496-97.

26. See, for instance, Harry J. McSorley, *Luther: Right or Wrong? An Ecumenical-Theological Study of Luther's Major Work, The Bondage of the Will* (New York: Newman, Minneapolis: Augsburg, 1969).

God."[27] At this time, however, Luther called only for the reform of an abuse, not for a theological revolution. And earlier the same year, in his *Disputation against Scholastic Theology,* it was not heresy but the strict Augustinian tradition he endorsed when he announced (in thesis 29) that "the best and infallible preparation for grace and the sole means of obtaining grace is the eternal election and predestination of God."[28]

If the Nominalists had pastoral motives at heart for teaching that grace goes to those who do their best, Luther had pastoral motives for opposing them. The conflict was not, for him, a merely doctrinaire matter but reflected the depths of his own experience of God, which drove him to bring the same gospel of grace to others. The crucial question is this: Who *are* the ones who are touched by grace? Is it those who, because their resources are limited, can climb no higher but may count on the assistance of grace because they have done all they can? Or is it those who can slip no lower because they have hit the bottom of frustration and despair and expect only condemnation? Is grace aid for the weak, or is it the promise of new life for the dead? To urge sinners to "do what is in them" was, in Luther's eyes, ruinous pastoral psychology because what is in them is the sickness of self-will, which shows itself either in presumption or in discouragement. Any new demand, even the modest demand to do what they can, will only move them to further outward expressions of their inner self-love. Hence the healing Word of God must be hidden under a diagnostic judgment, which breaks down over-confidence and makes despair the first step to salvation. The Word of God comes, when it comes, in a manner contrary to our expectations, announcing life hidden under death, salvation under damnation, heaven under hell.[29]

---

27. Luther, *Disputatio pro declaratione virtutis indulgentiarum* (emphasis mine), WA 1:236; LW 31:31.

28. Luther, *Disputatio contra scholasticam theologiam,* WA 1:225; LW 31:11.

29. I am summarizing the theme powerfully and provocatively developed in Luther's *Vorlesung über den Römerbrief,* partly under the influence of the mystics (see especially WA 56:392-93, 446-47; LW 25:382-83, 438-39). His description of the sinner as "bent in on himself" is a good Augustinian sentiment, but it may have come to him through the fourteenth-century mystical treatise that he titled *A Spiritually Noble Little Book* and published in 1516 — Luther's very first publication. Shortly afterward, he found a more complete manuscript of the treatise and published it under the title *Eyn deutsch Theologie* ("A

No doubt, there is a difference of tone from Thomas's sober Treatise on Grace when Luther rails against the obnoxious formula of the "pig theologians," but in substance his protest remains faithful to the mainline Catholic tradition.[30] This is not at all to conclude that Luther and those whom Calvin calls "the sounder Schoolmen" had nothing to quarrel about on the question of grace. True, Augustine, Thomas, Luther, and Calvin were of one mind in affirming the absolute priority of grace over human merit.[31] That was the issue with the Pelagians and the semi-Pelagians. Still, there were at least two points, already mentioned in passing, on which Luther did not merely repeat the Catholic tradition on grace. First, he left no room for the notion of *merit,* which Augustine and Thomas postponed (and carefully qualified) but did not exclude. Luther judged grace and merit to be simply incompatible, mutually exclusive concepts, and he took Paul to say in Romans 3:24 ("they are now justified by his grace as a gift") that "there is no such thing as merit."[32] Second, Luther rejected the description of grace as a *habit.* And this calls for a closer look, since it is the very definition of Lutheran grace that is at stake.

In his refutation of Latomus (Jacques Masson), a Roman Catholic theologian at the University of Louvain, Luther infers from Romans 5:15 that we are to distinguish God's "grace *(charis)*" from "the free gift in grace *(dôrea en chariti).*" *Grace* is the favor or good will of God that

German Theology," 1518). In his laudatory preface he wrote: "[N]o book except the Bible and St. Augustine has come to my attention from which I have learned more about God, Christ, man, and all things" (WA 1:378; LW 31:75). Likewise, thesis 18 of Luther's *Disputatio Heidelbergae habita* (1518) states: "It is certain man must utterly despair of his own ability before he is prepared to receive the grace of Christ" (WA 1:354; LW 31:40).

30. The qualifier "mainline" is required because some historians argue, correctly I think, that the authoritative Roman Catholic Council of Trent (1545-63) left room for the Nominalist view as at least a Catholic option. See Heiko A. Oberman, "The Tridentine Decree on Justification in the Light of Late Medieval Theology," in *Distinctive Protestant and Catholic Themes Reconsidered,* ed. Robert W. Funk, *Journal for Theology and Church,* vol. 3 (New York: Harper & Row, 1967), pp. 28-54. The opposing view is argued by Harry McSorley (n. 26 above).

31. "For on the beginning of justification there is no quarrel between us and the sounder Schoolmen." Calvin, *ICR* III, xiv.11 (1:778). The expanded comment in the French version, as translated in a footnote to the English (n. 15), reads: "It is quite true that the poor world has been seduced until now to think that man could of himself prepare to be justified by God. . . ."

32. "Nullum esse meritum prorsus." Luther, *De servo arbitrio* (1525), WA 18:769; LW 33:267.

accepts the sinner; the *gift* is the healing that comes from faith. "Here," he says, "as ought to be done, I take grace in the proper sense of the favor of God — not a quality of the soul [i.e., a habit], as is taught by our more recent writers." But there is also the gift, which works to purge away the sin of the person who is forgiven. There are thus two benefits of the gospel, one the opposite of wrath, the other the opposite of corruption; the first total, the second partial. "Everything is forgiven through grace, but as yet not everything is healed through the gift." Luther concludes that he only wants to speak in the simple, Pauline way, without any difficulty.[33]

The present-day reader may wonder where exactly this differs in substance, and not merely in terms, from the more technical Thomist way, which carefully distinguishes between the first and second meanings of the word "grace": as "favor" and "gift," respectively. Calvin, while agreeing with Luther in substance, moves closer to the Thomistic terminology when he speaks of a "double grace," including in the concept of grace what Luther distinguished as the healing gift. "By partaking of [Christ], we principally receive a double grace: namely, that being reconciled to God through Christ's blamelessness, we may have in heaven instead of a Judge a gracious Father; and secondly, that sanctified by Christ's spirit we may cultivate blamelessness and purity of life."[34] Unlike Thomas, however, Calvin does not see the healing gift as the effect of divine favor; he thinks rather of two distinct but mutually connected gifts that come from union with Christ. And there are other differences between Protestant and Thomist grace: the most important of them has to do with the way in which grace reaches us, since this says a good deal about how grace is understood.

The grace of God, as Luther puts it, is an *outward* good: the divine acceptance never depends on the healing that is going on *in* us, otherwise it would not be grace.[35] And behind this affirmation lies a funda-

33. Luther, *Rationis Latomianae confutatio* (1521), WA 8:105-8; LW 32:226-30. Note that Luther does not hesitate to apply the language of "infusion" to the gift, though not to grace. See also the preface to Romans in the *Deutsche Bibel* (1546), WADB 7:9; LW 35:369.

34. *ICR* III, xi.1 (1:725). I have had to dispense here with a more detailed discussion of Calvin's views on grace but may refer to my book *Grace and Gratitude;* see in particular pp. 69-70 n. 83, where I suggest a comparison between Calvin's usage and Thomas's.

35. Luther, *Rationis Latomianae confutatio*, WA 8:106, 114; LW 32:227, 239-40.

mental, if not irreconcilable, difference on the *means* of grace: whereas Thomistic grace is sacramental, Lutheran grace comes as a word, a proclamation, good news. "If you want to obtain grace, then see to it that you hear the Word of God attentively or meditate on it diligently. The Word, I say, and only the Word, is the vehicle of God's grace."[36] In short, the true treasure of the church is the gospel, good news.

There remains the problem of predestination! It has seldom been a divisive issue between Roman Catholics and Protestants: rather, it has occasioned party divisions within each of the two communions. Luther's cheerful truculence and fondness for overstatement may have appeared to make predestination a bone of contention between Rome and Wittenberg. (Erasmus suggested that Luther's honorific title should be *Doctor hyperbolicus*.)[37] It was surely unwise of Luther to argue for the bondage of the will by embracing Wycliffe's assertion, condemned by the Council of Constance (1414-18), that "everything happens by absolute necessity." It is one thing to say that by its own efforts the fallen will is unable to extricate itself from bondage to sin, quite another to say that to purpose anything either evil or good is in no one's control because everything is predetermined.[38] The sickness of self-will, bent in upon itself, is not the same as the determination of the will by divine necessity. It was absolute necessity that Erasmus took to be *the* Lutheran dogma, and Luther commended him for perceiving the central issue. As the controversy between the reformer and the humanist dragged on, Erasmus took his stand on the authority of the church and pronounced it a heresy to doubt free choice.[39] For the most part, however, the discussion of election and predestination in *The Bondage*

36. Luther, *In epistolam S. Pauli ad Galatas commentarius* (1519), on Gal. 3:2, WA 2:509; LW 27:249. I do not myself consider the contrast between sacramental and evangelical grace to be non-negotiable. What Luther discovered was precisely the sacramentality of the proclaimed word, and from there he reinterpreted the sacraments. But that is another large issue. See B. A. Gerrish, "By Faith Alone: Medium and Message in Luther's Gospel" (1963), revised and reprinted in *The Old Protestantism*, chap. 4.

37. Desiderius Erasmus, *Hyperaspistes II* (1527): *Desiderii Erasmi Roterodami opera omnia*, ed. Jean LeClerc, 10 vols. (Leiden, 1703-6), 10:1345D.

38. Luther, *Assertio omnium articulorum M. Lutheri per bullam Leonis X. novissimam damnatorum* (1520), WA 7:146.

39. Erasmus, *Hyperaspistes I* (1526); *Opera*, 10:1259D. See further my essay "*De libero arbitrio* (1524): Erasmus on Piety, Theology, and the Lutheran Dogma" (1978), in *The Old Protestantism*, chap. 1.

of the Will (1525), Luther's reply to Erasmus, moved within the lines of the Augustinian heritage.

In some ways, Calvin was more cautious than Luther on predestination and the bondage of the will.[40] But whereas after Luther the Lutherans said as little as possible about predestination, the later Calvinists became obsessed with it. The Calvinists even claimed that they were the real "Lutherans" because they were unembarrassed by Luther's predestinarianism.[41] They made the doctrine of predestination theirs, though they could find little or nothing new to say about it. "Sovereign grace," for them, meant grace that is irresistible because it is wholly an activity of the inflexible will of God, whose providence and predestination are the outworking of his eternal decrees. Calvin's own verdict remained axiomatic: "We shall never be clearly persuaded, as we ought to be, that our salvation flows from the wellspring of God's free mercy until we come to know his eternal election, which illumines God's grace by this contrast: that he does not indiscriminately adopt all into the hope of salvation but gives to some what he denies to others."[42] And it must be said of Calvin, too, that by tying sovereign grace to predestination, as Augustine had done, he made it easy for his followers and adversaries alike to divert the Reformed witness to grace into endless controversies over determinism and free will.

In Protestant folklore, Luther has been celebrated for replacing salvation by works with salvation by God's free grace through faith alone; in Roman Catholic folklore, he is deplored for undermining good works by imagining a grace that leaves sinners in their sin. The truth is more complicated. It would be hard to name a theologian who celebrated divine grace more assiduously than Thomas Aquinas, and not even Gabriel Biel believed in justification by works. For his part, Luther did not permit the unmerited favor of God to be invoked as an excuse for sin, any more than the apostle Paul did (Rom. 6:1); he simply thought that the healing of sin was not part of the meaning of the word "grace." He had his reason for so

40. See Chap. 6, at nn. 36, 37.

41. See the study by Fredrik Brosché, *Luther on Predestination: The Antinomy and the Unity between Love and Wrath in Luther's Concept of God,* Acta Universitatis Upsaliensis: Studia Doctrinae Christianae Upsaliensia, no. 18 (Stockholm: Almqvist & Wiksell, 1978).

42. Cited above: Chap. 6, at n. 6.

thinking: at no point can Christians stand before God on the grounds of their moral or spiritual attainments but must trust in the unmerited goodness of God. It is of course another question whether the restricted meaning Luther ascribed to "grace" is warranted by the New Testament Scriptures, which surely understand grace as also a transforming power (1 Cor. 15:10; 2 Cor. 12:9; Heb. 13:9; etc.). But the differences between the Protestant Reformers and the "sounder Schoolmen" are at least partly semantic. Calvin brought his language closer to Thomas by speaking of a "double grace" that comes from participation in Christ; and, as we have seen,[43] he was prepared to admit that even the quarrel over "merit" *could be* semantic.

Problems certainly remain for ecumenical theology; not least, the problem of grace and predestination in the Augustinian tradition. And it cannot be presumed that the dividing lines of sixteenth-century theology hold good for present-day dialogue between Protestants and Roman Catholics. It is sobering to recall that so eminent a Roman Catholic theologian as Louis Bouyer, who was brought up as a French Protestant, converted to Rome because only there, he decided, could *sola gratia* find a secure home. Though he noted the evidence of occasional revivals of the Reformation principles in Protestantism, the strange paradox, in his eyes, was that "the Reformation, begun to extol the work of grace, arrived at a Pelagianism never equalled before."[44] Here too, as elsewhere, "thinking with the church" is never finished.

---

43. See Chap. 6, pp. 111-15, above.

44. Louis Bouyer, *The Spirit and Forms of Protestantism,* trans. A. V. Littledale (Westminster, MD: Newman, 1956), p. 194.

Index of Names and Subjects

Index of Scripture References